Each volume of this series of companions to major philosophers contains specially commissioned essays by an international team of scholars, together with a substantial bibliography, and will serve as a reference work for students and nonspecialists. One aim of the series is to dispel the intimidation such readers often feel when faced with work of a difficult and challenging thinker.

Few thinkers have been so consistently misunderstood as Søren Kierkegaard (1813–1855). Amongst the many myths that have attached themselves to his work is the belief that Kierkegaard was an irrationalist who denied the value of clear and honest thinking. The truth is that Kierkegaard did deny the power of reason to uncover universal and objective truth in matters of value, but in the current philosophical climate there is nothing irrational about that.

The contributors to this companion probe the full depth of Kierkegaard's thought, revealing its distinctive subtlety. The topics covered include Kierkegaard's views on art and religion, ethics and psychology, theology and politics, and knowledge and virtue. Much attention is devoted to the pervasive influence of Kierkegaard on twentieth-century philosophy and theology.

New readers will find this the most convenient and accessible guide to Kierkegaard currently available. Advanced students and specialists will find a conspectus of recent developments in the interpretation of Kierkegaard.

THE CAMBRIDGE COMPANION TO

KIERKEGAARD

The Cambridge Companion to
KIERKEGAARD

Edited by

Alastair Hannay
University of Oslo

and

Gordon D. Marino
St. Olaf College

CAMBRIDGE
UNIVERSITY PRESS

Gordon D. Marino gratefully acknowledges the support of the Virginia Foundation for the Humanities and the American-Scandinavian Foundation. Thanks are also due to Philip Lickteig and Cynthia Lund for their bibliographic assistance and to Douglas MacLean, Phd., for his assistance with the index.

PUBLISHED BY THE PRESS SYNDICATE OF THE UNIVERSITY OF CAMBRIDGE
The Pitt Building, Trumpington Street, Cambridge, CB2 1RP, United Kingdom

CAMBRIDGE UNIVERSITY PRESS
The Edinburgh Building, Cambridge CB2 2RU, United Kingdom
40 West 20th Street, New York NY 10011–4211, USA
10 Stamford Road, Oakleigh, Melbourne 3166, Australia

© Cambridge University Press 1998

First published 1998

Printed in the United States of America

Typeset in Trump Medieval

Library of Congress Cataloging-in-Publication Data

The Cambridge companion to Kierkegaard / [edited by] Alastair Hannay,
    Gordon Marino.
        p.   cm.
    Includes bibliographical references.
    ISBN 0-521-47151-6 (hardcover). – ISBN 0-521-47719-0 (pbk.)
    1. Kierkegaard, Søren, 1813–1855.   I. Hannay, Alastair.
    II. Marino, Gordon Daniel, 1952–   .
    B4377.B29   1997
    198'.9 – dc21   97-617
                                                                                  CIP

A catalog record for this book is available from
the British Library

ISBN 0 521 47151 6 hardback
ISBN 0 521 47719 0 paperback

To the memory of
Edwin Ellis

CONTENTS

vii

CONTRIBUTORS

ANDREW CROSS, Assistant Professor of Philosophy at the University of California at Irvine, writes on Kierkegaard and the relations between ethics, agency, and self-interpretation.

HERMANN DEUSER, Professor of Systematic Theology at the Institute for Protestant Theology, the Justus Liebig University of Giessen, is the author of *Sören Kierkegaard. Die paradox Dialektik des politischen Christen* (1974), *Dialektische Theologie. Studien zu Adornos Metaphysik und zum Spätwerk Kierkegaards* (1980), and *Kierkegaard, Die Philosophie des religiösen Schriftstellers* (1985), as well as of numerous articles in philosophy of religion, systematic theology, and in Kierkegaard studies. He is translator and editor of Charles S. Peirce, *Religionsphilosophische Schriften* (1995) and co-editor of *Kierkegaard Studies Yearbook* (1996ff).

C. STEPHEN EVANS, Professor of Philosophy at Calvin College, is the author of numerous books including *Kierkegaard's "Fragments" and "Postscript," The Historical Christ and the Jesus of Faith*, and *Passionate Reason*. He serves on the International Scholarly Committee that oversees research at the Kierkegaard Research Centre at the University of Copenhagen.

M. JAMIE FERREIRA, Professor of Religious Studies and Philosophy at the University of Virginia at Charlottesville, is the author of *Doubt and Religious Commitment* (1980), *Scepticism and Reasonable Doubt* (1986) and *Transforming Vision: Imagination and Will in Kierkegaardian Faith* (1991).

RONALD M. GREEN, John Phillips Professor of Religion and Director of the Institute of Applied Ethics at Dartmouth College, is the author of *Kierkegaard and Kant: The Hidden Debt* (1992), *Religious Reason*, and *Religion and Moral Reason*. He has also written extensively on bioethics and business ethics.

ix

ALASTAIR HANNAY, Professor Emeritus of Philosophy, the University of Oslo, is the author of *Mental Images – a Defence* (1971), *Kierkegaard. The Arguments of the Philosophers* (1982, rev. ed. 1991), and *Human Consciousness* (1990). He is editor (with Andrew Feenberg) of *Technology and the Politics of Knowledge* (1995), and has published numerous articles in philosophy of mind, epistemology, ethics, and Kierkegaard studies. He is also translator of several works by Kierkegaard in Penguin Classics and is Editor of *Inquiry*.

TIMOTHY P. JACKSON, Assistant Professor of Christian Ethics in the Candler School of Theology at Emory University, has published numerous articles on moral theology and philosophy of religion and is the author of *The Priority of Agape: A Defense of Charity as First Virtue*, forthcoming from Cambridge University Press.

BRUCE H. KIRMMSE, Professor of History at Connecticut College and guest Lecturer at the Søren Kierkegaard Research Centre at the University of Copenhagen, is the author of *Kierkegaard in Golden Age Denmark* (1990), *Encounters with Kierkegaard* (1996), and many other scholarly articles. He is also an editor of *Kierkegaardiana*.

KLAUS-M. KODALLE, Professor of Philosophy at the University of Jena, is the author of *Thomas Hobbes – Logik der Herrschaft* (1972), *Politik als Macht und Mythos, Carl Schmitts Politische Theologie* (1973), *Die Eroberung des Nutzlosen* (1988) (on Kierkegaard), *Dietrich Bonhoeffer, Zur Kritik seiner Theologie* (1991), *Schockierende Fremdheit, Nachmetaphysische Ethik in der Weimarer Wendezeit* (1996), and of further books in the areas of Critical Theory (Frankfurt School), psychoanalysis and religion, philosophy of religion, and political philosophy.

GORDON D. MARINO, Associate Professor of Philosophy and Curator of the Hong/Kierkegaard Library at St. Olaf College, is the author of *Kierkegaard in the Present Age* (1997), and has written for both scholarly and popular journals in the areas of ethics and morality.

EDWARD F. MOONEY, Professor of Philosophy at Sonoma State University, is the author of *Knights of Faith and Resignation: Reading Kierkegaard's* Fear and Trembling (1991) and *Selves in Discord and Resolve: Kierkegaard's Moral-Religious Psychology from Either/Or to Sickness unto Death* (1996).

GEORGE PATTISON, Dean of Chapel at King's College, Cambridge, is the author of *Art, Modernity and Faith* (1991), *Kierkegaard: The Aesthetic and the Religious* (1992), and of *Agnosis: Theology in the Void* (1997). He has edited the collections of *Kierkegaard on Art and Communication* (1994) and (with Stephen Shakespeare) *Kierkegaard: The Self in Society* (1997). He has also published numerous articles and has broadcast for the BBC, mainly in the fields of art and religion, and Kierkegaard studies.

ROGER POOLE, Reader in Literary Theory, Department of English Studies at the University of Nottingham, is the author of *Towards Deep Subjectivity* (1972), *The Unknown Virginia Woolf* (1978, 4th ed. 1996); with Henrik Stangerup, of *Dansemesteren, Sider af Søren Kierkegaard* (1985), *A Kierkegaardian Reader: Texts and Narratives* (1989), and *The Laughter Is on My Side: An Imaginative Introduction to Kierkegaard* (1989); and of *Kierkegaard: The Indirect Communication* (1993). His play about Kierkegaard and Regine Olsen, *All Women and Quite a Few Men are Right*, has twice been performed at the Edinburgh Festival.

PHILIP L. QUINN, John A. O'Brien Professor of Philosophy at the University of Notre Dame, is the author of *Divine Commands and Moral Requirements* (1978) and is co-editor of *A Companion to Philosophy of Religion* (1997). He has also published numerous articles on the philosophy of religion and the philosophy of science.

ROBERT C. ROBERTS, Professor of Philosophy at Wheaton College, is the author of *Faith, Reason and History: Rethinking Kierkegaard's* Philosophical Fragments (1986) as well as *Taking the Word to Heart: Self and Other in an Age of Therapies* (1993).

MEROLD WESTPHAL, Professor of Philosophy at Fordham University, is the author of *Kierkegaard's Critique of Reason and Society* and *Becoming a Self: A Reading of Kierkegaard's* Concluding Unscientific Postscript. He has also written two books on Hegel.

ABBREVIATIONS

C	*The Crisis [and a Crisis] in the Life of an Actress*
CA	*The Concept of Anxiety*
CD	*Christian Discourses*
CI	*The Concept of Irony with Continual Reference to Socrates*
CUP	*Concluding Unscientific Postscript to the Philosophical Fragments* (volumes 1 and 2)
EO I	*Either/Or I*
EO II	*Either/Or II*
EO^h	*Either/Or* (Hannay)
EPW	*Early Polemical Writings*
EUD	*Eighteen Upbuilding Discourses*
FT	*Fear and Trembling*
FT^h	*Fear and Trembling* (Hannay)
JP	*Journals and Papers* (followed by volume and page or by entry number)
KAUC	*Kierkegaard's Attack upon "Christendom"*
OAR	*On Authority and Revelation*
Pap.	*Søren Kierkegaards Papirer*
PC	*Practice in Christianity*
PF	*Philosophical Fragments*
PV	*The Point of View for My Work as an Author*
R	*Repetition*
SLW	*Stages on Life's Way*
SUD	*The Sickness unto Death*
SUD^h	*The Sickness unto Death* (Hannay)
SV	*Samlede Værker* (superscripts denote edition)
UDVS	*Upbuilding Discourses in Various Spirits*

References to the works of Kierkegaard are to the Hannay and Hong translations, with the following exceptions: C (trans. Crites, 1967), CD (trans. Lowrie, 1940), KAUC (trans. Lowrie, 1944), OAR (trans. Lowrie, 1955), and PV (trans. Lowrie, 1939).

THE CAMBRIDGE COMPANION TO
KIERKEGAARD

Introduction

Myths attach rather easily to some thinkers, especially to those who like Hegel are hard to read or like Kierkegaard hard to place. Such myths are often based on hearsay or a superficial reading of the texts. One lingering myth about Kierkegaard is that he is an irrationalist in some sense that denies the value of clear and honest thinking. Kierkegaard did deny the ability of reasoned thought to arrive at universal and objective truth on matters of value, but today that is considered quite rational. This collection of previously unpublished essays is offered as proof of how wrong it is to suppose that if Kierkegaard's philosophical star is in the ascendant, as it now is, things must be going badly with philosophy.

Besides this general myth, though owing as much to them as they to it, are the particular myths – of Kierkegaard's uncontrolled predilection for paradox, a delight in exaggeration, and his writer's weakness for rhetoric over perspicuity – myths that have led in their turn to superficial renditions of the ideas and to failures to detect consistency or development in his multiauthored production. More than with any other recent thinker, and for good or ill, the reception of Kierkegaard's work has carried the subjective stamp of the receiver's own preferences. So much so that one might well ask if Kierkegaard has not so much enjoyed as "suffered" his several renaissances.

Emanuel Hirsch, whose influential German translations reflect personal political leanings, tried to weave Kierkegaard into the tangled web of an existence theology adapted to National Socialism. Herbert Marcuse, the revisionary Marxist, detected in Kierkegaard the makings of a deeply rooted social theory, while his Frankfurt School colleague Theodor Adorno saw in Kierkegaard a fellow cam-

I

paigner against the tyranny of the concept over the particular. The criticisms these two leveled at Kierkegaard's focus on religion and the individual are nevertheless hampered by narrowly focused visions of their own. Besides Hirsch, Kierkegaard was heralded by many other theologians. Attempts to see in him the provider of a radical Christian apologetic set in motion yet another school of interpretation. But he was also eagerly read in Max Weber's circle and welcomed by agnostic and atheistic thinkers of widely diverging political views. Heidegger's debt is still to be measured, but Kierkegaard's influence on the foremost Marxist intellectual of the century is well recorded. Though later in life Lukács criticized the "self-mortifying subjectivism" of Kierkegaard's critique of Hegel, in his youth he had held Kierkegaard in an esteem that bordered on hero worship.[1] As for yet another dominant twentieth-century tradition, analytical philosophy of language, it is no news that its leading twentieth-century exponent also felt the impact of Kierkegaard's thought. Wittgenstein once described Kierkegaard as the nineteenth century's most profound thinker.

This chameleon-like quality of the Kierkegaard reception can be, and has been, blamed on Kierkegaard himself, on his resort to pseudonymity and on the variety of his themes and writing styles; one gets the impression that behind the writings no one in particular is at home. Others, and not only those like Barthes and Foucault who proclaim "the death of the author," would find in this, on the contrary, a reason for praising the writings. Thus postmodern perspectivism provides yet another illustration of the versatile tenacity of Kierkegaard's appeal, bringing a very broad but perhaps precisely on that account still limited perspective of its own to bear on the varied texture of Kierkegaard's writings and on the many levels of meaning they can be made to disclose.

Given the huge span dividing this newest of renewals and straightforwardly theological readings of Kierkegaard, it is surely opportune to look again and carefully *into* as well as *at* the texts. Although some may take the width of the welcome Kierkegaard has enjoyed to be a reliable indication of the perennial topicality of his writings, the sheer heterogeneity of the banners under which the reception has occurred does suggest that justice has still to be done and that a vast middle ground may still be waiting to be charted and reclaimed.

Writing of himself Kierkegaard was reminded of what he had once written pseudonymously about Socrates (see the epigraph to Bruce H. Kirmmse's essay), that "his whole life was a personal preoccupation with himself, and then guidance comes along and adds something world-historical to it."[2] This was Kierkegaard's own perspective on his life in retrospect. He came to believe that he had had a religious mission from the start. The first part of the description seems fitting enough, but how far Kierkegaard's own life contained anything that might attract a biographer looking for a "world-historical" dimension is less clear. With regard to the influence of his writings, however, history has certainly proved Kierkegaard right.

Apart from four visits to Berlin and a trip to his family roots in Jutland, Kierkegaard's short life (like Kafka he lived to be only forty-two) was spent entirely in and around Copenhagen, a city with at the time a population of little over one hundred thousand. He was born there on 5 May 1813, the year being that which also saw the birth of Richard Wagner and of the father of Nietzsche, Wagner's youthful admirer-to-be and later critic. Kierkegaard was born eight years before Dostoevsky and five years before Marx. Among the thinkers who were to influence him, Hamann and Lessing had died a generation earlier, Hegel was forty-three and was to die in Kierkegaard's first year as a student. Schelling, whose famous lectures in Berlin in 1843 Kierkegaard attended along with many others who were to influence the course of European culture, including Marx, was thirty-eight.

The early years in Copenhagen were marked by forced proximity to a deeply religious father who had retired from business before Søren was born and by the deaths before he reached the age of twenty-one of his mother and five of the family of seven of which he was the youngest. Kierkegaard spent ten years at the university before completing his dissertation *On the Concept of Irony with Continual Reference to Socrates* (1841), in preparation, it seemed, for a career in the Church. His second major work *Either/Or* (1843) marked a postponement of that career and was the fruit of a fateful decision. In 1841 he broke off his engagement after one year to Regine Olsen, and there followed a period of intense creativity that lasted during and after a four-month trip to Berlin, ostensibly to hear Schelling's lectures. The publication of *Either/Or* in February

1843 (the manuscript was completed in November 1840) was followed in October of the same year by two slimmer volumes, *Repetition* and *Fear and Trembling* (both written for the most part on a second visit to Berlin following the publication of *Either/Or*). All these works may be said to express the author's "personal preoccupation with himself," in that they take up the question of the status of the "exception" in society with respect to a problem that Judge William in *Either/Or* calls "realizing the universal." In *Fear and Trembling* this problem is grasped first of all in terms of ethical participation, but the theme reappears soon after in *Stages on Life's Way* (1845), with a religious perspective brought more sharply into focus. Prior to that work, however, in June 1844, and within days of each other, there had appeared two books introducing new topics, *Philosophical Fragments* and *The Concept of Anxiety* (or *Dread*). The former, raising what seems on the surface to be an epistemological question, subtly distinguishes a Christian notion of knowledge from that of the philosophical tradition from Socrates to Hegel, a theme elaborated at much greater length in *Concluding Unscientific Postscript to the Philosophical Fragments* (1846). On the other hand, *The Concept of Anxiety* is an examination of the psychological background to the experience of sin and contains Kierkegaard's seminal account of anxiety (*Angest*) in the face of "nothing."

Alongside this already impressive and entirely pseudonymous production, Kierkegaard had also published in parallel twenty-one "edifying" (*opbyggelige*, also translated "upbuilding") discourses, signed works, some of them appearing simultaneously with works written under pseudonyms. As its full title indicates, *Postscript* was intended to "conclude" Kierkegaard's authorial career. However, in the guise of one of his pseudonyms (Frater Taciturnus, in this case), Kierkegaard provoked a feud with a satiric weekly, *The Corsair*, which instead of responding to the pseudonym turned ferociously on Kierkegaard himself. The affair had a deep and lasting effect on Kierkegaard's relationship with his fellow citizens on all social levels.

Partly, it seems, to avoid giving the impression that persecution by a weekly had forced his hand, Kierkegaard decided to abandon whatever plans he had formed for giving up authorship and becoming a cleric. In 1847 he published *Edifying Discourses in Different*

Spirits and the substantial *Works of Love*, followed in the spring of 1848 by *Christian Discourses*, and in 1849 by *The Lilies of the Field and the Birds of the Air* and *Three Discourses at Communion on Fridays*. All were on explicitly Christian themes and published under his own name, though in 1847 he briefly returned to the "aesthetic" genre in a *feuilleton* essay entitled *The Crisis [and a Crisis] in the Life of an Actress*. During this time Kierkegaard had financial problems, frequently changed apartments, and became increasingly concerned about his position *sub specie aeternitatis* as a writer. A retrospective justification of his authorship was prepared but withheld due to scruples about how its reception might falsify his own polemical position as he was beginning to see it (the work, *The Point of View of [for] My Activity [Virksomhed] as an Author* [the latter Danish term also has the connotation of "effectivity"; the Danish "for" is sometimes translated "for"] was published posthumously, by Kierkegaard's elder brother, in 1856).

At about the same time Kierkegaard was writing two works under a new pseudonym, Anti-Climacus: *The Sickness unto Death* (1849) and *Practice in Christianity* (1850). These, with their clear address to the world around him, mark the intrusion of a "world-historical" dimension. Its roots may be traced to a review Kierkegaard wrote just prior to publishing *Postscript*. The book reviewed was entitled *Two Ages*, and in his comments Kierkegaard brings together and develops certain social and political aspects of what had been written in that earlier pseudonymous period. These two later works, written during and in the aftermath of the 1848 upheavals in Europe, can be read against the background of the political changes brought about in Denmark at that time. These changes included the establishment of a constitutional monarchy and of a people's church, both of which flew in the face of the category of the "single individual" developed by Kierkegaard and which he now believed was of critical polemical importance.

Over the next few years little was to be seen of Kierkegaard. His relationship with the Church and its higher representatives, notably the primate, J. P. Mynster, was becoming increasingly embittered, but the conflict was not public. Kierkegaard appears to have been biding his time until the appropriate occasion for launching an all-out attack on the Church. That occasion was provided by the death of Mynster in 1854 and an address by his successor, Kierkegaard's former tutor H. L. Martensen, in which the late bishop was referred to as a "witness to the truth." Kierkegaard, however, still anxious that his own polemic should not be confused with those of others, held back for almost a year before unleashing the assault. When it came, he spent the remainder of his inheritance underwriting the publication of his own polemical broadsheet, *The Moment* (or *Instant*). This went through nine issues before Kierkegaard collapsed one day in the street. He died in a hospital some six weeks later, probably of a lung infection. He was forty-two years old. On his sickbed he confided to Emil Boesen, his friend from boyhood, indeed by that time his only friend, now a pastor and the only member of the Church he would see, including his own brother, that his life had been a "great and to others unknown and incomprehensible suffering." It had looked like "pride and vanity" but "wasn't" that. Kierkegaard said he regretted not having married and taken on an official position. His funeral was the occasion of a demonstration, led by his nephew who was an early supporter and who protested at the Church's insistence on officiating at the committal proceedings, contrary to the deceased's express wishes.

In a historical and biographical perspective, certain occurrences before and after Kierkegaard's death reveal his relationship to his family and country. In "Out with It!: The Modern Breakthrough, Kierkegaard and Denmark," Bruce H. Kirmmse connects these occurrences with Kierkegaard's constant intellectual preoccupation with the concept of authority and with his personal struggle to find a voice within his family and in the Copenhagen of his time. There is no denying Kierkegaard's special psychological makeup. Indeed, so special that during the heyday of psychoanalysis it was fashionable to reduce Kierkegaard's thought to its psychological background, as though there was nothing more to his writings than the workings of a melancholic mind. Although such reductive readings are too narrow, personal themes are clearly at work. One of these is the profound impact of his father on his life and works, acknowledged by Kierkegaard in many ways and on numerous occasions. Kirmmse's essay presents more than a glimpse of this complicated relationship, but also of the neglected but strife-ridden relationship between Kierkegaard and his elder brother. Kirmmse's essay fills this latter gap and also offers suggestions concerning the influence of Kierkegaard's filial and fraternal relationships on his final assault on Christendom.

Roger Poole records the influence of Kierkegaard upon others. His "The Unknown Kierkegaard: Twentieth-Century Receptions" surveys the full spectrum of Kierkegaard's impact on twentieth-century thought. Calling to mind what was referred to above as the chameleon-like character of the reception, Poole observes that thinkers who "fall under Kierkegaard's sway" do so for their own reasons, something that might also be said of those who reject him, as in the dismissive treatment of Kierkegaard in Denmark with which Poole begins. Among those Poole mentions who for their own reasons welcomed Kierkegaard are Jaspers, Heidegger, Bonhoeffer, and Sartre (who "existentialized" Kierkegaard though declined to own to any debt). Through Heidegger Poole also traces Derrida's debt to Kierkegaard. In a Derridian spirit, Poole believes the chameleon-like nature of the reception is in an important respect a good thing, since Kierkegaard intended that his works be received by individuals. The survey is therefore "critical" in the sense that it takes to task those who attempt to fit Kierkegaard into any "overarching-scheme." The extent to which this criticism is justified, and if so to whom it applies, is something individual readers may wish to judge for themselves. Poole also considers the important effect of interpretation on translation, which in the case of the British and American reception's initially "blunt" reading led to a need to rediscover Kierkegaard the writer, which, once done, belatedly allowed the tools of literary criticism to be applied. Poole notes how excesses in the deconstructionist turn have done Kierkegaard a disservice but finds an approach to the texts through their literary form truer to Kierkegaard than the attempts of theologians and philosophers at a systematic reconstruction that ignores the polypseudonymity and stylistic variety. Not only truer but more apt for giving the right kind of answer to the question, How should we read Kierkegaard here and now?

Perhaps there are several right kinds of answer, depending on the there and then of the provenance of the text in question. In the later, more "world-historical" phase, Kierkegaard's writing certainly acquired definable historical targets. The question may then be not so much how to *read* the texts as what can *be derived* from them. By placing one of Kierkegaard's most central concerns in its local context, George Pattison's "Art in an Age of Reflection" provides an opportunity to reflect on just that question. No theme recurs more consistently and problematically in Kierkegaard than "the aesthetic," and no one had more influence on Kierkegaard's understanding of art than the Danish writer and critic J. L. Heiberg. Pattison discusses this influence in the light of a coherent philosophy of art to be found in Kierkegaard that provides criteria for the evaluation of art works and a basis for a critique of art as such. Central to that critique is the notion of the limited role of the aesthetic in the psychological development of the individual. Pattison discusses Kierkegaard's diagnosis of his time as a reflective age, an age without passion, in which have been lost not only the immediacy required of great art but also the conditions for a religious understanding that allows us to see that what currently counts as Christianity is a form of aestheticism. He also notes that despite the narrow scope that Kierkegaard accorded art, he has been embraced by modern artists who, as Pattison explains, are attracted to Kierkegaard because of the tension in his works.

There is a continuing debate on the extent of Hegel's influence on the early Kierkegaard. Whatever the outcome of this debate, there is no doubt that the early pseudonymous authorship, notably *Concluding Unscientific Postscript*, contains a stinging and often satirical attack upon Hegel and his Danish epigones. In "Kierkegaard and Hegel," Merold Westphal explores several points of contact between the two thinkers. Regarding one issue, to be revisited in Andrew Cross's essay, Westphal notes that for different reasons both Kierkegaard and Hegel believed that irony, considered as an existence posture, had to be overcome. In an examination of *Fear and Trembling* Westphal argues that the issue for Kierkegaard was: either Hegel or Abraham, speculative philosophy or faith. Finally, Westphal, in examining the epistemology of *Concluding Unscientific Postscript*, offers a detailed analysis of Kierkegaard's critique of Hegel's quest for Absolute Knowledge. Of particular interest here is the fact that Westphal relates Kierkegaard's epistemological critique of speculative idealism to his ethico-religious critique of the same.

As Westphal's essay reveals, not only is Kierkegaard an ironical thinker, irony is a recurrent topic of his thought. Andrew Cross ("Neither Either Nor Or: The Perils of Reflexive Irony") scrutinizes

Kierkegaard's doctoral thesis, *The Concept of Irony with Continual Reference to Socrates*, and shows that the characteristics Kierkegaard finds in verbal irony, for instance the contradiction between internal and external, detachment, and the ironist's sense of superiority, become features of what some of Kierkegaard's pseudonyms, especially Johannes Climacus, were to treat as a distinctive orientation toward existence. In *Concluding Unscientific Postscript*, Johannes Climacus argues that irony is a transitional phase between the aesthetic and ethical modes of existence. Cross contends that ironists cannot take an ironical attitude toward their own lives, so that for this reason and others, the ironical perspective contains the seeds of its own downfall. It is a downfall, however, that from a Kierkegaardian point of view is not to be regretted.

C. Stephen Evans ("Realism and Antirealism in Kierkegaard's *Concluding Unscientific Postscript*") begins by observing that contemporary Kierkegaard scholarship is divided into two main camps, those who read Kierkegaard, however indirectly, as making truth claims, and those who see him as a proto-poststructuralist, a precursor of Derrida and Lacan. According to the latter, it is a mistake frequently made by bowdlerizing theologians to read Kierkegaard as offering anything akin to positive doctrines about anything. Evans argues that this conflict of interpretation can profitably be understood as a moment in the realism/antirealism debate. Indeed, if Evans is right, Kierkegaard himself is an untapped resource for participants in this debate. After offering a definition of "realism," Evans probes *Postscript*, a text that has been used to support both realist and antirealist readings. Tackling a number of passages that appear to support an antirealist interpretation, Evans forcefully argues that while no less skeptical than Kant about our access to "things in themselves," Kierkegaard did believe that through the "organ" of belief or faith we have access to other realities. Thus, on Evans's reading, Kierkegaard both acknowledges the limits of human knowledge and affirms the realistic and independent character of what is known.

Writing in the hand of Johannes Climacus, Kierkegaard pronounced the famous dictum "subjectivity is truth." While the source of many a myth, the statement indicates the enormous emphasis that Kierkegaard placed on subjectivity, inwardness, and what can loosely be referred to as the emotional life. Cross has provided an analysis of one form of subjectivity, namely, that of the ironical perspective. Robert C. Roberts ("Existence, Emotion, and Virtue: Classical Themes in Kierkegaard") reflects on the relation between thought, emotion, and character in a wide range of Kierkegaard's writings. Kierkegaard, no less than Aristotle, believed the good life to be characterized not just by action but by a certain quality of feeling. Roberts shows that on Kierkegaard's view our passions are not simply internal modulations that we passively endure; quite the contrary, we are to a degree responsible for how we interpret ourselves and our world, an interpretation that has everything to do with how we feel. Moreover, the patterns of our thought and feelings are the contours of our character. Finally, focusing on *Christian Discourses*, Roberts specifies a number of distinctively Christian passional dispositions, illustrating them, in the way of the psychologist he is discussing, with a rich gallery of exemplars of the various forms of subjectivity he has extracted from the writings.

Kierkegaard and his pseudonyms make generous use of the image of a leap to describe the transition to faith. Though poststructuralists would disagree, it might be argued that Kierkegaard was consumed with the project of veridically representing the inner transformation from unfaith to faith. In her study of this transformation ("Faith and the Kierkegaardian Leap") M. Jamie Ferreira argues that the idea of a qualitative transition is a structural element underlying and winding its way through the entire authorship. Focusing on *Philosophical Fragments* and *Concluding Unscientific Postscript*, Ferreira examines the variety of ways in which the leap can be understood, ranging from brute one-sided acts of will-power to an ineffable "happening." In the process, she reflects upon the important role attributed to both passion and imagination in Kierkegaard's account of religious transformation.

Ferreira's essay indicates that Kierkegaard's vision of faith is marked by a certain tension if not ambivalence. There are texts that invite a volitionist reading; that is, they would seem to suggest that faith is conditioned by an act of will. There are others, however, in which Kierkegaard stresses that it is only by the mercy and grace of God that God comes into our lives. Timothy P. Jackson ("Arminian Edification: Kierkegaard on Grace and Free Will") reads Kierkegaard as rejecting the claim that we are saved through irresistible grace as well as any "metaphysical account that would claim compatibility between determinism and freedom of the will." As his title suggests, Jackson submits that Kierkegaard's understanding of grace is similar to that of the Dutch Reformed theologian Jacob Arminius (1560-1609), in that both Kierkegaard and Arminius believed faith to be a universally offered gift that we are free either to accept or reject. But what does Kierkegaard mean when he stresses repeatedly that we are free? Jackson's essay is, among other things, a sustained attempt to answer this difficult but important question.

Ethico-religious phenomena, on Kierkegaard's view, often need to be communicated indirectly. The lack of directness he bestows on his own writings oblique method of communication shows what problems this can give rise to for the reader. Ronald M. Green's "'Developing' *Fear and Trembling*" finds at least five layers of meaning in that text. On one level, the story of Abraham is being used to present faith in all its primitivity, showing that faith is not a simple version of philosophy. Green argues that *Fear and Trembling* is also offered as a course in the psychology of religious transformation, the primary lesson here being the distinction drawn by the pseudonymous author, Johannes de silentio, between the movement of infinite resignation and the movement of faith. Other themes include a commentary on the relation between our moral duties and our duties to God. Green also contends that there is an underlying message about sin, grace, and salvation: If God can forgive Abraham his murderous intentions, surely he can work wonders in our lives too. Finally, Green illuminates the personal dimension of *Fear and Trembling* with respect to Kierkegaard's relationship with his father and his break with Regine.

Repetition appeared on the same day as *Fear and Trembling*. Written under the pseudonym Constantin Constantius, it remains one of Kierkegaard's most perplexing works. The author's concept of repetition is notoriously hard to grasp. He tells us that repetition is recollecting forward, that it is the interest of metaphysics, but also that on which metaphysics founders. The idea of repetition is connected also with repentance, atonement, and it is identified with eternity. It is also the "watchword of ethics." Edward F. Mooney ("*Repetition:* Getting the World Back") unravels the various strands in this tangle of meanings and argues that, first and foremost, repetition is a form of meaning-acquisition bound up with the double movement of giving up and receiving back the world. This brings the notion of repetition into close contact with the topics of *Fear and Trembling*. Mooney addresses an issue directly addressed by Ferreira and Jackson, namely, to what extent, if any, religious transformation – understood here as repetition – is an active process, concluding that repetition is best grasped as a receptive process rather than an act of acquisition.

One lesson conveyed by Kierkegaard's authorship is that an interest in leading the good life is to no avail unless you know what you are up against in yourself. Kierkegaard's two depth-psychologically oriented pseudonyms, Vigilius Haufniensis and Anti-Climacus, remind us that while anxiety and despair are indications of our spiritual nature, they are also states to be overcome. In "Anxiety in *The Concept of Anxiety*" Gordon D. Marino summarizes some of the major themes in that work (also translated as *The Concept of Dread*). These include Kierkegaard's view of the nature of psychology and its place among the sciences, and of the role played by anxiety in the account given of the Fall. Marino then evaluates the book's concept of anxiety and concludes with some reflections on the claim that anxiety can be a resource for the education of the spirit.

The same two pseudonyms all but predicted that we would one day come to understand both anxiety and despair as medical conditions to be treated pharmaceutically if necessary. Yet, as Alastair Hannay explains ("Kierkegaard and the Variety of Despair"), to think of despair as akin to a clinical depression that we passively suffer would simply be a manifestation of what Anti-Climacus calls "the cunning and sophistry present in all despair." After contrasting Kierkegaard's concept of despair with Hegel's, Hannay compares the presentation of despair in *Either/Or* with the systematic account given in *The Sickness unto Death*, pointing to significant similarities between the two. In the latter work the forms despair assumes, though many and varied, all reduce to the vain attempt to be rid of one's self. But what, asks Hannay, does Anti-Climacus mean by this self? Is it the self we just happen to be, or is it the self in view of some hard-to-fulfill spiritual expectation? Hannay defends the latter reading, identifies its reference to Kierkegaard himself and to Danish social life, and invites the question, what in this conception can be of interest to us today?

Whenever Kierkegaard speaks of ethico-religious phenomena, he strives to provide an account consistent with Scripture. Nowhere is this more true than when he and his pseudonyms articulate what he sometimes calls a "second" or "new ethics," that is, one that unlike Greek ethics assumes and takes into account the sinfulness of human beings. In an essay that, like Ronald M. Green's, relates Kierkegaard to Kant, Philip L. Quinn ("Kierkegaard's Christian Ethics") presents some central features and problems confronting Kierkegaard's ethico-religious position. Focusing on the signed *Works of Love* and the pseudonymous *Practice in Christianity*, Quinn examines Kierkegaard's insistence that Jesus commands us to a nonpreferential form of love. Quinn explains how Kierkegaard confronts the Kantian objection that love, as a feeling, is not subject to the will and so cannot be commanded. He notes that Kierkegaard took Christianity to call not for the admiration but the imitation of Christ and concludes with some of Kierkegaard's observations on how admiration can function as a self-serving ethical evasion.

Hermann Deuser's "Religious Dialectics and Christology" examines Kierkegaard's concept of religion. He sees it as forged in response to Protestant (Lutheran) Christology, Hegelian philosophy, and Kierkegaard's personal experience of mid-nineteenth-century European society. On Deuser's account Kierkegaard's writing is an attempt both to defend Christianity from its cultural despisers and to present a faithful specification of what it means to be a Christian. Kierkegaard's view contains a radicalization of traditional Christology in *Concluding Unscientific Postscript*'s "paradoxical" Religiousness B, in the role given to guilt and sin in the overcoming of the epistemological distance between a religious interest and its object, and in a transformation of traditional and idealist dialectics into an existential dialectic. Deuser is concerned throughout to point out how Kierkegaard's polemics influenced both the style and the content of his authorship, and especially the Christology of Anti-Climacus's *Practice in Christianity*. In conclusion he offers a Kierkegaardian evaluation of the prospects for and liabilities of a Christian social ethic, stressing that there is no hint of an anarchistic direction in Kierkegaard's concern to keep religion out of politics.

The theme of the separation of religion from politics is developed further in Klaus-M. Kodalle's "The Utilitarian Self and the 'Useless' Passion of Faith." Kodalle considers Kierkegaardian religiosity in the light of postmodernity's indifference and skepticism on the one hand and its proneness to irrational religious needs on the other. The rational way with religiosity has been to reduce it to its sociological and psychological functions, but Kierkegaard's notion of religiosity as (in Kodalle's term) "absolute spiritual presence" resists this reduction. The very attempt to capture the God-relationship in a utilitarian vocabulary betrays a fundamental misunderstanding. Kodalle cites, paraphrases, and discusses Kierkegaard's case for a religiosity that transcends the world of problem-solving strategies. The essay draws together many themes from the earlier essays: loss of passion (Pattison), loss of self (Hannay), what Kodalle terms "the courage to be powerless," which is also integral to the notion of a nonpreferential love (Quinn) as well as the leap (Ferreira). Kodalle adds to these themes the built-in utilitarianism of reason, its echo in the theology of God's having a "cause" that we can then "serve," the difficulty of thinking against the utilitarian grain of reason, the pull of conformity and of authority. Reverting to the myth of irrationalism, Kodalle shows that Kierkegaard's own view of faith, far from denying the value of clear and honest thinking, requires that reason "be brought to bear to the fullest extent possible."

NOTES

1 G. Lukács, *Soul and Form* (Cambridge: MIT Press, 1971); also in *The Lukács Reader*, ed. Arpad Kadarkay (Oxford and Cambridge, Mass.: Basil Blackwell, 1995). See also the editor's introduction (ibid., p. 4) for Lukács's recognition of his earlier "Kierkegaard phase."

2 *Pap.* X^I A 266 p. 177. The translation here is that of the Penguin Classics selection, *Kierkegaard's Papers and Journals*, trans. Alastair Hannay (Harmondsworth: Penguin Press, 1996), p. 382.

1 "Out with it!": The modern breakthrough, Kierkegaard and Denmark

His entire life was one of personal engagement with himself, and then [Divine] Guidance comes along and adds to it world-historical significance.

– *Søren Kierkegaards Papirer* (*Pap.* X¹ A 266, 177)

Has it ever occurred to you, dear reader, to entertain just a little doubt concerning the well-known principle that the outer is the inner and the inner is the outer? Well, frankly, this doubt has not plagued the present author so very much. Or at least a historian cannot be nearly as much a doubter on this score as Victor Eremita, opening his editorial remarks in *Either/Or*, would seem to want him to be.

Let us consider the following examples. On 19 October 1855, when he lay dying in Frederik's Hospital, Søren Kierkegaard had a caller. It was his brother, the theologian and pastor Peter Christian Kierkegaard, later a bishop and briefly a cabinet minister. Peter had traveled from his parish at Pedersborg-by-Sorø in west-central Zealand, in those days a considerable journey. Søren refused to receive his brother, who went home the next day.¹ That same day Søren admitted his friend Emil Boesen for a visit. Boesen asked him if he wished to receive the Eucharist. "Yes," answered Kierkegaard, "but from a layman, not a pastor." Boesen protested that this would be difficult to arrange. "Then I will die without it." Kierkegaard explained his position by stating that "pastors are civil servants of the Crown – they have nothing to do with Christianity."² These two deathbed refusals created scandals that followed Kierkegaard (and his brother) to the

15

grave and beyond, and it is important to realize that they were both *private* and *public* acts. Kierkegaard knew that his refusal to receive the Eucharist would soon become public knowledge, which it did almost immediately.[3] Similarly, he made sure to inquire as to whether his refusal to receive his brother had created a public stir.[4]

For historians and biographers, if there were not some important connection between the internal and the external, between the private and the public, the personal and the political, their jobs would not be worth doing, and they would presumably be doing something else. In the case of Kierkegaard, for instance, it has been impossible to resist the temptation to believe that when he talks in his works about the necessity of outgrowing "childish things" he is talking both about his society and about himself. This is not an essay in psychohistory. Rather, it is an attempt to investigate some of the factors in Kierkegaard's understanding of his family life that helped change his understanding of the life of *"familien Danmark"* – and vice versa. The boundary between "public" and "private" is arbitrary and ultimately artificial. Our lives are what they are, whole and complicated: lived alone, but with notions and structures received from others; and lived with others, but with ideas and actions for which the single individual is responsible. The boundary between history and biography is thus also arbitrary and is far more permeable than may be commonly supposed. The present essay is an attempt to explain and depict the connection between the two in the case of Kierkegaard.

I. DENMARK'S CHILDHOOD

Over the course of the 1840s Denmark's "childhood" was coming to an end. Since the latter part of the seventeenth century Denmark had been an absolute monarchy in which most political, social, and cultural power was concentrated in an oligarchical coalition of the crown and several hundred families. This group included the largest property holders, the most prosperous banking and mercantile houses, and the academically educated office holders in the upper echelons of the civil service. This was a tight, cozy, clubby, endogamous little society. The more than ninety percent of the Danish population who worked with their hands – primarily in agriculture – were not a part of this world. Then, within a comparatively short period of time it became impossible to continue to exclude the great majority of ordinary people from public life. In 1848 and 1849, for economic and political reasons – not the least of which was the need to assert Denmark's national identity and integrity in the face of German nationalism – Denmark was transformed into a constitutional monarchy with a representative government based on near-universal manhood suffrage, probably the broadest suffrage in the world at the time. Now the little people were to be a part of the shaping of public policy, and, equally important in our context, a part of the shaping of public taste, of the making of official culture.[5]

This transition was greeted with acclaim by some, including the Peasant Party and many National Liberals. After some initial hesitation it was warmly welcomed by the nationalistic "awakener" and theologian N. F. S. Grundtvig and his numerous supporters. Kierkegaard, too, despite a great many misgivings, eventually came to see the new democratic age as the inevitable way of the future and, indeed, as the will of "[Divine] Guidance" (*Styrelsen*). He came, for example, to see the atomism of the new age as fraught not merely with danger but also with the opportunity of developing each person into a full and responsible individual. In this, he differed greatly from the authority figures of the conservative mainstream of the Golden Age, the men who had once been his mentors. Bishop Jacob Peter Mynster, it is true, officially bade the new age welcome and sang the praises of the "new" Danish People's Church,[6] but it was obvious to all who knew him that he loathed this new democratic age and that his praise of its People's Church was merely a necessary political accommodation.[7] And the aloof, patrician Johan Ludvig Heiberg, who had no need to reach a compromise with the new political and cultural state of affairs, merely recited his litany about the dangers of atomism, heaped scorn upon the age, and withdrew from the follies of the human race into a lofty and bitter isolation. Nonetheless, in earlier years these men, Mynster and Heiberg – "the great coterie," as Kierkegaard called them[8] – had served as models (or even as father figures) for Kierkegaard in matters of religion and aesthetics, respectively.

II. DEAD SOULS: HEIBERG AND KIERKEGAARD

Heiberg would have been the first to insist, and quite properly, that he was no reactionary in matters of politics, culture, and public taste. As an Hegelian, he believed that people were capable of attaining higher levels of insight into their own individual lives and into the life of society as a whole, and that as their insights matured, they were entitled to an increasing share in the direction of public affairs. Heiberg believed that the intellect was the highest and most characteristically human faculty and thus quite fittingly adopted the model of the school or the classroom with respect to the social function of his own art. An artist (in this case a poet or playwright) is a tutor, and the individuals who constitute "the public" are his pupils. The artist's task is to instruct, to serve as the catalyst who assists the uncultivated (*udannet*) individual in gaining the higher outlook called "cultivation" (*Dannelse*), which will in turn enable the individual to find his appointed place in the differentiated and organic whole constituting society. Individuals as such have no place in Heiberg's polity. Those who have acquired the insight provided by cultivation "represent" the rest. Apart from representation, individual existence is mere "atomism." Heiberg expounded this theory in a series of essays from the early 1840s.[9] The problem was that Heiberg's intended pupils – the comfortably off and reasonably literate but (according to Heiberg's views) only half-educated Copenhagen middle class – were also the target of his increasingly pointed ridicule and sarcasm. This middle class was disinclined to play the obedient pupil, sitting quietly on the school benches in Heiberg's didactic temple of art.[10] They were bad pupils, naughty children who, at this rate, were never going to grow up to become responsible citizens, either of the world of art or of the civic realm. Nowhere did Heiberg heap his scorn and displeasure upon his "immature" public with as much trenchancy as in the stinging "apocalyptic" comedy, *A Soul after Death* [*En Sjæl efter Døden*] from the collection *New Poems* [*Nye Digte*], published in 1840.[11]

Heiberg's *A Soul after Death* is one of the most important works of Danish literature of the 1840s (and of the entire Danish Golden Age), and in some ways deserves to be ranked with Kierkegaard's remarkable output during the same decade. Both Heiberg and Kierkegaard were concerned with the individual's evasion of responsibility, with, as they both called it, "spiritlessness" (*Aandløshed*), the state of being dead while yet alive. For Heiberg this was the state of the respectable middle-class "Soul" who, after death, discovers that his entire earthly life, preoccupied as it had been with politics and the busyness of the world's finitude, had been "Hell," a sort of living death. The "Soul" can be granted admission neither to the Christian Paradise nor to the classical Elysium, because he has been a poor pupil and is lacking in cultivation. He is a shallow, pitiable, brainless wretch, the fit target of ridicule.

In many ways, Kierkegaard's *The Sickness unto Death* [*Sygdommen til Døden*] (written 1848, published 1849) invites comparison with *A Soul after Death*, and not merely because of the striking similarity of the titles. And as mentioned, both authors claimed to be concerned for the well-being of the "spirit" or "soul" and to be the enemies of souls that are not souls, enemies of "spiritlessness," a form of living death, which, both agreed, was found with great frequency among the "bourgeois philistines" (*Spidsborgerne*). But here they part company, and quite fundamentally. For Heiberg, the spokesman for cultivation, the spiritless are spiritless precisely because they are philistines. For Kierkegaard, on the other hand, the philistines are philistines because they are spiritless. This may seem like a distinction without a difference, but the difference is in fact enormous, because, unlike the intellectualist Heiberg, Kierkegaard equates spiritlessness not with a lack of education and cultivation but with a lack of *will*: "self" is "spirit," and "the more will, the more self" (*SV*¹ XI 127, 142). For Kierkegaard, being a fully fledged self, an adult, is quite specifically within the reach of every individual if he or she so wills, and in *The Sickness unto Death* he attacks the speculative intellectualism of Hegel, Heiberg, and others (227–38). No, according to Kierkegaard being an adult, being "an individual person, this particular individual person, alone before God, alone in that enormous effort and in that enormous responsibility" (117), is a possibility open to absolutely everyone, regardless of his or her intellectual capacity or level of "cultivation" in the sense in which the term is used by Heiberg – or for that matter by Hans Lassen Martensen, Mynster, and the other official representatives of Golden Age Christendom. According to Kierkegaard, the true cause of the sickness unto death has nothing to do with Heiberg's snobbish etiology in *A Soul after Death*. Indeed, so far is true spiritlessness removed from the Golden Age definition, that on the contrary, the principal stronghold of spiritlessness is Golden Age Christendom itself.[12]

Thus Heiberg and Kierkegaard agree that there is a plague of spiritlessness, an army of dead souls, but their diagnoses are diametrically opposite. That the two works should be quite similar is no surprise: Heiberg was the trend-setting author for much of fashionable Copenhagen in the 1830s and the early 1840s, and though twenty-two years younger Kierkegaard was at least a peripheral member of Heiberg's salon circle.[13] What is surprising is that the works are worlds apart. During the 1840s Kierkegaard had developed a radical critique of the entire taste-making clique that dominated polite Denmark. He was ready to move, and then came the political events of 1848, when "in the course of a couple of months, the past [was] ripped away from the present with such passion that it seemed like a generation had gone by" (SV¹ XIII 555). The two works about dead souls seemed worlds apart because, according to Søren Kierkegaard, they *were* worlds apart. Heiberg had failed to draw the consequences of the developments of recent times and wanted to close the door on the middle class that sought its salvation in politics. In his contempt for that middle class Heiberg lost touch with his constituency and with his own times and retreated from the scene. Kierkegaard, on the other hand, did not give up on the lost soul of the middle class, which on the contrary was his ideal interlocutor, a quiet, somewhat withdrawn ("encapsulated" [indesluttet]) individual who is

able to hold every extraneous person – i.e., everyone – away from his self, while externally he is entirely a "real person." He is an educated man, a husband, father, even an unusually capable official, a respectable father, pleasant to be with, very sweet to his wife, carefulness itself with his children. And a Christian? – well, yes, he is that, too – however, he prefers to avoid talking about it, even if he is happy to see, with a certain wistful joy, that his wife occupies herself edifyingly with godly things. He goes to church very rarely, because it seems to him that most of the pastors don't know what they are talking about. (SV¹ XI 175)

It is here, in the dawning consciousness of despair, that Kierkegaard sought his public, the very public that Heiberg consigned to Hell. Again, Kierkegaard was worlds away from his one-time mentor, very aware of the gulf that separated himself (Kierkegaard, i.e., "the graveyard,"[14] who was well acquainted with dead souls) from lofty Heiberg (i.e., "the mountain"). Kierkegaard was undoubtedly familiar with the puns on his deathly name and saw it as his task to awaken the dead, not to mock them; to save "souls," not to celebrate their perdition with an aristocratic smirk.

III. THE KIERKEGAARD FAMILY

Søren Aabye Kierkegaard was the youngest of seven children of a powerful and wealthy merchant, Michael Pedersen Kierkegaard, and a mother, Ane Sørensdatter Lund, who is nearly invisible to history. The story of the father is well known: a poor boy from the heaths of west Jutland, he traveled to Copenhagen, was apprenticed to an uncle who was a cloth merchant (a not unusual profession for Jutlanders-turned-cityfolk), struck out on his own at an early age, and soon became a wealthy man. He married a business partner's sister, but the marriage was childless and ended after less than two years with the death of the wife. Michael Pedersen subsequently married his serving maid and distant cousin, Ane Sørensdatter Lund, whom he had impregnated and then offered a marriage contract. He was known to be an astute businessman and a stubborn individual, and the contract for this hasty marriage was most unfavorable to his intended wife, who in the event of a divorce would have received almost nothing and certainly not custody of her child. The one-sidedness of the proposed contract provoked offense among the officials in the court where it was to be registered, and they attempted, with only limited success, to compel the wealthy widower to grant more generous terms.[15] The concern of the court officials turned out to be unfounded, as the marriage lasted some thirty-eight years and resulted in seven children.

Michael Pedersen was forty years old at the time of this second marriage and sufficiently wealthy to be able to retire from active business life and support a large household very comfortably on the income from his investments. He seems to have dominated the family more through his steady habits, firm manner, and his quiet and very serious, perhaps melancholic, religious temperament than through any external compulsion. Michael Pedersen was already fifty-six years old when Søren was born, and his youngest son al-

ways knew him as an old man. This is the way in which Kierkegaard's father has come down to us, primarily through his son
Søren's version of the story: a sternly religious old man, who was
rather wealthy but plainly had peasant roots. This peasant side of
Michael Pedersen Kierkegaard is illuminated further when one considers that he was one of nine children born to an apparently quite
ordinary (and therefore poor) farm family from the tiny west Jutland
settlement of Sædding. One of Michael Pedersen's brothers did
leave Sædding, but only in order to live with an uncle in southern
Jutland, where he died young and unmarried. Another brother spent
part of his adult life in Copenhagen, where he was well known as a
local madman who wore three overcoats in the summertime, but he
returned to Sædding in his later years and died there. The remaining six siblings spent their entire lives in obscurity in Sædding or
very close by. The one who was best off was apparently his sister
Else Pedersdatter, who married locally, inherited the family farm
from her brother, adding it to the holdings of her husband, with
whom she had one child, and lived to the age of seventy-five. But
despite her inheritance Else Pedersdatter led a pinched existence.
She regularly wrote to her wealthy Copenhagen relatives – her
brother Michael Pedersen and, after his death, her nephews Peter
Christian and Søren – in the hope of financial assistance, which she
received.[16]

Søren Kierkegaard's mother, about whom very little is known,
and who is never once mentioned by name in the thousands upon
thousands of pages of Kierkegaard's published and unpublished
writings, was a servant woman from a poor Jutland peasant family.
The only primary source the present author has been able to uncover in the archives tells us that her family owned "one cow and
four sheep"; that her father was a convivial man with a certain natural authority; and that her family "were all respectable and honor-
able people of their station." Ane Sørensdatter was one of six
siblings and the youngest of three sisters, all named "Ane," and was
therefore further specified as "little Ane."[17] She may have been little but was presumably not without a certain strength of character.
After she left her childhood home in Jutland to serve in the family
of her brother and sister-in-law in Copenhagen, Ane Sørensdatter reportedly had a disagreement and quit, becoming a servant in the

home of her distant cousin, Michael Pedersen Kierkegaard, by whom she became pregnant not long after he had been widowed. Forced marriage or not, Ane Sørensdatter managed to pass on her patronymic to three of her seven children, while her husband, by comparison, passed on his patronymic to two.[18]

These were "peasant roots" indeed, and must have been painfully obvious in Golden Age Copenhagen. The father had been compelled to build bridges between the Jutland heath and the respectable bourgeoisie of the capital. He was both shrewd at business and serious (and perhaps shrewd, as well) about religion. While retaining his rural pietist connection to the Herrnhut Congregation of Brothers, Michael Pedersen also made Jacob Peter Mynster his pastor. Depending on one's interpretation, one could say that by attending the Herrnhut congregation for evening prayer during the week and Mynster's Church of Our Lady on Sunday mornings, Michael Pedersen expressed the tension between independent peasant religiousness and respectable Copenhagen piety – or one could say that he was carefully hedging his bet socially. At any rate, given the social structure of early nineteenth-century Denmark, what is remarkable is not the very ordinary poverty of the family's origins, but the fact that Michael Pedersen and Ane Sørensdatter, alone of the total of fifteen siblings in the two families from which they stemmed, managed to make their way into the respectable upper-middle class. Of their seven children, two of their daughters married into a quite well-to-do family, while one of their sons became a respected theologian, bishop, and cabinet minister, and another became one of history's most famous philosophers. Nonetheless, being only one generation removed from the sheepherders of west Jutland and the heirs of a fortune made only too visibly and recently in the ignoble world of business, the Kierkegaard children could hardly avoid being regarded as parvenues in the polite society of Copenhagen.

By 1834, when he was twenty-one years old, Kierkegaard had lost his mother and five of his six siblings.[19] Four of these deaths, including the loss of his two favorite sisters, Petrea and Nicoline, as well as the death of his mother, had taken place within a span of about two years, from 1832 to 1834. Only the old man and his oldest and youngest sons, Peter Christian and Søren Aabye, survived.

IV. THE SONS OF THE FATHER

The relation between Søren and Peter cannot be understood apart from their rivalry in a triangular relation of desire for recognition by the father. There was a definite pecking order in the family, as is summed up by Peter's journal entry on the occasion of Søren's confirmation at fourteen. "Søren was confirmed on the 20th and received my watch; I [received] Father's."[20] It does not take a Freudian wizard to interpret this entry. The older brother was a forceful intellect, hardworking, a young man of impressive competence and credentials, perhaps a bit of a grind, but just the type that teachers love – a hard act to follow. It seems that wherever Søren went, the Borgerdyd School, the University, he had been preceded by his elder brother and had a good deal to live up to. Søren was extraordinarily clever, with a sharp tongue and a penchant for getting into trouble – the classic younger brother.

Søren was the youngest in a large family, the Benjamin, the spoilt favorite, perhaps, but prevented by that very status from having to – or being allowed to – grow up, to possess "authority" (*Myndighed*). For too much of his life, he was to survive by using the power of the weaker, the weapon of a boy, of one who is not taken seriously: *teasing*, whether this was his merciless teasing in school and at home, where he was known as "the fork," or his later insistent teasing of Heiberg, Martensen, and Mynster, a temptation he could never resist. It was always a question of growing up, of attaining adulthood, of reaching the age of majority, which was the "age of authority" (*Myndighedsalder*), in Kierkegaard's time twenty-five. In the officially Christian culture of the Golden Age, religious and earthly authority were closely intertwined, and thus it is not surprising that Kierkegaard's later wrestling with questions of authority applied not merely to the knotty problem of who had the right to claim *religious* authority, but as to whether an ordinary person, himself for example, had any authority at all vis-à-vis "the Establishment" (*det Bestaaende*) – the established order of things in church and state. In the end, Kierkegaard would decide that if he did not possess authority he did at least have the consent of Divine Guidance in his assumption of adult power as "a man of character" who could "overturn the Establishment." The question of adulthood – of growing up or of being permitted to grow up – was also of central importance in the life of the Danish common folk, the little people, who had been kept in a kind of "tutelage" (*Formynderskab*) by their social superiors. We will later return to "*familien Danmark*," but for now we will remain with the Kierkegaard family, where it would be Søren's task, as the youngest, to win not just his father's affection but his recognition, not just his elder brother's amused or irritated condescension but his respect.

Both Peter and Søren studied theology. Peter entered the university first, of course, in the 1820s, which were years of extreme turbulence in the Danish Church, thanks largely to the agitation of Grundtvig, whose (occasionally vacillating) follower Peter became. Grundtvig and Peter's Grundtvigian friends were regular guests at the Kierkegaard family home; they discussed church matters with Michael Pedersen and can scarcely have failed to have had an impact on Søren. The church politics of the 1820s and 1830s were much rougher than the gentle protest (if it was even that) that had been expressed by membership in the Herrnhut Congregation in the decade or two after the turn of the century, however, and although the cautious old man was intrigued with the Grundtvigians, he could hardly have been expected to give up his reverence for Mynster for the sake of these young troublemakers.[21]

While we don't have evidence concerning young Søren's reaction to all this, all indications are that he thought Grundtvig a fool and retained his father's deep respect for Mynster. Indeed, Søren later insisted quite plausibly that he had long maintained a loyalty to Mynster out of piety to his late father. It should be noted that this also had the effect of putting Søren in the same camp as his father, while leaving Peter to the troublesome Grundtvigians. Even worse, in Søren's eyes, Peter was a "moderate" Grundtvigian who did not always have the courage of his convictions and was repeatedly led to temporize. Peter was always plagued with scruples, with second and third thoughts. He lacked self-certainty, and his qualms of conscience often developed into depressive malingering. He accepted his first parish call, but immediately had doubts and backed out of it. The income attached to it was rather meager, as it turned out, and a few years later he accepted a call with a much more substantial living. This does not necessarily prove anything, of course, but Peter did seem to have a way of turning vacillation to advantage.

For Søren it could sometimes be difficult to discern the line between moderation and opportunism. Peter became a middle-of-the-road Grundtvigian, someone, for example, who could talk to Martensen. From Søren's point of view this was not a recommendation. Peter behaved cautiously and respectably, while Søren appeared at times crazy, even dissolute. Peter managed his money carefully, Søren was not nearly as careful.[22] Søren scandalously broke off his engagement and never married. Peter married carefully, even strategically, twice. First, he married Marie Boisen, whose father was Bishop of Lolland and whose brother was Grundtvig's son-in-law, and, when she died soon thereafter, he subsequently married Grundtvig's niece Henriette Glahn, who had spent part of her childhood in Grundtvig's home as a member of his family. This too was not necessarily a recommendation as far as Søren was concerned. And then there was Grundtvig himself, whom Søren perceived as full of bluster, always threatening to walk out of the Established Church, but meanwhile sitting quite comfortably in one of the snuggest sinecures in the country: nice pay, very little work (*Pap.* XI³ B 182 p. 300). Søren dismissed Grundtvig as unserious. Søren delighted in breaking up "coteries," and he took particular joy in stirring up confusion in the Grundtvigian camp (*Pap.* IX A 206 p. 104). From a fairly early period something close to a state of war prevailed between Søren and Peter. Søren stuck with Mynster, the man he called "his father's pastor," and thus, as he hoped, with his father.

V. BISHOP MYNSTER: "MY FATHER'S PASTOR"

The old man, Michael Pedersen Kierkegaard, then, was the object of the rivalry. Peter was the rival. Peter's paragon Grundtvig was a buffoon, while Søren cherished an apparently unlimited reverence for Denmark's other major clerical figure, Bishop Mynster, "my father's pastor." But from an early date – though we don't know how early – Søren's reverence for Mynster was only *apparently* unlimited. We must remember that Mynster was the urbane aristocrat, who deigned on occasion to visit the Kierkegaard residence and talk with Michael Pedersen, and that although wealthy the Kierkegaard family had retained a certain stubborn identification with its peasant origins. Søren was always sensitive to the least sign of condescension toward his father (whom Søren says he regarded as a spiritual giant) on the part of Mynster (whom Søren respected, but who nevertheless was tainted with an ineradicable scent of the perfume of *haute bourgeois* aestheticism).

For the sake of his father, whom Søren portrayed as a good, strong, pious, country man who had prostrated himself at the feet of Mynster, Søren did likewise. Things began to go badly, according to Søren's account, as soon as his father died, when he personally brought the word to the bishop, and Mynster – Søren alleges – shocked and dismayed Søren by seeming at first unable to remember who the old man was (*Pap.* XI² A 419 p. 409)! It is very revealing that although this episode supposedly took place on 9 August 1838, we only know about it from Kierkegaard's journal entry of 29 June 1855 (one of his very last); in other words, this incident apparently festered for seventeen years, right up to Kierkegaard's death. (It also ought to be noted that at the time of his father's death Søren Kierkegaard was twenty-five years old, the legal age of majority, though in a sense he had remained a minor (*umyndig*), now the spiritual ward or "parish child" (*sognebarn*) of Mynster as he had been the physical child of his father.) During these seventeen years Søren's journals recount an ever-accelerating demythologization of Mynster. He could never rid himself of his notion that Mynster had taken the old man – and the son, Søren – for fools! Starting in the mid-1840s matters became steadily worse, but as late as 1851 Søren could still summon up the filial piety he needed to pull himself together and have a conversation with Mynster on the anniversary of his father's death: "So I said that it had pleased me very much to talk with him today, because today was the anniversary of my father's death, and I wanted everything to be as it should be on this day" (*Pap.* X⁴ A 373 p. 221).

Mynster's crime, in Kierkegaard's eyes, was *personal*. It was a crime against his father – and through the father against the son. According to Søren's journals, Michael Pedersen Kierkegaard was a man who had struggled and suffered with Christianity all his life; he had been crushed by it. Søren's experience, through his father, was much the same. And here was the man on whom his father had depended, an earnest, well-spoken bishop, famous for his piety – who couldn't even remember who Michael Pedersen was on the day that he died! And this man, Mynster, had repeatedly humiliated Michael Pedersen's son Søren, whether merely by ignoring his efforts or – in studied obliviousness to the criticism contained in

Practice in Christianity – by deliberately misinterpreting Søren's views on church and state and turning them to account as support for his own position on the Established Church. In the worst incident, Mynster had added what he knew to be a gratuitous insult to the continuing injury he had heaped upon the Kierkegaards, father and son: He had publicly equated Søren Kierkegaard with M. A. Goldschmidt, editor of the satirical journal *The Corsair*, two peas in a pod![23]

And an important part of Mynster's crime was *social:* He could not recognize that a peasant like Michael Pedersen Kierkegaard could be an equal, an adult. Mynster's hauteur had a transitive effect. That is, we must remember, particularly in view of his lifelong, deadly earnest competition with his older brother, that Søren was desperate for his father to recognize *his* status as an adult, his manhood, his authority. Thus Søren saw himself as having to fight for his personal authority and adulthood on two fronts: against his weak and vacillating brother Peter, the moderate Grundtvigian, *and* against Mynster (and the entire Mynsterian establishment), who in blithe condescension had mocked the father and had deprived him of the ability to confer adult recognition on his youngest son. For Søren, the personal politics of the Kierkegaard family were inseparable from the church and cultural politics of Golden Age Denmark.

Of course Mynster's "Christianity" was self-serving hypocrisy, Kierkegaard insisted. Mynster hadn't permitted himself to be crushed by the God who had crushed Michael Pedersen and Søren Kierkegaard. In Søren's view, unlike Michael Pedersen, Mynster was *not* "a man of character, a man of principles, a man who stood fast when everything vacillated" (*SV*[1] XIV 10). Mynster survived the catastrophe of 1848 all too artfully. It would have been far preferable if he had lived up to his own words and "had had the character to fall along with everything else that fell" (*Pap.* XI[3] B 18,5; see also X[6] B 212 p. 335). No, "the truth was, that he was very worldly wise, but weak, pleasure-mad, and great only as an orator, . . . and *the misfortune of my life was that having been brought up by my late father with Mynster's sermons, I accepted this counterfeit note instead of protesting against it*" (*SV*[1] XIV 10). It cannot be more succinctly expressed: Kierkegaard was raised by his father, whom he portrayed as profoundly religious, to respect Mynster's Christianity, and according to Søren, it was out of filial piety to that father that he had refrained from calling attention to what he had long regarded as Mynster's glaring shortcomings.[24] But (again, in Søren's telling of the story) Mynster's unending condescension and pretended superiority, first to the father, and then to the son, released Søren from his obligation to respect his father's pastor. Indeed, the memory of his father obligated Søren to launch an all-out attack on Mynster's reputation and on the entire Golden Age Establishment he represented – and to speak up for what Søren called "the Christianity of the New Testament."

Søren bided his time until Mynster died and he could attack the man who had humiliated the father – and the son. That day came at the end of January 1854, and shortly thereafter Kierkegaard reflected in his journal on the importance of Mynster's death:

Bishop Mynster

Now he is dead. It would have been much preferable if he could have brought himself to conclude his life with the confession to Christianity that what he had represented had not really been Christianity but a toned-down version, because he carried an entire era. . . .

Dead without this confession, and everything is changed. Now the only thing remaining is the fact that his preaching has mired Christianity in a sensory illusion.

The situation is also changed with respect to my melancholy devotion to my late father's pastor. Because despite the fact that I know very well that I will always find something plausible in my old devotion to him and in my aesthetic appreciation, it would be too much if I could not talk more frankly about him, even after his death.

Originally I had wanted to transform my entire being into a triumph for Mynster. Later on, when I came to understand matters a bit more clearly, this remained my unchanged wish, but I had to require this little admission. This was not something I wanted for my own sake, and therefore I had the notion that it could certainly be done in such a way that it became a triumph for Bishop Mynster.

From then on there was a hidden misunderstanding between us, and I hoped that I could at least avoid attacking him while he was still alive. . . .

And yet it came close, close to the point where I thought I would have to attack him. I only missed one of his sermons, it was has last. I was not hindered by illness, but was in church to hear [another pastor] preach. What this signified to me was: now it must happen, now you must break your father's tradition. It was the last time that Mynster preached. God be praised, wasn't this as if it were [Divine] Guidance? (*Pap.* XI¹ A 1)

Then, with what Søren called the help of "Divine Guidance," the storm broke, and Kierkegaard unleashed his famous attack on the Church, which will not be discussed in detail here.[25] In the midst of the attack, in late September 1855, about a week before he collapsed on the street and was hospitalized with his final illness, Kierkegaard wrote one of his very last journal entries, dividing his judgment of Mynster into three categories – aesthetic, personal, and Christian:

Mynster was Great Indeed!

September 24, 1855

But from a Christian point of view he was not great. No. *Viewed aesthetically* he was great – as a counterfeiter.

Understood in this manner he had, aesthetically, my undivided admiration. *As a person* he had my undivided devotion, "also out of piety towards my late father." *Viewed from the Christian perspective,* [Divine] Guidance, in using me, assigned him the most dangerous of allies. (*Pap.* XI² A 437 p. 434; emphasis mine)

Here, shortly before his final illness and death, Kierkegaard again insists that his hand had been stayed out of personal considerations – specifically his filial obligation to his father – but that higher considerations ("Divine Guidance") had then compelled him to act against the man who had been his father's hero.

VI. KIERKEGAARD: OUTGROWING CHILDISH THINGS

Evidence of this connection between the inner and the outer, between Søren Kierkegaard's interpretation of the personal and family politics of recognition and adulthood in the Kierkegaard household and the larger politics of Denmark, can be traced in many fashions. Elsewhere, with evidence drawn principally from Kierkegaard's unpublished papers, the present author has traced Kierkegaard's evolving (negative) ecclesiology and his constantly escalating running polemic against Mynster.[26] Here we will take a brief look at a sample of how certain figures of adulthood (or manhood) assert themselves in Kierkegaard's published canon. Again and again, Kierkegaard's rhetoric constitutes a polemic against prolonged "childhood" and against "unmanliness." Kierkegaard equated childishness with unmanliness, which in turn was equated with being a "eunuch" and with "effeminacy," and so on. He assailed the established authority structure that denied him and other ordinary people the authority of their own adulthood. And according to Kierkegaard, this structure covered up for its own weakness ("effeminacy") by making sure that Kierkegaard and other "children of the parish" remained children. In its failure to be a strong and principled father, the established authority structure was transformed into a weak and wavering mother, who infantilizes her children.[27]

In his major treatment of ethics, *Works of Love* from 1847, Kierkegaard attacks those who have watered Christianity down by providing it with rational defenses, fit only for "unmanly" people and "eunuchs" (*Halvmænd*):

> Woe to him, who first thought of preaching Christianity without the possibility of offense. Woe to him who first flatteringly and triflingly, with recommendations and proofs, foisted off on people some unmanly stuff which was supposed to be Christianity! . . . [T]he more learned, the more excellent the *defense*, the more Christianity becomes as mutilated, as nullified, as exhausted as a eunuch. (*SV*[1] IX 190)

In *The Sickness unto Death*, written during the revolutionary months of 1848 and published the following year, the Pauline figure of the "child" and the "man" is used to illustrate the difference between the natural person and the Christian:

> The relation between the natural person and the Christian is like the relation between a child and a man: what the child shrinks from in horror is viewed as nothing by the man. The child does not know what is frightful. The man does know this, and he shrinks from it in horror. The child's imperfection is, first of all, not to know what is frightful, and secondly, implicit in this, the child shrinks from what is not frightful. (*SV*[1] XI 122–3)

Another example from *The Sickness unto Death*: "Despairing narrowmindedness is the lack of primality, or the state of having deprived oneself of one's primality, of having emasculated [*afmandet*, meaning "unmanned" or "castrated"] oneself in the spiritual sense" (*SV*[1] XI 146).

Not long thereafter, in 1851, Kierkegaard published *On My Activity as an Author*. The little tract reflected the revolutionary social and political changes of 1849, the year in which it was written and the year in which the Danish people received the democratic constitution that symbolized the new adulthood of the common people, who had outgrown the "childish stage" in which symbolic individuals from a higher social class could "represent" them, as in the aristocratic Heiberg's political theory:

> If the human race, or a large number of individuals in the race, have outgrown the childish stage in which another person can represent the Unconditioned [i.e., God] for them – well, nonetheless, the Unconditioned remains indispensable, indeed, it is more indispensable than ever. Then "the individual" himself must relate himself to the Unconditioned. (*SV*¹ XIII 509)

At about the same time that Kierkegaard published the above autobiographical fragment, he began writing *Judge for Yourself!*[28] Here he developed the childhood/adulthood figure quite explicitly, linking the end of childhood to the congregation's maturation into a sexually "knowing" being:

> There have been times when this sort of proclamation of Christianity was less offensive, even though it did not deserve unqualified praise, which it never does. These were times when the congregation was less knowing, less aware about the relation between working for something infinite and working for something finite. . . . As things now are, those who preach Christianity cannot come to openheartedness and a good conscience vis-à-vis an all-too-knowing congregation without making it clear which is which, whether it is the finite or the infinite which he wants. . . . It is like the situation with respect to modesty. In relation to a very little child modesty is one thing. As soon as it can be assumed that the child is sufficiently grown up to have acquired knowledge, then modesty is something different. To wish, after knowledge has been acquired, . . . to preserve the first sort of modesty would not only not be modesty but would be the most corrupt and corrupting immorality. . . . This is what is dangerous: when the congregation knows, and the preacher knows, and each knows that the other knows – *then* to refuse to come out with it, to wish to keep things on a more elevated, more formal plane, the untruth of which is clandestinely understood – *that* is what is dangerous and demoralizing. (*SV*¹ XII 410–11)

Near the end of his life, in *The Moment* (1855), Kierkegaard permitted himself the fun of mocking the pompous, robe-wearing clergy as a bunch of unmanly transvestites, whose clerical garb is "women's clothing." The message is clear: *they* (the clergy) are the immature, unmanly ones, and yet they are trying to keep *us* (the congregation, the ordinary people of Denmark) in an enforced tutelage, a prolonged childhood:

"Beware of those who wear long gowns." . . . It is women's attire, of course. And this leads us to think of something which is also characteristic of official Christianity: the unmanliness, the use of cunning, untruth, lies, in order to have power. . . . And this effeminacy is also characteristic of official Christianity in another way: the unconscious feminine coquettishness, which wants to and yet doesn't want to. . . . One must swoon, faint, when one is compelled to accept elevated and succulent sinecures, to which one is so definitely opposed that one only can decide to accept out of a feeling of duty. . . . Finally, there is of course something ambiguous and risqué about men in women's clothing. One is tempted to say that it conflicts with the police regulation which forbids men to wear women's clothing and vice versa. But in any case, it is something ambiguous, and ambiguity is precisely the most fitting expression for official Christianity.[29]

And in a subsequent issue of *The Moment* he turns directly to the question of Christianity and childhood:

[People say] "One must become a Christian as a child, it must be imbibed from childhood on." In other words, the parents do not want to have to be Christians, but must have a way of concealing this, namely by raising their children to be true Christians. The priests understand this secret very well, and this is why they often talk about Christian child-rearing, about this "serious business" by means of which the parents escape from the truly serious business. The situation of the parents in relation to their children is like that of the pastors in relation to their congregations. No more than the parents do the pastors have the desire to be Christians, but their congregations – *they* will be true Christians. . . .

So people raise their children to be Christians, as they say, which means that they stuff the child full of children's sweets – absolutely not the Christianity of the New Testament. And these children's sweets no more resemble the teachings about the cross, about suffering, about dying away, about hating oneself, any more than marmalade resembles cream of tartar. The parents taste a bit of the children's sweets and then become sentimental at the thought that they themselves are alas no longer Christians as they were when they were children, because only as a child can one really become a Christian. (*SV*[1] XIV 255)

Elsewhere in this same article Kierkegaard puts forward the rest of the argument, insisting that Christianity is not for the sort of children the Established Church urges us to become, but is in fact for *adults* and only for *adults*:

The truth is that one cannot become a Christian as a child. It is just as impossible as it is for a child to beget children. According to the New Testament, becoming a Christian presupposes a complete human existence, what in the natural person might be called a man's maturity. (*SV*¹ XIV 253)

In one of the very last entries in his journals, Kierkegaard gives an account of his personal journey. He maintains that he had needed to work through his youth, to reach maturity, and in so doing his understanding of his task had undergone a 180-degree reversal. Now, as a man, he understands that it is his task to destroy the Established Church that had played such an important role in denying adulthood, both in his own life and in the lives of ordinary people.

For many different reasons, and prompted by many different factors, I had the idea of defending the Established Church.

[Divine] Guidance has surely had the idea that I was precisely the person who was to be used to overturn the Establishment. But in order to prevent such an undertaking from being the impatient, perhaps arrogant, daring of a young man, I first had to come to understand my task as being just the opposite – and now, in what, inwardly understood, has been great torment, to be developed to take up the task when the moment came. (*Pap.* XI³ B 110)

Kierkegaard had grown up. He had become an adult. He was able to repair what he viewed as the private insult of Mynster to his father by breaking through into the public sphere, where he could finally speak in his own voice as a man of character. Kierkegaard had concluded that not "authority" but "character" was the issue.

VII. CONCLUSION: BREAKING THROUGH

At the beginning, we cited Kierkegaard's two private/public refusals on his deathbed: his refusal to receive his brother Peter, and his refusal to receive the Eucharist from the hands of a cleric. The present author has discussed the latter point, Søren Kierkegaard's falling out with the clergy and his ultimate break not only with the Danish Church but with *the* Church, with what he called "the concept of congregation," in more detail elsewhere.[30] What about Søren's refusal to see his brother? What had Peter done to deserve such treatment? As mentioned earlier, the record of the relationship between the two brothers is littered with evidence of feuding and ferocious rivalry.[31] The situation was greatly worsened in 1849, when Peter

held a public address, which he subsequently published, in which
he compared Søren's work with that of Hans Lassen Martensen, labeling Søren's "ecstasy" as opposed to Martensen's "sober-mindedness."[32] Rightly or wrongly, Søren felt that Peter's label, "ecstasy,"
was a codeword for "madness." (And as we will shortly see, in view
of Peter's eulogy a few years later, perhaps Søren was right to be sensitive on this point.) Stung, Søren counterattacked in his journals,
equating his brother and Martensen by linking them under the same
uncomplimentary heading: "The Martensen-Peter [Christian Kier-
kegaard] notion of sober-mindedness is to some extent an irreligious
notion of bourgeois-philistinism and complacency" (*Pap.* X^2 A 273
p. 201).

   If labeling Søren as "ecstatic" was one way of denying that his
younger brother was an adult, denying his "authority," and depriving him of a voice that was truly his own, Peter also had other ways.
In July 1855, at the height of Søren's campaign against the Church,
Peter ripped into his brother with a virulently critical speech, in
which he concluded by implying that Søren, even when he spoke
straightforwardly and in his own name, might not really stand behind his words. According to his own recollection, Peter concluded
his address with the following insinuation: "One could indeed almost come to imagine the possibility that even that which appeared
with the signature 'Søren Kierkegaard,' might not unconditionally
be his last word (but a point of view)."[33]

   In the light of the argument presented in the present essay concerning Kierkegaard's struggle to find his own voice and the "authority" with which to use it, it is not surprising that his brother
chose just this sort of weapon to use against him during the attack
on the Church. Peter's attempt to deprive Søren of the authority
with which to speak, even in his own name, should be viewed
against the larger background of Søren Kierkegaard's use of pseudonymity. One of the contentions of the present essay is that Søren
Kierkegaard's refusal to assert authority provides a framework for
understanding his use of pseudonyms. By distancing himself from
his own works, Kierkegaard was free to say whatever he wished.
One way to escape the problem of authority was to write under
pseudonyms. But after using pseudonyms that were "beneath" him,
Kierkegaard abandoned the tactic and wrote in his own name, reserving pseudonymity only for Anti-Climacus, who was indeed

"above" him. Then, during the attack on the Church, Kierkegaard decided, finally, that he did not need to have authority in order to speak as one adult to others; being "a person of character" was sufficient. So he revoked the foreword to *Practice in Christianity* as well as the pseudonymity that had established the distance of that work from his own person. Kierkegaard had finally found his own voice. And it was not surprising that even before he was dead, the campaign to deprive him of the right to speak, even in his own name, had begun.

Peter later implied rather disingenuously that he had prepared his July 1855 speech on the spur of the moment and that he had no notes. Neither claim is true. Peter's extensive notes are in the Manuscript Collection of the Royal Library, and if the talk was given on the spur of the moment it is hard to account for how Bishop Martensen, no friend of Peter Christian Kierkegaard, could have known about it *before* it was given.[34] At any rate, although Peter's speech was not published, Søren apparently knew a good deal about it and became very angry with his brother, as attested to by a number of journal entries (see *Pap.* XI³ B 154; 155; 164 pp. 270–2). Peter, for his part, must have known or at least suspected Søren's anger, for he seems to have attempted to visit his brother in Copenhagen in August, but Søren refused to see him, and he returned home.[35] Soon thereafter Peter fell ill and took to bed (as was not unusual for him in periods of stress),[36] arising only to make the journey to visit Søren in the hospital in October, where, as we have seen, he was heartlessly rebuffed.

Then Søren died. Despite his obvious wishes, and despite the fact that he had ceased attending church and had called upon all honest people "to cease participating in public worship" (*SV*¹ XIV 85), his funeral service was in the Church of Our Lady, the nation's principal place of worship, on a Sunday, between two regularly scheduled religious services. Peter Christian Kierkegaard gave the eulogy. He later said that he had lost the notes from which he spoke on that occasion, but he did manage to reconstruct his remarks, which included the intriguing:

confession that [I] not only deeply regretted but also felt a sincere shame and remorse, because during recent years none of us had understood that the vision of the deceased had become partially darkened and distorted from exertions and suffering in the heat of battle, causing his blows to fall wildly and blindly, as did *Ølver's* in the Norwegian saga; and that we should have acted as did Ølver's friends, and, with the confident gaze and the mild embraces of love, lured him *or compelled* him to take a long and quiet rest.[37]

This Ølver (or "Qlvir") is a figure in Snorri Sturluson's account of the history of the kings of Norway. It seems that during an attack by pagan Wends on southern Norway in the year 1135, a peasant named Ølver, who was at a beer-drinking party with his friends, stood up and announced that, despite lack of support from his fellows, he would go to the defense of the local townsmen. Incredibly, Ølver fought eight Wends simultaneously, and although surrounded, he killed six and put the other two to flight. Ølver himself was gravely wounded in his heroic struggle, however, and had to be taken away by his countrymen and nursed back to health.[38] There were many heroic figures, biblical, classical, and Norse, for Peter Christian Kierkegaard to choose among in eulogizing his brother, and this particular choice – a brave but foolhardy hero, who single-handedly fights off a pagan horde – is quite revealing. Even more revealing, perhaps, is the fact that Ølver's full name is "Qlvir miklimunnr," and means literally "Ølver Bigmouth." Nor should we forget the important ambiguity in the saga, namely, that at the time of his heroic deeds Ølver Bigmouth may well have been drunk, that is, as Peter Christian Kierkegaard more than hints with respect to his brother, the man was perhaps out of his mind. And as with Ølver, it would have been best if Søren had been forcibly taken away by his friends until he recovered. Søren Kierkegaard, the implication goes, was mad. In his speech of July 1855, Peter had started the campaign to deny his brother a voice by implying that Søren did not fully stand behind his own name; now, at Søren's funeral in November, Peter completed the job by implying that Søren had not been of sound mind.

This was Peter's final insult to the brother who had refused to receive him. But Peter felt a guilt that haunted him all his life. This is not the place to give a full account of Peter Christian Kierkegaard's guilt. It might be noted, however, that as early as 1834 Peter noted in his diary that he had been unable to "become truly reconciled with Søren," and cited Matthew 5:23–4 ("So if you are offering your gift at the altar, and there remember that your brother has something against you, leave your gift at the altar and go; first be reconciled to your brother, and then come and offer your gift").[39] Peter Christian was unable to rid himself of this sentiment. As the heir to Søren's estate, over a thirty-year period Peter received the royalties from the various editions of his brother's works. This became an increasing source of self-reproach, and toward the end of his life, from 1879 to 1883, he donated these sums to charity.[40] In 1875 Peter gave up his bishopric. In 1879 he returned his royal decorations to the government. In 1884 he voluntarily assumed the legal status of a child, "*borgerlig Umyndiggørelse,*" which literally means the loss of one's legal majority, of one's civil authority, an ironic end to a rivalry based upon the struggle for recognition and "authority." Peter died on 24 February 1888, aged eighty-two, as his biographer says, "in the darkness of insanity."[41] In a journal entry for February 1883, Peter noted that he had sent a letter to the Probate Court: "Wrote to the Probate Court out of sheer impulse on the 24th; started with I John 3:15...."[42] The contents of the letter are not known, but they were most probably some sort of rather embarrassing confession, because the letter was intercepted, opened, and returned by a friend of the family. I John 3:15 reads as follows: "Anyone who hates his brother is a murderer, and you know that no murderer has eternal life abiding in him."[43] Peter seems to have evolved from a sense of being unreconciled with his brother to the conviction that he had murdered him.

Despite Victor Eremita's views, there *is* an important connection between the inner and the outer. Our lives are whole and entire, biography *and* history, private *and* public. Shaped by the public, the private returns to reshape the public and, perhaps, find a sort of redemption in the satisfaction of having done so. The manner in which this takes place and the degree to which the private is successful in reshaping the public are of course dependent upon the particular historical circumstances in any given case. Luther's solution to his personal problem of the relation of faith and works was not original to him, but the circumstances were such that his personal response assumed major historical significance. As the American poet Robert Frost has written: "How hard it is to keep from being king, when it's in you and it's in the situation." The breakthrough into adulthood was both in Søren Kierkegaard and in the Danish historical situation. Kierkegaard's struggle for personal authority, for recognition in his family, led him to solutions that bore directly on larger questions of authority in Denmark as a whole. This was because families don't exist in isolation. An important player in the Kierkegaard family was Jacob Peter Mynster, who also happened to be a bishop and the Primate of the Danish Church. Private life isn't so private, and biography and history cannot be neatly separated.

Hounded to the end by the shame of having been rebuffed by the brother he had criticized, Peter Christian Kierkegaard died believing he had murdered Søren, and he apparently tried to put some sort of confession of this on the public record. But Søren died believing that he had become "a man of character." He had finally made his breakthrough, he had told what he insisted was the truth about Christendom, he had come "out with it" for his own sake and for the sake of ordinary people.

NOTES

1 See Peter Christian Kierkegaard's journals, located in the Manuscript Department of the Royal Library, Copenhagen (hereafter "KBHA"), Ny kongelige Samling (hereafter "NkS") 2656, 4⁰, bd. II, p. 15; see also Carl Weltzer, *Peter og Søren Kierkegaard* (Copenhagen: G. E. C. Gad, 1936), p. 266. See further Peter Christian Kierkegaard's entry in his account book for October 1855, where he writes: "Travelled in and out (18 & 20 Oct.) in connection with Søren's illness" (KBHA, NkS 3005, 4⁰, bd. II, p. 86), as well as the entries for 19 October and 25 October 1855 in Boesen's account of his hospital conversations with Kierkegaard in *Af Søren Kierkegaards efterladte Papirer. 1854–55*, ed. H. Gottsched (Copenhagen: C. A. Reitzels Boghandel, 1881), pp. 596–8. The textual bases for many of the biographical incidents and details mentioned in the present essay can be found in my book *Encounters with Kierkegaard* (Princeton: Princeton University Press, 1996) and (Danish version) *Søren Kierkegaard truffet* (Copenhagen: C. A. Reitzels Forlag, 1996).

2 From Kierkegaard's hospital conversations with Emil Boesen, in *Af Søren Kierkegaards efterladte Papirer. 1954–55*, pp. 596–7.

3 For example, in a letter to Peter Christian Kierkegaard, dated 1 November 1855 (in KBHA, NkS 3174, 4⁰) and in another letter to a friend, dated 14 November 1855 (in Henr. Bech [ed.], *Gunni Busck, Et Levnedsløb i en Præstegaard* [Copenhagen: Karl Schønbergs Forlag, 1878], p. 326), the Grundtvigian pastor Gunni Busck directly quotes some of Kierkegaard's remarks to Emil Boesen, demonstrating that Boesen communicated at

least some of the contents of his hospital conversations with Kierkegaard while the latter was still alive.

4 See Boesen's hospital conversations with Kierkegaard, *Af Søren Kierkegaards efterladte Papirer. 1854–55*, p. 598.

5 This transition has been discussed in more detail in my book *Kierkegaard in Golden Age Denmark* (Bloomington and Indianapolis: Indiana
University Press, 1990), pp. 1–81.

6 See, e.g., Mynster's sermon from 1852, "Vor evangeliske Folkekirke," in
Prædikener holdte i Aarene 1846 til 1852. Sommer-Halvaaret, 2nd ed.
(Copenhagen: Gyldendal, 1854), pp. 12–22.

7 Mynster's hypocrisy in this respect was immediately clear to Kierkegaard, who in his journals was highly critical of "the manner in which
[Mynster] is now trying, almost like a democrat, to ingratiate himself
with 'the People's Church' – him, the be-all and end-all of the State
Church" (*Pap.* X⁶ B 212 p. 335).

8 Mynster and Heiberg constituted the center of the leading circle that
dominated the Golden Age in the 1830s and 1840s. In 1848 Kierkegaard
wrote: "My tactic has always been to sow dissension in the coteries, and
now, after the fact, I can see how I have again been helped by [Divine]
Guidance. The great coterie is Mynster, Heiberg, Martensen, and company" (*Pap.* IX A 206 p. 103).

9 The most important of these were Heiberg's articles "Om Theatret"
(Johan Ludvig Heiberg, *Prosaiske Skrifter*, 11 vols. [Copenhagen: C. A.
Reitzels Forlag, 1861–62], 6:171–260); his reviews of Carsten Hauch's
Svend Grathe (ibid., 4:378–402) and Lope de Vega's *The King and the
Peasant* (ibid., 5:93–132); as well as his essays "Folket og Publicum"
(ibid., 6:263–83) and "Autoritet" (ibid., 10:328–49).

10 See, e.g., "Skuespilhuset. En Dialog," in *Danmark. Et malerisk Atlas*,
vol. 8 of *Johan Ludvig Heibergs poetiske Skrifter* (Copenhagen: C. A.
Reitzels Forlag, 1862), pp. 175–88.

11 *Nye Digte* came out in December 1840. It is available in *Johan Ludvig
Heibergs poetiske Skrifter*, 10:163–324 and in an excellent recent edition published for the Society for Danish Language and Literature:
Johan Ludvig Heiberg: Nye Digte. 1841, ed. Klaus P. Mortensen (Copenhagen: Borgen, 1990).

12 For example: "Christendom is . . . so far from being what its name implies, that most people's lives, from a Christian point of view, are too
spiritless even to be called sin in the strict Christian sense of the term"
(*SV*ⁱ XI 214; cf. also pp. 212, 226).

13 In the draft of her memoirs, Johanne Luise Heiberg writes that Søren
Kierkegaard was among those who could come by in the evening without having to be invited; see *Et Liv gjenoplevet i Erindringen*, 4th ed.,
ed. Aage Friis (Copenhagen: Gyldendal, 1944), 4:95.

14 In the autumn of 1838 Henrik Hertz remarked in his commonplace book, à propos of Kierkegaard's recently published book on Hans Christian Andersen: "What a peculiar churchyard [*Kirkegaard*]! To judge from various clues, it would appear that the trumpets have been sounded for resurrection from the grave – but if that is the case the dead have not yet recovered their bones, but are lying there quarreling over them. Because the confusion is great" (KBHA, NkS 2807, 4°, Henrik Hertz's optegnelsesbøger og efterladte papirer, I: Optegnelsesbøger A - J, bd. G, s. 11). See also the similar language in letters by B. S. Ingemann to H. L. Martensen, dated 28 January 1855 (published in *Breve til og fra Bernh. Sev. Ingemann*, ed. V. Heise [Copenhagen: C. A. Reitzel Boghandel, 1879], pp. 489–90) and to Carsten Hauch, dated 9 March 1855 (original letter is in KBHA, NkS 3751, 4°, bd. I, fasc. 8, no. 108; published in *Hauch og Ingemann. En Brevveksling*, ed. M. Hatting [Copenhagen: Gyldendal, 1933], p. 108).

15 See Sejer Kühle, "Søren Kierkegaards Fader," *Gads danske Magasin* 37 (1943): 469–70.

16 Of Michael Pedersen Kierkegaard's eight siblings: (1) Christen Pedersen Kierkegaard died shortly after birth in 1751; (2) another brother, also named Christen Pedersen Kierkegaard (born 1752), was the one who relocated to live with an uncle in southern Jutland and died there "young and unmarried"; (3) a third brother, Anders Pedersen Kierkegaard (1754–1802) remained in Sædding to take over the family farm, but died unmarried aged forty-seven, probably only having had possession of the farm for three years; (4) one sister, Karen Pedersdatter Kierkegaard (1759–1810) remained in Sædding and died there at the age of fifty-one, unmarried; (5) another sister, Maren Pedersdatter Kierkegaard (1761–1803) married locally and had four children before dying at the age of forty-two; (6) the fourth brother, Peder Pedersen Kierkegaard (1763–1834) was the madman who lived part of his adult life in Copenhagen and returned to Sædding where he died, unmarried, at the age of seventy; (7) a third sister, Sitsel Marie Kierkegaard (1766–1831) also remained in Sædding and died aged sixty-five, unmarried; (8) the fourth sister and youngest of the nine siblings was Else Pedersdatter Kierkegaard (1768–1844), who inherited the family farm but received financial assistance from Michael Pedersen and his sons. For more detail on Michael Pedersen Kierkegaard's family, see Olaf Kierkegaard and P. F. Parup, *Fæstebonden i Sædding. Christen Jespersen Kierkegaards Efterslægt* (Copenhagen: Thorsøe-Olsen's Bogtrykkeri, 1941).

17 The information on Ane Sørensdatter Lund in this paragraph is contained in a letter by P. Chr. Olesen to H. P. Barfod, dated 6 May 1868, in KBHA, Søren Kierkegaard Arkiv, D., pk. 5.

18 Ane Sørensdatter's father is commemorated in the names of Søren

Michael, Søren Aabye, and Petrea Severine, while Michael Pedersen's father's name was passed on to Peter Christian and Petrea Severine. This method of perpetuating the father's name was of particular importance now that Michael Pedersen and Ane Sørensdatter had moved to Copenhagen and adopted city ways. As far as is known, all previous generations of their families had automatically passed down the patronymic – i.e, the father's Christian name with the appropriate "-sen" or "datter" suffix – to all children in a family. But Søren Kierkegaard's parents had now become city people and had appropriated the modern fashion of giving their children middle names that could commemorate any of various family members, or even of close family friends.

19 Søren Michael (1807–1819) died aged twelve after a schoolyard accident; Søren Aabye was six years old. Maren Kirstine (1797–1822), the eldest child in the family, who bore the matronymic of both her parents, died unmarried when Søren was eight years old. Niels Andreas (1809–1833), reportedly having been forced by the stern father to seek his fortune abroad, died in Paterson, New Jersey, aged twenty-four; Søren was twenty at the time. Søren's two favorite sisters, Nicoline Christine (1799–1832) and Petrea Severine (1801–1834), married the promising and comfortably off brothers Johan Christian (1799–1875) and Henrik Ferdinand Lund (1803–1875), respectively, and each died following childbirth, Nicoline when Søren was nineteen, Petrea two years later, several months after the death of the matriarch Ane Sørensdatter; Søren was twenty-one years old.

20 Peter's journal is in KBHA, NkS 2656, 4°, bd. I, p. 3 from the end of volume. It has also been published (in slightly different form) in Weltzer, *Peter og Søren Kierkegaard*, p. 24.

21 Similarly, when a collection was taken up for Jacob Christian Lindberg, an evangelical radical and a forerunner of Grundtvig, Michael Pedersen shied away from participating – much to the surprise and disapproval of his house guests, Juliane and Christiane Rudelbach, sisters of the theologian A. G. Rudelbach (letter of Juliane and Christiane Rudelbach to A. G. Rudelbach, dated 2 July 1832, published in Weltzer, *Peter og Søren Kierkegaard*, p. 45).

22 There is no truth to the various myths according to which Kierkegaard gave the greater part of his money away. He spent most of it on himself, a good deal of it on luxuries. See Frithiof Brandt and Else Rammel, *Kierkegaard og Pengene* (Copenhagen: Levin og Munksgaard, 1935). In his journals for March 1842, Peter Christian Kierkegaard remarks that he has written his brother, counseling caution in financial matters and

noting that he will request Søren's written authorization for certain transactions, which he obviously believed to be ill considered (KBHA, NkS 2656, 4°, bd. I, p. 119).

23 See Mynster's "Yderligere Bidrag til Forhandlingerne om de kirkelige Forhold i Danmark" (1851), reprinted in Jacob Peter Mynster, *Blandede Skrivter* (Copenhagen: Gyldendal, 1853), 2:60–1.

24 In his recollections of Kierkegaard, Hans Brøchner makes this point quite definitely: "There had been a time when [Kierkegaard] had respected Mynster greatly, an attitude he had adopted largely because of his veneration for his father, who had set great store by Mynster" (in my *Encounters with Kierkegaard*, p. 247).

25 I have discussed the course and causes of Kierkegaard's attack on the Church elsewhere. See my article "'At voxe fra dette Barnlige': Kierkegaards angreb på kristenheden," *Berlingske Tidende* (Copenhagen), 4 October 1994; my book *Kierkegaard in Golden Age Denmark* (1990); and my essay "Tordenveiret. Kierkegaards Ekklesiologi," in *Vinduer til Guds Rige*, ed. Hans Raun Iversen (Copenhagen: Anis, 1995), pp. 97–114.

26 See my essay "Tordenveiret. Kierkegaards Ekklesiologi."

27 I suspect that Kierkegaard applied the sexual stereotypes and linguistic usages typical of his time, but only a thorough investigation of the literature of the period could reveal to what degree, if any, Kierkegaard deviated from what was then ordinary usage.

28 *Judge for Yourself!* was written in 1851–2, but was not published until 1876.

29 SV^I XIV 212–14. A propos of "ambiguity": "There is an ambiguity in [Mynster's] existence which is unavoidable, because the State Church is an ambiguity" (*Pap.* VIII^I A 415 p. 181).

30 See my article "Tordenveiret. Kierkegaard's Ekklesiologi." The development of Kierkegaard's ecclesiology can be summarized as the progress from rather severe criticism of the Church and of "the concept of congregation" (criticism that is nonetheless held in abeyance in the book *Practice in Christianity*), to the decision that there must be rigorous separation of church and state, and finally to an apparent rejection of the Church ("the concept of congregation") as such. The following passages indicate Kierkegaard's stations along this road:

> A. Despite the fact that "the concept of congregation is an impatient anticipation of eternity" (1848), one should not "overturn the Establishment" (1851).
>
> 1. A concept such as "congregation," . . . when applied to this life, is an impatient anticipation of eternity (SV^I XII 204).

2. *The Established Order – My Position*
Christianly understood, in the highest sense there is no Established Church, only a militant Church.

That is the first point.

The second point is that there is, however, in fact such an Established Church. It should not at all be overturned, no, but the higher ideal must hover over it as an awakening possibility. (*Pap.* X³ A 415; emphasis in original)

B. *"The concept of congregation has been Christianity's ruination" (1854) and the clergy will regret that they did not listen to Kierkegaard when it was still possible to carry out the separation of church and state in a gentle fashion (1855).*

1. *An Alarming Note.*

Those 3000 who were added to the congregation en masse at Pentecost – isn't there fraud here, right at the very beginning? Ought not the apostles have been uneasy about whether it really was right to have people become Christians by the thousands, all at once? . . . [Didn't the Apostles forget] that if the genuine imitation [of Christ] is to be Christianity, then these enormous conquests of 3000 at once just won't do? . . .

With Christ, Christianity is the individual, here the single individual. With the Apostles it immediately becomes the congregation. [*Added here in the margin:* And yet it is a question as to whether the principle of having to hate oneself – which is of course the principle of Christianity – of *whether that principle is not so unsocial that it cannot constitute a congregation.* In any case, from this point of view one gets a proper idea of what sort of nonsense State Churches and People's Churches and Christian countries are.] But here Christianity has been transposed into another conceptual sphere. And it is this concept [i.e., the concept of the congregation] that has become the ruination of Christianity. It is to this concept [i.e., the concept of congregation] that we owe the confusion about states, nations, peoples, empires, which are Christian (*Pap.* XI¹ A 189; my emphasis).

2. If the clergy unreservedly and in self-denial had been willing to consult the New Testament, it would have seen that the New Testament unconditionally requires the separation of Church and State and that it had therefore been the duty of the clergy to suggest it themselves. . . . [They would] have seen that from every sort of quarter the development of the world is pushing toward this point, the separation of Church and State, and that above all here in Denmark everything is undermined.

And if the clergy had been willing to understand this, it would have seen that in my hands the matter was in the best of hands, in hands that were as well-intentioned as possible toward the clergy. They have rejected this. I have continually had to force the matter to a higher and higher level and have had to put up with playing the role of a sort of madman – as compared with the wise clergy.

The clergy will come to regret this dearly. The decision is forcing its way through. It must come through. But then the clergy will have to deal with a completely different group of people.

The more promptly the clergy had been willing to opt for the decision, to opt for the divorce, the less they would have been unmasked in their untruth. The more active or passive resistance they make, the more they will be revealed in their untruth and the more wretched their situation will be when the matter is settled (*Pap.* XI² A 414).

C. *Although he had first understood his task to be the opposite (i.e., to prevent the establishment from being overturned – see A. 2 above), Kierkegaard asserts that he has in fact been called by Divine Guidance to overturn the establishment.*

For many different reasons, and prompted by many different factors, I had the idea of defending the Established Church.

[Divine] Guidance has surely had the idea that I was precisely the person who was to be used to overturn the Establishment. But in order to prevent such an undertaking from being the impatient, perhaps arrogant, daring of a young man, I first had to come to understand my task as just the opposite – and now, in what, inwardly understood, has been great torment, to be developed to take on the task when the moment came (*Pap.* XI³ B 110; this passage is also cited in the main text of the present essay).

31 In addition to the other incidents mentioned in the present essay, consider the following excerpt from P. C. Kierkegaard's journals (KBHA, NkS 2656, 4⁰, bd. I, p. 63; also cited in Weltzer, *Peter og Søren Kierkegaard*, p. 87):

[January 1835]
Nevertheless, praise God, on the 16th I did take communion with Father, after I had tried to make my peace with Søren, with whom I have recently got along reasonably well, inasmuch as we have each kept to ourselves.

There are many other passages in Søren Kierkegaard's journals that testify to his anger with his brother, but they need not be cited here. Søren

Kierkegaard's schoolmate Frederik Welding reported, as did a good number of others, that Søren was a tease in school and added that when Peter Christian Kierkegaard returned to teach Greek at his old school, Søren singled him out for embarrassment and abuse (see Welding's letters of 3 September and 23 October 1869 to H. P. Barfod, in KBHA, Søren Kierkegaard Arkiv, D. pk. 5). Hans Brøchner reports that Søren took great pleasure in misleading a German scholar who had come to meet him by explaining that there must have been some misunderstanding: "My brother, the doctor, is an exceedingly learned man, with whom it would surely interest you to become acquainted, but I am a beer dealer." Brøchner further reports that Søren was highly amused when observers thought the crowds attending his brother's lectures at the university were flocking to a dance (in my *Encounters with Kierkegaard*, pp. 238–9).

32 Peter Christian Kierkegaard's address was held before the Roskilde Ecclesiastical Convention, an association of clerics generally sympathetic to Grundtvig, on 30 October 1849 and published in *Dansk Kirketidende*, no. 219, vol. 5 (no. 11) (16 December 1849), cols. 171–9; it was subsequently republished in *Peter Christian Kierkegaards Samlede Skrifter*, ed. Poul Egede Glahn and Lavrids Nyegård (Copenhagen: Karl Schønbergs Forlag, 1903), 4:99–120.

33 *Dansk Kirketidende* 1881, no. 22; reprinted in *Peter Christian Kierkegaards Samlede Skrifter*, 4:125.

34 See the letter by Hans Lassen Martensen to his friend and follower, the cleric Ludvig J. M. Gude (1820–95), in KBHA, NkS 3450, 4°, bd. II; also published in *Biskop H. Martensens Breve*, ed. Bjørn Kornerup, vol. 1 of *Breve til L. Gude, 1848–1859* (Copenhagen: G.E.C. Gads Forlag, 1955), p. 148.

35 See Weltzer, *Peter og Søren Kierkegaard*, p. 255.

36 See Peter Christian Kierkegaard in *Dansk Kirketidende* 1881, no. 22; reprinted in *Peter Christian Kierkegaards Samlede Skrifter*, 4:124.

37 *Dansk Kirketidende* 1881, no. 22; reprinted in *Peter Christian Kierkegaards Samlede Skrifter*, 4:127; emphasis added on words "or compelled."

38 Ølver or "Qlvir miklimunnr" appears in Magnus Blinde's saga in Snorri Sturluson's account of the history of the kings of Norway; see *Heimskringla. Nóreg Konunga Sǫgur*, ed. Finnur Jónsson (Copenhagen: G. E. C. Gads Forlag, 1911), pp. 563–4. Peter Christian Kierkegaard presumably had his version of the story from one or both of the two translations that were current in his time, namely, *Snorre Sturlesons norske Kongers Sagaer*, trans. Jacob Aall (Christiania: Guldberg and Dzwonkowskis Officin, 1839), 2:145 and N. F. S. Grundtvig's translation, *Norges Konge-*

Krønike af Snorro Sturlesøn (Copenhagen: Schultz, 1822), 3:259–60. Good arguments can be made for Peter Christian Kierkegaard's acquaintance with either or both versions. He was interested in Scandinavian history and was a supporter of Grundtvig, so it is not unreasonable to suppose he owned Grundtvig's version. Similarly, Aall's translation was published in Christiania in 1839, the same year that Peter Christian spent time in that city. In both translations the name is spelled "Ølver" with on "Ø" and an "e," though in Aall's translation his full name is given as "Ølver Stormund," while in Grundtvig's it is the more colloquial "Ølver Gabmund." Both mean "Ølver Bigmouth."

39 From the entry for February 1834 in Peter Christian Kierkegaard's journals, located in KBHA, NkS 2656, 4°, bd. I, p. 52; it has also been published (in slightly different form) in Weltzer, *Peter og Søren Kierkegaard*, p. 79 and Sejer Kühle, "Nogle Oplysninger om Søren Kierkegaard, 1834–38," *Personalhistorisk Tidsskrift*, 9. Række. 4. Bd. 4. Hæfte. (1931), p. 2.

40 The rather incoherent record of these donations is in Peter Christian Kierkegaard's account book, in KBHA, NkS 3005, 4°, bd. II, pp. 143–58; see the discussion in Weltzer, *Peter og Søren Kierkegaard*, pp. 358–9.

41 Weltzer, *Peter og Søren Kierkegaard*, p. 359.

42 Peter Christian Kierkegaard's journals, in KBHA, NkS 2656, 4°, bd. II, p. 222; it is also published in Weltzer, *Peter og Søren Kierkegaard*, p. 358.

43 Interestingly, in his lecture notes on this same text from the winter of 1836–7, Peter Christian had written: "Just as, in the Old Testament, [a murderer] is subject to the death of the body, . . . in the New Testament he is naturally expelled from the church, i.e., the Kingdom of God is closed to him. . . . And here the Apostle says this same punishment is reserved for the person who commits murder in his heart, i.e., hates" (in KBHA, NkS 3013, 4°, bd. I). I John 3:15 is of course a parallel text to Matthew 5:23–24 ("If you are offering your gift at the altar . . . first be reconciled to your brother") which had so haunted Peter Christian's relation to his brother in February 1834 (see note 39 above), but in the epistle of John the point is made with much greater stringency: the fault of being unreconciled with one's brother has been escalated to murder.

2 The unknown Kierkegaard: Twentieth-century receptions

Søren Kierkegaard wrote his books for "that *individual*, whom with joy and gratitude, I call *my* reader." He opposed the ruling philosophical system of his day, despised lecturers and professors almost as much as paid churchmen, entered into dispute with his entire home town, and regarded having a disciple as the worst fate that could ever befall him. His books were written in an ironic, sophisticated, parodic style that allowed of no clear position for the reader and allowed of no definite result either.

It cannot be a matter of surprise, then, that the history of the reception of his work must be an account of the ways that individuals have reacted to his work. Time and time again, it is noticeable that, at a key point of their own thinking, philosophers, theologians, and writers have been influenced by the almost "random" encounter with Kierkegaard, both by his passionate and ambiguous private journal, which he kept throughout his lifetime, and the rich and ambivalent work he published between 1843 and 1855.

There can be no attempt, that is, to "fit" Kierkegaard into some overarching scheme, such as the history of German Romanticism, or of idealism, or even of the history of existentialism. However he is "placed" in any such history, Kierkegaard remains inassimilable to it. His irony and his many-voiced-ness, his *heteroglossia*, distance him from any position that could be asserted to be finally "his" position. In the last twenty years or so, much more attention has been paid than before to his actual manner of writing, his sheer literary virtuosity, which consists of playing just within, and yet just outside of, the conventions of the ruling "Romantic Irony" of his time, such that he has made any final "closure" on the matter of "his" meaning impossible. With this new "literary" perception of

48

his work he has taken on a new status as a postmodernist, someone who, in a certain sense, is writing "after Derrida" in what Harold Bloom would call an *apophrades*.

Kierkegaard wrote for "that individual," and through time he has in fact been read by "that individual," and remains important for those making an individual, dissonant, or even subversive, contribution to their own subject. Official, academic philosophy does not have much use for him, is given to denying him philosophical status, and quite often raises the question as to whether he is even of any philosophical interest. And all this is exactly the way Kierkegaard would have wanted it.

After a tempestuous life, he died amidst recrimination, odium, and scandal. When he died in 1855, the Danish public, exhausted by the demands he had made on it, consigned the man and his works to oblivion, hoping never to hear his name again. This attitude was encouraged by his brother, Bishop Peter Christian Kierkegaard, who had done his best to subvert Søren's cause while he was alive and included in his funeral oration some remarks that were little short of excuses for a brother who had become unhinged. Two assiduous scholars, H. P. Barfod and H. Gottsched, collected editions of Kierkegaard's papers, which appeared between 1869 and 1881. The bishop kept many of the papers back for himself, and, as they arranged their entries, Barfod threw away the originals, thus creating a problem that has bedeviled Kierkegaard scholarship ever since.

I. THE DANISH, GERMAN, AND FRENCH RECEPTION

Danish philosophy never took Kierkegaard up at a serious level. The first monograph about him (1877) was by the positivist philosopher Georg Brandes, and it is on record that Brandes himself said that, just as he had attacked German Romanticism in order to hit indirectly at the Danish Romantics, so he wrote about Kierkegaard to free the Danes from his influence. Brandes may not have had to try very hard, for the Danes were never in danger of being seriously under Kierkegaard's influence in the first place. Nevertheless, Brandes' book certainly gave the seal of philosophical disapproval that has kept Kierkegaard's writings unread and unpopular until very recent times.

Brandes must have had second thoughts, however, for ten years after his book came out, he wrote to Friedrich Nietzsche telling him that he must read Kierkegaard. Nietzsche replied that, on his next visit to Germany, he intended to work upon "the psychological problem" of Kierkegaard. That Nietzsche was interested enough to want to do so is interesting. Here is a major intellectual confrontation of the nineteenth century that never took place.

Subsequent Danish philosophical accounts of Kierkegaard were equally dismissive. Harald Høffding, another philosopher of a positivist persuasion, gave Kierkegaard very low marks for philosophical acumen in his *Søren Kierkegaard as a Philosopher* (1919). The noted historian Troels Frederik Troels-Lund, who was related to Kierkegaard, and a man of considerable influence in the literary circles of his day, opined, in his two autobiographical essays of 1922 and 1924, that Kierkegaard was little better than an eccentric, though obviously one of genius – a typically Danish evasion of the problem. Troels-Lund remembers the wandering philosopher with affection and admiration, admits that he was personally influenced by him in a way that changed the course of his entire life, and yet could not find it in his heart to say that Kierkegaard's existential thinking would or could have any lasting importance.

It was abroad that Kierkegaard's "indirect communication" began to fascinate individuals here and there. Kierkegaard's influence can only be decisive within a personal problematic that exists already. He modifies a worldview, in a suggestive and insidious way. Franz Kafka is a perfect example:

Today I got Kierkegaard's *Buch des Richters*. As I suspected, his case, despite essential differences, is very similar to mine, at least he is on the same side of the world. He bears me out like a friend.[1]

This is how the reading of Kierkegaard usually goes: a sudden self-identification with the thought of the man, which has a compelling existential significance, and which causes a reformulation of all existing personal thought-structures. Kafka continued to meditate on Kierkegaard, as a diary entry for 27 August 1916 shows:

Give up too those nonsensical comparisons you like to make between yourself and a Flaubert, a Kierkegaard, a Grillparzer. That is simply infantile . . . Flaubert and Kierkegaard knew very clearly how matters stood with them, were men of decision, did not calculate but acted. But in your case – a perpetual succession of calculations, a monstrous four years' up and down.[2]

There is a certain irony in considering Flaubert and Kierkegaard as men of decision, as men of action. This may be an indication of the extent to which Kafka needed to impose a strong misreading on the text of his own life. But it is typical of the way that the oblique effect of Kierkegaard's indirect communication has the power to generate new directions of thought.

It was the same in the case of the philosopher Karl Jaspers, who was at the time (1913) working in a psychiatric hospital in Heidelberg. The "treatments" were based upon the principles of Kraepelin. Kraepelin believed that mental illnesses were diseases of the brain, and so the patients were kept strapped down or immersed for hours in hot baths. Jaspers was appalled at the sheer philosophical primitiveness of this model of mental illness. It was in reading Kierkegaard that Jaspers became convinced that "mental illness" is most often nothing but an important event in the structure and development of the Existenz of the patient. The discovery of the concept of Existenz itself, and the emphasis and importance Jaspers attributed to it throughout an entire writing life, cannot but be derived from an attentive reading of Kierkegaard, where the concept of existence is foregrounded in so many works. Jaspers, in his work in psychiatry, began to wonder if some mental states did not actually allow us "fleeting glimpses of the ultimate source of Existenz." In the case of a Van Gogh, for instance, or Strindberg or Hölderlin or Swedenborg, could we actually speak of any of these as being "mad"? It was doubtless also due to an attentive reading of Kierkegaard's "indirect communication," that Jaspers came to regard the "will to total communication" as the basis of all true philosophical method. This doctrine he set out in his 1935 lectures, published as Reason and Existenz.[3] The importance of fully personal, authentic communication emerges again as late as the 1947 lecture at the university of Basel published as Der philosophische Glaube.[4]

Kierkegaard's communication, which he insisted upon calling "indirect," has most often been indirect in its effect and, quite often too, only indirectly alluded to, even by those who have fallen heavily under its influence. In the case of Heidegger, the affliction Harold Bloom calls "The Anxiety of Influence" is particularly marked. Heidegger, struggling with Husserl for the effective leadership of the phenomenological enterprise, remorselessly ransacks

Kierkegaard in his magisterial *Sein und Zeit* (1927). Although there are the minimal footnote acknowledgments demanded by academic custom, the extent to which Kierkegaard has supplied Heidegger with many if not most of his main poetical *trouvailles* is something Heidegger spends a great deal of art trying to hide.

Angest is one of the most striking ones, of course. It was Kierkegaard who, writing under the pseudonym Vigilius Haufniensis in 1844, had elevated *Angest* (dread) to the dignity of a concept. "If then we ask further what is the object of dread," writes Vigilius, "the answer as usual must be that it is nothing. Dread and nothing regularly correspond to one another."[5] The sheer audaciousness of this inspired Heidegger to his own flight of fancy:

That in the face of which one has anxiety is characterised by the fact that what threatens it is *nowhere*. Anxiety "does not know" what that, in the face of which it is anxious, is . . . it is already "there" and yet nowhere; it is so close that it is oppressive and stifles one's breath, and yet it is nowhere.[6]

The linguistic categories, too, are derived from Kierkegaard. Kierkegaard had written, in that passionate outpouring of bile he called "The Present Age" in *A Literary Review*, of "The Public" as "a monstrous Nothing."[7] The nature of public speech was itself "a monstrous Nothing." The linguistic categories of modernity are "talkativeness," "formlessness," "superficiality," "flirtation," and what is called "reasoning."[8]

The closeness of Heidegger's imitations should be a matter for a little embarrassment, perhaps. Heidegger writes out his own linguistic categories of modernity as "Idle Talk," "Curiosity," "Ambiguity," and "Falling and Thrownness."[9] All of these are uttered by that abstraction called *"Das Man,"* usually translated as "the 'They.' "[10] Kierkegaard had inveighed against loose public speech, comparing it to a masterless dog, which is free to bite all and sundry, but for which no one is responsible.[11] Heidegger's "Idle Talk" (*Gerede*) is defined as *"gossiping* and *passing the word along."* "Idle talk is the possibility of understanding everything without previously making the thing one's own."[12] It is impossible to reproduce Kierkegaard's meaning more closely than this, without actually quoting directly from the text. But this Heidegger will not do. *Dasein* itself, that master-trope of the Heideggerian discourse, is, in its various modalities of "Care," drawn directly from the Kierkegaardian analysis of *dread*. "*Dasein's* being reveals itself as *care*."[13] Vigilius Haufniensis describes the "vertigo" (*Svimmel*) before choice, which leads to the Fall. The relation of Heidegger's "Falling" and "Thrownness" to Kierkegaard's ironic treatment of "The Fall" in *The Concept of Dread* needs some properly ironic exposure.

Of course, Heidegger's philosophical purpose in borrowing thus shamelessly from Kierkegaard was his own. Concerned not to exis-tentialize but to phenomenologize and ontologize his concepts, he shrank from suggesting that individuals were ethically responsible in any real political or practical world. Patricia J. Huntington, in a recent essay, has described the results of this decision on Heidegger's part.[14] In a section of her essay called "Heidegger's De-Ethicization of Kierkegaard," she observes that "Heidegger's deliberate efforts to sever psychological matters from epistemology led him to underplay the role of interiority in how I engage, assume complicity with, or position myself in relation to reigning world-views. . . . Heidegger's tendency to attribute blame for his participation in National Socialism to destiny seems consistent with his de-ethicization of Kierkegaard's concept of guilt."[15]

Every thinker who falls under Kierkegaard's sway does so for his own reasons. Kierkegaard's effect on theologians has usually been because of the existential nature of his own theological thinking. The Paradox, the God in Time, the Moment, contemporaneous dis-cipleship, these themes, so strongly stated in the Kierkegaardian oeuvre, have had a great attractiveness to theologians trying to make sense of the literal and historical claims of Christianity in a modern skeptical world. One important theologian, whose life was brutally cut short by the Nazis in 1945, was Dietrich Bonhoeffer, whose *Letters and Papers from Prison* introduced to the world the idea of "religionless Christianity."[16]

Early influenced as an academic theologian by Kierkegaard, Bon-hoeffer later had reason to come to understand the existential or lived nature of Christianity when he was imprisoned in 1943 for his resistance to Hitler and for his involvement in a plot on his life. During the two years he wrote his *Letters and Papers* in Tegel prison, he was forced to conceive of a Christianity that would be-come entirely a matter of the individual conscience, a faith shorn of all the trappings of "religion" and one that might very well have to become an "arcane discipline" and go underground for a thousand years. In "a world come of age," there was no longer any place for religion as form, for religion as organized practice. In the Third Reich things had become too serious for that. In prison, Bonhoeffer was recognized, by fellow inmates and by warders alike, to be living out a form of the Imitatio Christi, and he had a copy of Thomas à Kempis' masterwork in the cell with him. His taking on of the secular authorities of his time, his deliberate entry into the political events of his own Germany, unheard of for a Lutheran pastor, was deeply indebted to that Kierkegaard who had found it his duty in his own time to enter into conflict with the whole established Danish Church.

If Heidegger had phenomenologized Kierkegaard, it was Jean-Paul Sartre who existentialized him. Sartre, however, as a Marxist could not accede to the Christianity of Kierkegaard and like Heidegger had to occlude the extent of his debt to him. Thus the reading of, say, *l'Être et le Néant* (1943) is an uncanny experience, in which Kierkegaard's influence is everywhere though his name is unspoken. The central idea, however, of personal authenticity, of the avoidance of *mauvaise foi*, indeed the entire scope of the existentialist notion of a free and responsible human life in a world of "bourgeois" hypocrisy and mediocrity, is in fact Kierkegaardian, however little it may be acknowledged. The phenomenological descriptions of the body, the debate with Kierkegaard on "vertigo" and "anguish" in the section called "The Origin of Nothingness," the concept of freedom laid upon us as an unavoidable fate, all these are derived from an anxious reading of the early pseudonymous works of Kierkegaard.[17] In his novel *l'Âge de Raison* (1945) for example:

All around him things were gathered in a circle, expectant, impassive, and indicative of nothing. He was alone, enveloped in this monstrous silence, free and alone, without assistance and without excuse, condemned to decide without support from any quarter, condemned for ever to be free.[18]

It is the world exactly as Kierkegaard described it, and by an act of magical fictional transformation Sartre has transformed it into an existentialist vision of the modern world. Nevertheless, Sartre never ceased trying to evade the issue of his debt to Kierkegaard; and as late as 1964, when UNESCO held a conference on Kierkegaard in Paris, of which the proceedings were published as *Kierkegaard Vivant*,[19] Sartre insisted blindly that he was free of debt to

Kierkegaard. It will hardly do. One has only to reread the Sartrean "empathetic" reconstructions of the lived worlds of Baudelaire, of Genet, of Flaubert to realize the extent to which Sartre derived from Kierkegaard the doctrine that "freedom alone can account for a person in his totality."[20]

Paradoxically enough, however, it was Hegelianism that was the most influential philosophical tendency during the Occupation of Paris by the Nazis. Alexandre Kojève's lectures on Hegel in the late 1930s had chimed in exactly with the mood of the moment. Just as Kierkegaard has been Hegelianized in the last twenty years, so in the Paris of the 1930s Hegel was being Kierkegaardianized. Sartre attended Kojève's lectures, as did Jean Wahl, Maurice Merleau-Ponty, Simone de Beauvoir, and Jean Hyppolite. All fell under the influence of Kojève's "Hegel" to a greater or less degree. But the political strain of reading Hegel while Paris was occupied proved too great for Simone de Beauvoir, who writes in her autobiography:

I went on reading Hegel, and was now beginning to understand him rather better. His amplitude of detail dazzled me, and his System as a whole made me feel giddy. It was indeed tempting to abolish one's individual self and merge with Universal Being, to observe one's own life in the perspective of Historical Necessity. . . . But the least flutter of my heart gave such speculations the lie. Hate, anger, expectation or misery would assert themselves against all my efforts to by-pass them, and this "flight into the Universal" merely formed one further episode in my private development. I turned back to Kierkegaard, and began to read him with passionate interest. . . . Neither History, nor the Hegelian System could, any more than the Devil in person, upset the living certainty of "I am, I exist, here and now, I am myself."[21]

In the mid-1940s, then, out of this conflict between Kierkegaard and Hegel, emerged the existentialism of the Left Bank, of the cafés and the Caves. The philosophical and political situation was experienced as one of diremption, of bad faith, of unwilling complicity. Simone de Beauvoir's *Pour une Morale de l'Ambiguité* (1947) gives the tone exactly. It is not surprising that the Kierkegaardian category of "The Absurd" was reconceived and projected into this modern moment. Sartre had used the idea in *La Nausée* (1938) in his brilliant cadenza on the "superfluousness" of the external world, and in particular the root of a chestnut tree. But the absurdity of the external world was a result of its being unnecessary. No God had created it, no force required its presence, it has no meaning.

It was doubtless this aspect of the Absurd, that everything existed without God, and in spite of there being no God, that led the young Albert Camus to give lapidary expression to the concept of the Absurd in *Le Mythe de Sisyphe* (1942). Kierkegaard's frank acceptance of the logical unthinkability of the central doctrine of Christianity, and his relegation of this problem to the Absurd, had allowed in turn, a hundred years later, of a translation into the secular world, in the form of a secular Absurd. Camus' text is, as it were, *Philosophical Fragments*, with all its premises, and yet taking its conclusion literally. The Absurd in Kierkegaard might best be seen as a category introduced to make livable something that is unthinkable. "The Absurd is sin without God" is Camus's answering proposal. Camus found in Kierkegaard an ideal model for an existentialism without God. The absence of God being so painful, the Absurd is the only way out. Camus, of course, is a militant atheist, but it is often to atheists, as Graham Greene suggests again and again in his novels, that powerful theological arguments most appeal.

In *Le Mythe de Sisyphe*, Camus sums it up in a question:

Kierkegaard can cry out, and warn: "If man did not have an eternal spirit, if, at the bottom of things, there were nothing but a wild and tempestuous power producing everything, the great as well as the mean in the whirlwind of obscure passions, if the bottomless emptiness which nothing can fill were hidden beneath everything, what would life be, if not despair?" This cry has nothing in it which could bring Absurd man to a halt. To look for that which is true must be distinguished from looking for that which would be desirable. If, in order to escape Kierkegaard's anguished question "What would life be?" it is necessary to feed, like the poor ass, on the roses of illusion rather than to resign itself to a lie, the Absurd spirit prefers to adopt Kierkegaard's answer: "despair." Everything considered, the resolute soul will manage to get along with that.[22]

II. THE BRITISH AND AMERICAN RECEPTION

The German period of phenomenology and the French period of existentialism had, of course, no corresponding movements in England. Postidealist philosophy in England, under the influence of Bertrand

Russell, G. E. Moore, Ludwig Wittgenstein, and eventually, after A. J. Ayer's *Language, Truth and Logic* of 1936, what came to be known as "Oxford" philosophy, was resolutely opposed to the "woolly abstractions" of "Continental philosophy," and developed along a parallel and entirely independent path. Indeed, sadly, even the most superficial connections between these two traditions of philosophy were hardly maintained. Edmund Husserl came to give four lectures in German at University College in 1922. His major work "The Crisis of European Sciences," Parts I and II of which were published in the Belgrade review *Philosophia* in 1936, went unnoticed. As the thirties darkened with the threat of war, only one spark of interest in Kierkegaard's work could have been observed in England, and that was the editorial effort of Charles Williams at the Oxford University Press.

Charles Williams was one of that group of Oxford intellectuals known as "The Inklings," a group that included J. R. Tolkien, C. S. Lewis and Owen Barfield. Charles Williams had come to perceive some prophetic quality in the writings of the Danish master and set out on a one-man crusade to get as much of it as possible into translation and into print as fast as he could. He entered into communication with Alexander Dru and invited him to translate a selection from the then unknown *Journals and Papers.* Dru responded with the magnificent *The Journals of Kierkegaard 1834–1854,* which appeared in 1938. It made Kierkegaard's inner thought-world available in English for the first time in any completeness and set the standard for Kierkegaard research for a generation.

But Charles Williams was also in contact with the retired American pastor Walter Lowrie, whose enthusiasm for Kierkegaard was just as great as Williams's own. Lowrie's great biography *Kierkegaard,* which also appeared in 1938, had the same trailblazing quality for the American reading public as Dru's translation of the *Journals* had for the British. It is typical of the pure and ascetic quality of Charles Williams's mind that he should have elected just these two men to act as translators for the Oxford University Press. They both understood Kierkegaard inwardly and translated him as a labor of love. Their translations seize the linguistic appropriateness and the accurate tonality every time, even when (as happens quite often in Lowrie's translations) there are errors at the level of the literal sense.

Thus it was that, from the New York office of the Oxford University Press, Walter Lowrie's translations appeared in a regular flow: *Christian Discourses* (1939); *The Point of View for My Work as an Author* (1939); (in collaboration with Alexander Dru) *The Present Age* and *Two Minor Ethico-Religious Treatises* (1940); *Training in Christianity* (1941); *For Self-Examination* and *Judge for Yourselves!* (1941); and, in a collaborative enterprise between Oxford University Press and Princeton University Press, appeared *Stages on Life's Way* (1940); *Repetition, Fear and Trembling, The Sickness unto Death* and the completion of David Swenson's monumental *Concluding Unscientific Postscript*, all in 1941; with *The Concept of Dread*, the completion of the second volume of *Either/Or* (again left unfinished by David Swenson), and *Attack upon "Christendom" 1854–1855*, all in 1944.[23]

Walter Lowrie's remarkably rapid productivity meshed in with a much more slowly paced, but nevertheless meticulous, activity of translation, that of David F. Swenson of Minnesota. As he tells it himself, Swenson's first encounter with Kierkegaard was a kind of conversion, and he spent the rest of his life trying, through his teaching and translating, to express a debt to Kierkegaard that he thought of as unpayable.[24] Thus it was that his early translation of *Philosophical Fragments* (1936) was followed by the translations of the two most extensive works in the *oeuvre*, *Concluding Unscientific Postscript* (1941) and *Either/Or* (1944). But his death in February 1940 meant that he left both of these vast works uncompleted, and it fell to Walter Lowrie to complete *Postscript* and the second volume of *Either/Or*. In a collaborative effort with his wife, Lillian Marvin Swenson, David Swenson also posthumously made available the "edifying" stream of the authorship. The four volumes of *Edifying Discourses* appeared between 1943 and 1946 from the Augsburg Publishing House in Minneapolis. *Works of Love* appeared in 1946, and *The Gospel of Suffering* and *The Lilies of the Field* in 1948.

III. BLUNT READING

The fact that the original translators were theologians or philosophers of religion has had a decisive effect upon the way that Kierkegaard has been received in the United States and indeed throughout the English-speaking world. There was from the first a remarkably impoverished awareness of Kierkegaard as a writer, as a stylist, and as a rhetorician.

Lowrie had spent his life as an ordained minister before he began to translate Kierkegaard in retirement. Swenson was a professor of religion at the University of Minnesota from 1898 until 1939. This emplacement within theology is the reason why Kierkegaard was translated as he was, to a very great extent translated as an orthodox Christian believer, and also translated in a manner that paid extraordinarily little attention to the contours of what Kierkegaard obsessively used to refer to as his "indirect communication."

Kierkegaard put a great deal of thought and reflection into the construction of his "indirect communication." It was his belief that what he had to say could not be proposed in some direct, blunt manner, like the "paragraph communication" of the Hegelian professors. His indirection consisted, then, partly in the use of pseudonyms for many of his works; partly in the use of an unremitting irony that did not allow of the reader's "placing" him as author within his own thought-process; partly in the fact that he issued a stream of "edifying discourses" to "accompany" the works that he called "aesthetic"; and partly in the fact that the indirection of the communication consisted very largely in setting up a "lived presence" in Copenhagen, the streets and squares of the town, that would "counteract" or "work against" (*modarbejde*) or in some other way dialectically inflect or subvert the expectations about him personally that had been set up by his works, both edifying and aesthetic. The "indirect communication," then, consisted of at least four elements from the start and was cunningly woven together in terms of a known cultural space. It was made even more complex than this four-part intention would allow for, when in early 1846 Kierkegaard found himself attacked and lampooned in the pages of a popular magazine called *The Corsair*. The effect upon his sensibility of the crude cartoons by P. Klaestrup, as well as the hurtful and spiteful articles, forced him to abandon his walks in the town and to modify in a dramatic way the structure of the fourth part of the "indirect communication." Thus, the "indirect communication" expanded from being a four-part to a five-part intention, and the demands made upon the reader became of an advanced degree of subtlety.[25]

Most of this subtlety was lost on the plain, honest mind of Walter

Lowrie. In his footnotes and prefaces, Lowrie consistently diminished the importance of the first three elements in the "indirect communication": he virtually disregarded the use of pseudonyms; very largely missed the irony; and he believed that the entire "aesthetic" stream was simply there to drive the reader into reading the "edifying" stream, thus, so to speak, "getting the point" of the whole enterprise. Thus, in his translator's preface to *The Concept of Dread*, for instance, probably the most ironic and certainly the most parodic of all the aesthetic works, Lowrie can quite seriously opine: "We need not therefore apply to this book S K's emphatic admonition not to attribute to him anything that is said by his pseudonyms. This was his first completely serious book, and everything we find in it may safely be regarded as his own way of thinking."[26] Why, then, one might ask, did Kierkegaard bother to write the work under a pseudonym at all? Why would he have been so "emphatic" in his "admonition" if he had intended Walter Lowrie to disregard it completely?

Lowrie's method of reading, however, spread widely, due to the prestige of his translations, and it might perhaps best be called "blunt reading." Blunt reading is that kind of reading that refuses, as a matter of principle, to accord a literary status to the text; that refuses the implications of the pseudonymous technique; that misses the irony; that is ignorant of the reigning Romantic ironic conditions obtaining when Kierkegaard wrote; and that will not acknowledge, on religious grounds, that an "indirect communication" is at least partly bound in with the *pathos* of the lived life.

The Lowrie translations were often carried out in haste, and Lowrie often made blunders at the literal level. Plainly a new and scholarly edition was necessary. It fell to the two dedicated Kierkegaard scholars and translators Howard V. Hong and Edna H. Hong to provide the learned world with what was required. First, they translated the *Journals and Papers*, which appeared from the Indiana University Press from 1967 to 1978. Then, in a major effort beginning in 1980 and which is nearing completion, they undertook the translation of all the works, which have appeared from the Princeton University Press under the title *Kierkegaard's Writings*.

It goes without saying that this major edition, especially with its massive annotation and addenda of relevant journal entries for each work, has changed the climate for Kierkegaard studies and made available an edition that can be used internationally. If there is a drawback, it consists in the fact that the translation of key terms, which Kierkegaard uses again and again in different contexts, has been decided upon by an editorial committee, and that these terms have always to be translated the same way, irrespective of context. The existential, humorous, continuously self-referring nature of Kierkegaard's syntax is expunged from the translation. In effect, what the Princeton translations do, is constantly to imply that Kierkegaard is laying down the law or proposing truth or telling us something, whereas, sufficiently understood, the Kierkegaardian text does not tell us something, it asks us something.

And Kierkegaard is, first and foremost, a writer. The parallel is surely with Plato. Plato used the dialogue form, so as to achieve a certain degree of "indirect communication" in his dialogues, that precluded the reader from deciding, once and for all, what his, Plato's, "own view" was. Plato also uses Socrates as a figure of irony, within the dialogues, such that the literal, final, "Hegelian" meaning is forever impossible quite to grasp hold of. He also uses mistakes and traps and apparent forgetfulnesses to achieve a dramatic structure. Above all, it has been necessary to distinguish, in Plato's work, the "written" and the "unwritten" doctrines.

In spite of the dramatic and dialectical structure of Kierkegaard's texts, though, the tradition of "blunt reading" insists on interpreting him as a "serious" writer who is didactic, soluble and at bottom, "edifying." His puzzles are only seemingly so. His meaning is, by assiduous effort, capable of final solution. Thus the tradition of scholarship represented by C. Stephen Evans, for instance, attempts to "solve" the mystery of *Philosophical Fragments*, first in a book of 1983, *Kierkegaard's Fragments and Postscript: The Religious Philosophy of Johannes Climacus*, and then, a decade later, in *Passionate Reason: Making Sense of Kierkegaard's Philosophical Fragments*.[27] It is this determined effort to "make sense" of something that is taken as being in a state of disarray, or confusion, from which it has to be rescued by the efforts of the academic philosopher, that provides the risible side of the tradition of "blunt reading." Would it be possible to entitle a book *Making Sense of Plato's Theaetetus?*

The efforts of the "blunt reader" are ultimately doomed to failure, though, because the direction of attention is 180 degrees in the wrong direction. Kierkegaard's text does not offer itself to be the object of the question "What does it mean?" It offers itself as the proponent of the question "What do you think?"

It goes without saying that, given these literalist and fundamentalist assumptions, given this kind of readerly intentionality, the entire dialectical structure of the Kierkegaardian text will be simply invisible. Kierkegaard will go on and on saying what the critics expect him to say, because they are always asking him the same question. Unless the critic is unusually candid and open, unless he or she is unusually aware that what you derive from a text will be very much what you put into it in the first place, the hermeneutic adventure will never begin.

It should by now have emerged clearly enough that the major problem in the reception of Kierkegaard has been the hermeneutic one: how, in what way, adequately to read Kierkegaard? Derrida could write, at the beginning of Glas,

Quoi du reste aujourd'hui, pour nous, ici, maintenant, d'un Hegel?

We might well then ask

What, after all, today, for us, here, now, about Kierkegaard?

The reason that so little satisfaction has been achieved is due largely to the refusal to take seriously the nature of the "indirect communication," the refusal to pay it more than lip service. Yet, an "authorship" so consciously crafted refuses to give up its secrets to those who choose to disregard the author's intentions. "My wish, my prayer," writes Kierkegaard in his own name, at the end of the Postscript, "is, that if it might occur to anyone to quote a particular saying from the books, he would do me the favour to cite the name of the respective pseudonymous author."[28] Since the learned world has refused him the fulfillment of his prayer, it is not surprising if his work resists all attempts at forcible entry.

Theologians, as well as philosophers of religion, have made heavy weather of his work. An early work by Paul Sponheim, Kierkegaard and Christian Coherence (1968), so far from facing the problems raised by the pseudonyms, subsumes them all under its overarching theme. His aim is to demonstrate the underlying harmony in the works, a harmony that would be based upon the figure, nature, and reality of Christ himself in Kierkegaard's thought. While of course, you *can* achieve such a reading by ignoring the fact that Climacus and Anti-Climacus disagree profoundly about the nature of Christ, you can only do so against the grain of the texts, and your result will be spurious. John Elrod, in his *Being and Existence in Kierkegaard's Pseudonymous Works* (1975), commits this error consciously and as a matter of policy. Refusing heterogeneity to the pseudonyms, Elrod mediates the distinctions set up by them and reads them as mere developments on the way to a conception of a unified "self," which would be, ultimately, consistent with the Christian doctrine, the Christian hope, of a self no longer at odds with itself. A harmonious and pleasing thought, though far from a Kierkegaardian one. Continuing this tradition of deliberate misreading, George Connell, as late as 1985, in his *To Be One Thing: Personal Unity in Kierkegaard's Thought*, makes the same resolute gesture of refusal to Kierkegaard's "wish and prayer." He refuses autonomy to the pseudonyms and insists that the works move through "varieties of turbulence" and "the negative oneness of the ironist" toward the unity of the religious self. Excellent, except that the Kierkegaardian originals work hard against any such easy assumption. By the constant use of "difference" between the views of the pseudonyms, Kierkegaard has made any such serendipitous "oneness of the Christian self" impossible. He insists on diremption to the last, and only the determinedly "theological" reading can manage to "unify" so many jarringly different accounts of what it is to be a "Christian self."

The same problem, the refusal of autonomy to the pseudonyms, is at the root of the unhappiness in expositions of Kierkegaard that concentrate on his "aesthetics." In the footsteps of Mark Taylor, George Pattison, in *Kierkegaard: The Aesthetic and the Religious* (1992), and Sylvia Walsh, in *Living Poetically, Kierkegaard's Existential Aesthetics* (1994), manage, by reducing the specificity and the sheer incompatibility of the pseudonyms' views, to impose a Hegelian pattern upon them, in which they become mere *Gestalten* in a kind of phenomenology of the aesthetic. Sylvia Walsh reads the pseudonyms as "moments" of a coming-to-comprehension-of-itself of a "Kierkegaardian" view of the aesthetic. She assumes that Kierkegaard was a philosopher of an aquiline and transcendental kind, staring down upon his creations from the height of a fixed, single "philosophy" of how the "aesthetic" relates to the "ethical" and the "religious." Like the translating committee of the Princeton edition of *Kierkegaard's Works*, she assumes that Kierkegaard was in perfect control of his work, whereas it is evident that Kierkegaard struggled with each and every work, at the limits of his endurance, aiming to *survive*, writing, as the poet Lorca says of Goya, "with his fists and his elbows."

Neither, ultimately, can the "indirect communication" and the devices of pseudonymity be simply, in the last analysis, abandoned, in order to come, as George Pattison believes that the theologian can come at last, once all the games are over, to a pure and uncontaminated *gnosis*. It is part of the convention of Kierkegaardian writing, as it is of Platonic writing, that the artistic devices of dialogue and displacement play their role until the very end, forbidding any withdrawal to "higher" conceptual ground.

Some philosophers have refused to take account of the "indirect communication" and the principle of pseudonymity, simply because they *will* not deal with it and are determined to talk "philosophy" with "Kierkegaard," whichever one of the strange many-colored costumes he may choose to turn up in. Stephen N. Dunning's *Kierkegaard's Dialectic of Inwardness: A Structural Analysis of the Theory of Stages* (1985), for instance, is one of the most brilliant pieces of straight philosophical reconstruction in the literature. But, as its title indicates, it moves straight through the aesthetic works and, as it goes, departs further and further from any possible verisimilitude. Hegel may well have thought like this, in "Stages" across "works," but Kierkegaard had made it a matter of principle to make sure that pseudonymity builds contradiction into the discourse and makes all linear or "structural" progress impossible.

There have been philosophers however, who have recognized the heterogeneity of the pseudonyms and chosen to argue strictly philosophically *within* those constraints, and this is going a very long way toward reading Kierkegaard as he desired to be read. H. A. Nielsen's *Where the Passion Is: A Reading of Kierkegaard's Philosophical Fragments* (1983) takes the pseudonymity of Climacus seriously and acknowledges straight away that he occupies a position *outside* Christianity. "Climacus offers himself as a sort of lens-grinder, a sharpener of perceptions. . . . Through his art the reader may be helped to discern sameness, and where there is not, to discern difference."[29] A refreshing change of emphasis. Robert C. Roberts's

Faith, Reason and History: Rethinking Kierkegaard's Philosophical Fragments (1986) is another such breakthrough study. "I am proposing to read Kierkegaard as he intended to be read . . . he does not want to be read as *Kierkegaard*. He wants, instead, to be a dispensable vehicle for his reader's coming to understand *other* things. . . . The present book is an experiment in honouring Kierkegaard's desire to be read in a more primitive way . . . I shall treat Climacus with experimental tentativeness and personal independence that befits reading such an ironic author." Roberts dismisses Niels Thulstrup's view (that *Fragments* represents Kierkegaard's "own views") with contempt. "Nowhere in Kierkegaard's writings is the irony as unwearied, incessant, dark and masterful as it is in this book."[30]

This shows that things, within philosophy as such, are on the move. Jeremy Walker, too, in his *The Descent into God* (1985) has a crisp, no-nonsense attitude toward reading the text that constitutes a very timely recall to priorities: "This situation should not continue. It is in the interests of scholarship in its widest sense, that we (a) pay Kierkegaard the elementary compliment of using his own chosen titles: (b) recall that he wrote and thought in Danish – just as Plato wrote in Greek, Aquinas in Latin, and Kant in German – and begin to read him in his own language; and (c) refrain from using English titles which cut English-language scholarship partially off from concurrent scholarly work in, say, French and German."[31]

Alastair Hannay, too, may be counted as one of those who take the pseudonymity seriously, and yet manage to argue consequently and rigorously within those constraints at a philosophical level. His *Kierkegaard* (1982, rev. ed. 1991) is a study determined to come to grips with what is living and what is dead in Kierkegaard's philosophy. In order to give Kierkegaard just that wider context that Jeremy Walker desiderates, Hannay discusses his thought in the context of Hegel, Kant, Feurbach, Marx, and Wittgenstein. "I found that the most effective way of bringing out the latent structure and logical content of Kierkegaard's writings was to compare and contrast his views with those of accredited philosophers whose thought is better known and more accessible."[32] Hannay translated that most contemporary of Kierkegaard's texts, *Fear and Trembling,* for the Penguin Classics in 1985, and it is significant that, as a result of that activity, he has almost entirely rewritten Chapter 3 in his new edition of 1991, in order to point up the debts to Kant in that work. Hannay wants, by this means, to make a serious philosophical claim about the importance of *Fear and Trembling* in the context of today. Like Ronald Green, whose work on Kierkegaard and Kant over the last fifteen years has been one of the ticking bombs in Kierkegaard scholarship,[33] Alastair Hannay believes that Kierkegaard's debts to Kant are at least as great as those to Hegel, and he cites Alasdair MacIntyre as the origin of that insight. After translating *Fear and Trembling* in 1985, Alastair Hannay translated, for the Penguin Classics series, *The Sickness unto Death* (1989), *Either/Or* (1995), and a selection from the *Journals* (1996). Hannay has restored much of the colloquial life and local semantic color to these works, which is a welcome move toward establishing the individual "tonality" of each aesthetic text, each one of which has quite a different "voice" behind it.

IV. THE DECONSTRUCTIVE TURN

A reaction to "blunt reading" set in eventually. In 1971, a pioneering book by Louis Mackey entitled *Kierkegaard: A Kind of Poet* appeared. The title is subtle, both making the claim and immediately modifying it in an important way, "a kind" of poet. What "kind" of poet, then, is Kierkegaard?

> The thesis of this book is neither difficult nor novel. Quite simply, it argues that Søren Kierkegaard is not, in the usual acceptation of these words, a philosopher or a theologian, but a poet. . . . Old and obvious as it is, the thesis still needs to be defended. For though the interpreters of Kierkegaard have conceded it in principle – they could scarcely do otherwise in view of his own abundant declarations – they have almost all abused it in fact.[34]

The thesis he advances in that book, however, certainly was, for its time, novel, and has been, for many, difficult. Mackey opens up the old Platonic distrust of the poets. Philosophers had for too long disregarded the literary nature of the books and attempted to secure univocal meaning. But Mackie argues sensitively and with detailed attention to the ambiguous and deceptive nature of Kierkegaard's texts, and proposes that considerable care has been taken to avoid univocal meaning, and that this was an authorial intention:

> The fact is, that if Kierkegaard is to be understood *as Kierkegaard*, he must be studied not merely or principally with the instruments of philosophic or

theological analysis, but also and chiefly with the tools of literary criticism. That is what this book tries to do.[35]

Louis Mackey followed his book with two major essays, "The View from Pisgah: A Reading of *Fear and Trembling*" and "The Loss of the World in Kierkegaard's Ethics," in a breakthrough collection of critical essays edited by Josiah Thompson, *Kierkegaard: A Collection of Critical Essays,* in 1972. In retrospect, this Thompson collection had a much greater importance in opening up a more "modern" phase of Kierkegaardian scholarship than was obvious at the time. After these two essays, Louis Mackey fell silent for a decade while he thought the matter through again, falling under the influence, as he did so, of contemporary deconstructive patterns of thought. When he finally issued his *Points of View: Readings of Kierkegaard* in 1986, he republished the two old essays, but accompanied them with two important essays of 1981 and 1984, as well as two spanking new essays in which the full draught of the Derridean wisdom had been drunk. "Starting from Scratch: Kierkegaard Unfair to Hegel," a brilliant transumption of Donald Barthelme's short story "Kierkegaard Unfair to Schlegel," insists that the entire job of reading Kierkegaard has to be started again. In the preface to his 1986 book Mackey writes:

Once it is recognised that Kierkegaard's writings are not to be arrayed under the rubrics of philosophy and theology, it is not sufficient (as some of us used to think) to call them "literary." . . . To double business bound, their tone is just as ambivalent as their purpose is devious and their method duplicitous. . . . By virtue of his authorial self-restraint, his texts exhibit an almost complete abstention from determinate meaning and an almost perfect recalcitrance to interpretation. Like poetry, they "resist the intelligence almost successfully" (Stevens, *Opus Posthumous,* 171).[36]

It is very much to Mackey's credit that he lays out so plainly both the necessity for a literary approach and the inevitability of its falling short. That insight has not been profitably absorbed by others who have also wanted to "apply" Derridean method. Some have decided that, in the face of the impossibility of establishing "determinate meaning," there is no reason why one should not play fast and loose with the Kierkegaardian text and make it mean anything that the fantast wishes to make it say. This was the path chosen by Mark C. Taylor.

Mark C. Taylor's opening book was a careful accounting for the literary reality of the Kierkegaardian technique. *Kierkegaard's Pseudonymous Authorship* (1975) is an admirable piece of scholarly work, laying out the principles according to which the pseudonymous authors have to be read. But at some point shortly thereafter he fell more profoundly under the influence of Hegel than he had previously been under that of the Danish master, and his *Journeys to Selfhood: Hegel and Kierkegaard* inaugurates a period of Hegelianization of the Kierkegaardian texts that has become both widespread and fashionable in his wake:

Unity *within* plurality; being *within* becoming; constancy *within* change; peace *within* flux; identity *within* difference; the union of union and nonunion – reconciliation *in the midst* of estrangement. The end of the journey to selfhood.[37]

In a string of subsequent books, Taylor sketched out, in ever more detail, a postmodern "A/theology" that uses Hegel as master both of thought and of method. In *Altarity* (1987) Taylor creates an intertextual palimpsest, in which the work of Hegel, Heidegger, Merleau-Ponty, Lacan, Bataille, Kristeva, Levinas, Blanchot, Derrida, and . . . Kierkegaard are interrelated and interwoven in a huge nihilistic tapestry. It is that last name that so ill fits its frame, for its own "altarity" from the others is so striking.

Mark Taylor's deconstructive approach to the Kierkegaardian text was helpful, then, while it restricted itself to exegesis but becomes distinctly unhelpful when a condition of textual "free play" is set loose across the page, and a kind of acoustic play, of punning jokiness, is substituted for the effort to explain some original meaning in the Kierkegaardian text. Occasionally the acoustic play becomes absurd, as when it simply hops over from one language to another. Commenting upon the fact that Kierkegaard's mother is never once named in the works or in the *Journals*, Taylor can write:

The silence of the mother repeatedly interrupts the é-cri-*ture* of the son with the incessant *cri: "Mor, Mor, Mor,"* To hear the echoes of this cry, it is important to note that *"Mor,"* the Danish word for mother, sounds much like the English word "more." The child's cry for *"Mor"* is the cry for an impossible "more." Neither the mother nor any of her substitutes can ever still this cry. The endless cry of *"Mor"* bespeaks a certain absence.[38]

Mark Taylor has come to interpret philosophical writing as a kind of "free play" of the subjective fantasy, an art form in which passing insights can be jotted down in the service of describing an ever greater nihilism of vision. He takes a licence to follow any line of assonance or consonance, whether or not the text permits this. This is clear already in *Erring: A Postmodern A/theology* (1984) and it descends through his work in the eighties, culminating in a four-part dialogue, *Theology at the End of the Century*, with Thomas Altizer, Charles E. Winquist, and Robert P. Scharlemann (1990).

This collection throws into relief the way in which A/theology has shrunk to a mere recitation of vatic names. "Nothing Ending Nothing," Mark Taylor's contribution, is a series of meditations upon canvases by Yves Klein and Lucio Fontana, upon which nothing, or very little, is painted. It is a discussion of the minimalist conditions of theological discourse, ending with a sculpture by Enrique Espinosa called "The Silence of Jesus." A/theological discourse has wound down to a Beckettian nihilism, where nothing can be asserted anymore. "In the aftermath of the death of God, religion no longer heals wounds by binding together the opposites that tear apart. To the contrary, religion exposes wounds that can never be cured."[39]

On the other hand, to his credit, Mark Taylor launched, in the mid 1980s, a series of books from the Florida State University Press at Tallahassee under the general title *Kierkegaard and Post/ Modernism*. Four volumes appeared between 1986 and 1988, and all of them make strong advances in the hermeneutic problem of how to read the Kierkegaardian text. Louis Mackey's *Points of View: Readings of Kierkegaard* (1986), I have already commented upon. John Vignaux Smyth, with *A Question of Eros: Irony in Sterne, Kierkegaard and Barthes* (1986), expands the field of reference in a most refreshing way, putting the Kierkegaardian irony into a wider modern context. His book shows the influence of Paul de Man and has much of the subtlety of reading which that implies. Pat Bigelow's *Kierkegaard and the Problem of Writing* (1987) makes an important conceptual leap by starting from a thorough knowledge of Husserl and of modern phenomenology generally, and thus manages to treat the problems of meaning, reference, text, and language far more accurately than was possible heretofore. Pat Bigelow's book is also a Kierkegaardian "text" in its own right, using all the forms of self-reference and self-reflection of *Either/Or* in order to achieve "The Poetic Poaching of Silence." Pat Bigelow is also the only thinker I know of who has integrated the acoustic world of James Joyce, particularly that of *Finnegans Wake,* into his analysis. With Husserl, Heidegger, and James Joyce as guides, it is not surprising that this book does actually produce some information that is both new and valuable. I instance, merely as an example, the interesting, responsible, and – yes – discussable conclusions at page 161. Pat Bigelow has made it possible to discuss Kierkegaard's "meaning" by the use of his phenomenological-acoustic method, and this is a genuine hermeneutic advance in the struggle against "blunt reading."

Aparté: Conceptions and Deaths of Søren Kierkegaard by Sylviane Agacinski (1988) is the fourth in the Tallahassee series and originally appeared in French in 1977. Agacinski starts from a fundamentally Freudian basis but thinks, and indeed often lays out her argument also, on Derridean lines. By following the "traces" and "supplements" across the works, she manages to pick up continuities at the level of sense, which lead her to some quite exciting and insightful hypotheses. These hypotheses are, of course, always offered "under erasure," but her reading of the events that lie behind "Solomon's Dream," for instance (240–55), achieve their verisimilitude precisely because the attention to the rhetorical-unconscious nature of the text itself is so sure.

Although not part of the *Kierkegaard and Post-Modernism* series, nor indeed from the same press, Roger Poole's *Kierkegaard: The Indirect Communication* (1993) should be mentioned in this context, for it too attempts to construct and reconstruct "meanings" in the texts by an attentive study of the rhetoric and of the "traces" and "supplements" through which, and only through which, Kierkegaard's intentions can be descried. The first half of the book examines certain key aesthetic texts in the authorship deconstructively, while the second half of the book, starting out from a detailed discussion of Derrida on Husserl, attempts to show how the indirect communication became "lived" after the attack of *The Corsair* in 1846.

It is in the field of ethics, indeed, that Kierkegaard has emerged recently as a major figure in contemporary American philosophy. In a philosophical climate brought to a conceptual standstill by the naive consumerism of Richard Rorty, Kierkegaard's little parable in *Fear and Trembling* has provoked new life in the debate about ethics. If Richard Rorty's aim is to make the idea of ethical obligation "as quaint and as old-fashioned as the divine right of kings," the emergence of Jacques Derrida's *The Gift of Death* in 1992 reinstated it as one of the most urgent of modern discussions:

> *The Gift of Death* starts from an analysis of an essay by the Czech philosopher Jan Patočka, who, along with Vaclav Havel and Jiri Hajek, was one of the three spokesmen for the Charta 77 human rights declaration of 1977. He died of a brain hemorrhage after eleven hours of police interrogation on 13 March 1977.[40]

So runs the translator's preface in the 1995 American translation. Derrida has divided his essay into four parts, of which the first deals with the notion of responsibility in the Platonic and Christian traditions and begins with the provocative "Secrets of European Responsibility." The fourth section is directly about economic and political reality in a recognizably twentieth-century world. In winding together the theme of responsibility for others and the theme of sacrifice, Derrida manages to arbitrate between Kierkegaard and Levinas, on whom he had written a major essay as early as *l'Ecriture et la différence* in 1967. But Derrida, animated by the spirit of Patočka, and those who are prepared to die for their belief in liberty, is in his most serious mood; and the third section, "Whom to give to," contains the essence of what Derrida has to say about *Fear and Trembling*. The argument is expertly summarized by John D. Caputo in *Kierkegaard in Post/Modernity*.[41]

Derrida's book appeared when John D. Caputo's *Against Ethics* (1993) was still in preparation. Caputo had taken *Fear and Trembling* seriously as a philosophical parable for our time, and his distinction between "ethics" (which is backed up by a "reassuring" philosophical discourse) and "obligation" (which affects the way we have to treat our neighbor here and now "in fact") is an attempt to mediate *Fear and Trembling* in a way that a modern philosophical community could engage with. In taking his distances from Levinas, who "weaves a fabulous, poetic story about absolute alterity," which is in the end unbelievable, and in examining the difference between "ethics" and "obligation" "close up" in the case of

Fear and Trembling, Caputo manages to free Kierkegaard into contemporary debate.[42]

The debate has been attempted recently by Martin J. Matuštík in a detailed analysis in which Habermas, Charles Taylor, and two versions of "Derrida" are run against Kierkegaard, in an attempt to disentangle the substantive issues between them. The critique of both versions of "Derrida" is particularly accurate and well defined, and yet the Kierkegaardian "individual" remains intact as a working and workable hypothesis. Once again, the theme of justice emerges as central. Caputo's remarkable fourth chapter in *Against Ethics* is reinforced by Matuštík. A dialogue with Kierkegaard, he concludes, would involve presenting "multiculturally positioned individuals with questions on how to become more responsible for a more just world."[43]

Kierkegaard then, is emerging after Rorty, after Habermas, after Taylor, after both versions of "Derrida," as a thinker who would enable us to reopen the question of justice in a mood of new optimism. He has evaded all the critiques that have been leveled against him and emerged as a powerful thinker who could continue the line of thought expressed so magisterially, for instance, in Edmund Husserl's *The Crisis of European Sciences*, a meditation in which science and philosophy would rejoin in a common concern for the *telos* of our civilization, and in a common concern for what Husserl called the *Lebenswelt*.[44] It is hardly too much to say that, in a philosophical world reduced to impotence by a naive and uncritical acceptance of the consumer society as a good in itself, Kierkegaard remains the best hope for renewal of philosophical conversation that we have.

All we have now to do, is to learn, at last, *how* to read his texts.

NOTES

1 *The Diaries of Franz Kafka*, ed. Max Brod (Harmondsworth: Penguin Press, 1972), p. 230. The entry is for 21 August 1913.
2 *The Diaries of Franz Kafka*, pp. 369–70.
3 Karl Jaspers, *Reason and Existenz*, five lectures, trans. William Earle (New York: The Noonday Press), 1955. See especially the third lecture, "Truth as Communicability."
4 Karl Jaspers *Der philosophische Glaube* (München: R. Piper and Co.

Verlag, 1963). See especially part 3 of the second lecture, "Vernunft und Kommunikation." "Vernunft fordert grenzenlose *Kommunikation*, sie ist selbst der totale Kommunikationswille" (p. 45).

5 Kierkegaard, *The Concept of Dread*, trans. Walter Lowrie (Princeton: Princeton University Press, 1957), p. 86.

6 Martin Heidegger, *Being and Time*, trans. John Macquarrie and Edward Robinson (London: SCM Press, 1962), p. 231.

7 Kierkegaard, *The Present Age*, trans. Alexander Dru (London: Collins, 1962), pp. 66–76 on "The Public."

8 *The Present Age*, pp. 76–90.

9 Heidegger, *Being and Time*, pp. 211–24.

10 Ibid., pp. 163–8.

11 *The Present Age*, pp. 73–5.

12 Heidegger, *Being and Time*, pp. 212–3.

13 Ibid., §6, "Care as the Being of Dasein," esp. pp. 227–35. Heidegger must have felt that his debts to Kierkegaard here were too flagrant to go without at least a formal acknowledgment, which he makes in a note at p. 492. ("The man who has gone farthest in analysing the phenomenon of anxiety . . . is Soren Kierkegaard.")

14 Patricia J. Huntington, "Heidegger's Reading of Kierkegaard Revisited: From Ontological Abstraction to Ethical Concretion," in *Kierkegaard in Post/Modernity*, ed. Martin J. Matuštík and Merold Westphal (Bloomington and Indianapolis: Indiana University Press, 1995), pp. 43–65.

15 Huntington, "Heidegger's Reading of Kierkegaard Revisited," pp. 47, 55.

16 Dietrich Bonhoeffer, *Letters and Papers from Prison*, ed. Eberhard Bethge (London: SCM Press, 1953); 2nd ed., enl., 1971. Kierkegaard's influence on Bonhoeffer is perhaps most marked in his book *The Cost of Discipleship*.

17 Jean-Paul Sartre, *Being and Nothingness*, trans. Hazel E. Barnes (London: Methuen, 1957). In that section of chap. 1 called "The Origin of Nothingness," pp. 21–45, it is difficult to say whether Sartre is more indebted to Kierkegaard or to Heidegger's reading of Kierkegaard: "In anguish freedom is anguished before itself inasmuch as it is instigated and bound by nothing" (35). Whatever the case, Sartre is no more prepared than Heidegger is to acknowledge the extent to which his early work is quarried out of *The Concept of Dread*.

18 Jean-Paul Sartre, *The Age of Reason*, trans. Eric Sutton (Harmondsworth: Penguin Press, 1961), pp. 242–3.

19 *Kierkegaard Vivant*, ed. Rene Maheu for UNESCO (Paris: Gallimard, Collection Idées, 1966). An account of the proceedings, and of Sartre's unwilling and half-hearted participation, is provided by William L. McBride in his essay "Sartre's Debts to Kierkegaard: A Partial Reckon-

ing," in *Kierkegaard and Post/Modernity*, ed. Matuštík and Westphal, pp. 18–42. Sartre's desire to evade the question of the "anxiety of influence" extended even to absenting himself from the discussions, "much to the annoyance of some of the others" (p. 39)!

20 Jean-Paul Sartre, *Saint Genet, Actor and Martyr*, trans. Bernard Frechtman (New York: George Braziller, Inc., 1964), p. 628. In a postface entitled "Please Use Genet Properly," Sartre writes: "I have tried to do the following: to indicate the limit of psychoanalytical interpretation and Marxist explanation and to demonstrate that freedom alone can account for a person in his totality . . . to prove that genius is not a gift but the way out that one invents in desperate cases."

21 Simone de Beauvoir, *The Prime of Life*, trans. Peter Green (Harmondsworth: Penguin Press, 1965), pp. 468–9.

22 Albert Camus, *Le Mythe de Sisyphe* (Paris: Gallimard, Collection Idées, 1962), p. 61, my translation.

23 A useful summary of translations and critical studies of Kierkegaard can be found in the bibliographical note, bibliographical supplement, and bibliographical note (1983) in the revised edition of James Collins's *The Mind of Kierkegaard* (Princeton: Princeton University Press, 1983).

24 David F. Swenson, *Something about Kierkegaard* (Minneapolis: Augsburg Publishing House, 1941; rev. ed. 1945).

25 On the way that the "indirect communication" moved from being a purely literary construct to one that involved the signifying activity of the "lived body," see Roger Poole, *Kierkegaard: The Indirect Communication* (Charlottesville: The University Press of Virginia, 1993).

26 *The Concept of Dread*, p. x. The whole translator's preface is of great interest in what it shows us of the presuppositions in Lowrie's mind as he translated.

27 C. Stephen Evans, *Passionate Reason: Making Sense of Kierkegaard's Philosophical Fragments* (Bloomington and Indianapolis: Indiana University Press, 1992). Evans's division of recent writing on Kierkegaard into "three broad types" (pp. 2–4) and his general methodical reflections in chap. 1, are useful insights into the structure of the problem as he perceives it.

28 Kierkegaard, *Concluding Unscientific Postscript*, trans. David Swenson and Walter Lowrie (Princeton: Princeton University Press, 1941), p. 552. The passage is of vital importance for a responsible hermeneutic approach to Kierkegaard.

29 H. A. Nielsen, *Where the Passion Is: A Reading of Kierkegaard's* Philosophical Fragments (Tallahassee: Florida State University Press, 1983), p. 3.

30 Robert C. Roberts, *Faith, Reason and History: Rethinking Kierke-*

gaard's Philosophical Fragments (Macon, Ga.: Mercer University Press, 1986), pp. 1–3, 10.

31 Jeremy Walker, *The Descent into God* (Kingston and Montreal: McGill-Queens University Press, 1985), p. 3.

32 Alastair Hannay, *Kierkegaard* (London: Routledge and Kegan Paul, 1982; rev. ed. 1991), p. xiv.

33 Ronald M. Green, *Kierkegaard and Kant: The Hidden Debt* (Albany: State University of New York Press, 1992).

34 Louis Mackey, *Kierkegaard: A Kind of Poet* (Philadelphia: University of Pennsylvania Press, 1971), p. ix.

35 Ibid., p. x.

36 Louis Mackey, *Points of View: Readings of Kierkegaard* (Tallahassee: Florida State University Press, 1986), p. xxii–xxiii.

37 Mark C. Taylor, *Journeys to Selfhood: Hegel and Kierkegaard* (Berkeley and Los Angeles: University of California Press, 1980), p. 276.

38 Mark C. Taylor, *Altarity* (Chicago: University of Chicago Press, 1987), p. 156. This passage is set inside the chapter called "Woman," which is on Julia Kristeva.

39 Robert P. Scharlemann, ed., *Theology at the End of the Century: A Dialogue on the Postmodern with Thomas J. J. Altizer, Mark C. Taylor, Charles E. Winquist, and Robert P. Scharlemann* (Charlottesville: The University Press of Virginia, 1990), p. 69.

40 Jacques Derrida, *The Gift of Death*, trans. David Wills (Chicago: University of Chicago Press, 1995), p. vii.

41 John D. Caputo, "Instants, Secrets, and Singularities: Dealing Death in Kierkegaard and Derrida," in *Kierkegaard in Post/Modernity*, ed. Matuštík and Westphal, pp. 216–38.

42 John D. Caputo, *Against Ethics* (Bloomington and Indianapolis: Indiana University Press, 1993). See especially chaps. 4 and 10.

43 Martin J. Matuštík, "Kierkegaard's Radical Existential Praxis, or Why the Individual Defies Liberal, Communitarian, and Postmodern Categories," in *Kierkegaard in Post/Modernity*, ed. Matuštík and Westphal, pp. 259–60.

44 Edmund Husserl, *The Crisis of European Sciences and Transcendental Phenomenology*, trans. David Carr (Evanston: Northwestern University Press, 1970). This massively documented and virtually unknown work is the context in which a reread Kierkegaard could make sense in our current philosophical vacuum. It offers hope for an intelligible future.

3 Art in an age of reflection

I. INTRODUCTION

In *The Point of View for My Work as an Author* Kierkegaard uses the concept of "the aesthetic" to establish one of the fundamental divisions of his authorship. Even more significantly, he seems to give to the question of whether the authorship is "aesthetic" or "religious" a pivotal place in defining the correct "point of view" from which to understand that authorship as a whole. We might therefore conclude that a concern with "the aesthetic" lies at the very heart of Kierkegaard's intellectual project.

But what is meant by "the aesthetic" here? When the aesthetic is defined as an "existence-sphere" in opposition to the religious, are we to assume that Kierkegaard has a particular grudge against the life-styles of artists and art lovers? Does writing a novel or going to the theatre exclude those who do such things from living ethically or religiously? Kierkegaard himself seems to have denied this quite conclusively in references to the *feuilleton* article *The Crisis [and a Crisis] in the Life of an Actress* he wrote in 1847, which paid tribute to Madame Heiberg's triumphant performance as Juliet, nineteen years after she had established her reputation as one of the stars of the Danish stage in that very role. The significance of this article, he claims, is that it refutes the view that "religion and Christianity are something one first has recourse to when one grows older" (*PV* 31). It showed that the religious aspect of his authorship did not simply replace the aesthetic. "That little article" (as he referred to it on several occasions) showed that an appropriate engagement with art could coexist alongside the religious.

Conversely, even complete philistines can be described as "aes-

76

thetic" in an existential sense. In *The Point of View* it is said that most nominal Christians actually "live in aesthetic, or, at the most, in aesthetic-ethical categories" (*PV* 35). Indeed, the clergy of the Established Church are also lambasted for being poets or actors in disguise in the final *Attack upon "Christendom" 1854–1855* (*KAUC* 197, 201–2, 289). Here Kierkegaard caustically remarks that the only difference between Church and theatre is that the Church doesn't allow you to claim your money back if you don't like the show! But if "the aesthetic" thus means something like existential inauthenticity, why has Kierkegaard chosen this particular term? What are the connotations that "the aesthetic" brings with it that makes it the one word needed to do this particular job? The answer to this question (and thus the key to unraveling the logic of "the aesthetic" in an existential sense) is to be found after all in the world of music and literature, art, and, above all, the theatre.

The concept of "the aesthetic" thus depends on an understanding of what is going on in the production and reception of works of art: But does Kierkegaard have an "aesthetic"? Clearly, he did not write an *Aesthetics* like that of Hegel or even his own philosophy professor, F. C. Sibbern. Nonetheless, the extent and coherence of all that Kierkegaard wrote on the arts does in fact enable us to reconstruct a critical aesthetic, and it is the aim of this essay to present an outline of that aesthetic.[1] Such a reconstruction will not only illuminate the existential sense of "the aesthetic" but also show how Kierkegaard's authorship belongs to a powerful stream of modern European reflection on art and the artist that situates the crisis of modern art in a wider crisis of meaning and value that since Nietzsche has been indicated by the term "nihilism."

I shall begin by examining three ways in which Kierkegaard contextualizes art: first, in purely aesthetic, formalistic terms; second, in the perspective of psychology; and third, within the wider orbit of history and society. In each of these contexts Kierkegaard offers both a theory of art, in the sense of what art can and should do, and a critique of art that serves to define the limits of what is and is not appropriate for art to attempt. In the purely aesthetic context these limits are determined by the requirements of art itself. In the sphere of psychology it is the interrelated phenomena of anxiety and freedom that mark the boundary beyond which art may not venture. Socially and historically, the ever-increasing dominance of what

Kierkegaard calls "reflection" generates a barrier to artistic development, in a sense not altogether remote from Hegel's dictum that since "thought and reflection have spread their wings above fine art . . . art, considered in its highest vocation, is and remains for us a thing of the past."[2]

In the course of this exposition we shall see how Kierkegaard's view of art is ultimately driven by religious motivations that lead to the negative judgment passed on the aesthetic as an existence-sphere.

The ordering of the texts and of the conceptual structure supported by those texts given here is not that of Kierkegaard himself. Nonetheless, in presenting Kierkegaard's aesthetics in this way, we venture to believe that we are not reading *into* his work concepts and categories that are essentially alien to it.

II. THE IDEAL FORM OF ART

The period of Kierkegaard's youth has been called "the golden age" of Danish literature, which – especially when set against the wider background of European Romanticism – meant that questions concerning the meaning and value of art were of great relevance to apologetically minded theologians. In his own early involvement with these issues Kierkegaard was influenced by the moderate Romanticism of philosopher-poets like F. C. Sibbern and Poul Martin Møller, yet he was also attracted by the Hegelian J. L. Heiberg, a leading dramatist and critic (and husband of the actress Madame Heiberg), whose idiosyncratic appropriation of Hegel's philosophy led him to a highly formalistic and logical theory of art.

Romantics and Hegelians alike understood art in an idealistic framework, and Kierkegaard shared this assumption. His understanding of what the ideality of art means is well illustrated in one of his earliest journal entries:

The reason that I cannot really say that I positively enjoy *nature* is that I do not quite realise *what* it is that I enjoy. A work of art, on the other hand, I can grasp, I can – if I may put it this way – find that Archimedean point, and as soon as I have found it, everything is readily clear for me. Then I am able to pursue this one main idea and see how all the details serve to illuminate it. I see the author's whole individuality as if it were the sea, in which every single detail is reflected. The author's spirit is kindred to me. . . . The works of the deity are too great for me; I always get lost in the details. (*JP* §117)

This emphasis on the privileged relationship between the artist and the recipient of the artwork does not involve denying that there is an ideal unity in nature, but it does single out art as a sphere in which we can anticipate the intuition of such a unity and experience the "harmonious joy" that it brings (*Pap.* I C 123). Art makes a single, cohesive whole out of a manifold of parts and reveals those parts in their essential unity. This is what distinguishes true art from the mere regurgitation of a mass of uncoordinated details (§5063). An exemplary instance of such a work is Goethe's *Wilhelm Meister* in which Kierkegaard discerns a "well-balanced guidance which pervades the whole" and a "moral world-order" that comes to be reduplicated in the life of the hero himself, so that the novel seems to be "truly the whole world seen in a mirror, a true microcosm" (§1455).

But if "an author's work should bear the imprint of his likeness" (*JP* §5351), the recipient of the work of art must also have the ability to perceive the unity in the work, which is a capacity most people lack (§2245). When the idea *is* perceived, however, and when the aesthetic union of artist and recipient in the idea is consummated, life is poetically "transfigured" (§1629) as if by "a refreshing, renewing bath" (§5287) in which the disparities and contradictions of life are reconciled (§1019).

Yet such aesthetic transfiguration is not generally found in life. Art's "poetic morning-dream of life" is related to reality as Moses is to Joshua: The one sees the promised land, but it is only the deputy, the epigone, who enters in (*JP* §859). Pharaoh's dreams may become more and more directly realistic, but they remain dreams that he cannot himself interpret. Similarly, although poetry can approach reality, it never coincides with it (§3651).

The indulgence in aesthetic pleasure thus comes to be seen not merely as a means of alleviating the contradictions and discords of actual existence, but as being itself motivated by a profound division in the individual's experience of reality. The poetic consciousness is, in Hegel's expression, necessarily an "unhappy consciousness."

When one understands Brorson's words
> When the heart is most oppressed
> Then the harp of joy is tuned

not religiously, as they were written, but aesthetically, then he has in them a motto for all poetic existence, which necessarily must be unhappy. (*JP* §800)

"The poetic life in the personality is the unconscious sacrifice," since it is suffering that generates aesthetic creativity and the poet, albeit unconsciously, sacrifices the achievement of wholeness in life for the sake of an ideal, poetic wholeness (*JP* §1027). At its most dangerous, an excessive preoccupation with the aesthetic can signal and even precipitate "the evaporation of the person . . . in which the authentic conscious existence is surrendered and everything is poetry . . ." (§3890).

This limitation of art vis-à-vis "authentic conscious existence" reflects the Romantic and Hegelian consensus that, as Hegel put it, "the work of art stands in the middle between immediate sensuousness and ideal thought. It is *not yet* pure thought; but, despite its sensuousness, it is *no longer* a purely material existent either, like stones, plants and organic life."[3] The various forms of art occupy a sequence of medial points on a scale that runs from the inarticulate world of nature to the standpoint of absolute self-reflection and freedom, the standpoint of absolute spirit. But art itself is never purely nature and, more importantly, never purely spirit.

The realm of art is, for Kierkegaard, logically regulated. If art is a labyrinth in which the unwary may lose themselves, knowledge of the laws governing the labyrinth can assist those seeking an exit from it. It is in this concern for the logic of art that Kierkegaard comes closest to the Hegelian aesthetics of J. L. Heiberg,[4] who has been described as "the Pontifex Maximus of Danish literature" of his time[5]– although Kierkegaard's relation to Heiberg was to bear all the marks of the intense ambiguity and even hostility that shadow all the father figures in his life.[6]

The key to Heiberg's aesthetics is the relationship between form and content as determined by the requirements of genre. In his own words: "every work which answers to the requirements of the genre to which it must be assigned is good and if it answers perfectly to its concept, then it is a masterpiece."[7] This definition provides the key to taste, which, according to Heiberg, cannot be merely a matter of our subjective response to the work. Taste depends on an objectively determined judgment regarding the internal structure of the artwork. It is "the acknowledgement of the objective element of art, and the individual's subordination to the sceptre of this power."[8]

But what principle determines the relationship between form and content, genre and idea? For Heiberg – and here we see the "Hegelian" aspect of his theory – the system of possible genres is determined by the dialectic of immediacy and reflection. Within the process of spirit's self-realization through the manifold forms of sensuous life, progressing from the immediacy of nature to absolute freedom, Heiberg sees all forms of art as subject to this dialectic. Immediacy is most purely expressed in the musical aspect of art and consequently in the lyrical element of poetry or in character and monologue in drama. Reflection is revealed in the plastic dimension of art, which includes the epic element in poetry and the situation in drama. True drama, incorporating both sides of the dialectic, is thus a "higher" form of art than is a painting (unmediated plasticity), a piece of music, or a sonnet. Within the sphere of dramatic art itself, comedy assumes a higher place than tragedy, since tragedy, as Heiberg understands it, hinges on the subjective, confessional quality of dramatic monologue, the self-expression of the tragic hero, whereas comedy subordinates character to the requirements of dialogue and situation, and presupposes irony in the sense of a reflective consciousness of the limitations that the dialectical elements within a work impose upon each other.

Motifs from Heiberg's aesthetics can be found at many points in Kierkegaard's writings on art. Particularly important are the principle of the determination of the relationship between form and content in terms of genre and the notion of a progress through the forms of art governed by the dialectics of immediacy and reflection. An outstanding example of this is the *Don Giovanni* essay in *Either/Or* Part I. Here Kierkegaard's A declares that a truly classic work is one in which there is an "absolute correlation" between the "two forces" of subject matter and form (*EO* I 49). This, he claims, is supremely instantiated in *Don Giovanni*. This claim is argued with respect to both form and content in terms of immediacy and reflection. The content of the opera, Kierkegaard states, is entirely and exclusively the character of the Don himself:

Don Giovanni is the hero in the opera; the main interest is concentrated upon him; not only that, but he also endows all the other characters with interest . . . the very secret of this opera is that its hero is also the force in the other characters. . . . Just as in the solar system the dark bodies that receive their light from the central sun are always only half-luminous, that is, luminous on the side turned to the sun, so it is also with the characters in this piece. Only that part of life, the side that is turned towards Don Giovanni, is illuminated; otherwise they are obscure and opaque. (*EO* I 118–24)

This character who gives the opera as a whole its character is the very incarnation of sensuous immediacy: he is "the elemental originality of the sensuous"; he is "desire as a principle," desire that "desires the particular absolutely . . . absolutely genuine, victorious, triumphant, irresistible, and demonic," irredeemably and utterly excluded from the realm of spirit (*EO* I 85). He does not even have the intellectual cunning of a seducer. Instead "He desires, and this desire acts seductively. . . . He needs no preparation, no plan, no time, for he is always ready; that is, the power is always in him, and the desire also. . . . He desires sensuously; he seduces with the demonic power of the sensuous; he seduces all" (99–102).

But why should such a character be particularly suited to musical representation?

In answering this question A explores the relationship between music and language against the historical background of Christianity's triumph over paganism. There is, he argues, a world of difference between the naive sensuous immediacy of a pre-Christian pagan culture and a return to sensuous immediacy in the wake of the Christian revelation. In a certain sense Christianity itself "brought sensuality into the world" (*EO* I 61) because only with the advent of Christianity was sensuality measured against the standard of spirit and thereby "first posited as a principle, as a power, as an independent system" (61). Christianity posits sensuality as a principle qualified by spirit but, precisely as such, as the principle of that which is excluded by spirit.

The relationship between language and music is analogous: "Language, regarded as medium, is the medium absolutely qualified by spirit. . . . In language, the sensuous as medium is reduced to a mere instrument and is continually negated. This is not the case with the other media. Neither in sculpture nor in painting is the sensuous a mere instrument; it is rather a component" (*EO* I 67). Music, like language, addresses itself to the ear, has time as its element, and, thus far, involves the negation of the immediate sensuousness. Yet if music stands closest to language in the hierarchy of media, it is not language and it is not party to the complete correlation that exists between language and spirit:

Not until spirit is posited is language installed in its rights, but when spirit is posited, everything that is not spirit is excluded. Yet this exclusion is a qualification of spirit, and consequently, insofar as that which is excluded is to affirm itself, it requires a medium that is qualified in relation to spirit, and this medium is music. (*EO* I 66–7)

The relationship between language and music thus exactly parallels the relationship between Christianity and sensuality, and it is in sensuous immediacy that music is said to find its absolute object. It is therefore no coincidence that, historically, the fullest development of music does not occur apart from Christianity (*EO* I 71).

In *Don Giovanni*, then, we see the complete congruence of content and form that is a prerequisite of a truly "classic" work. The working out of this congruence is also shown in the detail of the work, down to fine points of staging and performance. In this way A demonstrates in practice how the theoretical high ground of aesthetic principles can be used to gain a critical view of the work as a whole. In this vein Kierkegaard was later to criticize the overly reflective interpretation in a contemporary production of the Don's wooing of Zerlina, a small detail that signaled a complete misconstrual of the opera as a whole (*C* 95–105).

Though outside the realm of reflection, Don Giovanni, as the passionate sensuousness excluded and therefore posited by Christianity, does have a certain relation to spirit. This oblique relation is hinted at by A when he describes how, in the overture, the first flashing notes of the violin evoke the spirit of the Don:

There is an anxiety in that flash; it is as if in that deep darkness it were born in anxiety – just so is Don Giovanni's life. There is an anxiety in him, but this anxiety is his life. In him, it is not a subjectively reflected anxiety; it is a substantial anxiety. . . . Don Giovanni's life is not despair; it is, however, the full force of the sensuous, which is born in anxiety; and Don Giovanni himself is this anxiety, but this anxiety is precisely the demonic zest for life. (*EO* I 129)

Don Giovanni's anxiety is not "subjective" because he is not anxious for himself or aware of himself as anxiety; it is "substantial" because it belongs to the objectivity of his life situation. Anxiety is the reflection in his personality of the claims of a freedom, a spiritual life, that he does not, subjectively, acknowledge but Christianity declares to be a human being's ultimate goal.

The theme of Don Giovanni was one that had engaged Kierke-gaard's attention for some years prior to the writing of *Either/Or*, particularly as one of a trio of what he called the "representative fig-ures" of Don Juan, Faust, and the Wandering Jew. His scattered comments on these figures in the early journals provide a further in-dication of his indebtedness to Heiberg: the choice of specifically three ideas is scarcely coincidental in itself, against the background of Heiberg's triadic Hegelian logic of immediacy, reflection, and me-diated immediacy (or immediacy after reflection).

The aesthetic significance of these figures can be seen in the way that one entry in his *Journals and Papers* (§1179) speaks of the most appropriate means of representing them artistically as, respectively, music (Don Juan), epic (the Wandering Jew), and dramatic (Faust). Moreover, as ideas representing sensuousness (Don Juan), doubt (Faust), and despair (the Wandering Jew), Kierkegaard is concerned to demonstrate that any artistic portrayal must remain within the boundaries established by these ideas. Consequently, Goethe is wrong to let Faust convert, while Lenau is wrong to have him com-mit suicide. If an artist wants to show despair, he should not use Faust but allow "the idea hovering over all its actual forms" to po-tentiate itself in a new idea (or a new form of the idea) – the Wandering Jew (§1184). The world of each of these characters is also highly specific: Don Juan belongs to the Middle Ages, Faust to the Reformation, and the Wandering Jew to the modern period (§§1968, 737).[9] Each "idea" has its proper medium, its exclusive field of ideal content, and its own time and place. It is the task of the critic to dis-cern the objectivity of such correlations.

Although Don Giovanni and the other representative figures are defined in such a way as to be excluded from the world of Christian values, it is entirely inappropriate to judge them, *qua* aesthetic ideals, by moral or religious standards. Such judgment can only come into play if a person tries to live like a Don Juan or a Faust (*JP* §795). It is "fatuous" to call *Don Giovanni* immoral, because sur-rendering to the seductive power of the music occurs in an aesthetic context in which moral claims and actions do not arise (*EO* I 115).

If *Don Giovanni* represents the perfect congruence of form and content in the realm of musical art, the same principle of aesthetic excellence is exemplified in another work discussed in *Either/Or*, Augustin Eugène Scribe's play *The First Love*. Don Giovanni may

represent the volcanic power of pure desire, but Emmeline, the six-
teen-year old heroine of *The First Love*, represents the vacuousness
of fantasies bred by romantic fiction. The details of the plot are in-
consequential. "What the play revolves around is nothing; what
comes out of the play is nothing" (*EO* I 261). Equally inconsequen-
tial is Emmeline herself.

The play must be built on Emmeline; of that there can be no doubt. . . . She
has all possible qualities for becoming a heroine, not substantially, however,
but negatively. She is, then, comic, and because of her the play is a comedy.
She is in the habit of controlling, as befits a heroine, but that which she con-
trols is a fool of a father, the staff of servants, etc. She has pathos, but since
its content is nonsense, her pathos is essentially chatter; she has passion, but
since its content is a phantom, her passion is essentially madness; she has
enthusiasm, but since its content is nothing, her enthusiasm is essentially
frivolity; she wants to sacrifice everything for her passion – that is, she
wants to sacrifice everything for nothing. As a comic heroine, she is unparalleled. With her, everything revolves around a fantasy . . . watching it is tan-
tamount to gazing into an abyss of the ridiculous. (*EO* I 253)

Yet, because this is comedy and not tragedy, character needs to be
mediated through situation, immediacy transformed through reflection, so that the spectators must themselves bring a highly developed reflection to their enjoyment of the play. A writes:

The comic is commonly thought to be more a matter of the moment than
is the tragic. We laugh at it and forget it, whereas we often turn back to the
tragic and become immersed in it. . . . [Yet] the comic, if, that is, it is artistically correct, tempts one to become absorbed in it more than the
tragic. . . . [In the tragic situation] contemplation is completely in repose.
The comic situation . . . has a similar continuance for contemplation, but
at the same time reflection is in motion within; and the more it discovers – the more infinite the comic situation becomes inside itself, so to
speak – the dizzier one becomes, and yet one cannot stop staring into it.
(*EO* I 263)

The enjoyment that such infinitely empty reflection occasions is,
A adds, like the enjoyment that comes from a man gazing at the
swirling shapes made by his tobacco smoke – infinitely enjoyable
and altogether meaningless. This is the stance of the truly reflective
connoisseur of the comic. "The curtain falls; the play is over. Nothing remains but the large outline in which the fantastic *Schatten-*

spiel of the situation, directed by irony, discloses itself and remains afterward for contemplation" (*EO* I 277). The curtain falls, but the enjoyment of the connoisseur, who will return to it again and again in reflection, is only beginning, for the annihilation of immediacy is precisely his medium.

Even though Heiberg himself (who translated the play for the Danish stage) charged Kierkegaard with making a masterpiece of what was merely "a bagatelle," the essay on *The First Love* is exploiting Heiberg's own principles: The congruence of form and content and the dialectics of immediacy and reflection are the tools with which A goes to work.

No more than in the case of *Don Giovanni* should we attempt to justify the play in moralistic terms. To see it as the story of Emmeline's ethical maturation would change it "from a masterpiece to a theatrical triviality" (*EO* I 255). The moral vacuity of the story is integral to its comic potency.

It is striking that Kierkegaard (like Heiberg, though unlike Hegel) sees comedy as more reflective than tragedy and therefore, in a certain sense, a "higher" art form. Moreover, insofar as the potentiation of reflection is also a historical process, comedy is somehow distinctively modern. It thus approaches the frontiers of the aesthetic and it is no coincidence that already in his early journals, as later in *Concluding Unscientific Postscript*, Kierkegaard was to link the category of humor with the beginnings of the religious and even the Christian life.

Kierkegaard explores the problem of tragedy in the modern world in *Either/Or* (in "The Tragic in Ancient Drama Reflected in the Tragic in Modern Drama") and in *Stages on Life's Way* (in Frater Taciturnus's "Letter to the Reader").

"The Tragic in Ancient Drama" distinguishes between ancient and modern tragedy in terms of the degree or quality of self-conscious reflection on the part of the tragic hero who, A tells us, must be represented as both suffering his fate and responsible for it. If the hero is only the victim of fate, then the drama will lack essential interest. On the other hand, if he is represented as being completely responsible for his own downfall, then he is simply an evil man who receives his just deserts. "Tragic action contains an element of suffering, and tragic suffering an element of action; the aesthetic lies in their relativity" (*EO* I 150).

On the basis of this definition it is easy to see how the development of a reflective self-consciousness and of the accompanying sense of individuality and responsibility must transform the nature of tragic action.

> . . . just as the action in Greek tragedy is something intermediate between action and the suffering, so also is guilt, and therein lies the collision. But the more the subjectivity is reflective, the more Pelagianly one sees the individual thrown solely upon himself, the more ethical guilt becomes. Between these two extremes lies the tragic. If the individual has no guilt whatever, the tragic is annulled, for in that case the tragic collision is enervated. On the other hand, if he has absolute guilt, he no longer interests us tragically. (EO I 144)

Referring to Aristotle's dictum that tragedy evokes compassion in the spectator, A distinguishes between the ancient and modern forms of such compassion in terms of "sorrow" and "pain." "In ancient tragedy," he says, "the sorrow is more profound, the pain less; in modern tragedy, the pain is greater, the sorrow less" (EO I 147–8). Sorrow, he argues, reflects the hero's identification with a reality greater than his own private existence. It therefore has a "substantial" quality, it is "profound" and "gentle." Pain, on the other hand, presupposes the individual's recognition of his own culpability. "The most bitter pain is obviously repentance, but repentance has ethical, not aesthetic reality. . . . Repentance has a holiness that eclipses the aesthetic" (148–9).

These remarks, he notes, are made against the background of an age that "has lost all the substantial categories of family, state, kindred; [that] must turn the individual over to himself completely in such a way that, strictly speaking, he becomes his own creator" (EO I 149) – a situation that also throws into relief the view (propagated most notably by Heiberg) that "the whole age is working more toward the comic" (141), since in the comic we see the individual portrayed in the capriciousness of his isolated and arbitrary individual existence (Emmeline!).

A gives experimental shape to this account by describing a modern Antigone. In this modern Antigone, the guilt of Oedipus is not discovered. Only she knows the truth. With this knowledge she is

hurled with one blow into the arms of anxiety. Here at once I have a definition of the tragic in modern times, for an anxiety is a reflection and in that respect essentially different from sorrow. [Yet] anxiety is the vehicle by which the subject appropriates sorrow and assimilates it. Anxiety is the motive power by which sorrow penetrates a person's heart. . . . Anxiety, therefore, belongs essentially to the tragic. (*EO* I 154–5)

Her father dies. She falls in love and is loved. What can she do? To marry would be to enter into a relationship that demanded complete openness and mutual confidence – but to speak of her father's guilt would be to dishonor his memory. To betray her secret would be to destroy the possibility of her suitor finding happiness with her. How can the suitor know what feelings he unleashes when he pleads "in the name of the love she has for her father?" (*EO* I 164). The ancient Antigone's condemnation to being buried alive figures the fate of her modern counterpart: "she carries her secret in her heart like an arrow that life has continually plunged deeper and deeper, without depriving her of her life, for as long as it is in her heart she can live, but the instant it is taken out she must die" (164).

Such an Antigone, A claims, though authentically modern, is still tragic. But can a conflict that has been individualized and to such a degree really engage us aesthetically? "Quidam's Diary," in *Stages on Life's Way*, tells a not dissimilar story. Its narrator is a young man who is in love and has been engaged. He realizes that he cannot go through with the marriage for reasons that never become clear but concern a secret guilt that involves his father, as we learn from a sequence of vivid and expressionistic parables inserted into the diary. Incapable of the shared confidence that marriage requires, he breaks off the engagement. He now finds himself in an intensely ambiguous situation over against his former fiancée: Is he guilty with regard to the suffering she now endures? Would he be more guilty still if he had gone ahead with the marriage? Would his guilt have been greater if he had shared or withheld his secret? The absurdity of his situation is compounded by the fact that within a few months she is over the worst and loves another, while he continues to torment himself over the affair. The story ends with Quidam staring into the abyss, his life brought to an impasse by a fact that, in the eyes of the world, doesn't exist and by a guilt that he himself cannot determine. My diary, he concludes, "contains nothing, but if, as Cicero says, the easiest letters deal with nothing, then sometimes it is the hardest life that deals with nothing" (*SLW* 397).

In a "Letter to the Reader" that accompanies the diary, Frater

Taciturnus, the pseudonymous author, asks what kind of aesthetic hero Quidam makes. Is he tragic? Is he comic? And how does he stand with regard to the religious?

The tragic poet, Frater Taciturnus argues, will typically give his story a historical time and place, a fact that evidences the deeper point that tragedy demands the rootedness of substantiality or actuality. "But, now, does it help one to believe in what is great by knowing it is historical? No, not at all. . . . In order to grasp the ideality, I must be able to dissolve the historical in the ideality" (*SLW* 438–9). The historical is mere "raw material" that must be transformed into the ideality of possibility and only then appropriated existentially. In this respect tragedy reveals the characteristic limitation of the aesthetic. "The aesthetic result is in the external and can be shown . . . it can be shown and seen even by the most myopic that the hero conquers, that the magnanimous man falls in the battle and is carried in dead" (441) – or, perhaps, that the Greek Antigone is immured in a living tomb. Similarly the tragic collision itself has an objective, external form: Romeo and Juliet are separated by the feud between their families (407). When the contradiction that prevents the fulfillment of love lies in the consciousness of the lover himself, however, this is problematic with regard to poetry: "when love itself has become dialectical, poetry must relinquish it" (409).

Comedy might seem to be free from the constraints of history. "The comic poet . . . does not need a historical foothold. . . . He may give his characters whatever names he pleases, he may have the episode take place wherever he wants it, if only the comic ideality is there so there is sure to be laughter" (*SLW* 437). Similarly, comedy can make use of a contradiction that is in some sense internal to the consciousness of the lover(s). This was, for example, the case with *The First Love:* if Quidam's love, like Emmeline's, turns out to be much ado about nothing, is he, then, a suitable case for comic treatment? Yet whereas in the case of Emmeline and Charles there was never more than an imaginary love, Quidam and his fiancée are truly in love although unable to communicate that love to each other. Frater Taciturnus sees both comic and tragic elements in this. "The tragic is that the two lovers do not understand each other; the comic is that the two who do not understand each other love each other" (421). Such a situation lies at the very outermost limit of aesthetic possibility and, as such, "serves to illuminate the religious"

(422) that begins "in choosing the tragic higher passion out of the comic and the tragic" (422). In other words, the borderline between the aesthetic and the religious is crossed when the comic dimension has, through reflection, evacuated the substantiality and externality of the tragic and when the subject, in full consciousness of the objective meaninglessness of his situation, commits himself to that situation without reserve, a commitment that Frater Taciturnus names as repentance.

This, however, opens Quidam to the charge of being merely comic in another respect. For it is very possible to see Quidam's sufferings in their entirety as self-inflicted and "From the point of view of the aesthetic, every *heautontimorumenos* [self-tormentor] is comic" (*SLW* 465).[10] Frater Taciturnus acknowledges that Quidam is indeed "something of a self-tormentor" (472), but at this point the question of the viewpoint of the spectator is brought into play. For if we choose simply to laugh at Quidam's self-torment then we must ignore the religious perspective that sees self-torment as "reprehensible." "A religious healing is accomplished not by laughter but by repentance, self-torment is a sin like other sins" (468). Quidam is doubly ambiguous: On the one hand, from the standpoint of the spectator, he is simultaneously both laughable and pitiable, demonstrating to the full the ambiguity of the comic-tragic situation. On the other hand, he himself is confronted with the more serious dilemma: Is his predicament comprehensible in aesthetic terms or should he repent and embrace the religious?

Quidam thus represents an experimental testing of the boundaries of tragic and comic categories and so of the aesthetic as such. In him we see a subject poised at the point where the form-content correlation on which aesthetic judgment depends breaks down irretrievably. The inner is no longer manifest in the outer, and the outer can no longer express the self-contradictory passion of the inner.

III. ART IN THE DEVELOPMENT OF THE PERSONALITY

The very fact that art itself raises the question as to the limits of art invites reflection on what lies beyond those limits. One perspective on what transcends the aesthetic is provided by psychology in its concern for personal responsibility and the awakening of freedom.

In the development of the personality, as described by the psychologist, art can be seen to have a special relation to youth. Kierke-gaard notes the correlation between youth and art at many points in his authorship, and one of the clearest expositions of this corre-lation is in Constantin Constantius's excursus on the theatre in *Repetition*. "There is probably no young person with any imagina-tion," Constantin writes, "who has not at the same time been en-thralled by the magic of the theatre." (*R* 154). He goes on to describe the experience of adolescence as an experience of "coming out" from the hidden life of the child into the self-conscious responsibil-ity of adult life. In order to make this transition successfully, the adolescent must experiment with the various roles that life has to offer: If he is truly to *choose* himself, then his adult identity cannot be something imposed from without but must be his own choice. It is at this point that the magic of the theatre will exercise its power most profoundly. For in the theatre the young person is presented with a manifold of personalities that serve as models with whom he is able to identify or as whom he is able to imagine himself to be. Here he can try on and cast off a succession of personae without the responsibility of actual relationships and orient himself toward a fu-ture that he himself will have chosen from the multiplicity of pos-sibilities. In this process

Only the imagination is awakened to his dream about the personality; every-thing else is still fast asleep. In such a self-vision of the imagination, the in-dividual is not an actual shape but a shadow, or, more correctly, the actual shape is invisibly present and therefore is not satisfied to cast one shadow, but the individual has a variety of shadows, all of which resemble him and which momentarily have equal status as being himself. As yet the personal-ity is not discerned, and its energy is betokened only in the passion of pos-sibility. . . . [Thus] the individual's possibility wanders about in its own possibility, discovering now one possibility, now another. But the individ-ual's possibility . . . wants to be visible. (*R* 154-5)

The theatre provides a means by which this play of possibilities can become visible. Theatre is, in this sense, an exteriorization of the inner life of the imagination, an "artificial actuality" in which the nascent personality can "like a double . . . see himself and hear himself and . . . split himself up into every possible variation of him-self" (*R* 154).

Though not itself "real," this "shadow-play of the hidden indi-vidual" (*R* 156) is entirely appropriate to a particular stage of personal development. "The main point is that everything takes place at the right time" (155) since "this shadow-existence also demands satisfaction, and it is never beneficial to a person if this does not have time to live out its life" (154–5). On the other hand, if the shadow is confused with the reality, "if the individual makes the mistake of living out his life in it" the result is either tragic or comic in a quite different sense (155):

the cock crows and the twilight shapes vanish, the nocturnal voices fall silent. If they keep on, then we are in an altogether different realm where all this takes place under the disquieting supervision of responsibility, then we approach the demonic. (R 156)

When the play ends we must leave the theatre and face the real world, the child must put away childish things and confront the responsibilities of adult life. But does this therefore mean that art has no meaning or value for the adult?

This would not seem to be Kierkegaard's intended meaning. We have already noted his refusal to accept the strict equation that youth is to art as old age is to religion. Indeed, not only does he claim that his own review of Madame Heiberg as Juliet refutes that equation but the thrust of the review itself is that the mature Madame Heiberg has freed herself *artistically* from the accidentality of being merely "a damn pretty or a devil of a lively wench of eighteen" (C 70).

Moreover, there is one form of art at least in which ethical maturity is essential: the novel. In the course of his authorship Kierkegaard wrote extensively on three novels: *Only a Fiddler* by Hans Christian Andersen, *Lucinde* by Friedrich Schlegel, and *Two Ages* by Madame Gyllembourg (Heiberg's mother). In each case he confronts the work in question with the demands of what he calls a lifeview. This is a very specific concept that he has largely taken over from his philosophical mentor, Poul Martin Møller. Møller himself described this as being dependent on a personal experience of "the supersensuous in the sensuous, when it becomes the object of an experience of a higher kind," adding that

The Christian tradition, empirical experience, as well as the higher experience in which the supersensuous encounters us in a real form at particular times and places, give the discrete points which must have their place in a proper world-view, and the systematic, philosophical exposition only expresses with formal perfection that knowledge which is first present in an immediate way and in an inarticulate form.[11]

The structure of such a life-view is analogous to the structure of art itself since it is defined by the mutual interpenetration of ideal and real, inner and outer, in a manner that belongs to the immediacy of present experience more than to the reflection of philosophical investigation. The difference is, of course, that the achievement of a life-view must happen in life before it can be reflected in art.

In terms reminiscent of Møller, Kierkegaard describes the life-view so as to bring home even more forcefully its religious dimension:

it is more than experience. . . . It is . . . the transubstantiation of experience; it is an unshakeable certainty in oneself won from all experience, whether this has oriented itself only in worldly relationships (a purely human standpoint, Stoicism, for example) . . . or whether in its heavenward direction (the religious) it has found therein the centre as much for its heavenly as its earthly existence, has won the true Christian conviction "that neither death nor life, nor angels, nor principalities, nor powers, nor the present, nor the future, nor height, nor depth, nor any other creation will be able to separate us from the love of God in Christ Jesus our Lord." (EPW 76–7)

As such the life-view is a *conditio sine qua non* for the novelist who seeks to portray contemporary life. Such a one is Madame Gyllembourg, who is praised both in *From the Papers of One Still Living* and in *Two Ages* for the possession of a life-view that manifests itself as

The sublimate of joy in life, the battle-won confidence in the world, yielding a life-dividend, a confidence that the spring of the poetry of life has not gone dry in the world even in poetry's most inferior forms . . . a divine spark, which, carefully tended, can make the whole of life glow – in short, the verified congruence of youth's demands and life's achievements. (EPW 65–6)

In the absence of such a life-view a novel will either be merely a platform for a theory, what Kierkegaard calls a "dogmatic, doctrinaire novel," or have a "finite and incidental contact with the author's flesh and blood" (EPW 81). The former is the case with Friedrich Schlegel's *Lucinde;* the latter, with Andersen's *Only a Fiddler.*

A doctrinaire novel seeks to propagate an idea in a manner that is untrue to the concreteness of the empirical manifold of character, plot, and circumstance. In the case of *Lucinde* this idea is said to be

"irony." Schlegel's understanding of irony is judged by Kierkegaard
to be an illegitimate extension of Fichte's concept of the absolute
ego, revealing an arbitrary attitude to the world that makes itself
the sole arbiter of value. Kierkegaard labels this view "docetic" and
"acosmic," and regards it as "an attempt to suspend all ethics" (CI
289). For ethics depends on the acquisition of a life-view and the
life-view depends on the integration of ideality and reality, of the
transcendence of the subject and of the subject's involvement with
the daily detail of life. A similar critique seems to be implied in the
fragmentary journal entries discussing Clara Raphael, an early
Scandinavian feminist novel (JP §6709).

With regard to Andersen, however, the complete absence of a controlling idea means that what we end up with is an arbitrary and
self-indulgent expression of the author's own confused and resentful subjectivity. In terms that once more recall Heiberg, Kierkegaard
comments that "Andersen has skipped over his epic [stage]," understanding "epic" to mean "a deep and earnest embracing of a
given actuality" (EPW 70–1). As a result he is merely "a possibility
of a personality, wrapped up in . . . a web of arbitrary moods" (70).
Thus Andersen's novels are "to be regarded more as an amputation
than as a reproduction from himself" (84).

Both Constantin's excursus on the theatre and Kierkegaard's writings on the novel point to a moment of maturation in the development of the self that is decisive in determining the place of art. That
moment may be described as the transition to the freedom and responsibility of adult life or as the acquisition of a life-view in the
sense described. It is also the moment of anxiety. We recall that the
concept of anxiety is brought into play in such aesthetic representa-
tions as Don Giovanni and the modern Antigone, and it is not accidental that when Constantin Constantius speaks of "the disquieting
supervision of responsibility" frowning on the illegitimate extension
of the theatrical shadow-world into daylight hours, the word translated "disquieting" is the Danish ængstende, "causing anxiety."
Quidam, too, is an anxious figure, if we recall that he described his
own situation as revolving around an empty void, a life filled with
nothing, and that, as The Concept of Anxiety itself states, there is an
invariable correlation between nothingness and anxiety.

In Either-Or Part II Judge William challenges his young friend
with the image of Nero (what better example of an artist manqué?),

whom he describes as terrible precisely because the freedom of spirit has failed to break through the immediacy of his sensuousness.

The immediacy of the spirit cannot break through, and yet it requires a breakthrough; it requires a higher form of existence. . . . Then the spirit masses within him like a dark cloud; its wrath broods over his soul, and it becomes an anxiety that does not cease even in the moment of enjoyment. This, you see, is why his eyes are so dark that no one can bear to look into them, his glance so flashing that it alarms, for behind the eyes the soul lies like a gloomy darkness . . . and yet . . . a child who looks at him in a way different from what he is used to, an incidental glance, can terrify him. . . . He does not possess himself . . . [but] he is as if possessed, inwardly unfree. (*EO* II 186)

Nero causes anxiety in others not so much because he possesses tyrannical power but because he himself is hopelessly anxious: "his inner being is anxiety" (*EO* II 186). For all the glitter of the imperial throne and for all the corruption of his life, "despite all his experience, he is still a child or a young man" (186). A nightmarish Peter Pan, he is stuck forever in the twilight world of imaginative possibility, unable to break free and be the adult he is called to be.

Anxiety, then, marks the final frontier between the aesthetic and the religious, for it is in anxiety that the immediacy that is integral to the world of the aesthetic evaporates before the demands of freedom. In *The Concept of Anxiety* itself, that leap is characterized archetypally in terms of the Fall, yet it is also made clear that anxiety may mark the dawn of freedom. Insofar as the aesthetic culminates in anxiety, then, it is not unequivocally wicked. The experience of art may lie in a positive and constructive way along the path to freedom. But if this possibility is acknowledged in principle, can it be realized in practice?

With this question we turn to the social and religious contexts of Kierkegaard's aesthetics.

IV. ART AND SOCIETY

For all his protests against Hegel, Kierkegaard's own view of art is informed by a historical model of spirit's journey from the immediacy of nature toward its final self-realization as spirit, a journey recapitulated in the individual's development from the immediacy of childhood through adolescence to adult life. Yet the situation of the individual cannot be abstracted from society. When, for example, Kierkegaard compares Madame Gyllembourg and Hans Christian Andersen, he acknowledges that it is by no means accidental that Madame Gyllembourg, the possessor of a sound life-view, belongs to an older generation. In Møller's definition of a life-view, the Christian tradition had constituted an integral part of that which the individual internalized and appropriated in the acquisition of such a view. But, as both *From the Papers of One Still Living* and *Two Ages* make clear, that tradition has been undermined by rational criticism and by the fragmenting of social relationships that isolate the individual, thereby destroying the external basis of an authentic life-view. Kierkegaard admits that Andersen's failure to achieve a life-view is, at least in part, related to the fact that his formative years were spent in what Kierkegaard calls the "political period" (*EPW* 71), a term that, for Kierkegaard, denotes the fragmenting and leveling character of reflection, which abstracts from and absolves the individual from all personal responsibility.

Kierkegaard's *Zeitkritik* is most extensively developed, however, in the concluding section of *Two Ages*. Here "reflection" is made the decisive characteristic of "the present age," manifesting itself variously in the age's absence of passion, the short-term nature of its enthusiasm, its calculating prudence, its lack of action and decision, its craving for publicity, its indolence, its mercenary interests. Such an age "*lets everything remain but subtly drains the meaning out of it*" (*TA* 77). It is an age of envy, idle chatter, and leveling. The great symbols of religious doctrine are devalued and rendered meaningless. Should an apostle come among us in such an age he would be unrecognizable. His greatness could not find a corresponding expression in any external form but could only be consummated in the unrecognizability of suffering. Lacking the external authority of religion, the individual is therefore thrown back on his own resources and confronted, as no one in an earlier age had been confronted, with the stark choice between conforming to the uniformity of the crowd or seeking the religious in the absolute interiority of the self.

"Look . . . the cruelty of abstraction exposes the vanity of the finite in itself; look, the abyss of the infinite is opening up; look the sharp scythe of levelling permits all, every single one, to leap over the blade – look, God is waiting! Leap, then, into the embrace of God." But even the most trusted of the unrecognisable ones will not dare and will be unable to help anyone . . . they must make the leap by themselves, and God's infinite love will not become a second-hand relationship for them. (TA 108-9)

Reflection, by dissolving the structures linking inner and outer (and sense and meaning, form and content), is destroying not only the conditions for religious authority but also the conditions for the production of great art. It is by no means coincidental that this, Kierkegaard's most extensive critique of his contemporary society, is to be found in a work that is, essentially, a literary review. In this respect, then, the crisis of art and the crisis of religion in an age of reflection coincide in such a way that the impossibility of the aesthetic provokes and intensifies the question of the religious as never before.

This same complex of issues is also considered by Frater Taciturnus, who, with an eye to the love story of "Quidam's Diary," considers how even love has become "dialectical" in the modern age, as reflection has corroded the passion of the great lovers of the past. "An immediate love [such as that of Romeo and Juliet] is incomprehensible, and in our day even a grocer's boy would be able to tell Romeo and Juliet some astounding truths" (SLW 407). But when love itself has been drained of passion in favor of prudential self-interest, it can be of no further use to poetry, for "without passion, no poet, and without passion, no poetry" (405). Moreover, "The same reflection that corroded love will also corrode the infinite passion of politics" (410). Hence, "That the time of poetry is over really means that immediacy is at an end. . . . But if it is true that the time of immediacy is over, then it is a matter of attaining the religious – everything temporary serves no purpose" (412, 415).

When the choice facing the individual is focused in this way, then the aesthetic may no longer be regarded as a legitimate stage on the path to a religious awakening. To stay with the aesthetic is to refuse the religious. If art and religion are the two great resources that the modern world possesses by which to give meaning and value to life, this now means, for Kierkegaard, either art or religion. Although reflection has in one sense destroyed the possibility of great art, an age that fails to choose faith with the decisiveness of inward passion is, as it is characterized in The Point of View, an "aesthetic" age. The aesthetic has become the inauthentic.

Yet, despite all his polemics against "the aesthetic," Kierkegaard has been received in the community of modern artists as one of their own. Writers such as Ibsen, Strindberg, Kafka, and Mann reveal a Kierkegaardian influence, while painters such as Arshile Gorky and Mark Rothko have either incorporated Kierkegaardian themes into their work or appealed to Kierkegaard in explanation of their projects. Even musicians, most notably Samuel Barber, have turned to Kierkegaardian texts for inspiration.

This reception is less surprising if we consider that, despite Kierkegaard's strictures on "the aesthetic" and the implied critique of the world of art, his own writing has a powerful imaginative and poetic character, continually challenging the conventional boundaries between philosophy and poetry. Even in the guise of his most radically Christian pseudonym, Anti-Climacus, he offers a disturbing and, as he puts it, demonic self-portrait as a poet in the service of the religious. Indeed, this is the very point at which he is closest to artistic modernism. For if art since Romanticism has made art itself and the role of the artist into important themes of artistic work, that self-reflection has, since the ebbing of the first wave of Romantic inebriation, carried a characteristically critical stamp. Artists have been tormented by the pathos of Hölderlin's question "What are poets for in a barren age?" Hearing the hollowness of their best endeavours echoing in that question, the poets of the late nineteenth and twentieth centuries have turned from singing the praises of poetic inspiration to articulating the isolation, the failure, and the alienation of art in an age dominated by scientific rationalism, mass production, and social conformism. In this perspective "the death of art" has itself become a subject of artistic practice. In this context Kierkegaard's own critique of art appears very like the passionate and provocative gesture of one who himself writes out of the impossible tension that is the situation of the modern artist. Kierkegaard did not merely describe, he lived what Heidegger has called "the raging discordance between art and truth."

Of particular pathos in this respect is his own reworking in the period of his final attack on "Christendom" of the image of poetic life with which he began *Either/Or*. To the question "What is a poet?" he had then answered:

An unhappy person who conceals profound anguish in his heart but whose lips are so formed that as sighs and cries pass over them they sound like beautiful music. It is with him as with the poor wretches in Phalaris's bronze bull, who were slowly tortured over a slow fire; their screams could not reach the tyrant's ear to terrify him; to him they sounded like sweet music. And people crowd around the poet and say to him, "Sing again soon" – in other words may new sufferings torture your soul, and may your lips continue to be formed as before, because your screams would only alarm us, but the music is charming. (*EO* I 19)

Twelve years later, increasingly embattled in his opposition to established religion and increasingly rejected by his contemporaries, Kierkegaard recalls that image in his journal: "Like those in the ox of Phalaris whose screams sounded like music – those whom God uses are confined in an even worse way – for all their suffering is always taken by their contemporaries to be arrogance, which means that the contemporaries find joy in bringing more sufferings upon them – because of their arrogance. But so it must be, O infinite Love" (*JP* §6895).

The experience of the poet and of the unrecognized and unrecognizable witness to the truth is virtually indistinguishable in an age that has lost the immediacy of paradise. If the distinction between them is that in the situation of abandonment and misunderstanding the witness appeals to and on behalf of an infinite love, then surely we may yet ask why the poet should not do likewise and in that way also become "a kind of" witness.

NOTES

1 The counterview that there is no cohesion in Kierkegaard's comments on art and that Kierkegaard therefore has no aesthetic is, I suggest, best refuted by the exposition of that aesthetic itself and its power to make sense of the relevant texts.

2 G. W. F. Hegel, *Aesthetics: Lectures on Fine Art*, trans. T. M. Knox, 2 vols. (London: Oxford University Press, 1975), 2:10–11.

3 Ibid., 1:38.

4 A strong statement of the significance of Heiberg for Kierkegaard's development can be found in Frithiof Brandt's study of Kierkegaard's youth: "As an aesthetician Kierkegaard was spiritually akin to Heiberg in the highest degree and understood how to appreciate his work as few others did. He found in Heiberg a philosophically supported theory of criticism which understood the genres of art and their logical characteristics. Furthermore he found in Heiberg's person that elegant and witty

urbanity which was his ideal in his aesthetic youthful years." Frithiof Brandt, *Den Unge Søren Kierkegaard* (Copenhagen: Levin og Munksgaard, 1929), p. 126. Recent discussions of Kierkegaard and Heiberg can be found in H. Fenger, *Kierkegaard: The Myths and Their Origins* (New Haven: Yale University Press, 1980); Bruce Kirmmse, *Kierkegaard in Golden Age Denmark* (Bloomington and Indianapolis: Indiana University Press, 1990); and George Pattison, "Søren Kierkegaard: A Theatre Critic of the Heiberg School," *The British Journal of Aesthetics* 23, 1 (1983): 25–33.

5 P. M. Mitchell, *A History of Danish Literature* (Copenhagen: Gyldendal, 1957), p. 135.

6 The negative side of Kierkegaard's relation to Heiberg is most prominent in his responses to Heiberg's discussions of *Either-Or* and *Repetition*. See *EO* II 397–408; *R* 281ff. Many of these journal notes found their way into the text of *Forewords*.

7 J. L. Heiberg, *Om Vaudeville,* 2nd ed. (Copenhagen: Gyldendal, 1968), p. 43 (my translation).

8 Ibid., p. 32 (my translation).

9 We can, incidentally, see how the earlier order of Don Juan–the Wandering Jew–Faust has been subsequently rearranged in order to accentuate the correlation between the quantitative increase in reflection and the measure of despair represented by each of the figures.

10 The reference is to a play by Terence. We might also think of Molière's *Le Malade Imaginaire* as an example of a comic self-tormentor.

11 Poul Martin Møller, *Efterladte Skrifter* (Copenhagen, 1856), 5:69 (my translation). There are some very perceptive comments on the life-view in Peter Fenves's recent book *Chatter: Language and History in Kierkegaard* (Stanford: Stanford University Press, 1993), chap. 1 "Interrupting the Conversation."

4   Kierkegaard and Hegel

The story of German idealism is the story of Kant and the aftermath. By aftermath I mean the *Aufhebung* of critical philosophy in the speculative idealisms of Fichte, Schelling, and Hegel. The latter, of course, took himself to be the *Aufhebung* of Fichte and Schelling as well as Kant, to say nothing of Plato and Aristotle, Anselm and Aquinas, Descartes and Spinoza, and so forth.

The gods are jealous and do not tolerate such hubris. So German idealism involves a second aftermath, this time with Hegel rather than Kant as the subject of simultaneous critique (cancellation) and appropriation (preservation). Speculation, mediation, reconciliation, and the Idea are names by which Hegel designates a single strategy for trumping the tradition and becoming its fulfillment. The most unkindest cut of all for Hegel was to be himself outtrumped by Feuerbach, Marx, and Kierkegaard. The various ways in which his massive *Aufhebung* was *aufgehoben* in the 1840s make up one of the most fascinating stories in the history of philosophy.

Kierkegaard is a major figure in this story; he is one of the great anti-Hegelians. There are other illuminating ways to read his writings. He is a religious thinker in the Augustinian tradition. As such he is also an existentialist, a postmodernist,[1] and a critical social theorist.[2] But each of these stories will have to include an account of his complex relation to Hegel. The relation is complex precisely because it is an *Aufhebung*. There is appropriation as well as negation, and Kierkegaard is never simply anti-Hegelian.

Hegel writes,

The true shape in which truth exists can only be the scientific system of such truth. To help bring philosophy closer to the form of Science, to the goal where it can lay aside the title *"love* of knowing" and be *actual* knowing – that is what I have set myself to do. . . . To show that now is the time for philosophy to be raised to the status of a Science would therefore be the only true justification of any effort that has this aim, for to do so would demonstrate the necessity of the aim, would indeed at the same time be the accomplishing of it.[3]

Concluding Unscientific Postscript is a sustained satire against the idea that philosophy can be systematic science in this sense. Johannes Climacus, the pseudonymous author, finds this claim to be comical. First he states the objection. "Existence itself is a system – for God, but it cannot be a system for any existing spirit. System and conclusiveness correspond to each other, but existence is the very opposite. . . . Existence must be annulled in the eternal before the system concludes itself" (*CUP* 118, 122).[4] Then comes the satire.

If a dancer could leap very high, we would admire him, but if he wanted to give the impression that he could fly – even though he could leap higher than any dancer had ever leapt before – let laughter overtake him. Leaping means to belong essentially to the earth and to respect the law of gravity so that the leap is merely the momentary, but flying means to be set free from telluric conditions, something that is reserved exclusively for winged creatures, perhaps also for inhabitants of the moon, perhaps – and perhaps that is also where the system will at long last find its true readers. (*CUP* 124)

Two things especially should be noticed here. First, the issue is theological. For Climacus the gap between the human and divine is fundamental, while the system requires that it be compromised or even collapsed. We shall return to this point. Second, while finding Hegel to be absentminded to the point of being ludicrous (*CUP* 120–1, 125), Climacus pays him no small compliment. In conceding that this dancer leaps higher than any other dancer, he concedes that Hegel is the greatest of the philosophers, that his "system" is more comprehensive and more systematic than the great systems of, say, Aristotle, Aquinas, Spinoza, or Kant. It is just that he spoils his magnificent achievement by making an absurd claim about finality and completeness. Suddenly the great dancer looks ridiculous.

It is as if some new Whitehead and Russell were to develop a system of formal logic more powerful than any previously developed and then, after Gödel, to claim that it is at once consistent and complete. Their unparalleled brilliance would be spoiled by their unparalleled blindness.

Still, if Hegel is the most brilliant of the philosophers, it would not be surprising if Climacus, or other voices in which Kierkegaard offers a critique, including his own, were to incorporate Hegelian insights so that the critique would truly be an *Aufhebung*, a cancellation that preserves and a preservation that cancels.

The critique that culminates in *Postscript* begins in Kierkegaard's academic dissertation, *The Concept of Irony*.[5] This is widely recognized to be Kierkegaard's most Hegelian work. Those who find it necessary (but why?) to see Kierkegaard as simply anti-Hegelian suggest that the Hegelian features of *The Concept of Irony* are themselves ironical.[6] Those features are of two sorts. Formally speaking there are the triadic structures that give the book its shape; substantively speaking there is the critique of romantic irony.

It is Stephen N. Dunning who gives most careful attention to those triads. He acknowledges that such "Hegelian structures are perfectly obvious in the first part of *The Concept of Irony*" and that it is "startling that the very 'systematic *ein, zwei, drei*' ridiculed in *Concluding Unscientific Postscript*" (*CUP* 357; cf. 150n) should appear in Kierkegaard's own writings. But he tries to show that they not only structure the whole of *The Concept of Irony* but are to be found in five pseudonymous works as well, beginning with *Either/Or*, though "neither acknowledged nor obvious." His conclusion is that "Kierkegaard was quite unconscious of the extent to which he continued, even after breaking with Hegelianism, to think in terms that permit – and often seem to demand – a Hegelian structural analysis."[7]

We need not ask whether such a strong claim can be sustained. We only need notice that triadic structures as such would not compromise the positions normally attributed to Kierkegaard and his pseudonyms over against Hegel. Climacus, for example, insists that his own presentation is dialectical and rejects only the notion that it is a speculative dialectic, one that can be brought to closure. *The Critique of Pure Reason* is loaded with triads, but the difference between the human and the divine is not collapsed and the goals of philosophical speculation are quite famously renounced. Yet we must include Kant among the most ardent anti-Hegelians, even if we must speak anachronistically to do so. There is no need for Kierkegaard to undermine the triads of *The Concept of Irony* with irony. There is even less reason to treat *The Concept of Irony* as ironical at the substantive level, as if it were too Hegelian for the antispeculative posture of the pseudonymous authorship; for the critique of romantic irony that it contains is basically the same as is found in *Either/Or*.[8] From an ethical point of view, it represents excessive subjectivity.

The treatment of romanticism is indeed very Hegelian, not only in its ultimate conclusion, but in many of its details.[9] But there is no reason why Kierkegaard and Hegel should not agree in finding romanticism's flight from actuality to be problematic. Having a common enemy does not remove the differences between two people. Churchill did not become a totalitarian nor Stalin a democrat by virtue of their agreement that Hitler must be stopped.[10] A deep agreement about romanticism leaves room for Kierkegaard to distance himself quite decisively from Hegel. It need not be ironized away.

That distance already begins to appear in *The Concept of Irony*. Ironical negativity is seen as the birth of a subjectivity no longer completely submerged in society or the state (*CI* 168, 171, 178, 196, 228). This links Socrates to the sophists and provides whatever excuse there is for Aristophanes and for the jury whose verdict proved more fatal than his satire. But Kierkegaard also sharply distinguishes Socrates from the sophists as well as from Plato and the speculative impulse.[11]

The Socrates who emerges is quite ready to become the hero of the spirit that Climacus takes him to be in *Postscript*. He stands over against the established order, which he does not acknowledge as absolute. But his teleological suspension of the ethical, his recognition that he has a higher duty than his duty to Athens, is not a romanticism of personal preference (the aesthetic stage), as can be seen in his quarrel with the sophists. Nor is it that of Hegelian speculation (assimilated by Climacus to the aesthetic), as can be seen in his difference from Plato. The movement is not from the social institutions of Objective Spirit, which are unchallenged in their own sphere, to their philosophical self-consciousness in the higher realm of Absolute Spirit.[12]

Neither aesthetic, speculative, nor ethical (in the Hegelian sense

of the term that signifies a particular *Sittlichkeit*, the laws and customs of one's people), Socratic subjectivity as presented in *The Concept of Irony* is just the sort of ethico-religious subjectivity that
Climacus will explore in *Postscript* as an alternative to both the
theoretical complacency of Hegelianism and the practical complacency of Christendom. However deeply Hegelian Kierkegaard may
be in his dissertation, he is already on a collision course with the
system. Robert L. Perkins summarizes the situation eloquently:

> The similarities expressed between Kierkegaard and Hegel [in relation to
> romantic irony] also posit a real dissimilarity . . . in Hegel's dialectic, irony
> is overcome through the objective march and development of spirit in the
> actualities of family, civil society, state, and history, in which the individ-
> ual appears ultimately to be transcended, except insofar as he is caught up
> in art, religion, and philosophy as absolute moments of Spirit. On the other
> hand, for Kierkegaard as, we may say, also for Socrates, irony is not a move-
> ment or phase of world history and its overcoming is not achieved by the
> spirit or through the concrete universal, but rather irony is an individual
> manifestation and is overcome through the concrete individual. The move
> beyond irony is indeed in Kierkegaard as in Hegel the affirmation of this
> world, or ordinary human actuality; but according to Kierkegaard, within
> the new human actuality of ethical existence there remains irony. Human
> existence is not simply rounded off in the sphere of the ethical as defined
> by the ethics of Hegel. The infinite still calls.[13]

In *Either/Or* this call of the infinite comes in the sermon that concludes the second part, entitled "The Upbuilding That Lies in the
Thought That in Relation to God We Are Always in the Wrong"
(*EO* II 339). But in order fully to appreciate its force, we need to see
how deeply Hegelian the book is up to that point. Within the theory of the stages or spheres of existence, the aesthetic is perhaps
best described as the sphere in which preethical or amoral categories such as interesting/boring crowd out such ethical criteria as
right/wrong and good/evil in defining what shall count as the good
life. Excitement is in; duty and virtue are out.[14]

In the first part, the aesthetic mode of being-in-the-world is eloquently articulated in the papers written and collected by the young
man we know only as A. As already mentioned (note 8 above), he is
the embodiment of a romanticism that Hegel and Kierkegaard
would both find to be inordinately subjective, an immediate selfhood in need of mediation by ethical ideals and constraints. (Even

the highly reflective seducer whose diary A obviously cherishes is immediate in this sense.)

In the second part, B, whom we also know as Judge William, writes two long letters to A describing and defending the ethical sphere. He is clear about the categoreal character of the spheres and therefore clear that to enter the ethical is not the same as becoming good. "I only want to bring you to the point where this choice [between good and evil] truly has meaning for you. . . . Rather than designating the choice between good and evil, my Either/Or designates the choice by which one chooses good and evil or rules them out. Here the question is under what qualifications one will view all existence and personally live" (EO II 168–9).

Judge William describes this choice in two ways. He often describes it as an *absolute* choice of the self in its *eternal* validity (EO II 166–9, 178, 188–90, 214–19, 223–4). When he speaks this way it is easy to construe the ethical in Platonic, Thomistic, or Kantian contexts, as if one were choosing to make some eternal truth the criterion for one's life, whether this be the Form of the Good, the Natural Law, or the Categorical Imperative.

But most of the time Judge William talks about marriage, as if the ethical did not so much consist in becoming pure reason so as to apprehend some unchanging reality or principle, as in learning to participate in a specific social practice. As with Aristotle, socialization rather than science (*episteme, scientia, Wissenschaft*) is the basis of the ethical life. I choose myself in my eternal validity when I sincerely say, "I do. . . . With this ring I thee wed."

But this means that whether he knows it or not, Judge William is an Hegelian. For Hegel is an Aristotelian who repudiates the Platonic, Thomistic, and Kantian models in favor of an ethics in which the self has no immediate relation to the Good but only one mediated through the laws and customs of one's people. *Sittlichkeit* (ethical life) signifies the social institutions that mediate the Good to the individual. Not only does Hegel identify these as Family, Civil Society (the economic sector of a capitalist society), and State, but he focuses his analysis of family life on marriage.[15] Nothing could be more Hegelian than the move by which Judge William makes the meaning of marriage the key to the ethical sphere.

We can now appreciate the significance of the sermon with which *Either/Or* concludes: "The Upbuilding That Lies in the Thought

That in Relation to God We Are Always in the Wrong." To call it (as above) the call of the infinite is to see it as the disturbing reminder that the laws and customs of my people are finite. Even when such laws and customs sincerely seek to embody the Good, they are shot through with contingency and corruption. Both in their aspiration and in their achievement, ethically speaking, they are at best approximations. This means that when I have done all that my society requires of me and am an honored role model within it, I have still not fulfilled the infinite requirement that the ethical purports to express. A religious way of putting this is to say that in relation to God I am always in the wrong. No, that's not quite what the sermon title says. It is we, I and my *Sittlichkeit*, the laws and customs, institutions and practices of my society, that are always in the wrong once God is on the scene. For God is the Infinite and Eternal, while we are finite and sinful. "Woe is me! I am lost, for I am a man of unclean lips, and I live among a people of unclean lips; yet my eyes have seen the King, the Lord of hosts!"[16]

Either/Or is Janus faced by virtue of this ending, which in the fewest of words puts the long, Hegelian exposition of the ethical in question. It looks back to *The Concept of Irony* and its appreciation of a Socrates who refuses to make his society the absolute criterion for his life, not on the basis of private, preethical preferences (the sophist, the romantic, the aesthete) but on the basis of the Eternal, which has apprehended him without enabling him to comprehend it (Socratic ignorance). And it looks forward to the two texts in which the polemic against Hegel will find its most overt and most sustained expression: *Fear and Trembling* and *Concluding Unscientific Postscript*. It is two deeply Hegelian texts, *The Concept of Irony* and *Either/Or*, that set the stage for a religiously motivated critique of Hegel every bit as explosive as the antireligious critiques of Feuerbach and Marx.[17]

Hegel is the main target of *Fear and Trembling*, along with "our age," which is seen to be the everyday correlate of speculative philosophy. The evidence that Johannes de silentio, the pseudonymous author, has Hegel in mind is abundant. His preface makes it clear that his retelling of the Abraham story is directed at "our age" and its assumption that faith is easy and can be presupposed as given, while the really challenging task is to "go further" – presumably to understanding. Recalling the ancient skeptics for whom doubt was "a task for a whole lifetime," and anticipating the Abraham story, Johannes de silentio longs for the good old days. "Faith was then a task for a whole lifetime" (FT 5–7).[18]

Since it is Hegelian philosophy that embodies this urge (fatal to faith) to "go further" most explicitly and emphatically, Johannes de silentio concludes his preface with a paragraph in which he denies that he is a philosopher and identifies the philosophy he is challenging by calling it the "system" (nine times) and "science" (twice). To be sure that even the most inattentive reader does not miss the Hegelian reference, he further identifies philosophy as the attempt "to transpose the whole content of faith into conceptual form" (FT 7–8). But that is the central claim of Hegelian philosophy in its relation to religion, namely, that the content is the same but that philosophy replaces the inadequate, representational form (Vorstellung) with a properly conceptual form (Begriff).[19]

After the preface, Johannes de silentio turns his attention to Abraham, first in a "Eulogy on Abraham" and then in a "Preliminary Expectoration." What the latter is preliminary to is the main event, the heart of the text, spelled out in Problems I, II, and III. Each of these three reflections on the story of Abraham's willingness to sacrifice Isaac opens with the same formula, which goes like this. If such and such is the case, then Hegel is right; but then Abraham is lost (FT 54–6, 68–70, 82). In other words, Fear and Trembling is a confrontation between Abraham and Hegel. Its central theme is the incompatibility of Hegelian philosophy with biblical faith, of which Abraham is the paradigm in both the Jewish and the Christian Bibles. Contrary to its own central claim, the system is the abolition rather than the perfection of Christian faith.

This Hegelian focus of the text is more often than not overlooked. Then, when Johannes de silentio talks about a teleological suspension of the ethical, it is assumed that the ethical signifies the Moral Law in something like the Platonic, Thomistic, or Kantian senses mentioned above. Kierkegaard [sic] is then said to hold that religious faith is absurd and paradoxical because it is at odds with the Moral Law.[20] Or that the ethical, my duties to my neighbor and myself, is distinguished from the religious, my duties to God. Kierkegaard [sic] is then said to hold that religious faith is absurd and paradoxical because my duties to God are in conflict with my duties to my neighbor and myself.

But these conceptions of the ethical are imported into the text by the reader and impose a meaning on the text that cannot be found there. Over against his own view that moral insight is always embedded in the concreteness of the culture in which it occurs, Hegel usually uses the term *Moralität* for the historically unmediated ethics of pure reason that I have been calling Platonic or Thomistic or Kantian. Such theories abstract from moral experience too radically to be adequate to it. Moral philosophy needs to orient itself to the ethical life (*Sittlichkeit*), that is, the laws and customs, institutions and practices, of the people to whom the philosopher belongs. Far from distinguishing the ethical from the religious, this conception of the ethical as *Sittlichkeit* includes the religious within it, as one can easily see by reading either Hegel or Judge William.

Like Judge William, Johannes de silentio simply presupposes this Hegelian conception of the ethical. Two further indications of this turn up when he explicitly poses the question of a teleological suspension of the ethical. First, he writes, "For if the ethical – that is social morality – is the highest . . ." (*FT* 55; 346n7). The term here translated "social morality" is the Danish equivalent of Hegel's *Sittlichkeit*.

Second, Johannes de silentio distinguishes Abraham from the tragic hero. Jephthah and Agamemnon actually killed their daughters; Brutus actually killed his son. But they are tragic heroes who remain entirely within the ethical. The *Sittlichkeit* that justifies these killings and comforts the fathers in their sorrow is the laws and customs not only *of* their people but also *by* their people and above all *for* their people. Its highest requirements are the needs of the nation, the state, and society; and these needs prevail over the otherwise protected needs of the family. But no such larger social need motivates or justifies Abraham, whose society only asks that he love and protect his son (*FT* 57–9, 62).

Abraham is lost (a murderer) unless the laws and customs of his people are only the penultimate norms for his life, ultimately subordinate to a higher law. It is just such a claim that Johannes de silentio calls the teleological suspension of the ethical. This is not the claim that religious faith is in conflict with the Moral Law or with my duties to my neighbor and myself but the claim that to be seriously religious is to have a higher allegiance than to my people and their conception of the Good. What is at issue is the ultimate source of the Moral Law, including my duties to God, neighbor, and self. Is it society or God?

Johannes de silentio makes this point by distinguishing the universal from the absolute.

> Faith is precisely the paradox that the single individual as the single individual is higher than the universal, is justified before it, not as inferior to it but as superior – but in such a way . . . that the single individual as the single individual stands in an absolute relation to the absolute. . . . The paradox of faith, then, is this . . . that the single individual – to recall a distinction in dogmatics rather rare these days – determines his relation to the universal by his relation to the absolute, not his relation to the absolute by his relation to the universal. (FT 56, 70)

It is clear that the absolute to which the individual here is absolutely related is God.[21] If this were a Platonic, Thomistic, or Kantian context, the universal would be the Moral Law as a principle of pure reason. But in the Hegelian context that Johannes de silentio has so repeatedly emphasized, the universal is the concrete universal of the social order. What stands over against the particularity of the individual is not a principle but a polity and the practices that prevail within it. Thus, when he writes that for faith "the ethical is reduced to the relative" (FT 70), he means that the believing soul never identifies the law of the land with the law of God but gives absolute allegiance to the latter and only relative allegiance to the former. This "never" relativizes every *Sittlichkeit*, not just the historical precursors of modernity but modernity itself.

But in this case the self-consciousness of the modern world could not be Absolute Knowledge, as it is taken to be in Hegel's *Phenomenology*, nor could the modern state be the embodiment of reason or the teleological fulfillment of the historical process, as it is taken to be in Hegel's *Philosophy of Right* and *Lectures on the Philosophy of History*. Like the critique of political economy in Marx, the teleological suspension of the ethical is the rejection of modernity's ultimacy. In both cases Hegelian philosophy is seen as the illegitimate legitimizer of an order hostile to genuinely human life.[22]

This raises the epistemological question of how one might know the higher law that relativizes the norms of one's culture. In *Philosophical Fragments*, the very next pseudonymous text, Johannes Climacus explores two possible answers, reason and revelation.[23] This sets the stage for the next round of Hegel critique; for while reason is represented by the Platonic doctrine of recollection in *Fragments*, it is the Hegelian version of this speculative project that is the explicit target of the lengthy sequel to this little book, ironically entitled *Concluding Unscientific Postscript*.[24]

Here the difference between recollection and revelation intersects with the difference between objectivity and subjectivity. At the same time the difference between Socrates and Plato that disappeared in *Fragments* reappears. Speculation, whether Platonic or Hegelian, is a mode of objectivity in which the finitude of the subject is stripped away for the sake of an objective, universal, timeless apprehension of the truth. But Socrates develops the recollection motif in the subjective mode in which it is always in the service of the individual's infinite, personal, passionate concern for eternal happiness and never claims to deliver the individual from the conditions of temporal finitude. Hence the Socratic ignorance, the objective uncertainty that belongs to truth in its subjectivity, not only for the pagan Socrates but also for the authentic Christian believer.

Socratic faith (Religiousness A, immanence) will be distinguished from Christian faith (Religiousness B, transcendence) in due course. But this will only reinforce the anti-Hegelian point that has already been made by then. Hegelian speculation is not even playing the same game as Christian faith. *A fortiori* its conceptual moves cannot be the supreme mode of Christian faith. A triple somersault on a trampoline may be quite spectacular, but it is not the consummate form of the triple axel. Climacus is clear that this analysis does not establish the truth of Christianity; but he thinks it shows the falsehood of Hegelianism, which claims to be the highest form of Christianity.

The polemic begins in the introduction, which opposes dialectic to speculative thought in such a way as to make the surprising claim that Hegel is insufficiently dialectical (*CUP* 13). The distinction is Hegel's own, in Sections 79–82 of *The Encyclopedia Logic*. Whereas Kant had distinguished Understanding from Reason and portrayed the latter as falling into dialectical illusion, paralogism, antinomy, and so forth, Hegel distinguishes both a negative, dialectical mode of Reason and a positive, speculative mode. In Kantian fashion, the dialectical moment undermines the metaphysics of the Understanding, which employs finite categories suited to finite realities and is unable to attain the unconditioned totality to which it aspires. But the speculative moment puts Humpty-Dumpty together again both as the Idea (in the Logic) and in the light of the Idea (in the philosophies of Nature and of Spirit). As the skeptical overturning of Understanding's finitude, dialectical Reason is the herald of the infinite power of speculative Reason.[25]

Climacus introduces himself as a kind of Kantian thinker for whom the dialectical prevails over the speculative. He challenges the Hegelian attempts to make dissonance resolve into harmony and difference constitutive of identity. Then, as if he had just finished reading *Fear and Trembling*, Climacus points to faith as a paradigmatic resistance to the Procrustean embrace of the system (*CUP* 14). Neither Johannes (de silentio or Climacus) claims to be a man of faith; but both set out to rescue faith from a mode of reason that is its end, not as telos (the Hegelian claim) but as termination.

It is not reason as such that is opposed to faith but modes of human reason that have forgotten their limits as human and have lapsed into self-deification. This is why Socrates, who represented "the hypertrophy of the logical faculty" for Nietzsche,[26] can be an anti-Hegelian hero of subjectivity. Kierkegaard's sharp separation of Socrates from the sophists in *The Concept of Irony* is a reminder that we should not assume that subjectivity is synonymous with subjectivism in *Postscript* before reading the text. The synonym for "subjectivity" in Climacus's usage is "inwardness" not "arbitrariness." Far from being the release from all tasks, subjectivity is the highest task of all.

Part I of *Postscript* is devoted to a brief analysis of objectivity as an epistemological project. Part II is devoted to an expansive analysis of subjectivity and is fifteen times the length of Part I, which serves as little more than a foil. Hegel's insistence that philosophy must be scientific answers Kant's question whether metaphysics can be objective knowledge, free from the perspectival subjectivities of sense, opinion, tradition, authority, interest, and so forth. It is easy to recognize in this aspiration to objectivity not merely a modern awe of physical science but an ancient awe of mathematics that goes back to Pythagoras and Plato. When this awe gives place to envy and this envy in turn gives rise to the quest for the metaphysical comfort that comes from metaphysical certainty, we have a dominant tendency in Western philosophy.

Climacus takes the empiricist position that apart from purely formal systems, the search for objective knowledge never yields more than approximation. History and speculative philosophy are similar in that just as no final history of this or that can be written, so no final philosophical system can be written. Knowledge is a regulative ideal, and what counts as knowledge at any given moment is only the latest approximation.[27] This is especially troublesome for an anti-foundationalist system like Hegel's, for which truth is found not in the parts but only in the whole. When Climacus constantly taunts Hegel and his followers with the suggestion that the system is not finished (*CUP* 13, 76–7, 106–9, 119–24, 145), the incompleteness to which he points means that the whole is missing and with it, on Hegel's terms, the truth.[28]

Thus, when philosophy seeks to go beyond faith to something better, understanding as objective knowledge, it makes faith a promise it cannot keep. If faith is faith because it is not yet sight (full presence), philosophy, too, is at best partial and perspectival vision. But, Climacus says, let us grant for the sake of argument that philosophy could keep its promise. Should faith then join its bandwagon?

To do so faith would surely go beyond itself, precisely by committing suicide and ceasing to be faith. As an act of appropriation faith belongs to subjectivity or inwardness, to infinite, personal, passionate interest (*CUP* 51–6). This is because the question at issue is, as we have come to call it, an existential question, one about the meaning of my life and how I shall live it. But for the sake of objectivity the knower abandons first person discourse and seeks to become impersonal, dispassionate, and disinterested – systematically and intentionally cut off from all existential questions and *a fortiori* from faith.

Climacus gives the reader two images with which to make objectivity concrete. One is the Aristotelian portrait of the gods, whose "blissful pastime of thinking" (*CUP* 56) is completely devoid of either questions or decisions about how they should live their lives. But not only in Aristotle are they paradigms of the contemplative life. Since Hegel's system culminates in a quotation from Aristotle that portrays God as thought thinking itself in perfect repose, Climacus feels he has good reason to associate Aristotle's image with Hegelian speculation, which aspires to a repose free of questions and of tasks.

The other image is satirical. A man begins to wonder whether he is truly a Christian. His wife responds, "You are Danish, aren't you? Doesn't the geography book say that the predominant religion in Denmark is Lutheran-Christian? You aren't a Jew, are you, or a Mohammedan? What else would you be, then?" (CUP 50).

If we ask what this census bureau approach to religious identity has to do with Hegelian speculation, we find a clue in Climacus's earlier reference to "a speculative and almost Hegelian public" (CUP 34n). What is "speculative and almost Hegelian" about this wife, who quite possibly knows nothing at all about Hegel, is that she instinctively and in good conscience transforms a subjective question into an objective question. Her husband is asking, out of personal passion and interest, how he should live his life. By moving the discourse to the area of objective facts (of more interest to population statisticians than metaphysicians, to be sure), she tells him at one and the same time (1) that his question is already answered objectively so there is nothing for him to ponder or to choose, and (2) that for this reason his question is a silly one that should never have arisen in the first place. In this way the objectivity that purports to be the fulfillment of his subjectivity is in fact its obliteration. Climacus sees the move less as *Aufhebung* than as annihilation.

It is against the background of this account of objectivity and the dialectic of approximation and appropriation that Climacus later explores the hypothesis that truth is subjectivity. The point is not to deny objective truth but (1) to insist, with regard to the *what*, that human knowledge can never do more than approximate it and (2) to insist, with regard to the *how*, that the task of appropriation must not be supplanted by the quest for objective knowledge. Hence the following account of truth: "*An objective uncertainty, held fast through appropriation with the most passionate inwardness, is the truth*, the highest truth there is for an *existing* person." But this means that all substantive knowledge is a kind of faith rather than sight or sheer presence, and Climacus hastens to add that this definition of truth is "a paraphrasing of faith. Without risk, no faith.

Faith is the contradiction (tension, incongruity) between the infinite passion of inwardness and the objective uncertainty" (*CUP* 203–4). The Hegelian project of going beyond faith is doubly mistaken, as Climacus sees it. First, it promises to replace the objective uncertainty with certainty, which it cannot do. It, too, is an interpretation, a perspective.[29] But though Climacus sees the system as on a par with faith so far as certainty goes, he will not construe it as an instance of faith. For, in the second place, it eliminates the moment of passionate, inward appropriation, reducing the self to an impersonal observer devoid of existential identity. If the man who asked his wife if he were really a Christian would be foolish enough to turn to the system for help, it would respond just as his wife did. It would absorb the *what* of the question into objectivity and discard the *how* as superfluous and silly subjectivity.

Climacus himself has not made the movements of faith, nor does he recommend that his readers do so. But he fights doggedly to keep open the space in which decisions about such matters can be made.

As the dialectic of objectivity and subjectivity unfolds, it becomes clear that the tension between time and eternity is fundamental to it. But, since Climacus insists that only God inhabits eternity, this means for him that the underlying tension is that between the human and divine. In the forgetfulness of its limits as human, speculation is the self-deification of (human) reason (in its latest version), now identified simply (but deceptively) as Reason. If faith should turn out to be mad or absurd or paradoxical or contradictory in relation to this Wizard of Oz Reason (as both Johannes's insist it is), this does not mean that it is inherently mad or absurd or paradoxical or contradictory, but only that it is at odds with this version of human reason (and possibly others as well). This would be a fatal objection to faith only if this version of human reason (or perhaps some other version) were the highest standard of truth – were, in effect, the divine intellect.

It is the temporal character of human existence to which Climacus appeals against any such claim, Platonic, Hegelian, or whatever. The definition of truth given above is presented not as the highest truth there is but as the highest truth available to "an *existing* person." It is by making "existence" a technical term that applies uniquely to temporal modes of being that Kierkegaard (through Climacus) became simultaneously an existentialist and a postmodernist. His argument that we are not divine has a Cartesian flavor to it. If I were God I would not have left myself *in medias res,* given over to becoming, striving, and incompleteness.

This theme emerges with special clarity in the fourth and final thesis attributed by Climacus to Lessing:

If God held all truth enclosed in his right hand, and in his left hand the one and only ever-striving drive for truth, even with the corollary of erring forever and ever, and if he were to say to me: Choose! – I would humbly fall down to him at his left hand and say: Father, give! Pure truth is indeed only for you alone! (CUP 106)

The problem is that speculation needs to see the world *sub specie aeterni.* But since "to exist does not mean to be *sub specie aeterni,*" any such project will presuppose a "fictive objective subject" and the "illusory termination" of the quest for objective certainty (CUP 362, 81; cf. 189–93, 197–8, 217, 305–8, 361). In other words, existence itself "must be annulled in the eternal before the system concludes itself" (122).

In order to have a direct intuition of the forms, the Platonic soul must have reflected itself out of the cave so as to stand in an eternity prior to all worldly approximations of it. In order to have Absolute Knowledge, the Hegelian philosopher must both (1) possess the totality of the divine ideas and thus stand side by side with the Platonic soul[30] and (2) at the same time stand at the completion of the historical process so as to encompass the totality of the unfolding of the Idea. Standing at the Alpha and Omega points, the Hegelian philosopher would be reflected out of existence (becoming, striving, incompleteness) and into eternity – not once but twice.

Lessing recognizes that to see the world *sub specie aeterni* is to see the world as God sees it. But he also insists on the ineradicable temporality of human knowledge and thus on a distinction between human and divine that speculation cannot obliterate. "Pure truth is indeed only for you alone!" Perhaps Climacus loves this reaffirmation of Socratic ignorance all the more because it does not come from some romantic fideism but from a rationalist philosopher with strong links to Leibniz and Spinoza. In any case, he develops four versions of the claim that pure truth is for God alone:

A system of existence is for God alone. (*CUP* 118–19)
To be the spectator for whom *die Weltgeschichte ist das Weltgericht* is for God alone. (141, 158)
The identity of thought and being (subject and object, truth as objectivity) is for God alone. (190, 196)
To have the explanation of the paradox of Christian faith so that it ceases to be paradoxical is for God alone. (212, 562)

The first and third of these are directed against Hegel's Logic (either version), together with the *Phenomenology of Spirit* as the journey that initiates the thinker into the sphere in which it is possible. The second and fourth of these are directed against the Philosophy of Spirit developed in the *Phenomenology*, the *Encyclopedia*, the *Philosophy of Right*, and in the lectures on the *Philosophy of Religion*, and the *Philosophy of World History*. A look at the first will illustrate the strategy common to all four ways of resisting the collapse of the infinite qualitative difference between the human and the divine that Climacus sees as a necessary condition of speculative philosophy.

He claims that "*(a) a logical system can be given; (b) but a system of existence cannot be given*" (*CUP* 109). So that this will not be interpreted as a kind of Heraclitean assertion that deep down reality is chaos, he adds, "A system of existence cannot be given. Is there, then, not such a system? That is not at all the case. Neither is this implied in what has been said. Existence itself is a system – for God, but it cannot be a system for any existing spirit" (118). The original statement, then, presupposes the essential difference between God and human existence and makes a statement about what is available to the latter. God, but not Hegel, can be an Hegelian.

We might think that Climacus is granting to Hegel his Logic and challenging his *Realphilosophie*, the Philosophy of Nature and the Philosophy of Spirit. But that would be a mistake. We have already seen that Hegel's Logic is no mere formal system of deductive inference. He takes it to be "the exposition of God as he is in his eternal essence before the creation of nature and a finite mind."[31] But he also identifies his Logic with "*metaphysics*, with the science of *things* grasped in *thoughts* that used to be taken to express the *essentialities* of the *things*."[32] As such his logical system is a system of existence; for it not only gives us information about God, who simply is and thus dwells in eternity, but also about the things of the world that exist, that have come into being, that dwell in time.

It is in fact Hegel's Logic in particular that Climacus has in mind here, as is clear from his complaint "that Hegel's matchless and matchlessly admired invention – the importation of movement into logic . . . simply confuses logic" (*CUP* 109). But rather than focus on the way in which "everything flips over into its opposite by itself" (115) once we get started, Climacus turns to a question that exercised Hegel greatly, the problem of getting started.

According to Hegel's understanding, the beginning of philosophy as scientific system must be absolute, immediate, without presuppositions. But since Hegel takes two running starts to get to the starting line, Climacus doubts that he can satisfy his own criterion. In the first instance, there is the *Phenomenology*, a long journey that presupposes ordinary experience of many sorts in order to show that Absolute Knowledge is implicit within them. In the second instance, the *Science of Logic* opens with a chapter, "With What Must the Science Begin?" which argues as follows: "Thus the beginning must be an *absolute*, or what is synonymous here, an *abstract* beginning; and so it *may not presuppose anything*, must not be mediated by anything nor have a ground; rather it is to be itself the ground of the entire science. Consequently, it must be purely and simply *an* immediacy, or rather merely *immediacy* itself. . . . The beginning therefore is *pure being*."[33]

With reference to this second running start, and possibly also to the first, Climacus asks, "*How does the system begin with the immediate, that is, does it begin with it immediately?*" To which he replies, "The answer to this must certainly be an unconditional no. . . . The beginning of the system that begins with the immediate *is then itself achieved through reflection*" (*CUP* 111–12). But reflection, Climacus proceeds to argue, is something we do, not something that happens of its own accord. It requires "resolution" or decision, and with that we have left presuppositionlessness behind (112–13).

Ironically, this is a point Hegel seems already to have conceded. Just before the passage cited two paragraphs up, he writes, "All that is present [at the beginning of the Logic] is simply the resolve, which can also be regarded as arbitrary, that we propose to consider thought as such." Climacus's point is that this resolve is anything but innocent. By "arbitrary" Hegel no doubt means "contingent" rather that "capricious," but the dependence of the system on a contingent human decision raises questions that are made all the sharper when the substantive presuppositions of such a decision are noted. The resolve "to consider thought as such" presupposes both (1) that it is possible for an existing thinker to consider thought apart from the finite thinker who does the thinking, and (2) that it is desirable to do so. Climacus thinks it is neither (1) possible, since one would have to become the "fictive" subject who could see the world *sub specie aeterni* nor (2) desirable, since it would involve claiming, in effect, to be God. But it doesn't matter whether Climacus is right on these points. The decision to embark upon the system presupposes that he is wrong, thus violating the system's own requirement of a presuppositionless point of departure.

Moreover, an existing knower who cannot stand at the Alpha point required to get the system started will be equally unable to occupy the Omega point required to get it finished. To his doubts about the immediate starting point Climacus adds his previously expressed doubts about a totalizing conclusion. In existence, subject and object, thought and being are held apart by time. This is but another way of expressing the approximation motif from the earlier discussion of objectivity. If the system somehow could get started, it could only be completed with the help of "a conclusiveness that corresponds to the eternity into which the past has entered" (*CUP* 118). In other words, "Existence must be annulled in the eternal before the system concludes itself" (122). That Hegel wrote two versions of his Logic and revised them both suggests that no published version could claim to be more than the latest approximation of The Science of Logic.

There is really no new issue here. That the system must be presuppositionless and that it must be final are two sides of the same coin. In both cases the speculative philosopher needs to occupy a standpoint outside of time, and whether the eternity that must be achieved is represented as before or after time is not very important. In either case it involves the claim to have a God's eye view of the world.

While the details change as Climacus explores the other three forms of his claim that speculative philosophy arrogates to itself what properly belongs to God alone, the heart of the matter remains unchanged. He thinks that by collapsing the difference between God and human creatures the speculative philosopher becomes comical, and he is unsparing in the employment of his considerable satirical skills. But in the final analysis he is more offended than amused. He sees the speculative project as "impious, pantheistic self-worship" (CUP 124), though he is committed strategically to emphasizing the comical side of the story. But he shows his truest colors when he pleads, "Let us be human beings" (114) and when he writes, "I, Johannes Climacus, am neither more nor less than a human being; and I assume that the one with whom I have the honor of conversing is also a human being. If he wants to be speculative thought, I must give up conversing with him" (109).

Climacus is eager to return to the project initiated in *Philosophical Fragments*, that of comparing the modes of religious subjectivity embodied in Socratic and Christian faith. But before he can further distinguish the immanent pathos of Religiousness A from its teleological suspension in the transcendent dialectic of Reli-giousness B, he feels it necessary to devote considerable effort to point out the great divide that separates both Hegelian philosophy and "a speculative and almost Hegelian public" (CUP 34n), namely Christendom, from both Socrates and Christianity.

The centrality of *Postscript* in the Kierkegaardian corpus makes it easy to think that its richly developed contrast between Religiousness A and Religiousness B is the culmination of the authorship's presentation of the religious stage. But this is not the case. I have found it useful to designate central themes of post-*Postscript* accounts of faith as Religiousness C. Like Religiousness B, it is distinctively Christian, but whereas in Religiousness B Christ is the Paradox to be believed, in Religiousness C he is also the Pattern or Paradigm to be imitated, most particularly in his compassion for the poor and the powerless.[34]

Kierkegaard belongs to the tradition of ideology critique. His quarrel with prevailing theory has its telos in his quarrel with prevailing practice. In the writings of Johannes Climacus he charges Hegelian speculation with reducing the divine other to the human same in contrast to the welcoming of the divine other as other in a Christian faith oriented to the paradox of the Incarnation. But *Fragments* and *Postscript* are sandwiched between texts that focus on practice rather than theory. Over against Christendom (supported by Hegelian theory), which takes prevailing social practices to be divinely sanctioned (the ethical as presented in *Either/Or* and *Fear and Trembling*), Religiousness C presents an ethic of radical compassion that welcomes the neighbor even across the class boundaries of ethically sanctioned marginalization.

Kierkegaard's critique of Hegel is embedded in a larger project of trying to understand what it means to love God and neighbor in terms of overcoming our allergies to their alterity. The critique of modernity that emerges gives to the authorship a distinctively postmodern flavor.

NOTES

1 Those who stress the postmodern tendencies in Kierkegaard usually want to filter out the religious element, while those who emphasize the religious heart of his writings are, for this very reason, usually leery of linking him with postmodernism. But a religious postmodernism is to be found in the writings of Jean-Luc Marion as well as in works such as Walter Lowe, *Theology and Difference: The Wound of Reason* (Bloomington: Indiana University Press, 1993) and Kevin Hart, *The Trespass of the Sign* (Cambridge University Press, 1989). I have argued for a religious postmodernism in Kierkegaard in *Becoming a Self: A Reading of Kierkegaard's* Concluding Unscientific Postscript (West Lafayette, Ind.: Purdue University Press, 1996).

2 This category will surprise some readers. But Kierkegaard practices a (non-Marxist) form of ideology critique which is closely linked to a more direct critique of modern society. I have argued this in *Kierkegaard's Critique of Reason and Society* (University Park: The Pennsylvania State University Press, 1991), especially in chaps. 3, 4, 5, and 7.

3 *Hegel's Phenomenology of Spirit*, trans. A. V. Miller (Oxford: Clarendon Press, 1977), pp. 3–4.

4 The annulment of existence in the eternal has two senses in *Postscript*, individual and collective. Individually, the focus is on the Platonic escape from time, backing into eternity by means of recollection. Collectively, the focus is on the Hegelian completion of world history. Since both of these involve the attempt of philosophical speculation to see the world *sub specie aeterni*, Climacus treats them as variations on a single theme. Hegel's philosophy of world history is a footnote to Plato.

5 In a rather remarkable parallel, both Marx and Kierkegaard laid the foundations for their critiques of Hegel in their 1841 dissertations, but neither found his truly anti-Hegelian voice until writings of 1843.

6 See Lee M. Capel's translator's introduction to *The Concept of Irony* (Bloomington: Indiana University Press, 1965), pp. 34–5; Niels Thulstrup, *Kierkegaard's Relation to Hegel*, trans. George L. Stengren (Princeton: Princeton University Press, 1980), p. 257; and Sylviane Agacinski, *Aparté: Conceptions and Deaths of Søren Kierkegaard*, trans. Kevin Newmark (Tallahassee: Florida State University Press, 1988), pp. 65–77.

7 Stephen N. Dunning, *Kierkegaard's Dialectic of Inwardness: A Structural Analysis of the Theory of Stages* (Princeton: Princeton University Press, 1985), pp. 4–5.

8 The standard reading is not as careful to avoid identifying Judge William with Kierkegaard as it should be and therefore does not notice that the young aesthete of part I, known only as A, scores some rather damaging points against the judge. But it remains the case that (1) A is the spitting image of romanticism as portrayed in *The Concept of Irony* and (2) Judge William's critique parallels just as closely the critique developed in the dissertation.

9 For specifics, see Sylvia Walsh, *Living Poetically: Kierkegaard's Existential Aesthetics* (University Park: The Pennsylvania State University Press, 1994), pp. 55–6.

10 It is not the point of this analogy to Stalinize Hegel, politically speaking, though it is worth noting an affinity between the Kierkegaardian critique and postmodern accounts of the totalizing tendencies in Hegel's thought as a violent suppression of otherness.

11 For the sophists, see *CI* 201, 208–11; for Plato, see pp. 48, 87–8, 121.

12 Hegel suggests this reading of Plato's *Republic* when he says that far from being an empty ideal it "is in essence nothing but an interpretation of the nature of Greek ethical life [*Sittlichkeit*]." *Philosophy of Right*, trans. T. M. Knox (Oxford: Clarendon Press, 1942), p. 10.

13 Robert L. Perkins, "Hegel and Kierkegaard: Two Critics of Romantic Irony," *Review of National Literatures* 1, 2 (Fall, 1970): 250–1.

14 In contemporary culture it is perhaps the entertainment industry that most fully embodies the aesthetic standpoint.

15 This structure is developed briefly in the third part of Hegel's *Encyclopedia, The Philosophy of Mind* (*Geist*, Spirit) and more expansively in *The Philosophy of Right*. For an analysis of his little discussed view of marriage, see chap. 3 of my *Hegel, Freedom, and Modernity* (Albany: State University of New York Press, 1992).

16 Isaiah 6:5. In *Practice in Christianity*, Anti-Climacus puts it this way, "Every human being is to live in fear and trembling, and likewise no established order is to be exempted from fear and trembling . . . fear and trembling signify that there is a God – something every human being and every established order ought not to forget for a moment" (*PC* 88).

17 If we distinguish Kierkegaard's critique from Marx's on the grounds that they grow, respectively, out of religious and political/economic concerns, it will be necessary to remember that Marx is concerned in a major way with religion, while Kierkegaard's writings contain a radical social critique. See note 2 above.

18 In the epilogue a similar point is made with respect to love and faith as lifetime tasks. See *FT* 121–3.

19 For this theme in Hegel, see chap. 11 of *Hegel, Freedom, and Modernity,* and chap. 7 of my *History and Truth in Hegel's Phenomenology* (Atlantic Highlands, N.J.: Humanities Press International, 1990).

20 Attributing this view to Kierkegaard only compounds the primary error. For the author is Johannes de silentio, and Kierkegaard pleads with his readers not to attribute to him the words he puts in the mouths (or pens) of the authors he creates, just as a novelist might hope that his or her readers would not confuse any of a story's characters with their author. See *CUP* 625–30.

21 In *Postscript,* Climacus defines the religious as the task of being simultaneously related absolutely to the absolute and relatively to the relative. See *CUP* pp. 387, 407, 414, 422, and 431.

22 By putting Judge William's God radically in question, *Fear and Trembling* is a form of ideology critique not entirely unlike Marx's. But since Abraham's God is the relativizer rather than the legitimizer of the social order, it is not clear that the religious dimension of Marx's ideology critique has any critical bite against the conception of faith put forth in this text.

23 On the relation between Johannes Climacus and Johannes de silentio, see my essay, "Johannes and Johannes: Kierkegaard and Difference," in *International Kierkegaard Commentary: Philosophical Fragments and Johannes Climacus,* ed. Robert L. Perkins (Macon, Ga.: Mercer University Press, 1994).

24 In "Johannes and Johannes" I have argued that in spite of the explicit reference to Platonic doctrine *Fragments* should be read as ultimately directed against Hegel. The interpretation of *Postscript* that follows is developed in greater detail in *Becoming a Self.*

25 What Hegel says about skepticism in §81 of *The Encyclopedia Logic,* trans. T. F. Geraets, et al. (Indianapolis: Hackett, 1991), should be compared with what he says about it in §§24 (Addition 3), 32, 39, and 78. Cf. section 1B. of *History and Truth in Hegel's Phenomenology.*

26 *Twilight of the Idols,* in *The Portable Nietzsche,* trans. Walter Kaufmann (New York: Viking Press, 1954), p. 475.

27 From Climacus's perspective it does not matter whether we interpret the movement of the sciences in terms of progress or incommensurable paradigms.

28 On Hegel's holism, see *Phenomenology of Spirit*, pp. 3–11; and West-phal, *Hegel, Freedom, and Modernity*, pp. 75–81 and 118–22.

29 There are obvious affinities here with the perspectivism of Nietzsche, the fallibilism of Peirce and Dewey, the hermeneutics of Heidegger and Gadamer, and the undecidability of Derrida. Such a list could easily be lengthened.

30 Thus Hegel introduces his Logic by saying, "This realm is truth as it is without veil and in its own absolute nature. It can therefore be said that this content is the exposition of God as he is in his eternal essence before the creation of nature and a finite mind." *Hegel's Science of Logic*, trans. A. V. Miller (New York: Humanities Press, 1969), pp. 50, 43.

31 See note 30 above. Cf. *The Encyclopedia Logic*, §85, where Hegel claims that the categories of his Logic "may be looked upon as definitions of the Absolute, as the *metaphysical definitions of God.*"

32 Hegel, *The Encyclopedia Logic*, §24. Cf. *Science of Logic*, pp. 27, 63.

33 Hegel, *Science of Logic*, p. 70.

34 See "Kierkegaard's Teleological Suspension of Religiousness B," in *Foundations of Kierkegaard's Vision of Community*, ed. George B. Connell and C. Stephen Evans (Atlantic Highlands, N.J.: Humanities Press International, 1992). *Practice in Christianity* is the most important text for Religiousness C, but *For Self-Examination, Judge for Yourself*, and *Works of Love* are also very important.

ANDREW CROSS

5 Neither either nor or: The perils of reflexive irony

Irony ranks high among Kierkegaard's enduring philosophical pre-occupations. His writing career may be said to begin with his most sustained explicit treatment of the subject, his university thesis *On the Concept of Irony with Continual Reference to Socrates*. This was, as it turned out, far from his last word on the subject. Although he never again essayed a comprehensive theoretical account of irony, the subject recurs as a topic of discussion throughout his authorship, often accompanied by supporting references (or at least allusions) to the thesis. Even more pervasive than his remarks on irony is his employment of it, and of other varieties of verbal indirectness. Precisely how many, and which, of the utterances in Kierkegaard's texts should be taken as ironical (or in some way indirect) is a matter of considerable controversy – a controversy that has naturally intensified with the entry of poststructuralist critics onto the field of Kierkegaard interpretation. But one need not share the views of self-described postmodernists or poststructuralists to regard it as a truism that any adequate reading of Kierkegaard must confront both his announced views on irony and other modes of indirect discourse, and his highly deliberate and self-conscious employment of such modes.

Much has been written on Kierkegaard's conception and employment of verbal irony. What has received less attention is his conception of irony not as a verbal strategy but as a way of life. There are at least two reasons why this is not surprising. The first is the necessity just noted of coming to terms with Kierkegaard's own understanding of irony and other modes of indirect speech if one is to read his works with any sensitivity at all. The second is that, for many contemporary philosophers,[1] the word "irony" is thought to refer primarily to a certain mode of speech. Applications of the term to things other than speech acts are treated as derivative of this usage (as when the notion of an ironic person is understood as that of someone given to frequent ironic utterances) or as metaphorical or as simply confused.

Reading Kierkegaard from this view, it is easy to overlook the fact that for him, as for his contemporaries and near-contemporaries, irony is not exclusively, or even primarily, a particular kind of speech act. Rather, "irony" indicates a particular way of engaging in public (interpersonal) activity in general; speech (or writing) is only one of the activities that may be so engaged in. And in his discussions of ironic speech (as distinguished from his discussions of the more general phenomenon of "indirect communication"), Kierkegaard is interested primarily in articulating the distinctive structure of this more general phenomenon. He examines what it is to speak ironically, in short, in order to determine what is it to *live* ironically – to manifest in one's life, unqualifiedly, the attitudes and type of orientation toward the world that constitute irony. This question, the question of what it is to be an ironist "all the way down," is what he undertakes to answer in *The Concept of Irony*. And although he nowhere again lavished the same degree of attention upon this way of life – what I will call existential, as distinct from merely verbal, irony – this is not because his early interest in it was a mere youthful passion that he eventually moved beyond. Rather, existential irony comes to occupy a crucial place in the quasi-architectonic of the "spheres of existence" to which much of his "official authorship" is devoted. The conception of existential irony as an important stage in self-understanding and maturation, which in *The Concept of Irony* is expressed in the slogan that irony is "the awakening of subjectivity," remains largely intact in the later writings. And it returns, as an explicit theme, in *Concluding Unscientific Postscript*, where it is identified as a transitionary stage between the aesthetic and the ethical spheres. In *Postscript*, or so I will argue, Kierkegaard builds upon and in one crucial respect modifies his earlier conception of existential irony. What the earlier and later conceptions amount to and what motivated the modification are the subjects of this essay.

The structure of this essay is as follows. I begin with the account of verbal irony in *The Concept of Irony*, examining several characteristics that Kierkegaard presents as essential not only to verbal irony but to irony *simpliciter*. I then lay out the conception of "the ironist" – the person who manifests existential irony – provided in *The Concept of Irony*. I argue that the conception of existential irony in this work contains an internal tension that renders the ironist's way of life unstable, self-undermining. I then move to the later account of existential irony in *Concluding Unscientific Post-script*, arguing that this later account is modified so as to eliminate the tension in the earlier conception.

I. VERBAL AND EXISTENTIAL IRONY IN *THE CONCEPT OF IRONY*

I begin by exploring three features that Kierkegaard sees as essential to irony, starting with their instantiation in speech and extrapolating from that his conception of the distinctively ironic way of life.

Irony as contradiction between the external and internal

Irony always involves a contradiction (or opposition) between the external and the internal, between the ironist's inner state and his outward behavior. Few, I think, would argue that there is nothing right in this claim; the question is how it is to be interpreted. The most common interpretation is roughly as follows: ironic speech intends to convey the opposite of the literal meaning of what is said. To take a familiar example from Gregory Vlastos, a person in the middle of a torrential downpour says to the person next to him, "What lovely weather we're having," and intends thereby to convey that the weather is terrible.[2] Kierkegaard finds this way of interpreting the opposition manifested in ironic speech to capture only a deficient or attenuated mode of verbal irony, much as a metaphor that has become banal through widespread use may be thought to be a deficient example of metaphor; a borderline example, we might say, between metaphor and idiom. His reason is that where *p* is used as a means of expressing that not-*p*, the opposition between the speaker's observable condition and his inner state is merely superficial. When Vlastos's speaker makes his remark, his hearer understands, and is intended to understand, this remark to be a way of conveying displeasure at the weather. "This is lovely weather" becomes, in such a circumstance, simply another way of saying that the weather is lousy. The irony, in Kierkegaard's words, "cancels itself; it is like a riddle to which one at the same time has the solution" (CI 248). For Kierkegaard, an adequate interpretation of verbal irony – one that gets the distinctive point and nature of verbal irony, rather than substituting an analysis suitable only for borderline cases – must satisfy two conditions. The first is that the opposition it posits between the speaker's appearance and his internal state must not be merely superficial or "self-canceling" in this way. The second is that the opposition thus posited must not be such as to eradicate the distinction between ironic speech and mere lying. Attention to the further features of irony discussed below leads him to the conception of a more radical type of opposition than that involved either in "self-canceling" ironic speech or outright deception.

Irony as exclusionary

Consider, again, the humdrum ironic figure of speech. When I employ this trope, I speak in a kind of code. I say "Lovely weather," meaning "Lousy weather," and part of the point of using this trope is to call to mind a division between those who would naively take what I say at face value and those who are sufficiently perceptive to get what I really mean.[3] This implicit division and the feeling of superiority that the speaker and the discerning hearer get by taking themselves to be among the superior who are "in the know" explain the special delight in speaking ironically and understanding correctly ironic speech. As Kierkegaard writes,

The ironic figure of speech has [a] property that characterizes all irony, a certain superiority deriving from its not wanting to be understood immediately . . . with the result that this figure looks down, as it were, on plain and simple talk that everyone can promptly understand; it travels around, so to speak, in an exclusive incognito and looks down pitying from this high position on ordinary, prosaic talk. . . .

Just as kings and princes speak French, the higher circles (this, of course, must be understood according to an intellectual ordering of rank) speak ironically so that lay people will not be able to understand them, and to that extent irony is in the process of isolating itself; it does not wish to be generally understood. (CI 248-9)

In holding that irony involves an implicit division between an "inner circle" and the "uninitiated" (CI 249), Kierkegaard is not claiming that there must be actual representatives of each type present. In a flat case of irony like the remark "Lovely weather," the speaker hardly is to be understood as presupposing that some person is present who takes his remark literally. Rather, the point is that in this kind of locution the speaker and hearer see themselves and each other as "getting it," as contrasted with an implicit figure who does not "get it," and in this perception of themselves there is a feeling of superiority over the ingenuous person (real or imaginary). The pleasure of being in the know remains, akin to the pleasure lovers sometimes have when speaking to each other in their private code, even when they are by themselves.

By the same token, for Kierkegaard, speaking ironically does not require the actual presence of others who "get it." Kierkegaard's illuminating analogy between ironic speech and the encoded speech of the culturally sophisticated helps us to see why this is so. Ordinarily, when we make a joke that nobody gets, our intentions are frustrated. An esoteric allusion that nobody gets may be a failure if the point of making the allusion was to impress others with our own erudition. If the point, however, is not to impress others but simply to exercise our sophistication for our own pleasure – the pleasure we derive from seeing ourselves as sophisticated – then the allusion is still successful. Obviously, an esoteric allusion does not become any the less esoteric for the fact that nobody gets it. If anything, my actual audience's incomprehension reinforces my sense of my own sophistication. The point of an esoteric allusion is to separate the superior initiated from the inferior uninitiated and to establish the speaker as one of the former. The smaller the group of initiated, the greater the feeling of superiority; on the other hand, the more superior I feel myself to be, the less need I have of others' recognition of my superiority and the more I will take pleasure in making allusions that nobody around me is learned enough to get. This is also true of ironic speech. As Kierkegaard writes, "[I]t is only a secondary form of the ironic vanity that desires witnesses in order to assure and reassure itself of itself" (CI 249).

If we focus on this division of listeners into the discerning and the ingenuous, we will think of ironic speech not as a matter of expressing the opposite of what one seems to be saying but as one of seeming to some (the discerning) to be saying the opposite of what one seems to others (the undiscerning) to be saying. And the greater the discernment required, the greater the special pleasure elicited by the production or the penetration of such speech. Consider the following sentence in a letter of recommendation for a job candidate: "You will be lucky if you get this person to work for you."[4] Such a cleverly ambiguous remark looks, at first glance, like praise; but the reader soon sees the implied criticism in the sentence, and thus takes pleasure in seeing how the sentence has been crafted to mean the opposite of what it appears to mean. We see, that is, how the author could seem to mean one thing – and would so seem, to a more naive reader – but (probably) means something very different. In seeing this, we derive enjoyment from seeing the author's cleverness, and our own, at work; our sense of our own superior cleverness (which we share with the author) is reinforced.

Irony as liberating

When we speak in a direct, nonironic mode, we both express and make commitments of various kinds.[5] To make an assertion is, arguably, to pledge ourselves to the truth of what we assert; to stake, as it were, our reputation for reliability and sincerity on what we say. But when we deliberately say something that can be taken in a variety of ways, giving no explicit indication of which way it should be taken, we do not, as it were, put ourselves on record as believing any one of the propositions we could be interpreted as asserting. Whereas in an ordinary speech, I commit myself to what I say and leave myself open to criticism should what I say turn out to be false, in this kind of speech I make no such commitment. As Kierkegaard writes,

When I am aware as I speak that what I am saying is what I mean and that what I have said adequately expresses my meaning, and I assume that the person to whom I am talking grasps my meaning completely, then I am bound in what has been said. . . . I am also bound with respect to myself and cannot free myself any time I wish. If, however, what I said is not my meaning or the opposite of my meaning, then I am free in relation to others and to myself. (CI 247–8)

The ironic speaker is freed from responsibility for the hearer's having concluded what he did about the ironic speaker's inner state on the basis of his behavior. And, for Kierkegaard, the more one

speaks in this way – speaking in riddles that are left up to the hearer
to solve – the more one is an ironist. At its maximum, irony so conceived – both in respect of the speaker's freedom and in respect of
the heterogeneity between the inner and outer – is the type of
speech Kierkegaard attributes to Socrates, the type that I will call
"radical verbal irony." To speak in this way is to say something that
can be taken in a variety of ways, without intending the hearer to
take it in any one of those ways. What is said could be taken as an
expression that p or as an expression that $not\text{-}p$ or as an expression
that q; and S is unconcerned as to which of these H takes this to be.
He is interested only in producing these riddles; and since they are
riddles, saying them does not commit him, in the sense that he cannot be held to account for having expressed that p or that $not\text{-}p$ or
that q. He was expressing, literally, nothing; that the hearer takes
him to be expressing something, intending to communicate something, is the hearer's responsibility.

This may appear to be an exotic case. I think, however, that it is
simply an extension of a familiar phenomenon. We have all had the
experience of hearing someone utter a sentence that could be taken
as sincere and direct but where something makes us wonder whether
we are not somehow being taken in if we take it in that way. We may
then be so ingenuous as to ask, "What do you mean by that?"
Perhaps, with a hint of weary condescension, he explains himself,
lets us in on the joke; in which case he is no longer speaking in the
mode of radical verbal irony. He may in response, however, produce
a second piece of radical verbal irony, in which case our interpretative problems are only compounded and our worry that he may be
making fools of us increases. We become even more suspicious that
the speaker is not really engaging in conversation with us at all but
merely playing a kind of manipulative game at our expense.

This radical verbal irony is what Kierkegaard considers the most
extreme, and purest, form of ironic speech. It is not hard to see why.
The contradiction between the outer and the inner is here intensified. The letter writer, like the man who says "Lousy weather," has
at least this much consistency between his outward performance
and his inner state: the outward performance, considered simply as
an act of speaking, was an expression of an intent to express verbally
some belief or other; he, like the person who says "Lovely weather"

in the rainstorm, and like the mere liar, has such an intent; to that extent, neither is misrepresenting himself insofar as, by speaking, he represents his intent to convey some belief to the hearer.

Even this minimal homogeneity between inner and outer is lost in the case of radical verbal irony. In uttering the sentence, he represents himself as intending to communicate something; but this is a misrepresentation. Kierkegaard's ironist has no interest in communicating, directly or indirectly, deceptively or nondeceptively; his only interest is in luxuriating in the freedom that comes from playing at conversation, tossing out statements that can be taken in a variety of ways, and letting the hearer who takes this to be a real conversation flounder among interpretative possibilities. As Kierkegaard writes,

> [D]issimulation . . . has a purpose [i.e., the deception of the hearer by means of the utterance], but this purpose is an external objective foreign to the dissimulation itself. . . . [Irony's] purpose is nothing other than the irony itself. If, for example, the ironist appears as someone other than he actually is, his purpose might indeed seem to be to get others to believe this; but his actual purpose still is to feel free, but this he is precisely by means of irony. . . . (CI 256)

Such an ironic speaker is free in several ways. First, the ambiguity of his speech frees him from the responsibility he would have had had he said something with a single, clear-cut meaning. If he says that p, in such a way that a reasonably perceptive listener will recognize that he could be taken as meaning that p, could be taken as meaning that not-p, and could be taken as meaning something else altogether – and if his intention is simply to produce such an utterance, not to communicate anything at all – then the charge that he has lied or been culpably mistaken (in the event that p turns out not to be the case) is unfounded. Second, his orientation toward the practice of conversation itself is one of disengagement. It is all, for him, a kind of playacting; he is not really engaging in conversation at all but merely pretending to converse, like an actor speaking his part of the dialogue onstage. Third, he is free in the sense of being no longer reliant for the fulfillment of the intention with which he speaks upon the discernment of his hearer. When I produce a straightforward statement, the fulfillment of my intentions is contingent upon the hearer's interpreting the statement in the way that I wish. If, however, my intention is merely to produce answerless riddles and I am indifferent as to whether my hearer takes my statement in one way rather than another, then I am, as Kierkegaard says, free in relation to that hearer.

From this portrait of radical verbal irony, we can see an orientation toward the practice of conversation, and toward society generally, that Kierkegaard sees as crucial to irony *simpliciter*. To put the point bluntly, the ironic speaker is not taking this practice seriously. Superficially, he acts as one who is engaging in the practice but he does not have as his aim, nor adopt as his ideal, that which is the constitutive aim of the practice: communication. The person who says "Lovely weather," intending to convey that the weather is not lovely, engages in the practice of conversation in a more or less unproblematic way, using the full resources of the practice to achieve communication; the nontransparent ironist and the common liar abuse the practice but nevertheless adopt it as a means of communication just as the sincere direct speaker does. But the radical verbal ironist is using language in a far more deceptive way, for he is adopting the stance of one who intends to bring about communication without having any such intention.[6]

Kierkegaard generalizes this orientation toward the practice of conversation – outwardly engaging in it, while inwardly repudiating its goals and treating it all as a kind of game – to all the social practices of the person who lives ironically – the person I will from now on call the "ironist," as distinct from the ironic speaker. The person who lives, as opposed to merely speaking, ironically, converses, takes part in social life, pays taxes, goes to work, and attends PTA meetings. But for him, it's all a game; he does not take his participation in these practices, nor these practices themselves, seriously. Indeed, it is somewhat misleading to describe him as participating in these practices at all for he is merely playing at participating in them, without seeing himself as actually engaged in them. He does not have as his aim the aims that are constitutive for being a sincere participant in these practices. And in so rejecting the aims of these practices, he denies that these practices have any real point – denies that they merit being taken seriously and seriously engaged in. His particular way of rejecting these practices, however, is not by attacking them directly, by declaring his opposition to them, but by playing along, letting others come to their own conclusions as to whether he, like they, takes the practices seriously. Rather than engage with his social world either by taking part in or criticizing it, he lifts himself out of it altogether. Socrates, Kierkegaard's paradigm ironist, "in his relation to the established order of things, was entirely negative. . . . [H]e is suspended above all the qualifications of substantial life" (CI 217). "For him, the whole given actuality had entirely lost its validity; he had become alien to the actuality of the whole substantial world" (CI 264).

To adopt such a stance is to have a certain attitude not only toward the things that are done in one's social world but also toward the people in that world who do those things. Consider here the radical verbal ironist's attitude toward his hearers. He is indifferent to them, unconcerned as to how they take what he says; as a consequence, he is detached not only from the practice in which he (pretendingly) takes part but from those with whom he (pretendingly) engages within the practice. He does not take them as colleagues in a shared enterprise, nor even as witnesses to his displays of verbal cleverness. Their responses are irrelevant to his all-consuming activity of self-satisfied playacting.[7] This same attitude is present in intensified form in the ironist *simpliciter:* it is not only *qua* hearers or interlocutors that they are irrelevant to him but *qua* friends, neighbors, fellow citizens – even *qua* enemies. To invoke the metaphor Kierkegaard uses repeatedly, the ironist has risen above all society, all interpersonal interactions and relationships. Just as he is not personally invested in, or defined by, his social roles and activities, so he is no longer personally invested in, or defined by, his relations to others.

The ironist, then, is disengaged from his social world, in that he does not take the practices and norms that constitute that world seriously and does not take other individuals in that world seriously. And this disengagement is manifested in his going on just as if he were a sincere participant. Everything that he does, then, involves an extreme opposition between his outer behavior and his inner state. Outwardly, he seems to be a normal member of society, embracing its common aims, embracing the goods of mutual and reciprocally acknowledged participation in a common enterprise. Inwardly, for him, all of these aims, those goods, this society and its members are beneath him, beneath being taken seriously. As he conceives of himself, he is not the citizen of this community, the child of these parents, and so forth; all of these are things that he plays at being. And his play is the expression of the radical nature of his repudiation of human activity; to try to change his world or simply to inveigh against it or even to withdraw from it into some desert wilderness would be to attach some importance to his outward, observable mode of life, and to attach some importance to others' understanding him, or at least recognizing him to be different from them. To want to be seen as independent is, of course, to fail to be independent; the ironist, being truly independent, simply plays along, indifferent as to whether anybody suspects that that is all he is doing. As Kierkegaard writes of Socrates,

In a certain sense, he was revolutionary, yet not so much by doing something as by not doing something; but a partisan or leader of a conspiracy he was not. His irony saved him from that, for just as it deprived him of due civic sympathy for the state, due civic pathos, it also freed him from . . . being a partisan. On the whole, his position was far too personally isolated, and every relationship he contracted was too loosely joined to result in anything. . . . He stood ironically above every relationship. . . . His connection with the single individual was only momentary, and he himself was suspended high above all this in ironic contentment. (CI 182)

This pervasive character of irony is emphasized by Kierkegaard; Socrates "negates" the "whole given actuality" of his time, not by attacking it overtly but by going along with it while inwardly regarding this as simply a form of play. The ironist has "subjective pleasure as the subject frees himself by means of irony from the restraint in which the continuity of life's conditions holds him" (CI 255–6). He achieves a kind of radical separation from his social world, as is brought out in Kierkegaard's discussion of the significance of the phrase "know yourself":

[I]t is certainly true that the phrase "γνῶθι σαυτόν" can designate subjectivity in its fullness, inwardness in its utterly infinite wealth, but for Socrates this self-knowledge was not so copious; it actually contained nothing more than the separating, the singling out, of [the subject]. The phrase "know yourself" means: separate yourself from the other. (CI 177)

We must keep in mind, however, that the ironist not only separates or dissociates himself from "the other[s]" but in a very real sense dissociates himself from himself – from the social, embodied person that he has been and that he now merely plays at being.

Such an orientation toward one's society and one's self may seem sociopathic, schizophrenic. To put it bluntly, it seems to have little to recommend it. But Kierkegaard argues that this form of radical dissociation from one's society and one's social self, though not fully admirable or desirable as a way of life, constitutes an important improvement on the way of life that it rejects. For the movement of irony constitutes the self's break with "immediacy."

Immediacy and its cognates have several distinct usages in Kierkegaard's writings, usages that are linked by the notion of something's being unmediated, directly given. In the first usage, one's immediate nature (or one's immediacy) is simply those features of oneself that are merely given over to one's self: one's physical body and its characteristics, one's temporal position, one's socially determined identity, and so on. In the second usage, for one to stand in an immediate relation to something is for one's relation to it to be unmediated by critical reflection. Examples of such immediate relations abound in the authorship. They range from the spectacular extreme of "pure sensuous immediacy" personified by Don Giovanni, to the more humdrum forms of immediacy characterized by the child's unreflective trust in his parents and in the world, to the individual's unreflective pursuit of desire-satisfaction, to what may be called the "ethical immediacy" of the person who accepts and abides by the norms of his society without ever reflecting upon them or calling their authority into question.[8] In this usage, a person is always in an immediate relation to some x if that person lacks the detachment from x that comes from reflecting critically on it and on his relation to it (cf. *CI* 204–5).

In the third usage, to live a life of immediacy is to take life as it comes, to take one's life as a kind of happening in which one finds oneself, whose nature is determined by various conditions that are also, unreflectively, accepted as just "the way things are." One finds oneself in a given society, with certain dispositions and preferences, obligated to comply with various social norms; good things sometimes happen to one, and that's good luck, bad things happen to one, and that's bad luck. As Climacus writes in *Concluding Unscientific Postscript*, "the life-view of immediacy" – what the immediate person's view of life centers around – "is good fortune. If one were to ask from whence he [the immediate person] has this life-view, this essential relation to good fortune, he might naively answer: I do not understand it myself" (*CUP* 433; original emphasis removed). The immediate person pursues what he takes to be the good without reflecting upon or calling into question its goodness; he lives a life whose content is determined by his given desires and ideals, by the norms of his society, without considering, in abstract reflection, whether his conception of the good has any genuine merit, whether his desires and ideals should be transformed or modified, whether his society's norms have any genuine authority over him. He stands in an immediate relation both to his environing world and to himself: for his not calling "externalities" such as his societal norms into question – indeed, his failure to recognize these as externalities – is a manifestation of his failure to consider, in a detached and critical way, himself, whether the manner of life in which he "finds himself" is the only one available to him, whether he is living a type of life that is genuinely worthy of being lived.

For Kierkegaard, ceasing to live such a life of immediacy (in the third sense) requires that one dissociate oneself from, and regard as external to oneself, the whole of one's immediate or merely given nature. And this radical disengagement from what one has hitherto regarded as one's self is the movement or adoption of irony. The ironist separates himself from the self and the life that have hitherto been his; he ceases to identify himself with the identity and goals delivered to him by virtue of his particular location in a particular society, that is, his own history and upbringing, and so on. He asserts himself as something separate from this immediate nature; his ironic detachment, we might say, simply is the maintaining of this separateness. As Kierkegaard writes, discussing an aspect of Hegel's treatment of Socratic irony with which he is in agreement:

In the old Greek culture [in which Socrates found himself], the individual was by no means free . . . but was confined in the substantial ethic; he had not as yet taken himself out of, separated himself from, this immediate relationship, still did not know himself. Socrates brought this [separation] about . . . [and] made the individual alien to the immediacy in which he had previously lived. (*CI* 228)

Irony, Kierkegaard writes, is the "awakening of subjectivity"; that is, the awakening of the conception of oneself as a subject, something separate from, and undetermined by, a certain immediately given historical entity.

But – and for Kierkegaard, it is an important "but" – the ironist has no positive conception of a concrete form of life that would not reduce to this mere immediacy.

> For the ironic subject, the given actuality has lost its validity entirely; it has become for him an imperfect form that is a hindrance everywhere. But on the other hand, he does not possess the new. He knows only that the present does not match the idea. . . . [H]e is continually pointing to something impending, but what it is he does not know. (CI 261)

This is why, as Kierkegaard repeatedly says, the ironist's freedom is merely "negative": it is a freedom *from* the constraints of immediacy, but not the positive freedom that would consist in realizing a life that is genuinely his own, a life shaped in accordance with a substantive ideal that he embraces in freedom, as contrasted with an ideal merely given over to him in virtue of his immediacy. As Kierkegaard sometimes puts it, the ironist cannot have any "positive content"; he is nothing but this negating entity, this derogating and disengaging, carried on for its own sake rather than for the sake of some positive alternative. For him to have any such positive content would be for there to be something toward which he is not ironical – and if there is any such thing, then he is not a pure, which is to say total, ironist.

The ironist, then, has a nihilistic attitude toward social existence and toward all aspects of human life that are immediate and, hence, to be held apart from the self. His irony is the manifestation of, and the means of preserving, this radical detachment from the putatively purposeful activities and concerns that constitute social life. "In irony, the subject is continually retreating, talking every phenomenon out of its reality in order to save itself – that is, in order to preserve itself in negative independence of everything" (CI 257).

But what of the ironist's attitude toward himself – that is, toward the ironic self, the thing that is held apart from the embodied social being that it playfully manipulates?[9] Does the ironist identify himself with the activity of ironizing, and does he see this activity, the maintaining of this type of orientation, as having some point? Here, it seems, the ironist has been backed into a corner. If he does take this way of existing seriously, then his irony ceases to be comprehensive; there exists one way of life that he does not "negate" or repudiate, namely, the ironic life. To the extent that this is so, he is not a pure, total, ironist; he does not go so far, in his self-disengagement, as to disengage himself from his own self-disengaging.

Thus, if there is to be such a thing as a stance of total or comprehensive ironic disengagement, it must lie in the other possibility, that of dissociation from his own ironizing. This possibility immediately threatens us with an infinite regress of ironic disengagement from ironic disengagement from. . . . In speaking of the ironic subject as continually retreating, as in the passage cited above, Kierkegaard appears to posit precisely this regress. But there is another difficulty with the position of irony thus envisioned. If the ironist does adopt an ironic attitude toward his own ironizing, he loses another feature crucial to irony: the sense of his own difference from, and superiority to, that (and those) toward which his irony is directed. For insofar as he regards his own ironizing as a suitable object of ironic disengagement, he has the same attitude toward it as he has toward normal social activities; that is, he finds his ironizing an appropriate object of this attitude. Ironizing then becomes, for him, just one more pointless activity that he plays at engaging in, without taking it seriously or identifying with it. Talk of retreating infinitely to successive disengagings from disengagings will not help here, since what is being retreated to is just a repeated instance of the very thing being retreated from. Or, to put the point less opaquely, what is being retreated to is just another position whose suitability as an object of serious concern and identification has been ruled out in advance. The problem is not so much that the retreat is infinite as that it is not a retreat, since there is no material difference between the position retreated to and the position retreated from. The ironist cannot therefore consistently regard himself, *qua* ironist, as different from, or superior to, the others; and insofar as this sense of difference and superiority is essential to irony, he fails, once again, to be an ironist. Thus, either the ironist does not adopt an ironic attitude toward his own ironizing, in which case his irony is not total and he is not, by Kierkegaard's lights, a true (which is to say, total) ironist, or he does, in which case he can no longer regard himself as different from the others and is once again not an ironist.

Addressing this question of how the ironist is to view his own ironizing, Kierkegaard writes:

[I]nsofar as irony . . . pronounces the same thesis as the pious mentality [that is, that immediate existence is "vanity" and is not to be identified with], irony might seem to be a kind of religious devotion. If I may put it this way, in religious devotion the lower actuality, that is, the relationships with the world, loses its validity, but this occurs only insofar as the relationships with God simultaneously affirm their absolute reality. The devout mind also declares that all is vanity, but this is only insofar as through this negation all disturbing factors are set aside and the eternally existing order comes into view. Add to this the fact that if the devout mind finds everything to be vanity, it makes no exception of its own person. . . . Indeed, in the deeper devotional literature, we see that the pious mind regards its own finite personality as the most wretched of all.

In irony, however, since everything is shown to be vanity, the subject becomes free. The more vain everything becomes, all the lighter, emptier, and more volatilized the subject becomes. And while everything is in the process of becoming vanity, the ironic subject does not become vain in his own eyes but rescues his own vanity. (CI 257–8; translation modified)

Kierkegaard recognizes here that the ironist's judgment that "all is vanity" must somehow be prevented from turning upon itself. In order to preserve the differentiation of himself from that toward which he is ironical, the ironist must, unlike the "devout mind," except himself (his ironic self) from his derogating attitude. What Kierkegaard does not appear to have seen at this point is that the ironist can achieve this only by arbitrarily privileging his own stance (and thereby drawing a limit to his irony, an irony which is supposed to be, in Kierkegaard's word, infinite) or disengaging himself from his own stance (and thereby committing himself to an infinite regress that only keeps landing him in the same unstable position as before).

If this is correct, then so long as irony is seen as (to use the formula Kierkegaard appropriated from Hegel) "infinite absolute negativity" – as a purely and unconditionally negative orientation toward all human existence – it is inherently unstable. The position Kierkegaard names "irony" cannot be realized. I will argue in the next section that in the later *Concluding Unscientific Postscript,* Kierkegaard grappled with and attempted to resolve this apparent tension in the account of irony he offered in *The Concept of Irony.* Writing as Johannes Climacus, he argues that the ironist's self-contentment and sense of superiority over the ways of life he ironically engages in can only be achieved if the ironist, like the devout mentality mentioned above, relates himself not just negatively toward human existence but positively toward an absolute that is of a qualitatively different kind from the ideals that shape the ordinary person's life. I will now turn to the discussion of Climacus's account, showing how it elaborates on, and in this important respect modifies, Kierkegaard's earlier conception of irony.

II. IRONY IN *CONCLUDING UNSCIENTIFIC POSTSCRIPT*

Like Kierkegaard, Climacus sees verbal irony as at most a manifestation of an ironic life – often not even that. "Irony is an existence-qualification, and thus nothing is more ludicrous than regarding it as a style of speaking or an author's counting himself lucky to express himself ironically once in a while" (*CUP* 503–4). And like Kierkegaard Climacus finds that the essence of irony lies in manifesting "the contradiction that the outer is not the inner" (323). Moreover, the ironist, for Climacus, eschews sincere participation in conversation with others and in so doing eschews direct engagement with others altogether. Climacus writes of a comment of Socrates' that it

is proper irony; it is devoid of the sympathy with which Socrates could create a mutual situation with another (and the law for teasing irony is quite simply this: the ironist's cunning prevents the conversation from being a conversation, although in every way it looks like a conversation, perhaps even a sincere conversation). (*CUP* 552; Climacus's footnote)

Finally, Climacus, like Kierkegaard, sees in the ironic life a kind of radical detachment of oneself from all others and from one's surrounding world; as he somewhat obscurely puts it, "In irony there is no sympathy; it is self-assertion" (*CUP* 553), the asserting of oneself as a radically independent entity.

To understand why Climacus thinks this to be an important stage in the maturation of the individual, one must understand the stage that he thinks precedes irony, as well as the stage that follows it. Beginning with the first of these stages, one immediately encounters a difficulty. In one passage of *Postscript*, Climacus writes that there are three existential spheres, the aesthetic, the ethical, and the religious, and that irony constitutes the *confinium* between the aesthetic and the ethical, while the stance he calls "humor" constitutes the *confinium* between the ethical and the religious (*CUP* 501–2). (A *confinium*, as Kierkegaard writes in *The Concept of Irony*, is a "transitional element" lying between two things, a sort of border zone that "actually belongs neither to the one nor to the other" [*CI* 121].) In another passage, however, he asserts that irony lies between immediacy and the ethical (*CUP* 531; Climacus's footnote). To understand Kierkegaard's notion of irony, we must clarify the spheres that irony, as seen by him, lies between. And in order to do that, we must briefly discuss the "aesthetic" and see what it has in common with, and why he apparently equates it with, immediacy.

Climacus's conception of immediacy is essentially the same as Kierkegaard's. For Climacus, the immediate person is one who has not become sufficiently detached from his given existence and his given pursuits for the notion of responsibility for his manner of existing even to arise for him. Happiness is perceived as a product of good fortune; unhappiness, as one of misfortune. And the extent to which one fails to achieve a satisfying life is due to one's luck, that is, to circumstances beyond one's control. "Misfortune is like a narrow pass on the way of immediacy. Now he [the immediate person] is in it, but essentially his life-view must continually imagine that it will in turn end because it is something alien" (*CUP* 434).

At first glance, such immediacy would seem to be considerably removed from the way of life of one in Kierkegaard's "aesthetic" sphere – the way of life embodied by A, the pseudonymous author of Part I of *Either/Or*.[10] Whereas the person of immediacy has at best a low degree of self-consciousness, the self-absorbed A seems self-conscious to a fault; he is constantly reflecting on his own condition, on the varieties of experience he pursues, on what is implied in the pursuit of such varieties of experience, and on what the rationale for that pursuit is, and jotting down his observations *ad nauseum*. Whereas the immediate person simply accepts his life as he finds it, A has consciously committed himself to an aesthetic life. Whereas the person of immediacy uncritically accepts his social world, blending in with that social world and accepting on face value its norms' authority, A scornfully rejects what he sees as the humdrum, bourgeois, passionless manner of life he sees being lived all around him. Finally, whereas the immediate person seeks immediate enjoyment – a day on the beach, a steak dinner – A scorns all such enjoyment. Instead, he expounds on the virtues of increasingly reflective forms of enjoyment; he moves from the immediate enjoyment of listening to *Don Giovanni* to the enjoyment of reflecting upon and recollecting that enjoyment, and from there to the enjoyment of reducing his immediate experiences to source materials for reflection and fantasy, and from there to the reflective enjoyment of reflecting on, and imagining, the experiences of others. Each of these projects, moreover, is provided with an elaborate rationale, the product of much reflection upon his past efforts to find absolutely significant experiences and upon what it would take to have such an experience. If the mark of immediacy is a lack of reflection, A seems anything but immediate.

Climacus, in his commentary on *Either/Or*, accentuates A's reflective character. "As a thinker," he writes, "A is advanced. . . . He possesses all the seductive gifts of understanding and intellect" (*CUP* 253). A's aesthetic life is a "fantasy-existence," rich in imagination; his writings have "rich intrinsic thought-content" (253). A's problem, according to Climacus, is not that he is lacking in reflection but that he devotes himself too thoroughly to it. He gives himself over so much to the activity of reflecting that he never, as the current phrase goes, "gets a life"; in Climacus's less direct terms, he is "an existence-possibility that cannot attain existence" (253). Occupying himself with reflective fantasy, he never puts any of his reflections into practice; he prefers to live vicariously, through fantasizing about the lives of others. A "holds existence at bay by the most subtle of all deceptions, by thinking. He has thought everything possible, and yet he has not existed at all" (253).

Why, then, does Climacus appear to associate the aesthetic with immediacy in the conjunction of quotations with which we began this section? The answer comes via Judge William's second letter to A in Part II of *Either/Or*, in which he describes and diagnoses A's position. William describes the difference between the immediate pursuit of enjoyment, finite common sense, and the pursuit of more reflective enjoyment as follows:

[There is a] life-view which thinks one must live to satisfy desire [the pursuit of immediate enjoyment]. A prudent common sense readily perceives that this cannot be carried through and that it is therefore not worth starting on. A refined egoism perceives that it misses the point in pleasure. Here, then, we have a life-view which teaches "Enjoy life," and then expresses itself again thus: "Enjoy yourself; it is you yourself in the enjoyment that you must enjoy." This is a higher reflection. Naturally, however, it does not penetrate into the personality itself; this remains in its accidental immediacy. After all, here too the condition for enjoyment is external and not within the individual's control; for although he, as he says, enjoys himself, he still only enjoys himself in the enjoyment. . . . The only difference is that his enjoyment is reflective, not immediate. $(EO^h$ 500)

The difference between reflective and immediate enjoyment is not, for William, the difference between an immediate life and a life that has transcended immediacy. "In desire itself the individual is immediate, and however cultivated or refined the desire, however artful, the individual is nevertheless in it *qua* immediate, in the enjoyment he is in the moment" $(EO^h$ 496). The self-conscious A, occupying himself with reflecting on his own immediate experiences and on the experiences of others, absorbs himself in his experiences just as much as does the naive pleasure pursuer. He remains in immediacy, in two respects. First, A's absorption in reflective experience is still an absorption in experience; the fact that the experiences he absorbs himself in are the products of his own imagination does not differentiate his activity in any significant way from the person who absorbs himself in direct sensory experience. Whether his experiences are generated by reflection or by perception is of no importance; experience, as such, is always something that is directly given. Second, and more importantly, as a reflective aesthete his reflection does not "penetrate into the personality itself"; while A reflects on his life, on the variety of experiences he has had, on the variety of experiences he can have, he does not reflect critically upon his own devotion to experience. He does not, that is, "penetrate" his "personality" by calling into question why it is that he is devoted to enjoyment or whether a life devoted to enjoyment is all that he takes it to be. The pursuit of enjoyment is a project that he simply inherits, one might say, from the earlier stage of immediate pleasure-pursuit. He concocts increasingly elaborate and reflective means of carrying out that project, but that this project itself is to be carried out is, for him, simply a given.

Although the aesthete is more reflective in certain respects than the "immediate person" is, and even more self-conscious (in the sense of thinking about himself) than that person, his relation to the objects of his pursuits, and to himself *qua* pursuer of these objects, remains immediate. He absorbs himself in feelings and fantasies, and although these feelings and fantasies are reflective in that they are products of his imagination and thought rather than his senses, they are, *qua* experiences, as immediate as his sensory experiences. Furthermore, though he energetically pursues a life of reflective enjoyment and reflects on the best ways to realize such a life, he does not call the value of such a life into question. He takes it as given that only experiences can make one's life meaningful for one; reflection for him is simply a means for satisfying his immediately given desire for enjoyment. To that extent, he allows the content of his life to be determined for him by a merely given, immediate, characteristic. And, again like the "immediate person," he regards himself as having only limited responsibility for the manner of his own life. He sees himself as determined by a condition that is not within his control; with regard to the shaping of his own life, he remains fundamentally passive. As Climacus writes, "Fortune, misfortune, fate, immediate enthusiasm, despair – these are what the aesthetic life-view has at its disposal" (*CUP* 434). These are precisely the same categories as those under which, as Climacus wrote in the passage quoted above, the "immediate person" comprehends his existence. Like the immediate person, the aesthete unreflectively takes certain given conditions as determinative of his life. And insofar as this is so – insofar as, as William wrote, he is reliant upon "external conditions," that is, conditions he does not regard as products of his own agency – he ultimately forsakes responsibility for whether that life goes well or poorly.

This is so even, perhaps especially, at the final stage of the aesthetic, the position represented in A's essay "The Unhappiest One" and in his introductory "Diapsalmata." A eventually realizes that the attempt to ground his life on meaningful experience cannot be achieved; even the varieties of reflective enjoyment fall prey to the deterioration that he saw as inevitably ending immediate enjoyment but hoped to escape by turning to reflective enjoyment. Having realized this, he reaches the position that I will call that of the "defeated aesthete," the position that William calls "the laughter of despair" (*EO*[h] 508). Realizing that his project must fail, A regards this not as evidence that he has erred in devoting himself to this project but as evidence that the necessary conditions of a worthwhile and meaningful life cannot be met. His attempt to give his life a stable meaning by devoting himself to reflective experiences that, being reflective, are under his control fails; and his conclusion from this is not that meaningfulness is to be found in a life oriented toward something besides enjoyable experiences, but rather that life can never be meaningful. To be human, in his final view, is just to be caught in this trap; and the meaninglessness of his own life is not something for which he is responsible but is a result of the tragic and unalterable conditions of human existence.

A's progress through the various stages of the aesthetic life concludes at this point, a point that verges on irony; he concludes that life is inescapably meaningless, that his own realization of this is itself a form of despair, and that all there is to do is mock every human activity, including one's own activity of mocking.

> If you marry, you will regret it; if you do not marry, you will regret it. . . . Laugh at the world's follies, you will regret it; weep over them, you will also regret it. . . . Believe a girl, you will regret it; if you do not believe her, you will also regret it. . . . If you hang yourself, you will regret it; if you do not hang yourself, you will also regret it. . . . This, gentlemen, is the sum of all practical wisdom. (EO^h 54; translation modified)

What the aesthete, even the defeated aesthete, has in common with others in immediacy, then, is that he regards the self as something given. Reflection is regarded as an instrument to be utilized in the service of the demands with which the self already finds itself, be they the moral and conventional demands of one's society or the demands, which the aesthete seeks to satisfy, that follow from one's nature as a self-conscious bearer of experiences. Whereas the aesthete does not stand in an immediate relation to his social world – he calls that world, and the way of life of its members, into question, reflects upon it, and achieves detachment from it – he remains in an immediate relation to himself. He takes himself as a person who happens to have been born with, or to have acquired, this particular set of inclinations, talents, dispositions, and so forth, and sets about devoting his talents to the satisfaction of the inclinations that he happens to find within himself. His reflection "penetrates" just far enough to reach an understanding of the content of his desires, but not far enough to identify, and call into question, the ground of those desires. He fails, that is, to assume responsibility for himself; when his life-project founders, this is seen not as evidence that he has made an unwise choice of life-projects but as evidence that no life can be meaningful.

The way to escape this despairing position, according to William, Climacus, and Kierkegaard,[12] is by taking a more active role in the shaping of the self and its projects. One moves into the "ethical" sphere, adopting a different orientation toward one's given nature. This change in orientation is brought about in the movement described as "choosing oneself."

Kierkegaard's conception of "ethical self-choice" is intricate and cannot be laid out in complete detail here. The core idea is that of an unrestricted taking of responsibility for oneself, a taking of responsibility extending toward one's immediacy, one's past, and one's future. This taking of responsibility involves a double movement toward one's empirical self in both its physical and social aspects. The first movement is a ceasing to identify with this self; one regards oneself as essentially not such-and-such an embodied person but an autonomous will, a thing with an unbounded capacity for choice.[13] The second movement, which is the actual "choosing" in ethical self-choice, is a partial reunification of this willing self with the embodied person; being this embodied person is taken on as an act of one's own will. Retrospectively, one's past actions, character, inclinations, even those features of oneself that are standardly regarded as given determinations of oneself that are not products of one's own agency are regarded as objects of one's own present willing. This is the retrospective movement William terms "repentance." Prospectively, ethical self-choice entails the perception of one's embodied self, the self that has such-and-such psychological traits, inclinations, social position, and so forth, as a task – as, so to speak, raw material to be shaped in accordance with an ideal posited in freedom. In both directions, one assumes responsibility for one's immediacy, first by seeing oneself as something distinct from and unconstrained by this immediate nature, and second by regarding this nature as "one's own," not in the sense of being identical with it but in the sense of being morally accountable – perhaps even causally resonsible – for it.

This broadly Kantian project has, on Kierkegaard's view, problems of its own.[14] But it does constitute a means – the means – of escape from the trap in which the defeated aesthete finds himself. The defeated aesthete sees the meaningfulness of his life as depending, in virtue of his given nature, on the satisfaction of conditions that turn out, also in virtue of his given nature, to be unsatisfiable. For the person in the ethical sphere, on the other hand, meaningfulness is to be found in the realization of one's capacity for autonomous choice and willing; the embodied social self with all its given attributes is then regarded as something external to the self, upon and through which this capacity for choice is exercised.

From what has been said so far, it should be clear why Climacus sees irony as a border zone between immediacy (which includes the aesthetic) and the ethical. Between the position of the person who takes his given immediate nature as brute data for the pursuit of a meaningful life (and as determining what would constitute a meaningful life) and the person who takes his immediate nature as an object of choice, there is the position of the person who has dissociated himself from his immediate nature but not yet achieved the partial reintegration with that nature that ethical self-choice involves. This intermediary position in which one is entirely dissociated from one's immediacy, without identifying oneself with anything other than this dissociating, is the position of irony.

The question now is, does irony as Climacus construes it fall prey to the same internal tension as did irony as construed in *The Concept of Irony*? Kierkegaard's ironist, as we have seen, goes through the motions of his daily life while regarding what he does as no more than a kind of play. Climacus's ironist has a similar stance of derogation toward and disengagement from immediacy and his immediate self; he finds all of these as things that are beneath him. However, in tracking down the source of this feeling of superiority and condescending amusement – the distinctive type of self-differentiation essential to irony – Climacus finds cause to criticize Kierkegaard's conception of irony as presented in *The Concept of Irony*.[15] Kierkegaard, Climacus writes, has, "consciously or unconsciously, [wanted] to bring out only the one side" (*CUP* 503); he has overly accentuated the negative aspects of irony, failing to see that the purely negative stance he describes cannot ultimately sustain the sense of differentness and superiority that gives irony its special form of amusement and pleasure.

The ironist as Kierkegaard describes him in *The Concept of Irony*, dissociated as he is from his immediate self, is free. But, as we have seen, this freedom is merely negative; though the ironist derogates and repudiates his immediate nature with its pursuits and goals, he has nothing positive to put in its place. And as we have seen, this leaves the ironist in a precarious position. If he arbitrarily excludes his own mode of existence from his ironizing, his ironizing is not fully carried through; if he does not, he is forced to see his position as no better (no less worth ironic scorn) than the immediacy he derogates, in which case he will see that he has not really transcended anything and will succumb to a tragically nihilistic view of human possibilities like the defeated aesthete (who reduces his own laughing at the world's follies to the same level of meaninglessness as marriage and suicide).

Climacus addresses this issue by identifying two types of response to the conflict between one's immediately given nature and one's capacity for transcendence of that nature. He labels these responses the "tragic" and the "comic." The person who sees himself as the battleground of this conflict, but has no substantive conception of how to realize his capacity for self-determination, gives this conflict a tragic interpretation. One's immediacy is, in this case, experienced as a burden; one's capacity for transcendence is experienced as the sense of being under a demand that one has no notion of how to fulfill. Such a stance, precisely because it is tragic, cannot on Climacus's view be the ironist's way of experiencing this contradiction.

Climacus's ironist gives this contradiction a comic interpretation; and the reason his interpretation is comic, the reason he escapes the trap in which Kierkegaard's ironist was caught, is that he has a more contentful conception of a life that is both available to him and based on a genuine ideal. He perceives, that is, ethical self-choice as a way of integrating his immediate nature with his capacity for self-determination; he does not take the step of choosing himself ethically, but he sees that and how it can be done. He understands the ethical and understands that the ethical is precisely what would put his life on a genuinely worthy basis. "The irony emerges by continually joining the particulars of the finite with the ethical infinite requirement and allowing the contradiction to come into existence" (*CUP* 502). Climacus's ironist is able to "join himself as a vanishing particular together with the absolute requirement" (502–3), to see himself as both an immediate being (and, as such, incommensurate with the ideal) and as a being capable of basing his life on an ideal that transcends immediacy; and, since he understands what that ideal is, and how the apparent conflict between his finite and infinite aspects can be resolved, the contradiction is no longer painful.

[W]here there is life there is contradiction. . . . The tragic and the comic are the same inasmuch as both are contradiction, but *the tragic is suffering contradiction, and the comic is painless contradiction*. . . . The comic interpretation produces the contradiction or allows it to become apparent by having *in mente* [in mind] the way out; therefore the contradiction is painless. The tragic interpretation sees the contradiction and despairs over the way out. (*CUP* 513–16)

The ironist, then, sees the contradiction in his nature; he holds that the contradictory elements can be reconciled if he, in his freedom, undertakes the shaping of his immediate, finite self – if he takes upon himself fulfillment of the "absolute requirement." He sees that there is a way out, sees that the reconciliation of his contradictory aspects is within his power; as a consequence, the pain engendered by being aware of oneself as composed of contradictory aspects and being unaware of how to reconcile these aspects is canceled for him. Having always in mind the never-foreclosed possibility of ethical self-choice, the ironist is able to view both his immediate existence and his ironizing toward immediacy as games that he plays because he enjoys the play, not as meaningless strivings to which there is no alternative. "Irony," Climacus writes, "is only a possibility" (*CUP* 505) – the unactualized, but consciously understood, possibility of ethical self-choice.

In this way, Climacus's ironist is able to achieve the transcendence of immediacy that Kierkegaard's ironist can only vainly struggle toward. Since he "sees the way out" and knows that this way out is an option of which he can avail himself at any moment, his immediate existence, even his existence *qua* ironist, is seen by him, not as a set of inescapable constraints but as a home in which he chooses to dwell. He is thus able to include his own mode of existence within the scope of his irony, view his ironic play as just one more baseless form of human existence among others, and at the same time regard himself as not simply a victim of a tragic and universal human condition of confinement within immediacy. In having acquired the resources for an escape from the merely immediate life, he has already transcended it, in the sense that he is no longer restricted to it. Looking, as it were, both backward at his immediate existence and forward toward the possibility of ethical self-choice, the ironist sees himself as essentially neither the one nor the other type of self.

Climacus's conception of irony, then, escapes the difficulties inherent in Kierkegaard's earlier conception. Those difficulties arose as a result of Kierkegaard's recognizing, as Climacus writes, only one side of irony: its negating, depreciating aspect. If one wants to be true to the phenomenon of irony and allow for its involving a kind of freedom from and superiority over that toward which it is directed and claim that a consistent ironist must be ironic toward his own mode of existence as much as toward that of the others, then, it seems, one must ascribe to the ironist some positive conception of an alternative to his present mode and that of the others. In Climacus's ironist, reflexive self-understanding – the seeing of oneself as subject to, and falling short of, the same standards by which the others are judged and found laughable – is made compatible with the feeling of transcendence. This ironist is free to laugh without the bitterness shared by the defeated aesthete and the ironist of *The Concept of Irony* – at himself.

NOTES

I would like to thank the editors of this anthology for helpful criticisms and suggestions. Ralph Kennedy suggested this title to me.

1 Richard Rorty is a striking counterexample to this trend, interested as he is in the more Kierkegaardian notion of irony as a position or way of life.
2 Gregory Vlastos, "Socratic Irony," in *Socrates: Ironist and Moral Philosopher* (Ithaca: Cornell University Press, 1991).
3 The suggestion that verbal irony involves this type of "implicit division" has been defended and explored at some length by proponents of the "echoic reminder" theory of irony. See Roger J. Kreuz and Sam Glucksberg, "How to Be Sarcastic: The Echoic Reminder Theory of Verbal Irony," *Journal of Experimental Psychology* 118 (December 1989): 374–86, and the works there referenced, especially the works of Daniel Sperber. In an important work largely informed by thoughtful reading of *CI*, Wayne C. Booth argues against including this exclusionary character among the features of verbal irony and emphasizes the

community-building aspect of irony in opposition to Kierkegaard's conception of irony as isolating; however, he seems to think that the "victims," the parties excluded by irony, must be actual hearers or readers whom the ironist intends to exclude. In contrast, as I read Kierkegaard, his claim is that the speaker may not intend to exclude anyone actually attending to his utterance, while still invoking in his hearers the sense of being part of an exclusive group that is "in the know." See Booth, *A Rhetoric of Irony* (Chicago and London: University of Chicago Press, 1974), esp. pp. 27–31.

4 I owe this example to Jamie Tappenden.

5 For a useful discussion pertaining to this, see Robert Brandom, "Asserting," *Nous* 17 (1983): 637–50.

6 Kierkegaard represents Socrates' conversation as this kind of pseudo-conversational play in several places. Cf. his discussion of the *Protagoras* in *CI* 56–7, where he makes much of Socrates' ironic satisfaction at the exchange in which he and Protagoras wind up each converting the other to his own point of view; also, his interpretation of Socratic questioning as not sincere questioning in pursuit of an answer, but pseudo-questioning with the aim of "showing that when all was said and done they [both he and his interlocutor] knew nothing whatever" (36–7).

7 One might think that this statement is too strong; for it can seem that the ironist has the goal of tricking the others so as to establish his own superiority, and that as a result his intentions will be frustrated if his hearers are not taken in. On Kierkegaard's view, however, the ironist speaks not in order to trick the others and establish himself as superior; his irony is its own end, not something employed in the pursuit of some separate end. Cf. *CI* 256.

8 As Kierkegaard writes in *CI*, "The immediate consciousness, secure and confident as it relies upon what it receives from the past, like a sacred treasure, scarcely ever notices that life is full of contradictions. Reflection, on the other hand, discovers this at once. It discovers that what is supposed to be absolutely certain, determinative for men (laws, customs, etc.), places the individual in conflict with himself; it also discovers that all this is something external to a person, and as such he cannot accept it" (204).

9 The question raised here of the ability of irony to include itself within its own scope has been illuminatingly discussed, in connection with the "irony" of Richard Rorty, by Ermanno Bencivenga in "The Irony of It," *The Philosophical Forum* 25, 2 (Winter 1993): 125–33.

10 The interpretation of the aesthetic sphere offered here owes much to Jane Rubin, "Too Much of Nothing: Modern Culture, the Self and Salvation in Kier-kegaard's Thought," Ph.D. diss., University of California

at Berkeley, 1984, as well as to Mark C. Taylor, *Kierkegaard's Pseudony-mous Authorship: A Study of Time and the Self* (Princeton: Princeton University Press, 1975).

11 It should be noted that the depiction of the "defeated aesthete" in *EO* appears to be largely drawn from a conception of "modern," Romantic irony presented in Part II of *CI*. Kierkegaard appears at this early stage to have had the idea of what Climacus terms the "tragic" interpretation of the ironist's dilemma. "Irony," he writes, "is indeed free, free from the sorrows of actuality, but also free from its joys, free from its bless-ing, for *inasmuch as it has nothing higher than itself* [i.e., inasmuch as it has no conception of something higher than itself], it can receive no blessing" (*CI* 279; emphasis added). What he does not seem to have thought at this point is that the very tragic character of this interpreta-tion vitiates its claim to be ironical, and that the ironist as presented in *CI* both must and cannot succumb to this tragic interpretation.

12 It should be noted that neither Climacus nor Kierkegaard appears to hold that the project described below is successful; each, in other words, seems to regard this as the appropriate means of escape from the despair of the aesthetic, albeit a means that leads to yet another form of despair. For evidence that this is Climacus's position, see *CUP* 253–8.

13 As William writes, "The first form the choice takes is a complete isola-tion. For in choosing myself I sever myself from my relationship to the whole world until, in this separation, I end in an abstract identity" (*EO^h* 534).

14 The extent to which the position defended by Judge William is intended by Kierkegaard to be a Kantian one is a matter of some debate. For a re-cent and sensitive criticism of Kantian readings of William, see George B. Connell, "Judge William's Theonomous Ethics," in *Foundations of Kierkegaard's Vision of Community: Religion, Ethics, and Politics in Kierkegaard,* ed. George B. Connell and C. Stephen Evans (Atlantic Highlands, N.J., and London: Humanities Press International, 1992).

15 Climacus is not alone among Kierkegaardian voices in criticizing *CI*; Kierkegaard himself harshly criticizes the dissertation in a pair of jour-nal entries. In both entries, the criticism pertains not to the conception of irony offered in the dissertation but to specifically Hegelian positions asserted there regarding the proper relation between the individual and the state. *CI* 453; *JP* §4281; *Pap.* X³ A 477, and also *CI* 453–4; *JP* §4238; *Pap.* XI² A 108. In a draft from the *Postscript,* Climacus also chides the earlier Kierkegaard for his Hegelianism; *CI* 452; *JP* §5796; *Pap.* VI B 35 p. 24.

6 Realism and antirealism in Kierkegaard's *Concluding Unscientific Postscript*

If a reader should go into a good library and browse through the books about Kierkegaard, she would, I think, be struck immediately by a significant difference between most of the older books and quite a few, though certainly not all, of the more recent volumes. Older books, such as James Collins's *The Mind of Kierkegaard*, tended to see Kierkegaard primarily as a philosopher, albeit an unusual one with poetic gifts and religious interests. By and large, they approached Kierkegaard as one would approach other philosophers, inquiring as to his views on ethics, epistemology, and other standard philosophical issues. The underlying assumption is that Kierkegaard had convictions about such issues, and that those convictions might be, in part or as a whole, true or false, correct or incorrect.

Roger Poole's *Kierkegaard: The Indirect Communication* may serve as a good example of the type of later book I have in mind, though works by such authors as Louis Mackey, Sylviane Agacinski, John Vignaux Smythe, and John D. Caputo would serve equally well. Poole explicitly distances himself from the tradition, one that he stigmatizes as "theological," that understands Kierkegaard's pseudonymous works as containing philosophical doctrines.[1] On his view, "Kierkegaard writes text after text whose aim is not to state a truth, not to clarify an issue, not to propose a definite doctrine, not to offer some meaning that could be directly appropriated."[2] Kierkegaard cannot offer us objective truth because he is seen as committed to a view of language and meaning similar to that of Derrida and Lacan. In order for propositions to have fixed truth values, they must be about something, and Kierkegaard's texts do not refer in this way. "The texts demonstrate to a nicety the

154

Lacanian perception that all we are ever offered in a text is an end-less succession of signifiers."[3]

One way of understanding the difference between these two ap-proaches is in terms of the contemporary philosophical debate be-tween *realism* and *antirealism*. I mean by this the debate as to whether there is a mind-independent reality, a reality that exists in-dependently of human judgments and by virtue of which those judg-ments are true or false. Of course the antirealist accepts what we all call "the real world" in one sense. What the antirealist denies is that human language can refer to the world as it is *in itself*, apart from our human concepts and classifications, which in turn reflect our human activities and interests.

This debate could be characterized in terms of a disagreement about language, a dispute about meaning and reference, or as a dis-agreement about truth and the existence of mind-independent real-ity. Although each way of describing the dispute could provide a basis for an illuminating look at Kierkegaard, I wish to focus on the concepts of truth and mind-independent reality. That these con-cepts are central to the debate can hardly be denied. For example, William Alston describes realism as the claim that "whatever there is is what it is regardless of how we think of it," combined with the belief that there is in fact something.[4] Alvin Plantinga says that the dispute centers on the antirealist claim that "objects . . . are not on-tologically independent of persons and their ways of thinking and behaving."[5] Sometimes the dependence of truth on human knowers is characterized epistemically. Thus, Hilary Putnam describes the realism he wishes to reject in the following terms: "a distinguishing feature of the realistic sense of 'true' is it is logically possible for even the best attested statement to be false."[6]

Despite the fact that Kierkegaard is famous (or infamous) for the claim in *Concluding Unscientific Postscript* that "truth is subjec-tivity," the contemporary debate about realism and antirealism has not paid a great deal of attention to Kierkegaard.[7] There are occa-sional references and hints that Kierkegaard has something to say about these issues. For example, Richard Rorty identifies Kierke-gaard as one who rejects the Socratic assumption that humans have a timeless "truth-tracking faculty called Reason" in favor of the view that the point of departure of human knowers may simply be a contingent historical event.[8] Still, by and large, Kierkegaard's voice has not been prominent, at least in the Anglo-American venue for the debate. So it seems quite appropriate to take a closer look at Kierkegaard, and particularly at *Concluding Unscientific Post-script*, to see what Kierkegaard might have to say about this dispute. Such a look may have the added bonus of clarifying the way we read Kierkegaard himself, and giving critical perspective on both of the streams of scholarly literature that continue to appear about him. Is Kierkegaard a realist or is he better understood as at least a precursor of contemporary antirealism?

I. ANTIREALISTIC TEXTS IN *POSTSCRIPT*

It is hardly surprising that Kierkegaard should be read as an antirealist in the sense of someone who denies there is any mind-independent reality. After all, Kierkegaard is known preeminently as the philosopher of subjectivity, and so it seems reasonable to take him as agreeing with Putnam that "the worm of the human" lies over everything, including our knowledge of reality. Nevertheless, such a general impression of Kierkegaard as a philosopher of subjectivity hardly settles the issue, since it leaves vague the nature of subjectivity and what Kierkegaard's emphasis on subjectivity means and implies. We must therefore look at specific texts.

However, I should like to say at the outset that the question as to whether Kierkegaard is a realist or antirealist in *Concluding Unscientific Postscript* cannot be settled in a simple "proof-text" manner by producing passages that appear to favor one view. For one thing, as I shall presently show by illustration, there are passages that appear to support each side of the debate, as well as plenty that are ambiguous. For another, as we shall see, there are plausible explanations each side can give of the passages that appear to support the other side. Nevertheless, it is helpful to begin by considering some passages that appear to support both antirealism and realism, to give some content to the argument. I shall begin with some passages that appear to be antirealist in their thrust.

An important test case concerns the nature of God and the knowledge of God. Is God a metaphysical reality who exists independently of human consciousness? If so some kind of realism would seem to be presupposed. However, there are numerous passages in *Postscript* that appear to take an antirealist view of God. In these passages, God is not regarded as an objective reality existing independently of human consciousness, but is in some way "constituted" by subjectivity: "But freedom, that is the wonderful lamp. When a person rubs it with ethical passion, God comes into existence for him" (*CUP* 138).

How can God "come into existence" for a person? One possible answer is suggested somewhat later: "God is not something external, as is a wife, whom I can ask whether she is now satisfied with me. . . . God is not something external, but is the infinite itself, is not something external that quarrels with me when I do wrong but the infinite itself that does not need scolding words, but whose vengeance is terrible – the vengeance that God does not exist for me at all, even though I pray" (163). Though this passage is, to say the least, somewhat obscure, one might construe it to mean that awareness of God's reality is simply awareness of some infinite "idea" in consciousness, perhaps consciousness of an infinite moral demand, which has no existence independent of consciousness. On this reading, belief in God would be something rather like belief in an absolute moral standard. Of course one might construe this moral standard as an objective reality and thus assume a realistic posture toward it, but one might also think of it in quasi-Kantian terms, as a moral law that the moral agent himself creates. (Of course Kant himself also says that moral duties are to be seen as divine commands, but one could imagine someone who took such talk as being a poetic way of emphasizing the objectivity or absoluteness of the moral law.)

Such passages can be construed in ways consistent with realism. One might say, for example, that Kierkegaard means only that God comes into existence for a person in the sense that the person first becomes aware of God's reality when she acts freely and responsibly. And we have just seen that the "infinite" that consciousness discovers could be construed metaphysically as having some ontological status independent of the consciousness that conceives of the demand. Nonetheless, I think one must admit that these passages, taken alone, do not require such a realistic reading, and that the antirealistic construal might be regarded as providing a more natural interpretation.

One might also argue that even if Kierkegaard takes an antirealistic view of God, this does not imply any general commitment to antirealism. Perhaps it is only moral and religious truths that are to be construed in an antirealist manner. Such a position is suggested by passages such as the following: "If Christianity is essentially something objective, it behooves the observer to be objective. But if Christianity is essentially subjectivity, it is a mistake if the observer is objective. In all knowing in which it holds true that the object of cognition is the inwardness of the subjective individual himself, it holds true that the knower must be in that state" (53). The commitment to antirealism seems very strong here; in the case of Christianity the "object of cognition" is not a reality existing independently of the knower, but something internal to the consciousness of the individual. Nevertheless, one might argue that this does not involve any general commitment to philosophical antirealism. On the contrary, there is in the passage an implied contrast between knowing that has a realistic object and knowing that takes "inwardness" itself as its object. Nevertheless, such an antirealism about moral and religious truth, even if it is not a universal antirealism, is very significant, since for many readers of Kierkegaard, and doubtless for Kierkegaard himself, moral and religious truth is fundamentally important.

II. REALISTIC TEXTS IN *POSTSCRIPT*

From a purely textual point of view, such antirealistic passages are by no means the whole story, however. There are many texts that, on the surface at least, seem to presuppose a more traditional, realistic view of God.

For example, God is frequently described as the creator of the natural world, but it seems evident that only an objectively existing being could create a world. An infinite moral demand that I place upon myself hardly seems up to the job of creation. Though God is not directly present in his creation, it is nonetheless his creation: "Nature is certainly the work of God, but only the work is directly present, not God" (*CUP* 243). Subjectivity, on this view, does not bring God into existence, but is rather the condition for epistemic awareness of God: "Nature, the totality of creation, is God's work, and yet God is not there, but within the individual human being there is a possibility (he is spirit according to his possibility) that in inwardness is awakened to a God-relationship, and then it is possible to see God everywhere" (246–7).

There are many similar passages that describe God as creator, as the one who needs no human person to carry out his plans, and as the one who assigns to humans tasks that may or may not have world-historical significance (see, e.g., *CUP* 136, 137, 139). Nevertheless, such passages, while certainly appearing to presuppose a realistic view of God, are no more decisive than are those that appear to take a more antirealistic view. Readers who view Kierkegaard as thoroughly elusive may well read such passages ironically and suggest that it is a mistake to try to read his texts "straight," as if they contained doctrines. (Of course taking this line implies that one must be similarly suspicious of passages that appear to propound in a "straight" manner antirealistic views.) Even if one does not assume that a kind of global ironical perspective undermines the possibility of taking such apparent assertions as assertions, one might still hold that the apparently realistic language is not to be taken literally. Rather, Kierkegaard may be using traditional religious language, but infusing it with radically new existential and pragmatic content, speaking poetically and not literally.

III. THE QUESTION OF METHOD

One might think that the question of Kierkegaard's view of the realism debate could be resolved if we had some general guidance as to how such texts as the above disputed ones should be read. Can we presuppose some hermeneutical method, some theory as to how to approach philosophical texts in general and Kierkegaard's texts in particular? There are of course general interpretative perspectives that will resolve the issues, but the adoption of such a perspective is hardly the adoption of a neutral method that will resolve the dispute impartially. Rather, in this case it is clear that the interpretative perspective one takes presupposes some view on the very issues under consideration.

For example, if one argues that every text in some sense "deconstructs" by failing to communicate what the author intended, and that it is impossible for a text to affirm propositions that are "objectively true," then it is quite clear that Kierkegaard's texts will not function in the way realists assume. Furthermore, if one assumes that Kierkegaard himself realized this, then one can go on to interpret his whole edifice of pseudonyms and irony and humor as attempts to express this insight, perhaps as an attempt to "show" what cannot be "said," to use Wittgenstein's language. On such a reading Kierkegaard is an antirealist who recognized that it would be incoherent to *assert* the objective truth of antirealism and hence tried to express his insights in an appropriately elusive manner. That such an approach is possible is demonstrated by the newer type of literature I began by describing, but the perspective adopted by this mode of reading is hardly dispassionate and objective with respect to the dispute about realism. Rather, it amounts to a demonstration that if one assumes the truth of antirealism, and assumes that Kierkegaard realized this truth, then one can read Kierkegaard as an antirealist.

Of course, realist readings may be equally question-begging. To go to the opposite extreme from radical deconstructionism, if one assumes that the meaning of a text is fixed objectively by the author's intentions and assumes there is a fact of the matter as to what Kierkegaard intended, then presumably one can take seriously some of Kierkegaard's seemingly objective claims about God if one has reason to think that Kierkegaard intended those claims to be read as objectively true. But once more a realistic account of truth seems to be presupposed by the hermeneutical theory employed, and it is also assumed that Kierkegaard accepted such a view. It is hardly surprising that if we assume realism and that Kierkegaard accepted realism, we can successfully read Kierkegaard as a realist.

Obviously there are theories of meaning that lie in between radical deconstructionism and objective authorial intent. However, my point is that there are no neutral, noncontroversial theories that will give us a method for objectively settling the question as to how Kierkegaard should be read. One's readings of Kierkegaard will inevitably be shaped, to a greater or less degree, by one's global commitments about meaning in general and Kierkegaard's literature as a whole.

I do not believe that the impossibility of a "method" in this case means that meaningful conversation and dispute between the antagonists is impossible. Rather, it seems to me that each differing view can develop both overall comprehensive readings as well as readings of particular texts and books. Opponents can imaginatively "try on" alternative readings, and test them by their ability to illuminate and clarify the text and resolve problems that are posed therein. Although no neutral ground can be found to resolve the dispute once and for all, conversions may happen, and even without conversion, give and take is possible in which each side may learn from others in the conversation.

The story that follows is one that fits with the broader story I have given about Kierkegaard other places.[9] It is in one sense a "realistic" reading in that I take seriously the philosophical claims made in the text as claims that can be defended or criticized by arguments. Pragmatically, this seems to me to be the best approach to the text, since even if Kierkegaard's writings are ironical through and through, there is a sense in which the irony will be undermined if we do not "play along" and take the particular claims and arguments seriously. A "global" sense that "everything in the text is ironical" can, ironically enough, make it impossible for us to recognize whatever ironical elements are present. Roger Poole's claim that Kierkegaard's texts consist of "literary machines that . . . actually work but carry out no function at all"[10] can be just the kind of *a priori* straightjacket that Poole argues characterizes what he calls "theologically-driven" readings of Kierkegaard. I believe that taking Kierkegaard seriously as a philosopher can illuminate the realism debate, because Kierkegaard seems to accept the kinds of epistemological premises that are often regarded as justifying antirealism, but he combines these epistemological views with a quite traditional acceptance of realism.

IV. KIERKEGAARD ON KANT AND HEGEL

The contemporary debate about realism and antirealism is preeminently a debate about Kantian issues. Antirealists such as Putnam are not Berkeleyan idealists; in some sense they recognize that there is a "real world" that is objective over against the individual, and that in ordinary life we distinguish between true and false statements about that world. The debate concerns the status of that world. Is it in some sense the world *as it appears to us*, a phenomenal world, or is there such a thing as the world *as it is in itself*? Hilary Putnam's 1976 Presidential Address to the Eastern American Philosophical Association makes this Kantian structure explicit.

After discussing Kant's view that knowledge is a "representation" that is the work of a "transcendental me," Putnam explains his own position: "I would modify Kant's image in two ways. The authors (in the plural – my image of knowledge is social) don't write just *one* story: they write many versions. And the authors *in* the stories are the *real* authors. This would be 'crazy' if these stories were *fictions*. A fictitious character can't also be a real author. But these are true stories."[11]

In light of this Kantian framing of the problem, it is illuminating to examine Kierkegaard's own comments on Kant in Chapter III of *Postscript*, which contains a discussion as to whether Hegel has given an adequate answer to "Kantian skepticism." This discussion is initially puzzling in a number of ways. In the debate Kant is viewed as a skeptic who denied the possibility of knowledge of the "real world." Hegel on the other hand is described as a purported realist who attempted to answer this Kantian skepticism.

One might also wonder what this debate about skepticism has to do with the debate about realism. After all, it would seem that one could be a skeptic and a realist, affirming that there is an independent reality while denying we have any knowledge about that reality. I think Kierkegaard would affirm the coherence of such a position. However, though it appears possible to be a skeptic and still be a realist, the refutation of skepticism would seem to require the triumph of realism, unless the triumph over skepticism is itself an illusion. As we shall see, this is precisely what Kierkegaard thinks Hegel's overcoming of Kant amounts to.

It might seem that Kierkegaard has the positions of Kant and Hegel reversed. After all, Hegel is known as the proponent of philosophical idealism, while Kant's philosophy can be seen as committed to realism in at least two respects. First, there is Kant's "empirical realism," where Kant sees himself as refuting Humean skepticism and vindicating the objectivity of scientific knowledge. Though it is true that this knowledge turns out to be knowledge of appearances, it is still in one sense "objective" for Kant. Second, one must also recognize Kant's defense of noumenal reality, his contention that even if knowledge is in some sense of reality as it appears to us, there is such a thing as reality in itself, a reality that turns out to be significant for moral and religious ends in the second *Critique*.

A closer look at Kierkegaard's text shows that he is not really confused. Since the point of the chapter is to criticize Hegel's claim to have successfully answered Kant, it is reasonable for Kierkegaard to view Kant through Hegelian eyes. And the picture sketched is precisely the portrait Hegel paints: Hegel sees himself as vindicating "absolute knowledge" against the Kantian "idealism" that limits human knowledge to appearances. Kierkegaard's own critical perspective on Hegel is that in fact Hegel's answer to Kant is no answer at all. Hegel's vindication of "absolute knowledge" is an illusion, and his answer to what Hegel sees as Kant's skepticism is actually a deeper and more insidious form of skepticism. As we shall see, Kierkegaard's own view turns out to be quite similar to Kant's, though it is not clear whether Kierkegaard is aware of this.[12]

As Kierkegaard tells the tale, Hegel's answer to Kant's skepticism rests on the validity of Hegel's "method." Hegel's dialectical method was supposed to enable the thinker to reach the standpoint of "pure thought," the exalted viewpoint of "reason" that leaves behind the thinking of the understanding, which is tied to the traditional Aristotelian principle of noncontradiction. From this exalted viewpoint, the thinker can "mediate" philosophical disagreements, seeing the truth contained in rival viewpoints and incorporating those truths in increasingly adequate and more comprehensive perspectives. Kantian skepticism is not merely confronted with a dogmatic denial. Rather, the standpoint of absolute knowledge is supposed to emerge from the process of reflection that has itself generated Kantian skepticism. The skeptical standpoint is in some way supposed to "overcome itself." Though there is an obvious Cartesian flavor to this idea (we discover absolute certainty by an attempt at universal doubt), at the heart of it lies the Hegelian conviction that skepticism, like every other one-sided philosophical doctrine, contains the seeds of its own destruction, but that this is a destruction which does not merely negate but also constructively preserves what is right about skepticism.

Kierkegaard makes several criticisms of this Hegelian project. First of all, he rejects the idea that doubt can overcome itself. Echoing his own earlier discussion of skepticism in *Philosophical Fragments*, he claims that skepticism is in some sense a willed standpoint (*CUP* 335–6n). He does not mean, I think, as is sometimes thought, that people can in general voluntarily control their beliefs. Rather, he means that those who adopt a global skeptical attitude basically do so because they want to be skeptics. To the degree that skepticism rests on a resolution, it can only be ended by a resolution.

The second charge he makes is that the knowledge of noumenal reality that "pure thought" is supposed to achieve is illusory. From Kierkegaard's viewpoint, thinking always employs universal concepts; to think about some concrete reality is always to apply to it some concept and for Kierkegaard a concept is essentially a *possibility, a possible way of being*. This means that the concrete actuality of the object of thought cannot itself be made an object of thought. The "identity of thought and being" reached by "pure thought" is an illusion because when "being" is thought, it is transformed into possibility and one "abstracts" from its actuality, which is bound up with its concrete particularity. So, ideally speaking, thought and being are identical, but that means only that being as thought is equivalent to thought. The "union of thought and being" is far from a vindication of realism; it in fact is a sign that thinking has totally abandoned any attempt to make contact with actuality and is content with the world of possibility (331).

Kierkegaard's claim that thinking necessarily fails to grasp being in its concrete actuality seems to put him on the side of the skeptic. However, he has his own answer to the skeptic, one that emphasizes what might be called the noumenal quality of the thinker's own *existence*. The existing individual can know himself as actuality without transforming that actuality into possibility. The individual subject "is able to know what lives within him – the only actuality that does not become a possibility by being known and is not something that can be known only by being thought" (320; my translation). I take this to mean that the individual's own existential reality can therefore be thought and known, and that it is the only concrete actuality for which this is the case. It is not known only by being thought and it can be thought without its actuality being annulled. So Kierkegaard's alternative solution to the problem of "Kantian" skepticism turns out to look remarkably like Kant's own perspective, which limits theoretical reason to knowledge of the phenomenal world so as to allow room for the perspective of the rational agent, who has rational faith in his own existence as a free being and grounds his belief in God and immortality on this practical faith.

This is not a reversion to the Cartesian *cogito*, because the reality known is not merely the reality of consciousness, which would merely be awareness of possibility, but the reality of agency, the passionate transformation of possibility into actuality. It does threaten, like the Cartesian *cogito*, to imply some kind of solipsism, or "acosmism," as Kierkegaard himself notes.[13] That is, one might take Kierkegaard here to be saying that the only "thing in itself" that can be known is the agent's own reality, and thus that one must take a skeptical position about "the external world."

That Kierkegaard has a genuine sympathy for skepticism cannot be denied. In the last analysis, however, he is not himself a skeptic. To see this one must recognize that Kierkegaard uses the term "knowledge" in two different ways. At times he uses "knowledge" as requiring the kind of certainty that classical foundationalism thought was required to know. It is in this sense that he claims that the only actuality an individual can know is his or her own ethical actuality. At other times Kierkegaard uses the term "knowledge" in a different and much looser sense. He recognizes that there is a broad class of things that in everyday life are regarded as known. For example, in *Philosophical Fragments* he says that he assumes that there is such a thing as knowledge of the past and only wants to know how this knowledge is acquired (*PF* 81).

This looks like a contradiction: we only know our own existence; we know many things. However, no contradiction is really implied. The underlying issue is the demand for objective certainty present in classical epistemologies. If one accepts this demand, Kierkegaard argues, nothing can be known except the individual's own ethical reality. Kierkegaard himself, however, is not committed to this ideal and seeks to undermine it by showing that much of what we accept as knowledge in ordinary life does not meet it.

If we consider the comments Kierkegaard makes about skepticism in *Philosophical Fragments*, as well as his thoughts on historical knowledge in *Postscript*, the following picture emerges: Kierkegaard's view is not that human knowers can never make contact with an external world but that all such contact involves *faith* or *belief* (Danish *tro*) (*PF* 72–88). The idea is not that people are imprisoned within their own consciousness but that knowledge of the external world is never objectively certain. All such knowledge involves a risk, the possibility of error, and such a possibility must be annulled by the decision not to take the skeptical attitude. Once more this claim does not have to be understood as implying direct voluntary control over individual beliefs but as a claim that knowledge of the external world requires one to reject what might be called the life-view of the skeptic.

In *Philosophical Fragments* this claim is illustrated enigmatically via a discussion of faith or belief. There Kierkegaard[14] says that "immediate sensation and cognition cannot deceive" (*PF* 81). Thus, when a person sees a star or experiences an event, *something* is immediately present and certain. However, as soon as the person forms a judgment about the content of the experience, for example, by holding the belief that the star is a *star*, an objective part of the physical world, then there is uncertainty, because the reality of the star as a public object with a history cannot be immediately sensed (81). One could say that uncertainty is present as soon as the star is viewed as a *thing in itself*, a mind-independent reality whose existence transcends my consciousness of it. Kierkegaard argues that this uncertainty must in some way be negated, and that the attitude that in fact carries out the task is known as faith or belief. Since the object of historical inquiry is by definition such a real event, something that really happened, it follows that faith is an essential component in what we normally call historical knowledge (81–2). (And it is important to note that Kierkegaard does not deny that there is such a thing as historical knowledge.)

In all of this Kierkegaard seems to be committed to a kind of metaphysical realism. It is precisely the objectivity and mind-independent character of existent objects that makes knowledge of such objects uncertain in character. For example, Kierkegaard describes historical knowledge as "approximative" in character. But if our knowledge of history is approximative, this seems to imply that there is some kind of ideal to be approximated, and what else can such an ideal be but that of an accurate representation of the object of knowledge? In claiming that historical knowledge can never be more than approximative, Kierkegaard is not denying the independence of the object of knowledge. On the contrary, he is presupposing it. Even the best and most exact human knowledge is subject to error, because existing objects have an "illusiveness" that is grounded in their independence of us and our concepts and methods of knowing.

But is this realism consistent with the claims that all thought "abstracts from existence" and that all thinking involves a transformation of actuality into possibility? How can I know a reality that I must think as a possibility? It is here that the significance of Kierkegaard's claim that my own existence can be both thought and known as actuality becomes apparent. It is not that I attempt to infer the existence of an external reality from my own existence in a Cartesian fashion. There is no way to obtain objective certainty with regard to existing realities other than myself. If we adopt the epistemic standards of modern classical foundationalism, we will become skeptics about the external world, and Kierkegaard thinks that Greek skepticism should have taught us this already. We arrive at the external world only through faith or belief. Nevertheless, we can arrive there. We can do so because we have a sense of what it means to exist in actuality, and we have such a sense because we know ourselves as actual agents.

Kierkegaard says that existence is not a concept, and hence it is incorrect to say we learn the meaning of "existence" from our own case in the sense that we might learn the meaning of "white" by seeing white objects. Nevertheless, we do have a sense of what it means to exist, and we do make judgments about what things exist and what things do not, and the attitude Kierkegaard calls "belief" is an expression of this distinction. One way of expressing this would be to say that one must analyze an individual's belief about an independent reality as a linking of thought-possibilities with that individual's own existence. Though I have no *concept* of existence, I know what it means to exist by existing.[15] Believing that my friend John exists amounts to linking John in some ways to that concrete actuality that is thought without becoming a mere possibility, namely, my own actuality. John is *my* friend, the one I went through high school and college with.

Kierkegaard says explicitly that knowledge of past historical figures requires a link to my own existence. To understand the actions of a person in the past, I must conceive of that individual as an agent like myself, either by imaginatively placing myself in his shoes or imaginatively placing him in mine (*CUP* 146). Historical knowledge, however, is tied to my own existence in two other ways. First, this knowledge is rooted in a passion-driven attitude we call belief, and since passion is the heart of existence, we can say that belief or faith is itself a part of my existence. Second, the content of faith or belief is linked to existence. What does it mean to believe that Julius Caesar existed, as opposed to merely contemplating the possibility of his existence? It means that in some very complicated ways I believe that Julius Caesar is tied to that stream of passionate doings that I know as my own existence. Whether I see Caesar as my forerunner, my causal antecedent, the creator of monuments I or others I know might visit, or whatever, in thinking of him as *actual* I necessarily link him in my thought to the only actuality that I know as actual.

In looking at Kierkegaard's critical perspectives on the Hegelian claim to have overcome "Kantian skepticism," we see then an interesting blend of epistemic attitudes. There is on the one hand a strong dose of epistemological humility, an attitude that borders on skepticism; the only "thing in itself" humans can know with any certainty *as actual* is the reality of their own existence as agents. The actuality of other realities is only apprehended through faith or belief. Nevertheless, it is the *actuality* of those other realities that is believed, and faith or belief makes possible what Kierkegaard calls an "approximative" type of knowledge. This approximative character is an indicator both of the limits of human knowledge and the realistic and independent character of what is known.

V. REALISM AND TRUTH

What light does all this throw on Kierkegaard's famous discussion of truth and his claim that "truth is subjectivity" in *Postscript*? The discussion begins with a brief look at two theories of truth: the "empirical" (correspondence) definition of truth as "the agreement of thinking with being" and the idealistic definition of truth as "the agreement of being with thinking" (*CUP* 189–90). Summary criticisms are made of each view.

The idealistic formula is described as merely tautological, for as we have just seen, the "being" that is the object of thought is not actual being but being *as thought*. Hence the agreement between being and thought in this case is merely the agreement of thinking with thinking (*CUP* 190). The heart of this criticism is the claim that abstract thought deals not with actual existence but with ideal conceptualizations. Thus, the point made is essentially the same as that implied by the discussion of "systems," where it is asserted that, for human beings, a "logical system is possible," but an "existential system" is not possible (109). Human beings can develop conceptual systems or models, but as soon as they are applied to actual being they become approximations or hypotheses (110).[16]

This last point leads directly to the criticism made of the "empiricist" or correspondence theory of truth, which is that truth on this account becomes an ideal that can never be fully realized. This is so because both the actuality that is being represented and the knower are "unfinished" and in process. Kierkegaard here can be understood as emphasizing the tentative, never-final character of empirical inquiry, which is rooted both in the complexity and flux-suffused character of what is known as well as the finitude and uncertainty linked to the temporal character of the knower. The objection here seems not to be to correspondence as an *ideal*.[17] Indeed, Kierkegaard seems to assume that no other ideal makes any sense. Rather, the objection is to any claim that the ideal can be finally and fully actualized. As I have already argued, such a claim, while it may be subject to criticism for being overly skeptical, is not antirealistic. Rather, it rests on what Hilary Putnam has termed the defining tenet of realism, the radically nonepistemic character of truth. It is just because reality is ultimately independent of human minds that human attempts to know that reality must always be approximations.

Kierkegaard thus seems to combine an epistemology that rejects classical foundationalism with a traditional "realistic" account of the aim of knowing. He seems "postmodern" in his account of knowledge, yet "modern" or really "premodern" in his understanding of truth. Such a combination is puzzling to many. How can one believe in an objective, mind-independent reality and at the same time deny that human beings have final knowledge of such a reality? Can we view our beliefs as "approximations" of an ideal truth if we never possess that truth? How can one say there is a thing in itself and then deny that we humans ever finally know what that is? At this point the antirealist argues that the thing in itself is a meaningless or perhaps useless ideal. Richard Rorty, for example, argues that realism only makes sense if one asserts that humans have some kind of direct access to reality, some mode of "givenness" such that we can compare our ideas with a reality that is known independently of those ideas. But since we have no such access to reality, Rorty asserts we must give up the ideal of truth as "contact with reality" in favor of truth as "what it is good for us to believe."[18]

It is just at this point that Kierkegaard's view is most illuminating. For he rejects an often unnoticed premise that is common both to the classical foundationalist and the antirealist postmodernist. Both agree that *if* there is to be knowledge of objective reality, there must be some method of obtaining certain knowledge about that reality. The classical foundationalist, from Descartes through Husserl, concludes that since there is objective knowledge there must be such a method. The antirealist concludes that since there is no such method there is no knowledge of objective reality. We can see lurking behind Rorty's antirealism the dashed hopes and disappointments of the classical foundationalist.

On Kierkegaard's view, though there is no "absolute given" and no "method" that can be relied upon to produce certain, objective knowledge, empirical knowledge necessarily aims at such knowledge. He never doubts that this ideal of objective knowledge is valid as an ideal or that there is a reality independent of us that we are attempting to know. But if we don't *know* this objective reality with certainty, how can we be *certain* it is even there? If we don't have absolute truth, how can we be sure it is there as an ideal to approximate?

One might think that Kierkegaard could appeal to God's omniscience at this point, since he clearly asserts that although no existential system is possible for humans, reality is indeed a system for God. There is absolute, objective truth about the actual world; it is found in God's view of that world. On this point Merold Westphal is quite right to point out that there are different forms of antirealism, and that Kant and Kierkegaard should be understood in the context of their theistic beliefs.[19] Like Kant himself, when Kierkegaard insists that human knowledge is always approximative in character, he is not denying there is absolute truth but affirming the finitude of human attempts to realize that truth.

However, though there is clearly a link between belief in God and belief in objective truth, I am inclined to think that the inference goes the other way for Kierkegaard. That is, I think he would be more inclined to say we must believe in God because we believe in an objective truth than that we believe in objective truth because we believe in God. Certainly, Kierkegaard cannot here appeal to God to complete his own "system." He rejects objective proofs of God's existence, and any objective assurance of God's reality, so he cannot appeal to God as an *objective* proof that there is objective truth. In any case, to believe in God we must already believe in objective truth, since we can hardly believe in God, trust God, place our hope in God, and at the same time fail to believe in God's objective reality.

If we ask why Kierkegaard believes in an objective reality as what knowledge attempts to "approximate," the answer seems to be that this is part of the structure of "belief" or "faith." That is just what a belief *is* or *does*. The mind-independent character of reality is precisely what gives belief its risky character. Belief just is the human attitude that takes this risk and takes what is apprehended as *real*.

As I have repeatedly said, this is not to say that individual beliefs are voluntary actions, and it does not mean that beliefs are always hard to come by. On the contrary, Kierkegaard seems to be of the opinion, shared by Hume and Reid and Moore, that certain kinds of beliefs are just natural though perhaps not inevitable; they are called forth by life itself.[20] Skepticism, then, is difficult; one must work to be a skeptic.

VI. TRUTH AND SUBJECTIVITY

If Kierkegaard is a realist and accepts objective truth as an ideal to be approximated, then in what sense does he hold that "truth is subjectivity"? First of all, it should be noted that the claim that truth is subjectivity, far from denying the objectivity of propositional truth, includes an affirmation of such truth:

> When the question about truth is asked objectively, truth is reflected upon objectively as an object to which the knower relates himself. What is reflected upon is not the relation but that what he relates himself to is the truth, the true. If only that to which he relates himself is the truth, the true, then the subject is in the truth. When the question about truth is asked subjectively, the individual's relation is reflected upon subjectively. If only the how of this relation is in truth, the individual is in truth, even if he in this way were to relate himself to untruth. (CUP 199)

This paragraph assumes that there is such a thing as objective propositional truth. That is, it assumes that it is possible for an individual to believe what is not (objectively) true even if the individual herself is in some sense in the truth, just as it assumes that an individual can believe what is objectively true while being personally in untruth. Kierkegaard illustrates this claim by the famous comparison between the pagan who prays with the passion of infinity, even though he lacks objective knowledge of God, and the Christian who prays in a false spirit, even though he presumably has objective knowledge (*CUP* 201). The life of the pagan in such a case is the one that contains "more truth."

The thesis that truth is subjectivity is explicitly said to apply only to a particular kind of truth, the truth that is "essential" to human existence, and it is clear enough that for Kierkegaard this means moral and religious truth, the truth about how human life should be lived. The point is not to deny that there are objective moral and religious truths, but to raise the question as to how a person can learn to live truly. What is it that makes a person's life true?

But can a life be true? Or is this merely using the word "true" in a misleading, metaphorical way? For Kierkegaard, human existence curiously mirrors human knowing, but with what might be called a reverse directionality. In knowing we attempt to "reproduce" or reduplicate reality, and though we speak of some of these attempts as knowledge and regard knowing as a case where our thought accurately mirrors reality, Kierkegaard says that such efforts are never final but always approximative and tentative. In any case the propositions we believe are themselves ideal objects, not spatio-temporal actualities. Propositions do not *exist*, though believings of them are acts of or states of existing beings.

Existence, like knowing, involves a "reduplication," because it involves the actualization of conceived possibilities. A life can correspond, or fail to correspond, to its ideals. The question concerns how a life can truly "correspond" in this way. Does a person live truly if and only if that person has the right beliefs, that is, objectively true moral and religious beliefs? Or is it rather the case that a person can have objectively true beliefs about morality and human life and still live falsely? And can a person whose beliefs are objectively false still be a person whose life contains truth?

Kierkegaard says, with respect to such questions, that "there can be no doubt about the answer for anyone who is not totally botched by scholarship and science" (*CUP* 201). It is not hard to see why he thinks the answer is so easy. We all know people who hold what we take to be objectively false beliefs about moral and religious matters but who live lives that seem to exhibit those qualities human existence is supposed to manifest. And we all know people who appear to have objectively correct beliefs but whose lives are characterized by moral failure and hypocrisy. The crucial question for Kierkegaard then is not whether a person's beliefs are objectively right but whether the person has the right kind of relationship to what is believed.

Such a position appears to be naive. What about the sincere Nazi? One might agree that it is important existentially to realize one's ideals, but surely it is also important that one have the right ideals. The "how" may be important, but the "what" seems important as well.

I think Kierkegaard can accommodate this worry. In the end, his position is not that what a person believes is unimportant but that how a person believes is crucially important. In comparing the pagan who prays to the idol with the passion of infinity and the Christian who prays to the true God in a false spirit, the point is not that the pagan has supremely realized the truth. The claim made is that there is *more* truth in the life of the pagan. In effect, Kierkegaard says that if you had to choose between these two options, you would be much better off if you chose to be the pagan. But that is compatible with saying the pagan would be better off still if he had true beliefs.

In fact, one reason the pagan is better off than the hypocritical Christian is precisely that he is more likely to gain true beliefs. For what Kierkegaard finally wishes to claim about moral and religious truth is that whatever knowledge we gain about such matters is gained through having the right kind of subjectivity. It is for this reason that the person who rubs the lamp of freedom with ethical passion finds God. This is the case not because there is no objective truth about such matters but because God has providentially arranged that moral and religious insight is gained only through moral and religious striving.

Whether this is an adequate answer to the problem of the "sincere Nazi" I shall not attempt to say. But I can say that Kierkegaard's conviction that truth is gained through and realized in subjectivity is not a repudiation of realism with respect to propositional truth about anything, including religious issues. God's reality is not founded in any human activity. Rather, it is because it is objectively true that there is a God who desires humans to live truly that the world has been arranged in such a manner that finding moral and religious truth is linked to the development of the right kind of subjectivity. It is because of God that finding the truth about God is logically dependent on learning to live truly.

NOTES

1 Roger Poole, *Kierkegaard: The Indirect Communication* (Charlottesville: The University Press of Virginia, 1993), p. 6.

2 Ibid., p. 7.

3 Ibid., p. 9.

4 William Alston, "Yes, Virginia, There Is a Real World," *Proceedings and Addresses of the American Philosophical Association* 52, 6 (August 1979): 779–80.

5 Alvin Plantinga, "How To Be an Anti-Realist," *Proceedings and Addresses of the American Philosophical Association* 56, 1 (September 1982): 48.

6 Hilary Putnam, "Realism and Reason," *Proceedings and Addresses of the American Philosophical Association* 50, 6 (August, 1977): 485.

7 There is a big debate about the status of Kierkegaard's pseudonyms. Though I have a well-developed position on this issue, and I side wholeheartedly with those who affirm the significance and autonomy of the pseudonyms, in this essay I shall not deal with the issue. Since the views of Kierkegaard are often discussed with reference to things his pseudonyms say, it is appropriate to evaluate those discussions as discussions of Kierkegaard. In this essay "Kierkegaard" will simply be a term for the figure speaking in the literature under discussion, which in reality means that in the case of *Concluding Unscientific Postscript* the views under discussion are actually those of the pseudonymous author, Johannes Climacus. I don't want to assume that the views of Climacus, or the Kierkegaard I am discussing, are the same as the historical Kierkegaard's, but neither do I wish to assume in advance that they must be different from the actual views of Kierkegaard.

8 Richard Rorty, "The Priority of Democracy to Philosophy," in *Philosophical Papers* (Cambridge University Press, 1991), 1:188. This claim is echoed in volume 2 of Rorty's *Philosophical Papers* as well; see 2:32.

9 See my *Passionate Reason: Making Sense of Kierkegaard's Philosophical Fragments* (Bloomington and Indianapolis: Indiana University Press,

1992) and *Kierkegaard's* Fragments *and* Postscript: *The Religious Philosophy of Johannes Climacus* (Atlantic Highlands, N.J.: Humanities Press International, 1983).

10 Poole, *Kierkegaard: The Indirect Communication,* p. 7.

11 Hilary Putnam, *Meaning and the Moral Sciences* (Boston: Routledge and Kegan Paul, 1978), p. 138.

12 See Ronald Green, *Kierkegaard and Kant: The Hidden Debt* (Albany: State University of New York Press, 1992) for an account of the many similarities between Kant and Kierkegaard, as well as an intriguing but speculative suggestion that Kierkegaard suppressed any acknowledgment of his indebtedness to Kant.

13 The accusation Kierkegaard himself raises as a problem is pressed forcefully in Louis Mackey's "The Loss of the World in Kierkegaard's Ethics," in *Points of View: Readings of Kierkegaard* (Tallahassee: Florida State University Press, 1986).

14 Really, of course, it is the pseudonym Johannes Climacus who says this. See note 7 above.

15 Kierkegaard's view here can be compared with the view of Thomas Reid and other philosophers that humans acquire such concepts as those of "power" and "cause" from a "first-person" perspective. We know what it means for something to be a cause because we are conscious of our own causal activity. The difference is that Kierkegaard does not wish to say that "existence" is a *concept* but explicitly denies this. When we think of a tiger as existing, the concept of a tiger has not changed. Nevertheless, our attitude toward the concept does change, and Kierkegaard wants to claim that our sense of what this attitude involves is acquired by existing.

16 Kierkegaard's claim is interestingly similar to a well-known claim of Einstein: "As far as the laws of mathematics refer to reality, they are not certain; and as far as they are certain, they do not refer to reality." From "Geometry and Experience," an expanded form of an address to the Prussian Academy of Sciences, Berlin, 27 January 1921, quoted from Einstein's *Sidelights of Relativity* (London, 1922). I found the quote in Henry Margenau, "Einstein's Conception of Reality," in *Albert Einstein: Philosopher-Scientist,* ed. Paul Arthur Schilpp (La Salle, Ill.: Open Court Publishing, 1949), 1:250.

17 A good example of the way the ideal of correspondence with reality is assumed as an ideal can be found in *Philosophical Fragments,* where Hegelian accounts of history as "necessary" are criticized on the grounds that the character of what is known (history as involving contingency) is altered by the knowing, rather than by the knower seeking to make his thought correspond to reality. See *PF* 81–2.

18 Richard Rorty, *Philosophy and the Mirror of Nature* (Princeton: Princeton University Press, 1979), p. 176. See William Alston's discussion of this point in "Yes, Virginia, There is a Real World," pp. 780–6.

19 See Merold Westphal, "Christian Philosophers and the Copernican Revolution," in *Christian Perspectives on Religious Knowledge*, ed. C. Stephen Evans and Merold Westphal (Grand Rapids, Mich.: Wm. B. Eerdmans, 1993).

20 In *Postscript* Kierkegaard emphasizes the impossibility of universal doubt. Doubt is a task that requires effort; doubting universally would require an infinite effort that an existing human being could never realize (318). Very similar themes can be found in *Fragments*, where it is emphasized that skepticism is not a natural or necessary result of thought, but is grounded in the will (*PF* 82–5).

7 Existence, emotion, and virtue: Classical themes in Kierkegaard

I. KIERKEGAARD AS CLASSICAL MORAL PSYCHOLOGIST

In an explanatory note appended to the last book in his pseudonymous authorship, Kierkegaard declared that the importance of his pseudonymous authors "unconditionally does not consist in making any new proposal."[1] In his intentionally provocative readings of the human existence-relationships, Kierkegaard stamps such words as "subjectivity" and "existence" with his distinctive mark (this is especially true of "existence"). These words have fostered his reputation as one who holds that, in matters of ethics and religion anyway, "truth" is created by human decisions rather than discovered or known; the words have encouraged a conventionality associating Kierkegaard with the epistemological claims and departures of existentialists and their postmodernist successors.[2] Other items in his vocabulary of human existence, such as "character," "pathos," "passion," and "inwardness" suggest other historical associations and a more classical orientation. Still others, such as "personality" and "self," have a modern rather than postmodern ring.[3]

In this essay I want to take seriously Kierkegaard's disclaimer to be making any radically new proposal. I shall read Kierkegaard more as a successor of Aristotle and Thomas Aquinas than as a predecessor of Sartre and Foucault. On this reading, "subjectivity" and "existence" will evoke the thought of *character* rather than *subjectivism* and *radical choice*. I shall hear the declaration of Johannes Climacus, the pseudonymous author of *Concluding Unscientific Postscript*, that his generation has "forgotten what it means *to exist* and what *inwardness* is" (*CUP* 249; italics by Climacus; *SV*[1] VII 210) as saying that members of his generation have forgotten what it is to be a person of integrity, of character; they are oblivious to the serious possibility of living a life of intense virtue, ethical or Christian.

"Existence," "inwardness," "subjectivity," being an "individual," and "character," while closely related, are not perfectly interchangeable. Since Kierkegaard's choice of vocabulary is usually motivated by polemical considerations, understanding is aided by keeping in mind the targets of his disputes. "Subjectivity" (*Subjektivitet*) suggests a contrast with the interests, attitudes, and compulsions (that is, the character-formation) associated with the activities of speculative philosophy and professional historical scholarship. Climacus calls this formation of personality "objectivity."[4] "Inwardness" (*Inderlighed*) often implies a different contrast – with "externalities" such as social position, reputation, the "results" of one's actions, and publicly observable natural phenomena (see, e.g., *CUP* 243–7; *SV*[1] VII 205–8). A life characterized by "outwardness" would be a formation of personality all right, but in a sort of oblivion that an outwardly successful life can mask a corrupt, trivial, or empty "heart." "Self" (*Selv*) is sometimes used in a similar way. Some people

use their capacities, amass money, carry on secular enterprises, calculate shrewdly, etc., perhaps make a name in history, but themselves they are not; spiritually speaking, they have no self [*Selv*]. (*SUD* 35; *SV*[1] XI 148)

"Existence" (*Existents*) denotes the concreteness and individuality of a life lived in time and the requirements on personality that are implied by these features of selfhood, as contrasted with and contravened by the efforts of aesthetes and "pure thinkers" to conduct their lives abstractly *sub specie aeterni*, neglecting the particular self (oneself!) to be formed in accordance with the noble concepts and chosen from among the interesting possibilities (see, e.g., *CUP* 92; *SV*[1] VII 72). "Individual" (*Enkelte, Individet*) is similarly defined in polemical contrast to a life oriented to and by "the crowd." To be an "individual" is to be so constituted as to be able to act and feel with a high degree of social independency – that is, *not* to be so subject to the approval and disapproval of one's significant peers as to be emotionally enslaved by them (see, e.g., *PV* 81; *SV*[1] XIII 507). Such a constitution is largely a matter of passionate commitment to an "idea" (goal or life-ideal) and is thus exemplified in emotional response as well as in action. I shall say more about "character" (*Charakteer*) in a moment.

In support of my classical reading of Kierkegaard, I shall stress his preoccupation with emotions. Aristotle defined moral virtues as mean dispositions with respect to actions and *pathē* (feelings, emotions, passions), and vices as failures to find the mean with respect to them.[5] To exist as a genuine, fully blooming human being is, on this view, to be disposed to feel emotions such as fear, anger, hope, confidence, grief, pity, and the like in ways that are proper both to being human and to the particular situations in which one finds oneself. If we leave out Aristotle's doctrine of the mean – the idea that proper emotions and actions are somehow intermediate between two extremes – we are left with the idea that virtue consists in the disposition to *right* emotion and action. But virtues are not dispositions to respond automatically – either in emotion or behavior – to some kind of stimulus. A virtue is, as Aristotle says, "a state of character *concerned with choice*" (1107a1). It is concerned with choice in two ways: First, the right emotion or action often needs to be chosen, *given the virtue;* and second, it is in choosing the right emotion or action that *the virtue is acquired.*

All of this is also Kierkegaard's teaching on the nature and formation of character. His writings are all about proper and improper emotions and action, and he stresses, as strongly as Aristotle does, the role of choice in acquiring and exemplifying these. If we may paraphrase Aristotle as saying that virtues are dispositions to proper emotional response, we may in parallel paraphrase Kierkegaard as saying that genuine existence, or subjectivity (when it is truth, and not just "subjectivity of a sort") is proper pathos. We are reminded, too, that Thomas Aquinas devoted questions 22–48 of his *Summa Theologiae* (Ia2ae), which precedes his extensive discussions of the virtues, to a very sophisticated account of the emotions. For Kierkegaard, as for these earlier thinkers, educating the emotions is essential to "the inward transformation of the whole mind" (*CD* 249; *SV*[1] X 243).

Lamenting, with transparent irony, that unlike the "good people," he has no time to devote to "the future of world history" and has "to sit at home and mourn over [him]self," Johannes Climacus says that "in strong passions and the like, I have material enough, and therefore pain enough in forming something good out of it with the aid of reason." Then in a footnote attached to this last sentence, he comments, "With these words I wish to call to mind Plutarch's splendid definition of virtue: 'Ethical virtue has the passions for its material, reason for its form.' See his little book on the virtues" (*CUP* 161–2; *SV*ᴵ VII 133).⁶ I shall claim that this rather uncharacteristic reference to virtue and reason is in fact a good summary of what preoccupies Kierkegaard throughout his writings.

II. THE CONCEPT OF CHARACTER

Postscript is the *locus classicus* for the terms "subjectivity," "existence," and "inwardness." In *Two Ages*, which was published about a month after *Postscript*, Kierkegaard uses the word "character" (*Charakteer*) several times in the manner that I have mentioned. Here "character" means something like "sustained dispositional ethical enthusiasm or interest" (we might also say "commitment," though this is not a typical word for Kierkegaard). Character contrasts with the personality formation typical of the present age, which is *"devoid of passion, flaring up in superficial, short-lived enthusiasm and prudentially relaxing in indolence"* (*TA* 68, *SV*ᴵ VIII 64; emphasis in the original). Character is psychological continuity,⁷ stability in the face of changing circumstances. "Morality is character [*Charakteer*]; character is something engraved (χαράσσω); but the sea has no character, nor does the sand, nor abstract common sense, either, for character is inwardness (*TA* 77f; *SV*ᴵ VIII 73)." A person with character offers something "to dwell upon," something real, something stable, whereas a person without character is an "unstable emptiness" that stands only in "transitory relations" to other persons (see *TA* 54; *SV*ᴵ VIII 51). Lacking "essential passion," he or she is "an uncomfortable lack of specific quality" (*TA* 62; *SV*ᴵ VIII 59). These descriptions remind one of Judge William's descriptions of the personality (or rather, lack thereof) of the main aesthete of *Either/Or*, who from the judge's point of view is insubstantial, unconsolidated, lacking a definite personal identity because he never chooses himself in a decisive way, never becomes, "finite" and "temporal" but drifts in realms of possibility (see *EO* II 163; *SV*ᴵ II 148).

One might think that abstract common sense is inwardness too, since it is mental. But "inwardness" does not refer just to those operations that are private or relatively so (inward in the sense of hidden or concealable from other persons). Kierkegaard does frequently stress the hiddenness of inwardness, but the reference here is to what is at the *core* of the self conceived spiritually. "Inwardness" is a metaphor for centrality to the self. This core of the self is its concerns (enthusiasms, interests, passions) and what flows from them: emotions, intentions, decisions, actions. "If the essential passion [*væsentlige Lidenskab*] is taken away, the one motivation, and everything becomes meaningless externality, devoid of character, then the spring of ideality stops flowing and life together becomes stagnant water" (*TA* 62; *SV*^{I} VIII 59). Passion of the appropriate kind gives substance, shape, and direction to the self – in other words, its character. One might think that passion is "unruly," but unruly affections are not what Kierkegaard calls "passion." Being ethical or religious (a passion for the good and the true), "essential passion" produces and is produced by a strict sense of propriety. As contrasted with prose, poetry imposes strict constraints on the writer, and so does essential passion:

[Propriety] is feeling's [*Følelsens*] and passion's [*Lidenskabens*] own invention, and just as prose is unconstrained language, so also prosiness is unconstraint that does not know propriety; it is not the lack of discipline that produces terrible prosiness but instead a dismal lack of character [*Charakteerløshed*]. Fundamentally, essential passion [*den væsentlig Lidenskab*] is its own guarantee that there is something sacred, and this gives rise to the determinant propriety. (*TA* 64; *SV*^{I} VIII 61)

Kierkegaard distinguishes ethical envy, which retains an enthusiasm for the good and a sense for the excellent, and for *this* reason envies the person who displays ethical excellence, from characterless envy, in which the envier really has no interest in excellence, but is willing to do away with all excellence for the sake of having no superiors. Again, character is a matter of personality-integrating enthusiasm (interest, passion); but not every interest is capable of integrating the personality. In particular, an interest in being superior to other people is not capable of it, and so the envy that arises on the basis of this interest is "characterless." The ability of a passion to consolidate the personality seems to be, for Kierkegaard, what qualifies it as "essential" (*væsentlig Lidenskab*), and what the passion is essential *to* is the human being, thought of as having a nature that demands a formation of this type. The idea of an essential passion contains an idea very similar to Aristotle's idea of the human telos. Such a passion integrates the personality because the self, as a synthesis of the finite and the infinite, the temporal and the eternal, is *designed* to be actualized in such a passion.

III. PRACTICAL WISDOM

Two Ages and *Postscript* are both deeply preoccupied with the nature of thought and the life of the mind. In these places Kierkegaard and Climacus emphasize the practical effects and involvements of thought, whether in the "subjective thinking" that Climacus commends and the "objective thinking" that he exposes as a disease of the spirit or in the "reflection" that Kierkegaard analyzes as leading to passionlessness and characterless envy.[8] So if we ask what virtues these two books are about, they are certainly about a version of what has traditionally been called "practical wisdom" (they are of course about much more). Kierkegaard's focus on the connection between passion and reflection goes to the heart of his conception of the well-formed and fully functioning person. His basic position is that *the mature self is a proper synthesis of passion and reflection.* Passion without reflection is immature, unformed, chaotic, and childish "immediacy," and reflection without passion is the kind of personal emptiness that is the chief target of *Two Ages* pages 68 through 112 (*SV*[1] VIII 64–105). Kierkegaard's thought on this topic bears a strong resemblance to Aristotle's in the latter's stress on choice as a synthesis of desire and reasoning:

... moral virtue is a state of character concerned with choice ... and choice is deliberate desire. . . . The origin of action . . . is choice, and that of choice is desire and reasoning with a view to an end. This is why choice cannot exist either without reason and intellect or without a moral state; for good action and its opposite cannot exist without a combination of intellect and character.[9]

Aristotle's identification of character with proper desire (having the proper end in view) is reminiscent of Kierkegaard's identification of character with essential passion. Aristotle would agree with Kierkegaard that a person whose interests and enthusiasms were disconnected from reflection would be rather childish; and someone whose reflection was mere unpractical, idling ratiocination would be some kind of professorial monstrosity.[10]

To get an idea of the similarity, as well as the difference, between what Kierkegaard is promoting and what might ordinarily be called practical wisdom, consider the following:

... it must always be kept in mind that reflection itself is not something pernicious, that on the contrary the prerequisite for acting more intensively is the thorough kneading of reflection. Antecedent to inspired, enthusiastic action are: first of all, the immediate, spontaneous inspiration, then the period of prudence, which, because immediate inspiration does not deliberate, seems to be superior by virtue of its ingenuity in deliberation, and then finally the highest and most intensive enthusiasm which follows on the heels of prudence and therefore perceives what is the most prudent thing to do but rejects it and thereby gains the intensity of infinite enthusiasm. (*TA* 110–22; *SV*^{I} VIII 103)

The individual that Kierkegaard holds up to us as ideal is one whose passion is directed by reflection and whose reflection is given ethical and religious substance by passion. Note two peculiarities.

First, Kierkegaard couches the connection between passion and reflection in terms of a temporal sequence, which is a little artificial. Surely it is not characteristic of the mature individual that every decision is *preceded* by "immediate, spontaneous inspiration" that then is *followed* by a "period of prudence." Rather, the individual's enthusiasm is *shaped* by a certain understanding of himself and the world, in terms of which he "reflects." Once the subject has become a certain kind of pathetic-reflective thinker, his immediate responses are already, as immediate, shaped by his characteristic ways of thinking. It is clear from other contexts in Kierkegaard's writings that the concept of shaped passion that is expressed in Aristotle's phrase "desiderative reason or ratiocinative desire,"[11] is Kierkegaard's more usual pattern of thought (see the discussion of thought and emotion below).

Second, Kierkegaard is more sensitive to the *pitfalls* of deliberation than Aristotle, and is, in particular, concerned to alert his reader to the difference between ethical-religious reasoning, on the one hand, and the kind of reasoning that is the corrupt norm in Christendom, on the other. So he says that the wise person "perceives what is the most prudent thing to do but rejects it," and a little farther down on the same page says that the highest enthusiasm "acts against the understanding." But Kierkegaard is not rejecting understanding. There is Christian understanding and ethical understanding, after all, and he has just spent one hundred pages or so trying to get some of it across to his reader. The "prudence" of which he writes here, which must be rejected, is that self-serving, cowardly, leveled and leveling indolence that he has been holding up to his reader throughout *Two Ages*. That is the pattern of thought that he has mostly identified with "reflection" (*Reflexion*), but it must be remembered that there is also Christian reflection (note that *Works of Love* is subtitled "Christian Reflections [*Overveielser*] in the Form of Discourses").

IV. SOME FACTS ABOUT EMOTIONS

A number of claims about the nature of emotions are derivable from Kierkegaard's writings. First, emotions are based on concerns (interests, passions, enthusiasms) that, as we have begun to see, are constitutive of character. This implies that emotions themselves (episodes of emotion) are, or can be, indices or manifestations of character. Second, emotions depend on thought. One implication of the thought-dependency of emotions is that they may depend on spiritual outlook; thus there can be aesthetic emotions, ethical emotions, Christian emotions. Another implication of thought-dependency is that emotions are susceptible to the will; by choosing to think in one way rather than another about our situation, we can to some extent choose our emotions. However, since emotions are not identical with thoughts, there is no guarantee that by thinking in a certain way about our life or the world we can in any given instance make our emotions more virtuous. Yet another implication of emotions' dependency on thought is that they have a logic or "dialectic" the knowledge of which is a kind of moral wisdom. Kierkegaard's writings consist, to a large degree, in explorations of this emotion-dialectic, a "dialectic of existence" or dialectic of character. Since such exploration is a large and central task of "virtue ethics," Kierkegaard can and should count as an eminent virtue ethicist. Third, emotions are perceptual states of a certain sort and so give epistemic access to the moral and spiritual qualities of the situations they are about. (It is because emotions are thought-dependent perceptual states, not just thoughts, and because these perceptions are based on concerns, that thinking in certain terms cannot guarantee the production or inhibition of emotions.) Fourth, the moral and spiritual emotions have simulacra, which we might call "mere feelings," which can easily deceive a person into regarding himself as more virtuous than he is. And fifth, emotions can be dissociated from. That is, even though, in general, emotions are indices or manifestations of character, human beings have the capacity to stand back from certain emotions and say, as it were, "what is manifested there is not really *me*." And this need not be false denial; it may be resolute dissociation.

V. EMOTIONS AND CONCERNS

Kierkegaard does not, to my knowledge, distinguish emotions from concerns, nor does he claim that emotions are based on concerns. However, once we distinguish emotions and concerns, and relate them in the proposed way, it is easy to see that there is, in Kierkegaard's writings, a difference between them and that the proposed relationship is expressed in his usage of such words as *"Lidenskab"* (passion) and *"Pathos"* (pathos) and their cognates. The difference is marked not by vocabulary, but by usage. That is, *"Lidenskab"* is used sometimes for emotion, sometimes for concern; and so is *"Pathos."* But this should not surprise speakers of English, since the same shiftiness characterizes parts of our emotion-vocabulary.

Notice how a range of very different emotions can be based on the same concern. Consider somebody who is deeply "involved" in the business that she has created, a specialty bookbinding workshop. We could say that she is "attached" to her work, that her work is a major "concern" of her life, that her shop is her "passion." We could say that she is "interested" in her work, though this sounds a little pale; that she is "enthusiastic" about her shop. To say such things is to say something importantly characterizing about *her*; but it is not yet to say that she is in any one emotional state or other. We can know she is passionate about her shop without knowing how she is feeling. If the shop is flourishing, then on the basis of her concern for it, she will be glad (happy, joyful). If it is not quite thriving but she notes signs of its beginning to do so, she will be hopeful. If business is going badly and she is aware of the prospect of having to close the shop, we can expect her to be anxious. If the shop fails and irrevocably closes, but she continues to care about it as before, she will experience grief. If a friend of hers takes difficult or heroic action to keep the shop solvent in time of need, she will feel grateful to him.

If someone intentionally or through negligence undermines the business, she will be angry. And so on. What I am calling emotions are particular states based on one concern or another, mental states such as joy, hopefulness, anxiety, grief, gratitude, anger, pride, guilt, shame, nostalgia, and so on. These mental states vary with the circumstances, or, more precisely, they vary with the subject's construal of her circumstances, how she "sees" them.[12] But virtually any concern (passion, interest, enthusiasm, attachment, involvement) can give rise to any or all of the whole range of emotions, depending on how the subject views the circumstances insofar as they impinge on the concern.

In English, the word "emotion" does not do natural service as a synonym for "concern" in the sense I attach to it in the above paragraph. But the words "passion" and "concern" do double service. For example, we can say not only that the individual has a passion for her shop but also that when she found out that her competitor had been rumoring about that she uses low-grade leather in her fancy bindings, she flew into a passion and started yelling. And we can say not only that she has an ongoing concern for everything relating to her shop but also that when business slows up, she begins to get concerned. Thus "passion" sometimes doubles for "anger" and "concern" often doubles for "anxiety" or "worry." In an earlier vocabulary, "passion" was a generic term for emotions, as well as for related states such as desires and aversions and love (which in one central usage is not an emotion but an attachment or passion). For example, much of what David Hume writes of in the second book of his *Treatise of Human Nature* – "Of the Passions" – are what we call emotions; as are the mental states of which Descartes writes in *Les Passions de l'Âme* and Thomas Aquinas in *Summa Theologiae* 1a2æ.22–48, under the name of *passiones*. Many of what Aristotle calls *pathē* are emotions. "*Lidenskab*" as Kierkegaard uses it often refers to emotion; but just about as often it does not.

In *The Point of View for My Work as an Author* (28; *SV*[1] XIII 533), Kierkegaard speaks of the difficulty of communicating with an angry man; Lowrie translates "a man who is passionately angry," but Kierkegaard's text reads "*et Menneske i Lidenskab*" [a man in a passion]. In the following passage from Kierkegaard's journal it is clear that "*Lidenskab*" designates some emotion, though whether it is annoyance, envy, anger, or something else is not entirely clear:

It is rather odd how men whom I generally regard as good-natured and who generally are not unfriendly toward me, when they get into a passion [*komme i Lidenskab*] are then able to lie to the high heaven and scarcely be aware of it themselves. Passion [*Lidenskaben*] does have a strange power, and therefore how foolish all this modern thing about systems and systems, as if there were help in them; no, passion [*Lidenskaben*] must be purified. (*JP* §3128; *Pap.* VII¹ A 102)

That is, not much moral change is to be expected from the quarter of standard philosophizing; the kind of change that is needed is a change of the dispositions to emotional response. If, instead of becoming angry or envious in response to Kierkegaard, they began to feel appropriate contrition, they would neither lie nor be obscure to themselves, but would both speak and perceive the truth. We can see that such a change of emotion would in all likelihood signal a change of concern. The concern on which their present emotional response is based is (probably) a concern to seem justified, morally and spiritually; the concern that contrition would show forth would be the purer concern for righteousness itself (see Matt. 5:6).

Thus a couple of passages in which "*Lidenskab*" quite clearly designates the kind of state that we usually call emotion – a response to particular features (as the subject sees it) of the subject's world. On the other hand, "*Lidenskab*" often designates the concern on which such responses are contingent.[13] For example, immediately following the passage I just referred to from *Point of View*, Kierkegaard calls a romantic attachment a *Lidenskab* (throughout his writings, this kind of attachment is a favorite example of passion). A romantic attachment is clearly not an emotion, but instead the ground of a whole range of quite various emotions that the lovers may feel, depending on how they take things to be going in their relationship – joy, anxiety, sadness, hopefulness, disappointment, anger, and so on. Toward the beginning of *Postscript* Climacus uses "passion" in close juxtaposition, indeed interchangeably, with the word "interest" (see *CUP* 16, 21, 27; *SV*¹ VII 7, 11–12, 16): In such passages it seems clear that "*Lidenskab*" refers to a caring, an enthusiasm, a yearning. Climacus contrasts an interest in scholarly results with the yearning for an eternal happiness. He says that this latter interest or passion is "the possibility of faith and then faith" (*CUP* 27; *SV*¹ VII 16). I take this to say that at first a person yearns for an eternal happiness, without having found it. At this stage, depending on what the individual believes and how deeply he involves himself in the search for an eternal happiness, he may have a number of emotions, such as frustration, disappointment, guilt, or possibly hopefulness. A person would not have such emotions if he lacked the infinite interest, but the emotions are not the same as the infinite interest; they are manifestations of it. But faith is more than just the yearning and striving for an eternal happiness; it is in some sense a resting in it, a having found it. Then the dominant emotions, based on the same interest, will be joy and gratitude (see *PV* 103, 150–1; *SV*ᴵ XIII 582, 500–1). Thus when Climacus calls faith a "happy passion" (*lykkelig Lidenskab*) (*JC* 54; *SV*ᴵ IV 221), he has in mind a *satisfaction* of the yearning for an eternal happiness.

Sometimes both senses of "*Lidenskab*" – passion as emotion and passion as interest or concern – occur in the same passage. For example, in his journal, Kierkegaard writes,

It is often pointed out . . . that it takes just a little trifle to arouse the greatest passion [*Lidenskab*]. In my opinion this can be explained by the fact that there is an unsound or half-demented relationship between passion [*Lidenskab*] and object; once passion [*Lidenskab*] has arisen, it is inflamed by the senselessness that the whole thing revolves around a mere trifle.

If, as an example . . . of how a trifle sets the strongest passion [*Lidenskab*] in motion, reference is made to the fact that partisan or schismatic disputes, religious disputes, and civil wars always are the most violent – and this despite the fact that the contenders are so close to each other that it must indeed be a trifle which most often disunites them – it must be pointed out that here the matter is altogether different, because at the root of the disunity lies all the passion [*Lidenskab*] which also had expected or desired unity. At the root of controversy or enmity between strangers lies indifference – at the root of the other controversy lies friendship [*Venskab*], a spirit of solidarity [*Sammenhold*]. (*JP* §3131; *Pap*. X³ A 583)

In the first four occurrences of "passion" in this passage, Kierkegaard clearly has reference to the emotions of communal strife: anger, resentment, bitterness, perhaps envy, and the like. He is trying to explain why such emotions reach a higher pitch of intensity, and require less to provoke them, among family, friends, and compatriots than among persons who are not so connected. His answer is that in the background of the strife of the connected is a passion – now in the sense of a concern or interest (as in the last occurrence of "passion" in the passage) – namely, the passion of friendship (which obviously is not an emotion, but a basis for any number of different emotions). Irritations among the connected flame up more readily and more brightly because these people sense, dimly no doubt, that the attitudes and behavior characteristic of strife "sense-lessly" undercut the concern for harmony that is ingredient in their friendship. Thus a secondary set of emotions – embarrassment, shame, anxiety about the relationship and their undercutting of it – arise and exacerbate the emotions of strife. It is not clear from the text *how* the secondary emotions aggravate the emotions of strife, but perhaps some thesis about defense could supply the connection: The intensity of the anger somehow reassures or justifies the parties, giving them a sense of being in the right, thus defending them against their self-perception as in the wrong that is ingredient in their embarrassment, shame, and anxiety about senselessly undercutting the relationships that they care about. This explanation requires us to posit yet another passion in the sense of a concern or interest, namely, a rather intense interest in being in the right. In any case, it is clear that, while Kierkegaard does not theorize about the distinction that I am pressing, it is to be found in his use of "*Lidenskab*," and the distinction is a significant contribution to the understanding of his moral psychology.

VI. EMOTIONS AS SHAPED BY THOUGHT

Following a line of thought about the emotions that goes back at least to Aristotle's *Rhetoric* and is much traded on by the Stoics and other Hellenistic schools,[14] Kierkegaard stresses the connection between emotions and thoughts (concepts). The problem of becoming a Christian is "pathos-filled[15] and dialectical" (*CUP* 555; *SV*[1] VII 484);[16] as an existence-problem, as a problem of developing a character befitting an actual individual human being, it is at once the task of developing a certain pattern of emotional receptivity, and of thinking about oneself, God, and the world in certain definite ways, expressible in propositions.[17] Getting one's emotions right and getting one's thoughts right are intimately connected. Climacus makes fun of the "turbulent religious address" that neglects its conceptual *p*'s and *q*'s and ends up "at times a jumbled, noisy pathos of all sorts, esthetics, ethics, Religiousness A, and Christianity" (555) and thus has the disadvantage of being incapable of existential assimilation.

Kierkegaard faults Pastor Adler for using the language of Christianity but not the concepts, with the result that the emotions (*Grebedheden*) he tries to pass off as Christian are in fact not specifically Christian (see *OAR* 163–5; *Pap.* VII² pp. 199–202).

In his upbuilding discourses Kierkegaard repeatedly instructs us on how to *think* so as to have, or not to have, a given emotion. The key to getting free from the heathen anxiety (*Bekymring*) of abundance is not to change one's physical and social circumstances (which may seem to the unreflective to be the source of their anxiety) but to change one's way of thinking about one's situation.

But is there not something that is able so to take away from a man riches and abundance that he is deprived of it without becoming a . . . formerly rich man, that he is deprived of it and still is the rich man? Indeed there is such a thing. What power then is this? It is thought [*Tanken*] and the power of thought. (*CD* 30; *SV*ᴵ X 32).

A crucial difference between the emotional life of the heathen and that of the Christian is in the leading thoughts by which they conceptualize their goods: The rich heathen's mind is shaped by "the thought of *possession*, the thought that he owns and possesses this wealth and abundance as *his*." (*CD* 30; *SV*ᴵ X 32 Kierkegaard's italics). The Christian, by contrast, avoids the anxiety of riches and abundance, "bearing in mind [*betænkende*]" (*CD* 29; *SV*ᴵ X 29) that he is a *traveller* through this life, like a man who sits down on benches that are not his, sleeps in hotel rooms that are not his, eats in dining rooms that are not his. The rich Christian is like the heathen in taking joy (*Glæde*) in his possessions, but with the difference that he thinks of those possessions in distinctively Christian terms: as *gifts of his heavenly Father*, and as *resources for doing good for others and serving God* (see *CD* 35–6; *SV*ᴵ X 37–8). To cure the anxiety of highness one must "reform his notions [*forandre sin Forestilling*]" (*CD* 53; *SV*ᴵ X 54).

In another place (*UDVS Gospel of Sufferings*, fifth discourse), Kierkegaard counsels his reader how to experience a distinctively religious joy. This joy is not ordinary, for it takes tribulation as its object. The natural person experiences joy upon *recovering* from an illness, *avoiding* tribulation, and so on, and when hardship comes is more likely to feel sorrow, self-pity, and resentment. But joy in suffering is possible because of the Christian teaching that "tribulation is the way" (that is, it is the normal way to enter the kingdom of God – Acts 14:22, I Thess. 3:3, James 2:2–4). Imagine someone who is crippled for life in an accident. The natural thoughts about this circumstance are that his life is spoiled, that he is confronting an obstacle to fulfillment, that he is unfortunate. But with the help of the thought that tribulation is the way, the disability is seen not as spoiling his life but as enhancing it, not as an obstacle but as a special path, not as a misfortune but as a peculiar sort of blessing.

Religious thoughts are thus the basis for a configuration of emotional responses very different from the "ordinary" or "natural" ones. Where the heathen responds with anxiety, the Christian responds with calm trust; where the heathen becomes resentful and self-pitying, the Christian experiences joy. And these patterns of response, if they become stable dispositions of the personality rather than flashes of feeling tied to very special circumstances (say, formal worship services or the high rhetoric of the religious address) are a significant dimension of the religious virtues. They exemplify proper "existence," "inwardness," "subjectivity," "character," in the normative sense of these words.

In light of these considerations, let us return to Plutarch's saying that "virtue has the passions for its material, reason for its form." Kierkegaard's idea would be that in human beings emotions are shaped (defined, given particular identity) by the "reasons" that can be given for them – that is, by the thoughts in consideration of which the subject feels emotionally as he does. Some of these thoughts are false or unreasonable. For example, a thought may ascribe great importance to things that have little importance, or may misidentify its objects or fail to consider important objects or aspects of objects. Goods may be identified as permanent possessions, sufferings may be identified as unmitigated catastrophes. In this kind of case the resultant passions do not provide the "material" of virtue, but instead, of vice. In other cases, the thoughts are right and reasonable. Ascriptions of normative rationality are, as Kierkegaard never tires to point out, contestable in matters of ethics and religion.[18] But whatever emotion-shaping propositions are taken to be correct will, within a given spiritual outlook, be taken by the adherents of that outlook to be normative, and in that sense reflective of "reason." In the upbuilding discourses from which I am illustrating Kierkegaard's treatment of emotions, certain propositions about possessions, social status, tribulations, and so forth are taken to be true and therefore reflective of reason in the last mentioned sense. When those norms are exemplified in a person's habitual emotional responses, then those responses are the "material" of the virtues.

The reader may wonder how the emotional suffering that *exemplifies* the religious personality, which Johannes Climacus discusses in *Postscript* (385–555; *SV*¹ VII 333–484),[19] relates to the suffering whose *absence* exemplifies the religious personality, which we find discussed in some of the upbuilding discourses. The former suffering is composed of emotions overlapping in type with the emotions that are overcome by the thought that tribulation is the way. For example, frustration, disappointment, and anger may belong to the suffering of the person at the second stage of existential pathos (*CUP* 431–525; *SV*¹ VII 374–458), just as frustration, disappointment and anger are the nonreligious person's characteristic responses to tribulation. But the former exemplify the religious personality while the latter do not, not only because of the different thoughts that shape these different frustrations, disappointments, and angers but also because of the different concerns on which they are based. The religious person suffers as a result of a frustrated desire to relate absolutely to his absolute telos, while the nonreligious person suffering as a cripple suffers from a frustrated desire to function as normal limbs allow. The fact that a person experiences an emotion of a given *type* (say, joy, disappointment, hope, or anger) tells us next to nothing about the individual's character. It begins to do so only if we know what concern the emotion is based on and the patterns of thought that shape it.

The reader may also wonder about the relationship between the concern or concerns on which an emotion is based and the thoughts that shape it. The answer is that the concern belongs to the world of the thoughts, so that the thoughts can impinge on the concern. The concern to relate absolutely to one's absolute telos, for example, can become a conscious commitment only if one has some thought of the absolute telos, and the concept of an absolute end is of course utilized in the thought *I am backsliding from my absolute end* or *I find myself absolutely committed to relative ends* – thoughts that impinge on the concern to relate absolutely to one's absolute telos and provide the shape for such emotions of "religious suffering" (*CUP* 431–525; *SV*¹ VII 374–458) as self-anger and sorrow over one's religious failures. This reference to the "world of the thoughts" that shape an emotion leads us to the first of three implications, found in Kierkegaard's writings, of the fact that emotions depend on thoughts.

(a) I have already quoted Climacus's remark about the sentimental preacher's "jumbled, noisy pathos of all sorts, esthetics, ethics, Religiousness A, and Christianity" (*CUP* 555; *SV*[I] VII 485).[20] The comment suggests that emotions and the traits (virtues and vices) they exemplify are always indexible to one or another existence sphere or "stage." Joy or anxiety, for example, may come in a number of sorts, depending on the sphere-identity of the concerns and thoughts involved. There is aesthetic joy (say, the joy of romantic love, not yet transfigured by a sense of marital duty), ethical joy (say, a joy in some act *as* a fulfillment of duty), Religiousness A joy (say, Socrates' joy in his own independence of the temporal world as he drinks the hemlock) and Christian joy (a joy in being received by Jesus Christ, the God-man). Each existence sphere has its characteristic concerns and interests, as well as its characteristic ways of thinking about the issues of life; and these generate sphere-distinctive versions of pretty much the whole range of emotion types. Episodes of these emotions are distinctive manifestations of the kinds of inwardness or character that belong to each of the spheres.

(b) If emotions depend on thoughts, then they are to some extent within the command of the will. In "A Hearty Longing" (*CD* 259–68; *SV*[I] X 255–68), Kierkegaard talks about what is in effect the active promotion of Christian emotions, especially ones associated with the sacrament of Holy Communion. Longing (*Længsel*) comes and goes like the Holy Spirit, is a gift of God, but moments of longing for the eternal can be exploited to one's spiritual benefit by thinking certain kinds of thoughts, in particular, thoughts about the insecurity of one's finite life and thoughts about one's sinfulness.

Or think of a lily growing on an ancient dunghill out of sight behind a ruined chicken coop.

"It is hard, it is not to be endured, when one is a lily and beautiful as a lily, then to be allotted a place in such a situation, to bloom there in an environment which is as unfavourable as possible, as though expressly calculated to annihilate the impression of one's beauty; no, that is not to be put up with, that is indeed a self-contradiction on the part of the Creator!" So it is we men would likely think and talk, if we were in the situation of the lily, and thereupon we would wither with grief [*Græmmelse*]. But the lily thinks [*tænker*] differently, it thinks thus: "I myself have not been able to determine the situation and the circumstances, and so it is not in the remotest way my affair; that I stand where I stand is God's will." (*CD* 339; *SV*¹ XI 29–30).

Because of its way of thinking, the lily experiences no vexation, no despair; its life expresses perfect obedience. By choosing to think like a lily, someone, a brilliant philosopher, say, consigned to a crushing work load in a second-rate university, may be able to control his frustration and discontent analogously, turning them into calm trust and joy. Kierkegaard is aware that what comes naturally to the lily takes laborious, long-term, and sometimes violent self-discipline for a human being. It is one thing for the philosopher, as an adept with ideas, to think the thought, "God is in control; God is wise; what matters is not that I show my brilliance and have a brilliant effect on the intellectual élite of my generation, but that I submit to his will and find my happiness in that; for there is certainly happiness in that." When we say that, in virtue of their dependency on thoughts, emotions are partially subject to the will, we do not ascribe to Kierkegaard any simplistic identification of thinking and feeling, or any automatic causal connection between them. But it remains the case that, given a certain stage of character cultivation, the subject will be able, sometimes, to choose his emotions by choosing to think about the emotions' objects in one way or another. Not just any philosopher in a second-rate institution can think his way out of the emotions of professional frustration. But one who, through habitual, active obedience to God, has gained the power actually to perceive his world in terms of the thought of God, will often have it within his power to "yield" emotionally to that thought, *or* to its emotional rival. And everybody makes some choices of emotion.

(c) A third implication of the thought-dependency of emotions is that they have a grammar or dialectic that to know is an important part of practical wisdom. Kierkegaard describes himself as a dialectician of existence, and we have seen that this means he is an explorer of possibilities of human character, and that this is in large measure an exploration of possible patterns of emotional responsiveness. The possibility of this wisdom rests directly on the "dialectical" character of emotions, and thus on the dialectical character of the traits that are composed largely of dispositions to those emotions. But in the spirit of Kierkegaard we must distinguish a truly "existential" or practical wisdom from a merely philosophical or "theoretical" wisdom with the same content.[21]

The chief difference between these is in the power or readiness of application ("practice"). The person of merely philosophical wisdom has facility with the concepts in question – for example, is able to diagnose the anxiety of poverty, talk coherently about the cure of it, explain the feelings of people under its grip, and so forth (in other words, has the knowledge of a competent therapist) – but this knowledge does not make much difference in his own life. He himself may be in the grip of one of the anxieties of the heathen and, committed to the truth of Kierkegaard's account of this anxiety, able to diagnose it in himself and other people, but he does not put this knowledge to the practical work of relieving his own anxiety and improving his character. Instead, he lectures on the topic or writes articles.

VII. EMOTIONS AS ASPECT PERCEPTIONS

Following the theme of the bird, which is ignorant of its poverty or its abundance, as the case may be, Kierkegaard depicts the Christian, too, as "ignorant" of his earthly poverty or his earthly riches, as the case may be (*CD* 35; *SV*¹ X 37). In the human case, "ignorant" (*uvidende*) is not quite the right word. A highly developed Christian does typically know about his poverty or abundance. It would be better to say that riches and poverty are not salient for the Christian; he is not absorbed by them. Instead, he is absorbed by God and his kingdom, hungers and thirsts for righteousness, labors and is heavy laden under the burden of his sin; these are the issues that concern him, the principles of saliency in his attention. Such concerns and saliencies are less bases of knowledge and ignorance than of perception and imperception of a certain sort. Particular emotions in which the concerns of the poor and rich heathen come out are anxiety (*Bekymring*) for what they will eat and put on, and anxiety to retain what they have, respectively. In these anxieties they do not merely "know" that they lack or have wealth, but are "impressed" with this fact with a perception-like immediacy. They are "in touch" with their poverty or wealth; they "feel" it. While the poor and rich Christian *know about* their poverty or wealth, they are not *impressed with* their condition.

While emotions are shaped by thoughts, the fact that they focus specific kinds of features of the situations they are about, and do so in terms of the concerns on which they are based, makes them as much like perceptions as like *mere* thoughts. One is reminded of Wittgenstein's comment (about some experiences that have a much more salient *sense* perceptual aspect than the present cases) that "the flashing of an aspect on us seems half visual experience, half thought."[22] That emotions are impressions of the situations they are about in terms of the situations' personal importance qualifies emotions as mental states of central importance for existence (subjectivity, inwardness, character). Not only are they expressions of the individual's concerns and ways of conceptualizing issues of importance to him or her; they are also immediate, though in the case of ethical and spiritual emotions, theirs is a "second" or "new" immediacy (*SLW* 162; *SV*¹ VI 155). It is this immediacy or perceptual quality that distinguishes an emotion from the mere thought or belief that "such-and-such is so-and-so, and it is very important that it is so-and-so." It is this perception that fails to be achieved in cases where a person tries to change his emotion by changing his way of thinking about something, but fails. However assiduously he may rehearse to himself the thought that, say, it is more important to serve God gladly in Fort Hays than to be showered with fame and prestige in New Haven, and no matter how sincerely he may believe this, the rival view of things keeps *impressing* him. The unhealthy thought, rather than the healthy one, shapes the perceptions of his heart. It is the spiritual analog of a sense-perceptual illusion. No matter how convinced one may be that the two lines of the Mueller-Lyer illusion are of equal length, for most people the one continues to *look* longer than the other.

In speaking of emotional change, Kierkegaard frequently uses heavily perceptual imagery. For example,

[A] believer is . . . a blind man, his eyes are blinded by the splendour of the all which he gains, he cannot see anything of the all wherein the world has its life and its pleasure, he can see nothing of this all because he has seen that it is nothing. . . . But a believer is likewise a deaf man, his ears echo with the glory of the all which he gains, he can hear nothing of the all wherein the world has its life and its pleasure. (*CD* 152; *SV*¹ X 150)

The worldly person and the spiritual person differ in what they "notice," what they "look at." The spiritual person "looks" and "sees" using religious thoughts, such as that *what one loses temporally one gains eternally.*

. . . he who in truth would save his soul looks at [*seer paa*] that which should be looked at, and precisely by looking at that he discovers [*opdager*] at the same time the joy of it that what one loses temporally one gains eternally. Ah, and as the severity of the teacher is sometimes necessary, not to punish inattention, but to punish attention, to compel the pupil to look at that which should be looked at, instead of sitting abstractedly and being lured to look at all sorts of things – so must the fear of perdition help the sufferer to look at that which should be looked at, and thereby help him to discover the joy. (*CD* 147; *SV*¹ X 145)

To someone who doubts that joy is to be found in the thought that the weaker you become, the stronger does God become in you, Kierkegaard answers that "as in all these discourses, everything depends on how the situation is viewed [*sees*]." It depends on whether the thought is used in such a way that the beauty in the situation is made perceptible, striking. To experience the joy is to see the situation in its "[more] joyful aspect" (*glædeligere Side*). To "stare fixedly upon" (*stirre paa*) one's own weakness is to be "despondent, low-spirited, perhaps in despair." If the persecuted one "fix[es] his gaze on" (*stirre paa*) his oppressors' strength rather than on God's sustaining of him, "it is merely an error of vision [*Feilsyn*] on the part of the sufferer" (*CD* 131; *SV*¹ X 131).

For Kierkegaard the thoughts that enter into and shape the life of an individual in a "stage" are not mere thoughts. It is, after all, not much trouble to think after Kierkegaard the thoughts that he explores in his upbuilding discourses and other writings. Any intelligent and moderately patient reader can do that. But it is quite another thing to "exist" in these thoughts, for them to become the thoughts that shape one's character. I am suggesting that for Kierkegaard, so to "exist" is in large part for those thoughts to shape one's emotional responses, and that such responses, in turn, are a kind of immediate impression of the way things are (the way God is, the way oneself is, the way the world is), the most natural metaphor for which is sense perception.

VIII. FEELINGS WITHOUT DEPTH

The reader, even if sympathetic to the general direction of my argument, may have followed it with a certain uneasiness whose magnetic center is the word "emotion." My argument is that for Kierkegaard emotions, like actions, are indicators of character, inwardness, subjectivity, and existential depth; nay, "indicator" and "symptom" are words too weak for the relation between emotion and character. It is as though the person at his or her core is not just manifested in emotion, but is somehow actualized or made present in a special way in emotion, just as he is actualized or made present in his action. In emotion and passionate action the *person* is actually present in a way that he or she is not when sleeping, day-dreaming, calculating in a "disengaged" and disinterested way, and so forth. It is something like this that Kierkegaard is trying to capture with his innovative use of the word "existence": people who lack essential passion and passionate action are not quite "all there" as persons. We could also say, as I have argued here, that they are without character: they are mushy, inchoate, indefinite, shallow things. And I have argued that Kierkegaard's concern with character, and his construal of it in terms of emotion-dispositions, is a classical theme, found most notably in Aristotle and his successors.

But there is in Kierkegaard's writings a subtheme concerning emotion and character (existence, subjectivity, selfhood) that is less Aristotelian. It is a *suspicion* of emotion, in particular cases, as artificial and disconnected from the self, one that parallels the suspicion I noted in the section on practical wisdom, where we saw that Kierkegaard is more alert than Aristotle to the possibility that reflection (deliberation) may lose its connection with character and in this idling condition undermine it.

If the reader is uneasy with the word "emotion," perhaps it is because what we call emotion in contemporary English seems to be something superficial, disconnected from the depths of personality. Emotion is a symptom of moral and spiritual immaturity. Thus it may be thought that whatever mental states exemplify moral character, it is better not to call them emotions. The truth is that in contemporary English we use "emotion" sometimes to indicate shallowness and sometimes to indicate depth. We may dismiss a political speech or sermon as "mindless, merely appealing to the emotions" and dismiss persons, with a moral sort of dismissal, by saying that they are "emotional." "Emotional" people and people who are moved by "emotional" speeches are thought to lack a certain kind of integrity, solidity, objectivity, and moral intelligence; their decisions and judgments are not to be trusted because of the superficial and mindless way they are arrived at. On the other hand, we may speak of moral novels like Alan Paton's *Cry, the Beloved Country* or George Eliot's *The Mill on the Floss* as written with emotion and as evoking emotion in their readers; and the sadness, indignation, compassion, admiration, and joy expressed in and evoked by various scenes of these novels may be anything but superficial, soft and stupid, or unconnected with moral character and moral intelligence. So the honor of "emotion" varies with context. But we must admit that a significant domain of the word's usage does not commend it for the suggestions of moral and spiritual depth characteristic of Kierkegaard's usual usage of "passion" (*Lidenskab*) and "pathos" (*Pathos*).

Kierkegaard is well aware of the possibility of emotions or emotion-like states of mind that are morally and spiritually shallow. In *Postscript*, Johannes Climacus distinguishes existential pathos, which expresses character (subjectivity, inwardness, existence), from aesthetic pathos, which is the superficial kind.[23] Here, however, I want to focus on a somewhat different emotion-related concept in Kierkegaard's writings, that of feeling (*Følelse*). "*Følelse*" is, like its English counterpart, a word of ranging use. It can refer to a physical sensation (*SUD* 31; *SV*¹ XI 144), say of heat or cold (pleasant or unpleasant or neither). It can refer to a sort of intuitive awareness or judgment – for example, a feeling that something is about to happen or that someone is upset – or to the sensitivity or power of intuition by which such judgments are made. It translates some senses of "sense" – for example, a sense of duty, a sense of one's own lowliness (*CD* 56; *SV*¹ X 57). In one important use it translates the English "emotion" or "feeling" (where "emotion" and "feeling" are more or less interchangeable). Thus Johannes Climacus speaks of his mixed feelings of admiration and despondency as he contemplated the work of historical scholars (*CUP* 11; *SV*¹ VII 3). Sometimes "*Følelse*" is used to commend emotion as morally and spiritually important, as "*Lidenskab*" and "*Pathos*" typically are used (see *CUP* 350; *SV*¹ VII 303. *CD* 69; *SV*¹ X 69–70), but more often it occurs in passages where Kierkegaard is voicing criticisms and suspicions of emotions (or rather, their simulacra) – pointing out that these can be morally and spiritually superficial and/or deceptive.

As I have said, "*Følelse*" is sometimes an equivalent of our word "emotion," just as our word "feeling" sometimes is. But "*Følelse*," like "feeling," strongly suggests the *awareness* of something (very often, but not always, of a state of the self), in a way that other words for emotion, such as *"Lidenskab," "Pathos," "Grebedhed," "Bevægthed,"* and *"Rørelse"* do not. An emotional *Følelse*, one might say, is a perception of oneself as in one emotional state or another. Thus it can be veridical, or in one degree or another inaccurate, artificial, or misleading. In this way emotional *Følelse* is like other kinds of perception: it can be *experientially* very real, while being quite unreliable as a representation of its object (the self). Note that we are not always *deceived* by our inaccurate perceptions; sometimes we know that we are not seeing things as they are. The same is true of the emotional feelings that Kierkegaard subjects to suspicion and criticism: sometimes we are deceived or half-deceived by them, and sometimes we are clearly aware that they are not good indicators of our character.

The chief aesthete of *Either/Or* is not much deceived about himself by his feelings; at least he is not deceived about their artificiality and lack of connection to a solid self. By the strategy of poetization, he intentionally turns his emotional states into "productions" from which he dissociates himself by a distance of aesthetic contemplation. Anti-Climacus, the pseudonymous author of *The Sickness unto Death*, comments about the consequences for character or selfhood:

When feeling [*Følelsen*] becomes fantastic in this way, the self becomes only more and more volatilized and finally comes to be a kind of abstract sentimentality [*Følsomhed*] that inhumanly belongs to no human being but inhumanly combines sentimentally [*følsomt*], as it were, with some abstract fate – for example, humanity *in abstracto*. Just as the rheumatic is not master of his physical sensations [*sandselige Følelse*], which are so subject to the wind and weather that he involuntarily detects any change in the weather etc., so also the person whose feeling [*Følelse*] has become fantastic is in a way infinitized, but not in such a manner that he becomes more and more himself, for he loses himself more and more. (*SUD* 31; *SV*¹ XI 144)

If emotions when genuine exemplify character, it is not surprising that a vaporized self should be exemplified in fantastic, dissociated emotions. The extreme of personality development to which Anti-Climacus refers is that of someone who feels emotions only when they are not his own. He feels emotions only in the theater, or when reading novels, or when thinking about his own remote childhood (or somebody else's), or when watching a documentary about suffering persons half way around the globe. Or if he does feel compassion for people in his immediate surroundings, this feeling too is "fantastic," that is, it works by converting the present individual into a merely poetic, merely "possible" reality, with respect to which no action needs to be taken. Dostoevski's underground man is an example of what Anti-Climacus has in mind:

And do you know, gentlemen, what was the chief point about my spitefulness? Well, the whole point of it, I mean, the whole nasty, disgusting part of it was that all the time I was shamefully conscious – even at the moments of my greatest exasperation – that I was not at all a spiteful or even an exasperated man, but that I was merely frightening sparrows for no reason in the world, and being hugely amused by this pastime.[24]

Throughout Dostoevski's story, this psychological wreck has disconnected emotions, the artificiality of which he nearly always recognizes. He, like the aesthete, experiences his most satisfying emotions in relation to objects he reads about in books, and he experiences the out-of-controlness of emotion suggested by Anti-Climacus's comparison with the rheumatic's physical sensations and shown in some of the Diapsalmata of *Either/Or* (see, e.g., *EO* I 23, 24, 31–2, 34; *SV*[I] I 8, 16, 18–19). (For a rich discussion of dissociated *Følelse* in which self-deception figures more prominently, see *UDVS* 68–72; *SV*[I] VIII 171–3).[25]

IX. DISSOCIATION FROM EMOTIONS

I have argued that for Kierkegaard subjectivity is character and character is in large part constituted of dispositions to emotion. This classical idea is that, by and large, if you want to know what "stage" a person is existing in – that is, what moral species of traits constitute his or her deepest personality – one of the best indicators is the pattern of the individual's emotions. In the preceding section, however, I noted Kierkegaard's rather nonclassical insight that emotions (not just their characteristic behavior) can be faked, thus being potentially misleading indicators of character. And I characterized their fakeness by speaking of their dissociation from the self and its character-constituting concerns. Dissociated *Følelse* is feeling that is not rooted in passion as interest or concern. But Kierkegaard is also aware of a different kind of dissociation from emotion, this time from emotion that is not fake, but is morally and spiritually repugnant to its subject. Here the emotion is rooted in passion and therefore expressive of character, but the subject takes his own passion to be improper and his character distorted. This, too, is a non-Aristotelian insight, though it is present in the ancient world, notably in Romans 7 and Augustine's *Confessions*.

Aristotle so identifies character with emotional response patterns that he denies continence (self-mastery) to be a virtue.[26] True, to be the sort of person who struggles against his own vicious emotions is, for Aristotle, better than being complacent about them (intemperance). But the power of self-dissociation from one's vicious emotional responses does not count as a virtue, as it does in Christianity (see Gal. 5:23). By contrast with Aristotle, Kierkegaard does not flatly identify being a Christian, say, with being disposed to experience Christian emotions and being undisposed to experience the contrary, heathen ones.

The ungodliness does not consist after all in being anxious, though certainly it is not Christian to be so; the ungodliness consists in not being willing to know anything else, and not being willing to know that this anxiety is sinful. (CD 23; SV¹ X 25)

In Kierkegaard's view, a person's moral identity is not flatly identified with his or her character, in the sense of emotional dispositions. The reason is that, in the always incomplete world of temporal existence, persons who are engaged in the more strenuous "stages" of spiritual development will always find in themselves vestiges of contrary character. An example would be one of the heathen anxieties that Kierkegaard delineates. As he suggests in the quotation, the moral identity of the individual is now not simply a question of what emotions he experiences but of *how* he experiences them. The heathen lives in his heathen anxiety; he is, by default or perhaps even by explicit commitment, identified with it. But the Christian who experiences heathen anxiety says to himself, as it were, "that is not the real me." And *that* dissociation – a dissociation from his own character – is in the interest of Christian spiritual growth.

Yet even when the Christian dissociates himself from his own character, he does not do so without character. He is instead a conflict of two characters, one with which he identifies and another from which he dissociates. Typically (though not necessarily in every instance) he will have a secondary emotional response to the emotion – a Christian sadness or alarm about his heathen anxiety – and it is *that* emotion that exemplifies his Christian character and partially embodies his dissociation from the heathen character expressed in his anxiety.

The concept of an emotion is central to Kierkegaard's thinking about subjectivity, inwardness, existence, and character. I have argued that, as in the classical conception, character is for Kierkegaard constituted in large part of dispositions to emotion – good character (virtues) being dispositions to proper emotions, and bad character (vices) dispositions to improper ones. Human emotions incorporate thought as well as interest or concern for what the thought is about, thoughts that may be right or wrong. Thus to exist well is to incorporate right thinking into a pathos-filled life. As Plutarch comments, summarizing classical moral psychology, "Ethical virtue has the passions for its material, reason for its form." Kierkegaard differs from Aristotle, however, in two suspicions: He is more attentive than Aristotle is to the fact that reflection, when separated from passion, can undermine it further and become an enemy of the virtues; and he is aware that emotions, or their simulacra, can likewise be dissociated from selfhood in such a way that the self is "volatilized." He also affirms, with the Christian tradition and against Aristotle, that it can be virtuous to dissociate oneself from aspects of one's character.

NOTES

I am grateful to the Pew Charitable Trusts for financial support that enabled me to write this essay, and to C. Stephen Evans, Alastair Hannay, and Gordon Marino for suggestions that led to improvements of it.

1 Printed without page numbers at the end of *Concluding Unscientific Postscript.* "First and Last Explanation," at the end; *SV*¹ VII 548.

2 I discuss Alasdair MacIntyre's interpretation of Kierkegaard as an advocate of radical choice in "Kierkegaard, Wittgenstein, and a Method of 'Virtue Ethics,'" in *Kierkegaard in Post/Modernity*, ed. Martin Matuštík and Merold Westphal (Bloomington and Indianapolis: Indiana University Press, 1995). See pp. 148–51.

3 "Personality" (*Personlighed*) is used fairly frequently in Judge William's

second letter in *Either/Or* II; "self" (*Selv*) dominates in *The Sickness unto Death* and is also used in *Either/Or* II. "Subjectivity," "existence," "inwardness," "pathos" (*Pathos*), and "passion" (*Lidenskab*) are all richly employed in *Postscript*. "Character" (*Charakteer*) occurs most often, to my knowledge, in *Two Ages*. "Individual" (*Enkelte, Individet*), another term with strong characterological implications, occurs frequently in many of Kierkegaard's works.

4 I have explored these matters in "Thinking Subjectively," *International Journal for Philosophy of Religion* 11 (1980): 71–92.

5 See *Nicomachean Ethics* 1106b16–23.

6 The Hongs give the reference as Plutarch's *Moralia* 440 (Loeb VI 18–19).

7 See also Judge William's discussion of ethical continuity in the self or personality and its connection with choice, *EO* II 258–63; *SV*¹ II 232–6.

8 I have explored the latter connection in "Passion and Reflection," in *International Kierkegaard Commentary: Two Ages*, ed. Robert L. Perkins (Macon, Ga: Mercer University Press, 1984), pp., 87–106.

9 *Nicomachean Ethics* 1107a1; 1113a12, 1139a32–35. Translation is by David Ross (Oxford University Press, 1980).

10 As Aristotle remarks, we pursue philosophical ethics not just to know something but to become good people (1103b27). Aristotle and Kierkegaard are similar in the degree to which they think conceptual insight can effect changes in character. Aristotle holds that only people whose desires and habits of action are ethically well formed will benefit from ethical knowledge (1095a5–10), and that therefore one's early upbringing is crucial (making "all the difference") to the formation of character (1103b7–25). Kierkegaard, in discussing the personality deficiencies of Magister Adler, comments that in former times a high value was placed on the upbringing (*Opdragelse*) of children, "understanding by this a harmonious development of that which was to support the various gifts and talents and peculiarities of personality ethically in the direction of character [*Charakteer*]," whereas in his own time the emphasis is on instruction (*Underviisning*) in such subjects as "languages, mathematics, religion, etc." (*OAR* 180; *Pap.* VII² B 235 p. 220). On the other side, we have seen that Kierkegaard, like Aristotle, takes reflection to be essential to character and that he cannot have thought that adult reflection has no value at all in the moral and spiritual life, since he presumably believes that his own writings may have some salutary effect on their readers.

11 *Nicomachean Ethics* 1139b5.

12 See my "What An Emotion Is: A Sketch," *Philosophical Review* 97 (1988): 183–209.

13 "Concern" seems to me the best generic word for designating the inter-

est or yearning that is basic to emotions. Other words, such as "interest," "passion," "yearning," "attachment," seem to have more specialized connections. Kierkegaard sometimes uses "concern" as a substitute for "passion." See *CUP* 201; *SV*¹ VII 168, where Climacus speaks of a person as being "infinitely concerned" (*uendelig bekymret*).

14 See Martha C. Nussbaum, *The Therapy of Desire* (Princeton: Princeton University Press, 1994). Kierkegaard is more nearly Aristotelian than he is like any of the other Hellenistic schools on the issue of emotions and virtues, since he has a strong sense of *proper*, as well as improper emotions; while the other schools were all, in their various ways, suspicious of emotions and intent on limiting or extirpating them *as such*. This contrast is vividly brought out in Nussbaum's book.

15 For a discussion of Johannes Climacus's use of "pathos" (*Pathos*) and "pathos-filled" (*Pathetisk*), as well as more discussion of "*Lidenskab*," see my "Dialectical Emotions and the Virtue of Faith," in *International Kierkegaard Commentary*: Concluding Unscientific Postscript, ed. Robert L. Perkins (Macon, Ga.: Mercer University Press, 1997).

16 The second division of chapter IV of *Postscript* is divided into two parts – A: Pathos, and B: Dialectic. Since the A also corresponds to Religiousness A (a generic or "Socratic" religiousness) and B corresponds to Religiousness B (Christianity), one might get the impression that Christianity is dialectical and Religiousness A is not. This would be a false impression, for as Climacus remarks, "Religiousness A is by no means undialectical, but it is not paradoxically dialectical" (556; *SV*¹ VII 485). In the present subsection I am pointing out that all the stages, insofar as they are existence-stages, are pathetic-dialectic, since they are all characterized by distinctive patterns of emotional response shaped by characteristic ways of thinking.

17 The propositional characteristic of emotions is especially evident in the series of discourses "Joyful Notes in the Strife of Suffering" (*CD*) in which each of the seven discourses is devoted to a consideration – e.g., "that what thou dost lose temporally thou dost gain eternally" (fifth discourse) – which when understood and taken to heart yields distinctively Christian joy.

18 For deft discussions of Kierkegaard's concept of reason, see Merold Westphal's *Kierkegaard's Critique of Reason and Society* (University Park: The Pennsylvania State University Press, 1991) and C. Stephen Evan's *Passionate Reason: Making Sense of Kierkegaard's Philosophical Fragments* (Bloomington and Indianapolis: Indiana University Press, 1992).

19 For a short discussion of these emotions, see my "Dialectical Emotions and the Virtue of Faith."

20 See Kierkegaard's reference to "emotion [*Grebedheden*] [that] is of a spe-

cific, qualitative sort, the Christian emotion [*christelige Grebedhed*]," which is tied to a language that results from "skill and schooling in the definition of Christian concepts" (*OAR* 164; *Pap.* VII² B 235 p. 201).

21 For more developed discussions of the nature of such wisdom, see my "Kierkegaard, Wittgenstein, and a Method of 'Virtue Ethics'" and "The Philosopher as Sage," *Journal of Religious Ethics* 22, 2 (Fall 1994): 409–31.

22 *Philosophical Investigations*, trans. G. E. M. Anscombe (New York: Macmillan, 1953), 2:197.

23 See *CUP* 387–8; *SV*¹ VII 335–6. I discuss aesthetic pathos in "Dialectical Emotions and the Virtue of Faith."

24 *Notes from the Underground*, trans. David Magarshack (New York: Modern Library, n.d.), pp. 108–9. It is also interesting that the underground man several times contrasts his own personality constitution with that of "the man of action and character."

25 I have discussed the nature and origin of nonveridical feelings of emotion and presented criteria of veridicality in "Feeling One's Emotions and Knowing Oneself," *Philosophical Studies* 77 (1995): 319–38.

26 *Nicomachean Ethics* 1145a17.

8 Faith and the Kierkegaardian leap

In a journal entry from 1842–3 Kierkegaard asks rhetorically, "Can there be a transition from quantitative qualification to a qualitative one without a leap? And does not the whole of life rest in that" (*JP* I 110)? He thus strikingly and unambiguously sets the leap in perspective – the leap, the form of qualitative transformation, lies at the heart of all life. Later in his journals this master of polemic against the theoretical makes two intriguing references to what he calls "my theory of the leap" (*JP* III 20). Whether or not he has a theory as such, the concept of a leap is appropriately associated with the name of Kierkegaard, since the leap is a structural element that winds its way throughout his whole authorship: it informs his various accounts of the peculiar character of transitions between radically different ways of life as well as his challenge to the philosophical and romantic accounts of such transitions that were influential in his day.

The popular association of the leap with Kierkegaard is often couched in terms of the leap *of* faith. It is worthwhile to be reminded, however, and interesting to note, that Kierkegaard never uses any Danish equivalent of the English phrase "leap of faith," a phrase that involves a circularity insofar as it seems to imply that the leap is made *by* faith.[1] He does, however, clearly and often refer to the concept of a leap (*Spring*) and to the concept of a transition (*Overgang*) that is qualitative (*qvalitativ*) or, alternatively, a *meta-basis eis allo genos* (transition from one genus to another); moreover, he clearly and often refers to such a qualitative transition to religiousness and to faith in an eminent sense, namely, Christian religiousness. Thus, even if the concept of a leap of (made by) faith is foreign to the terminology of Kierkegaard, the concept of a leap *to* faith remains cen-

tral to his writings. Since the popular understanding of the leap usually derives from the works Kierkegaard wrote under the pseudonym
of Johannes Climacus, I want to explore what is at stake in Climacus's affirmation of the leap required for faith. Although Kierkegaard's references to the leap are not limited to his Climacus
writings, such an exploration will illuminate a significant part of
Kierkegaard's contribution to the study of religious transformations.

I. THE LEAP: GENERIC AND RELIGIOUS

Climacus introduces the leap in *Philosophical Fragments*, the "pam-
phlet" intended to present an alternative to the Socratic model of
recollection as the way to attaining truth; this alternative, drawing
out the radical implications of the unknown, illuminates the notion
of the genuinely other or absolutely different (*PF* 5, 44–7). Any attempt to learn about the leap must, of course, take account of
Climacus's self-assessment of *Fragments:* the "most mistaken impression one can have of it" is that it is "didactic." On the contrary,
it is, he notes, riddled with irony, parody, and satire (*CUP* 275n). It is
indirect communication; we will not, therefore, obtain a theory of
the leap as a piece of information or what Climacus and Kierkegaard
derisively call a "result" (65, 73, 78, 242). But the imaginative strategy and textual crafting of an indirect communication *can* communicate; insofar as indirect communication can impart or call forth or
communicate an ability (*JP* I 281–2, 284, 303–8), it can communicate
a concept. Still, any attempt to identify Climacus's leap with
Kierkegaard's understanding must take into account the fact that
Climacus confesses himself not to be a Christian (*CUP* 451, 466,
501, 511, 557, 597, 617, 619).

Although the notion of a leap is implicit throughout *Fragments*,
it only receives explicit treatment in the third version of the non-
Socratic story. The first three chapters of *Fragments* can be seen as
an example of repetition, of spiraling action in which we circle back
to what seems to be the same place, yet with at least one different
coordinate. The presentation of a genuine alternative to the Socratic
model of the way things are is offered first in the speculative abstractness of a "Thought-Project" (Chapter I), with the focus on
teachers, conditions, and truth, and is then taken up in a "Poetical
Venture" (Chapter II), which explores the concreteness of lovers,

suffering, and lilies. Climacus then begins a third version (in Chapter III) of the non-Socratic alternative, elaborating the theme of the unknown through metaphysical musings on paradox, from Socratic to absolute; the emphasis on the passion of thought and the analogy with erotic love echo both of the earlier dimensions of the story (as does the subtitle, "Metaphysical Caprice"). It is here that Climacus brings in the leap as part of the discussion of how the limits of the theoretical require and exemplify the notion of a qualitative transition.

Before examining this in detail, it is worth noting that despite its relatively underplayed role in *Fragments*, the importance of the discussion of the leap is made clear by Climacus's further treatment of it in *Concluding Unscientific Postscript*. In this work, which he says is a "renewed attempt," a "new approach to the issue of *Fragments*," he focuses at greater length and with much more explicitness on the category of leap (*CUP* 17). Of this postscript to *Fragments*, which is the heart of Climacus's attempt to address "the qualitative transition of the leap from unbeliever to believer" [*Springets qvalitative Overgang fra Ikke-Troende til Troende*], he says that "what has been intimated here [in the introduction] has been emphasized in *Fragments* frequently enough, namely, that there is no direct and immediate transition to Christianity" (12, 49).

While the impossibility of a direct and immediate transition may have been emphasized in *Fragments*, the character of the transition that occurs receives very little explicit attention there. We first learn about the leap in the context of Climacus's assessment of the all-too-common attempt to "demonstrate the existence of God," and there it is tied to the concept of letting go. Climacus highlights the limits of demonstration when he remarks that what passes for demonstration is usually only a case of developing "the definition of a concept" (*PF* 40). But he includes under demonstration inductive as well as deductive reasoning, teleological as well as ontological arguments, calling attention to the way in which the premises we accept in order to begin (as Socrates knew) must already be infused with the ideas with which we conclude (44). Climacus stresses not only the conditional nature of such reasoning, but also its tentativeness: real dependence implies real vulnerability, living "*in suspenso* lest something so terrible happen that my fragment of demonstration would be ruined" (42). He goes on to ask "how does the existence of the god emerge from the demonstration?" – in the same breath he answers: "I have to let go of it" (42). That is, demonstration falls loose at both ends – at its beginning, where premises must be assumed, and at its conclusion, where letting go must occur, accepting the whole of premises and process as good enough. "So long as I am holding on to the demonstration (that is, continue to be the one who is demonstrating), the existence does not emerge, if for no other reason than that I am in the process of demonstrating it, but when I let go of the demonstration, the existence is there." Insofar as I reach existence at all, I leap: "Yet this letting go, even that is surely something; it is, after all, *meine Zuthat* [my contribution]. Does it not have to be taken into account, this diminutive moment, however, brief it is – it does not have to be long, because it is a *leap*" (43).

Climacus reinforces his claim that the moment of the leap is, however diminutive, a crucial or decisive moment with an anecdote about Carneades's desire to "grasp the point at which the quality [in the syllogistic chain of a sorites] actually made its appearance"; Chrysippus's teasing response to Carneades foreshadows Climacus's later caricature of the attempt to disguise the discontinuity of a qualitative transition. What becomes clear is that the direct and immediate transition he rejects is precisely not the qualitative transition at issue. Rather, "direct and immediate" refers to the cumulative, automatic, Hegelian type of transition in which something passively "flops over" by "immanental necessity" (*JP* III 21); the immediacy that is rejected is that involved in the Hegelian view that "the one standpoint on its own necessarily determine[s] its transition over to another" (*CUP* 295).

Aligning the leap, as Climacus does, with letting go already hints at the leap as something curiously active yet passive. Climacus's references to the activity of letting go emphasize the active dimension of the leap that can easily be forgotten in our tendency to see demonstration as compelling us to assent, but in the context of evidence and judgments of adequacy, they belie the notion of leap as a one-sidedly volitional activity.

Reference to the *reservatio finalis*, "that the existence itself emerges from the demonstration by a leap," ends Climacus's brief explicit treatment of the leap. Later on, in the interlude's discussion of "belief," we are given two relevant pieces of information: (a) the reference to the "*metabasis eis allo genos* [transition from one genus to another]" that occurs "if that which comes into existence does not in itself remain unchanged in the change of coming into existence" (*PF* 73), and (*b*) the claims that "belief is not a knowledge but an act of freedom, an expression of will" (83) and that neither belief nor doubt is a "cognitive act," for "they are opposite passions" (84). All this information is sandwiched in between two chapters that indirectly refer to a leap in terms of the incommensurability between the historical and the faith response; Climacus later reminds us that this was *Fragments'* presentation of the "impossibility of becoming contemporary (in an immediate sense) with a paradox" (*CUP* 96n).

The quasi-sequel[2] to *Fragments* found in *Concluding Unscientific Postscript* takes up the substance of the leap in its rejection of cumulative, quantitative transitions to the religious, insisting that "there is *no approximation*, that *wanting to quantify oneself into faith*" is a "misunderstanding, a *delusion* (*CUP* 11). The claim made early on that the one in faith has "made the qualitative transition of the leap from unbeliever to believer" is carried through to the uncompromising conclusion that "there is no direct transition to becoming a Christian, but, on the contrary, this is the qualitative leap" (12, 381). An early footnote reference to the leap from essence to existence (39n) echoes *Fragments'* discussion of the relation between concept (or thought) and existence, but Climacus's most elaborate treatment of the leap is found in Section 1 of Part 2, entitled "Something about Lessing" (*CUP* 63–125). Here Climacus develops his view of subjectivity by reference to G. E. Lessing, the eighteenth-century German dramatist and critic whose claims about the incommensurability (the "broad ugly ditch") between truths of history and truths of reason would have been familiar to his readers.

Despite the fact that Lessing is clearly singled out for attention, it has been suggested that perhaps Kierkegaard's understanding of the leap owes more to Kant than to Lessing.[3] However surprising this might at first appear, there is a *prima facie* plausibility about it. The leap is central to Kierkegaard's general reaction against Hegelian system and method: he writes that "Hegel has never done justice to the category of transition" (*JP* I 110) and Climacus insists that "the leap is the most decisive protest against the inverse operation of the [Hegelian] method" (*CUP* 105). Since Kierkegaard was reacting against Hegel and Hegel was himself reacting against Kant, it should not surprise us that there would be a kinship between Kierkegaard and Kant. It is true that both Kant and Kierkegaard affirm the limits of theoretical reason, distinguish between faith and knowledge, and claim that religious faith does not issue from the sphere of objectivity; such congeniality in making "room for faith" is indeed significant and deserves to be explored further.[4] Still, it is Lessing, rather than Kant, to whom Kierkegaard through Climacus makes detailed and explicit reference in developing the notion of the leap, and that discussion should provide the most direct source of information on what is at stake in Climacus's leap.[5]

The "something about Lessing" to which our attention is called by Climacus begins with an expression of gratitude. Despite the fact that irony is piled on irony in these chapters, with Climacus commenting ironically on the ironic Lessing, jesting with the jester Lessing,[6] the acknowledgment of gratitude is sincere: Lessing

did not allow himself to be tricked into becoming world-historical or systematic with regard to the religious, but he understood, and knew how to maintain that the religious pertained to Lessing and Lessing alone, just as it pertains to every human being in the same way, understood that he had infinitely to do with God, but nothing, nothing to do directly with any human being. (*CUP* 65)

Climacus concedes the difficulty in determining Lessing's position, but it is obviously with tongue in cheek that he complains that it is "disturbing not to be able to abandon oneself to Lessing with the same confidence as to the presentation of those who with genuine speculative earnestness make everything out of one thing and thus have everything finished" (*CUP* 91). Lessing's methodological or pedagogical commitments are inconsistent with direct communication (65, 67, 69). Lessing's preferred status as an enigma is a function of his wanting "to make everyone free in relation to him" (72) and of his reluctance to be "world-historically butchered, salted, and packed in a paragraph" (107) – the communication of subjectivity can neither be appealed to or made determinate (66–8). The difficulty in pinning Lessing down seems to stem from his appreciation of the isolation of the God-relationship and the consequent relevance of indirect communication and double-reflection – thus, Climacus affirms a significant agreement between his own position and the one he attributes (albeit hesitantly) to Lessing (72).

Climacus alludes to Lessing's style somewhat haughtily as a "mixture of jest and earnestness that makes it impossible for a third person to know definitely which is which – unless the third person knows it by himself" (*CUP* 69). Nonetheless, Climacus himself admittedly speaks in earnestness and jest, and allows that even if (or perhaps when) a jest is "explicit," "the remark itself need not therefore be merely jest" (104). Referring to Socrates, he hints that jesting "may also be the highest earnestness, and the speaker, while jesting with someone, may be in the presence of the god" (88); extending this to the preeminently religious, he intriguingly suggests that the "unity of jest and earnestness" is the point at which "all Christian categories are situated" (104).

Climacus explores the depth of his debt of gratitude to Lessing in relation to two "possible theses" by Lessing – theses that affirm subjective existence, indirect communication, and striving or becoming. He then turns to two "actual theses" by Lessing, the subject of the first of which (the "broad ugly ditch") can be "traced more definitely to Lessing" (*CUP* 93).[7] Here the agreement is more explicit: "Lessing opposes what I would call quantifying oneself into a qualitative decision" (95); the heart of their agreement lies in their common appreciation of the qualitativeness of the shift necessary, for Lessing understands "the incommensurability between a historical truth and an eternal decision" (98). Indeed, for both thinkers "the transition whereby something historical and the relation to this becomes decisive for an eternal happiness is a *metabasis eis allo genos* [shifting from one genus to another]"; clarifying the latter point, Climacus immediately adds that "Lessing even says that if it is not that, then I do not know what Aristotle has understood by it" (98). Attending to the very word Lessing uses (*der Sprung*) and appreciating the very expression Lessing borrows from Aristotle (*metabasis eis allo genos*), Climacus examines what Lessing rightly understood about the leap – that it is an act of isolation and that there is no possible mitigation. He explores Lessing's references to the broadness of the ditch and the earnestness of the leap to make us aware, as perhaps Lessing himself was, of the all-or-nothing character of the leap. Lessing, Climacus concludes, "perceives very well that the leap, as decisive, is qualitatively dialectical and permits no approximating transition" (103).

Thus, although Lessing obscured his understanding of the leap by employing it within the "illusory distinction between contemporaneity and non-contemporaneity" (*CUP* 98), and although his relation to the leap is not clear and must always be affirmed with a parenthetical "perhaps," Lessing was (to his credit) aware of it (105). Climacus's initial expression of gratitude to Lessing, who gave hope and joy to the "poor private thinker" in his little garret room (63) is maintained to the end – despite their differences as to the possibility of such a transition, Lessing has been important and encouraging to Climacus (105) in highlighting its radical qualitativeness.

The qualitativeness of the transition, which is seen by Kierkegaard in contrast to the Hegelian category of transition, is also elaborated by him in relation to the orthodox Lutheran tradition: "Here as everywhere we must pay attention to the qualitative leap, that there is no direct transition (for example, as from reading and studying in the bible as an ordinary human book – to taking it as God's word, as Holy Scripture), but everywhere a *metabasis eis allo genos*, a leap, whereby I burst the whole progression of reason and define a qualitative newness, but a newness *allo genos*" (*JP* III 22). Because Climacus, too, emphasizes so strongly his rejection of the quantitative transition that comes cumulatively or automatically, the leap has come to be treated all too often by commentators as if it were an intentional, purposeful, deliberate, self-conscious, or reflective act of will or volition, through which the agent selects from a variety of alternative options. The leap is seen as something we still have to do (to bridge a gap) after we have appreciated the options.[8] The result is a volitionalist reading that interprets the claim that the "the leap is the category of decision" (*CUP* 99) along the lines of radical discontinuity and even arbitrariness, on the model of a decision to do something when all the alternatives are able to be formulated independently of our attraction to them. In this way, attention to the leap as decision has diverted attention from other ways in which the leap could be seen as decisive. But Climacus's discussion of Lessing tells us something that should qualify such a volitionalist view. Climacus reveals something more about how "the leap is the category of decision" when he goes on to contrast his view of the qualitative achievement with the brute willpower character of a "Münchausen" type of leap, where "one closes one's eyes, grabs oneself by the neck . . . and then one stands on the other side" (99). I suggest that Climacus is here taking pains to preclude a misunderstanding of the leap as serious as that of supposing it to be a cumulative achievement: he is opposing himself to such a caricature of the leap (regardless of where one ends up) as a deliberate act of willpower as much as to the caricature of the leap that becomes easier because one inches oneself up to it gradually.

That willpower caricature is also later corrected when Climacus notes that "The inwardness and the unutterable sighs of prayer are incommensurate with the muscular" (*CUP* 91). This is perhaps why Climacus admits there is something "rather well said" in Jacobi's claim that "If you will just step on the elastic spot that catapults me, it will come by itself" (102): although obviously Jacobi fails to realize that the hard part is to "just step," there is a sense in which "it will come by itself." And this also perhaps explains Climacus's otherwise curious comment that Mendelssohn "has indicated quite correctly the lyrical culmination of thought in the leap" (95).

What then is the character of the leap, if it is not either the Jacobean quantitative (and social) leap or the Münchausen muscular willpower leap? Some suggestions about what is really at stake in the qualitative decision that constitutes the leap can be found in Kierkegaard's two journal references to his "theory of the leap."

The first reference makes clear that the qualitativeness of a leap is correlated with freedom: "Regrettably one finds almost no examination of the ethical in logic, which arouses in my thought a suspicion about logic and serves to support my theory of the leap, which is essentially at home in the realm of freedom" (*JP* III 20). In addition to this *sine qua non* limiting condition of the leap, the second reference suggests something about its positive content; he writes: "This will be an investigation of importance for my theory of the leap and of the difference between a dialectical transition and a transition of pathos. In the final analysis, what I call a transition of pathos Aristotle called an enthymeme" (20). In what follows I will explore both the requirement of freedom and the suggestion of pathos-filled motivation.

II. FREE AND NONVOLITIONAL QUALITATIVE TRANSITIONS

Climacus unambiguously sees the leap to Christian faith as a transition that is "qualitative" and a "break in immanence (*CUP* 12, 95, 103, 381). What is at stake is that the transition not be an experience of simple continuity, whether as a necessary unfolding or otherwise merely cumulative result. This rejection of continuity is the rejection of rational necessity or compulsion – what is at stake is that the transition be a free act.[9] Indeed, Climacus often uses the phrases freedom and act of will (or expression of will) as appositives, and he contrasts what is done by will with what is done by way of necessity (*JC* 265; *PF* 82). But neither qualitative nor free change need be brought about by a brute act of willpower.

To appreciate the range of the activity that might constitute a leap, we need to recall that for Climacus what is constitutive of "subjective acceptance" is that the conclusion not follow "directly of its own accord" (*CUP* 130). But conclusions that do not follow as a matter of course are seen by Kierkegaard as leaps. He repeatedly refers to the "leap of inference in induction and analogy," claiming that in such cases "the conclusion can be reached only by a LEAP" and "all other conclusions are essentially tautological (*JP* III 19, 16]. An inductive inference is, in a sense, a decision that p is true, but it is as different from a deliberate, self-conscious, act of willpower as it is from an immanental determination or necessary "flopping over." The reorienting shift in perspective which occurs in such leaps of inference can be both qualitative and free, and the fact that all nontautological conclusions can be seen as leaps certainly broadens the notion of decision and willing involved in a leap.

But is this a strong enough notion of change and freedom to illuminate the category of Christian faith? Although Kierkegaard concedes that the change from possibility to actuality is a leap (*CUP* 342; *JP* I 109–10), he notes that the leap to Christian categories is like the change from nonbeing to being: "Christianity holds that the central issue is a qualitative transformation, a total character transformation in time (just as qualitative as the change from not being to being which is birth). Anything which is merely a development of what man is originally is not essentially Christian" (*JP* III 416). The "quality of the divine," which Christianity introduces, goes beyond "the idea that the divine is the superlative of the most superlative superlative of the human" (417). Consider what is arguably a more perspicuous example of a qualitative change – namely, a *Gestalt* shift. Such a model of transition is found at its simplest in the duck/rabbit picture, but it can assume far more complex and subtle forms. Acquaintance with such a model reminds us that qualitative and free transitions can be accounted for without invoking a deliberate, self-reflective act of willpower.

In a situation in which a *Gestalt* shift occurs, we initially see only one possibility; at some point, after concentrated attention or perhaps coaching, a different figure comes into focus for us. Seeing the latter figure is not the direct or immediate result of any decision or volition, nor is it a choice in any standard sense since at the outset we recognize no other equally real possibilities from which to choose. We can decide to *look for* the figure we are told is there and cannot yet see, but we cannot decide to see (recognize) it. Recognizing the new and qualitatively different figure is not the direct result of willing or the necessary result of the effort to look for it.

In a *Gestalt* shift a new quality emerges at a critical threshold; the broader model of critical threshold change, however, can illustrate the directionality and decisiveness of the transition in religious conversion better than the simple *Gestalt*-shift model (which involves an in-principle symmetry and hence a reversible conclusion, and also lacks any real relation between the two pictures – the duck and the rabbit).[10] A threshold concept refers to a state or condition that is not expressed gradually or by degrees – for example, water gets hotter and hotter by degrees, but it doesn't boil gradually; it doesn't boil at all until it reaches a critical threshold. Explosive material gets hotter and hotter, but it doesn't explode gradually; it doesn't explode at all until it reaches a critical threshold. The latter example shows the extreme of asymmetry and directionality. The qualitative change at a critical threshold is decisive since any increases after that threshold are superfluous, but such a change is a function of what precedes it; although the change is not just cumulative, it is integrally related to what goes before. Something is *registered* during the process leading to the shift; in the case of the boiling water or the explosive, heat is registered all the while. Although the transition is a qualitative one – that is, it is an all-or-nothing kind of movement, rather than a quantitative accumulation by degrees – it is nevertheless anchored in what precedes it. Evidence, like heat, can be registered during a process, even though the qualitative transition occurs only when the critical threshold is reached.

The category of critical threshold thus illustrates not only the directionality of change but also how continuity can be incorporated and accommodated in a model of qualitative shift. The transition is a function of what precedes it, without, however, coming by degrees with increases of evidence or attentive effort. The transition leads to a qualitatively different conclusion (in this sense it might be considered discontinuous with what preceded it), but it cannot occur unless much preliminary material is registered and so depends on what precedes (in this sense it might be considered continuous with it). In this connection it is intriguing to note Kierkegaard's explicit appreciation of continuity; he writes that "This, precisely, is the irregularity in the paradox, continuity is lacking, or at any rate it has continuity only in reverse, that is, at the beginning it does not manifest itself as continuity" (JP III 399–400). Such continuity, assessable retrospectively, is compatible with qualitative change.

Kierkegaard himself connects the concept of the leap with the idea of such critical thresholds when he speaks of "the leap by which water turns to ice, the leap by which I understand an author, and the leap which is the transition from good to evil" (JP III 17). These examples are cited in reference to the question "Is this leap then entirely homogeneous," and are admittedly presented in a context of examples that illustrate a "qualitative difference between leaps." But interestingly the example of a qualitatively different kind of leap is "The paradox. Christ's entry into the world." That is, the qualitatively different (nonhomogeneous) leap is the one made by God coming into Time, *not by us*. On *our* side a transition may be a leap (that is, a qualitative transition) even if homogeneous in contrast to the leap made by God into the world. Since a critical threshold and a qualitative shift occur even in these homogeneous leaps, I suggest that the category of critical threshold sheds light on the kind of activity Kierkegaard thinks we engage in, the kind of free and qualitative change that occurs, when, for example, "The thought of God emerges with a leap" or when there is "the leap of sin-consciousness" (JP III 19).

The emergence of a qualitatively different awareness at a critical threshold is an example of a qualitative transition that is distinguishable from a quantitative, cumulative process as well as from a momentary, separable, act of will or decision that fills a gap. It is, so to speak, a creative culmination rather than a mechanical accumulation – and it can be an exercise of freedom.

Moreover, the qualitative change that occurs in a *Gestalt* shift can be free in the sense that it is not compelled (either physically or rationally), yet it is not self-consciously intentional nor does it involve an explicit acknowledgment of a variety of options. Qualitative changes can be free without being arbitrary, since freedom does not require a total absence of constraint, though of course it is incompatible with compulsion. An uncompelled activity might nevertheless be subject to some constraint – a response can be free even while it is a *response* to something. Climacus's emphatic rejection of the category of necessity can, in principle, be maintained without turning either to intentional or arbitrary decision, and the qualitative and free transition that is at stake for Climacus can, in principle, be achieved in ways that have little to do with the emasculated model of decision as a discrete, direct ("muscular") act of will in contrast to other activities. Thus, where freedom is understood by contrast with a necessary or compelled reaction, the idiom of will can well be used to emphasize the freedom of the acceptance.

It might be thought that Kierkegaard's (and Climacus's) Biblical commitment to faith as obedience (for which blame and reward are appropriate) assumes and/or requires a stronger sense of freedom, involving more discontinuity and effectively more arbitrariness. But freedom, for Kierkegaard, never requires *liberum arbitrium* (freedom of indifference) (*JP* II 61–2; see also 74, 68). We learn from his journals that human freedom is compatible with absolute divine governance and omnipotence and that constraint is compatible with freedom (62–3, 70–2); we learn that the choice he means to guarantee is not "abstract freedom of choice," "bare and naked," "contentless," achieved through a "perfectly disinterested will" (73, 67, 59). Freedom is always an interested, contextualized freedom. Moreover, he distinguishes between "freedom of choice" and "true freedom" and the latter is compatible with there being, in some meaningful sense, "no *choice*" (74, 68). This complex understanding of freedom and choice illuminates (and qualifies) any Biblical commitment to faith as obedience, and opens the way to a more subtle understanding of the necessary conditions for a *free* qualitative transition.

Even if one rejects such a compatibilist view of "true freedom," it is still possible to guarantee a significant notion of responsibility in the larger picture of faith by allowing that there are important and sufficient loci for deliberate (by *fiat*) choices or straightforward decisions surrounding the transition. There are decisions for which we can be held responsible, which prepare the way for the transition to faith or confirm it, which cultivate it or stifle it, even if the actual transition is not achieved directly by such a choice; there are decisions (recalling the *Gestalt*-shift model) by which we look patiently and attentively or close our eyes stubbornly and rebelliously, even though we cannot decide by *fiat* to see a new vision.

This discussion of freedom in relation to obedience and responsibility reveals the need to address another kind of question: namely, whether such a model can do justice to Climacus's insistence on the *risk* involved in leaps to faith. We are all familiar with Climacus's repeated refrain, "Without risk, no faith," and his graphic illustrations of such risk in terms of being out over seventy thousand fathoms of water or in a leaking boat refusing to seek harbor (*CUP* 204, 210; 140, 204, 225n). Can one "take a risk" other than through the sort of deliberate volition I have been arguing against; how is risk involved in the kind of transition or shift I have been suggesting? At the very least, risk remains relevant in that the "picture" one comes to see in ethico-religious cases is neither objectively certain nor demonstrable; risk is not eliminated by the *Gestalt*-shift model. Admittedly, the simple *Gestalt* model does not highlight the way in which one can put oneself at risk by engaging in, or being engaged by, a process or activity that can lead one to lose one's bearings entirely; it can obscure the ways in which risk is taken in the experience of the shift. It is possible, nevertheless, to imagine more subtle and complex shifts in perspective, and to imagine that the pictures at issue could be far more engaging and consequential than the simple model suggests. Climacus writes that "To be infinitely interested and to ask about an actuality that is not one's own is to will to believe" (*CUP* 323). To ask in an infinitely interested way is to dare to be radically changed, to face a demand, our response to which (whatever it is) will necessarily change us radically – this is to take a real risk, to put oneself out over seventy thousand fathoms.

One can take a risk, be threatened with loss, even if one does not know *exactly* what will be lost (or gained). Although one cannot beforehand see precisely what one might come to see, one can know beforehand that there is the chance that all one's former certainties can be undone. The threat is the absolute demand one might face. To choose to look may be an act of will (though not unconditioned will) requiring courage, even if the seeing – the transition – itself is not achievable by choice. Risk attends the looking as much as the seeing.

III. PATHOS-FILLED QUALITATIVE TRANSITIONS

The notion of a conceptual shift in perspective and the category of critical threshold broaden the possibilities for understanding leaps as qualitative and free yet nonvolitional transitions, but this does not yet tell us what generates the letting-go – it does not yet reveal what Kierkegaard will call the "substance" of the leap. To determine this we need to reconsider Kierkegaard's appeal to the distinctive category of a "transition of pathos," found in his second reference to his theory of the leap:

This will be an investigation of importance for my theory of the leap and of the difference between a dialectical transition and a transition of pathos. In the final analysis, what I call a transition of pathos Aristotle called an enthymeme. (*JP* III 20)

This same contrast between kinds of transition is found elsewhere in the journals, when he contrasts a "dialectical" transition with a "pathos-filled" one and explains that "dialectically nothing can be derived."[11] We can then infer that a dialectical transition is one that merely unfolds what is already there, with no substantive derivation; by contrast, a "transition of pathos" would be a transition that constitutes genuine derivation. But what this means is illuminated by Kierkegaard's intriguing and unexpected reference to the Aristotelian category of "enthymeme."

What do we learn from the claim that a "transition of pathos" is what Aristotle called an "enthymeme"? An Aristotelian "enthymeme" is a *rhetorical* syllogism[12] – what distinguishes such a syllogism from a *"dialectical"* one is that the premises are derived from the popular (nonexpert) opinion of those in its audience. Working with their pathos in this way such a syllogism is intended to create a practical, concrete, nonnecessary, transition in the audience. Insofar as a "transition of pathos" is like an Aristotelian enthymeme, it would intend a rhetorical transition – that is, concrete and practical change, generated by pathos. Lest the appeal to pathos be misleading, however, it is worth noting that Kierkegaard would have been well aware that Aristotle's enthymeme was technically a *syllogism*. This is significant insofar as it invokes the idea of structure, however implicit. This suggests that a pathos-filled transition is not an arbitrary or ungrounded transition, that there may be an implicit structure that could be reconstructed.[13] It suggests, too, that his rejection of the Hegelian "System" is not a rejection of structured transitions as such, but rather of transitions that were necessary and premised on abstractions. A passage in *Postscript* is revealing in this respect:

There are examples enough of a mistaken effort to assert the pathos-filled and earnestness in a ludicrous, superstitious sense as a beatifying universal balm, as if earnestness in itself were a good or something to be taken without prescription; then everything would be good just as long as one is earnest, even if it so happened that one was never earnest in the right place. No, everything has its dialectic – not, please note, a dialectic by which it is made sophistically relative (this is mediation), but by which the absolute becomes distinguishable as the absolute by means of the dialectical. Therefore, it is just as questionable, precisely as questionable, to be pathos-filled and earnest in the wrong place as it is to laugh in the wrong place. (*CUP* 525)

This passage, too, like the reference to "enthymeme," suggests that the pathos-filled is capable of being critically assessed; it is not simply lovely feeling, totally formless or arbitrary – indeed, "everything has its dialectic."[14] It allows enthymematic structure in the sense of a tension-filled reflective interplay – what is at stake is the rejection of the relativizing synthesis and mediated resolution with which Hegel ends the dialectical interplay.

Kierkegaard connects this "pathos-filled transition" or "transition of pathos" directly with a leap when he writes that "pathos" is "the substance of the leap"; he connects it with a leap indirectly when he refers to the "transition to the infinite, which consists in pathos." These journal references suggest that it would be fruitful to reconsider *Fragments* and *Postscript* in order to determine the Climacus's view of the relevance of pathos to the leap.

In *Postscript* Climacus ties "pathos" (*Pathos*) together, not unexpectedly, with the category of "passion" (*Lidenskab*): "Inwardness is subjectivity; subjectivity is essentially passion" (*CUP* 33) and "pathos is . . . inwardness" (242). This is consistent with Kierkegaard's tendency to equate pathos and passion: "Let no one misinterpret all my talk about pathos and passion to mean that I intend to sanction every uncircumcised immediacy, every unshaved passion."[15] His explicit and lengthy discussions of various expressions of "existential pathos" later in the work explore the role of passion, developing earlier suggestions about both the "how" of subjective appropriation (203, 419n, 427, 495, 509, 540, 574, 610–12) and the role of passion as "existence at its highest" (197) and the culmination of subjectivity (230).

Climacus's claim that the "requirement of existence [is]: *to join together*" (*CUP* 531, 535) recalls his earlier discussion of the "difficult" task of maintaining oneself in the "prodigious contradiction" of existence: namely, "to understand extreme opposites together and, existing, to understand oneself in them" (350, 354). That task involves passion because "passion is the very tension in the contradiction" (385). While aesthetic pathos is the "pathos of possibility" in the sense of "disinterestedness," "ethically the highest pathos is the pathos of interestedness (namely, that I acting, transform my whole existence in relation to the object of interest)" (389–90). When this "interestedness" is expressed in a "pathos-filled relation to an eternal happiness" (443), or more precisely, in relating absolutely to an "absolute telos," we have a "truly pathos-filled existing person" (409). When a "person's passion culminates in the pathos-filled relation to an eternal happiness," we have "plain and simple pathos" (385) – thus, "the religious is the purest pathos" (462).

The pure pathos of the religious consists in the way that "the individual, existing, venture[s] everything" in relation to an eternal happiness as absolute telos (*CUP* 429). But this is not a plain and simple relation – there is a tension in an *individual's* relation to an *eternal* happiness, to an *absolute* telos. To repeat, "everything has its dialectic." Even within immanence, then, there is an element that "creates a resistance that intensifies pathos" (535). That pathos is "sharpened" in Christianity (581) because Christianity requires, in addition, that one "venture to believe against the understanding (the dialectical)" (429). Presumably, the need for this "risk" of one's "thought" is what constitutes the "additional qualifications" that "work as an incitement that brings passion to its extreme" (385). In Christianity the dialectical distancing is raised to a second order, to the paradoxically dialectical – the incomprehensible yields the ultimate "pathos of separation" (557, 561, 582).

The "pathos-filled" is thus, for Climacus as for Kierkegaard, *different* from the "dialectical" (the believing against the understanding [*CUP* 429], the distance within relation [535], and the repulsion from the incomprehensible [611]), but whereas the journal passage presents them as alternatives, Climacus highlights in *Postscript* the way both should be part of any qualitative transitional movement (385). The pathos of religiousness is sharpened, thus qualitatively changing the character of the religiousness, by the "dialectical" dimensions of the "consciousness of sin" – that is, "both because it cannot be thought and because it is isolating" (585). Thus, Climacus presents a dialectical relation between pathos and dialectic (535, 555); indeed, the dialectical works dialectically to intensify passion (607, 611) – passion plus distance and repulsion generates deeper passion. The category of the pathos-filled as it is revealed in *Postscript* clearly emphasizes the interestedness of passion as intense appropriation, but what is at stake in a "pathos-filled transition" is further clarified by a backward look at *Fragments*.

Passion is introduced in *Fragments* in a rather different way. Climacus there makes the striking claim that faith is *a* "passion," indeed, *a* "happy passion" (*PF* 54, 59, 61). Faith is more than an act done with passion, more than an activity experienced with passion – it is itself a passion, a passion (presumably) analogous in some significant ways to passions like love, hate, or fear. Indeed, Climacus introduces the happy passion that is faith in terms of happy (vs. unhappy) love and in both *Fragments* and *Postscript* he repeatedly draws analogies between faith and love.[16]

The category of passion substantively qualifies what leap or decision means in the case of faith. Climacus writes that "the something in which this [transition] occurs" is the happy passion of faith (*PF* 59): that is, the transition that is called a leap is said to achieve a passion or, conversely, the onset of the passion is coextensive with the leap. The attributions of "leap" and "passion" are not directed to discrete or successive moments of the phenomenon of faith – they both refer to the transition.[17]

At the very least this shared attribution undermines any one-dimensional voluntarist reading of the leap. Popular English usage associates passion or emotion with both feeling and passivity, emphasizing the original sense of the term: namely, "the condition of being acted upon or affected by external agency." The Danish "passion" (*Lidenskab*) likewise shares a root with the verb "to suffer" (*lide*). Kierkegaard's appreciation of Aristotle, however, lends more nuance to his use of the term "passion." The leap is not qualified by simple passivity – passion is itself a more complex phenomenon, as is suggested in other dictionary definitions that follow Aristotle's lead in treating passions under the rubric of "the things men do of themselves, the acts of which they themselves are authors"; these definitions posit passion as "an eager outreaching of the mind toward something; an overmastering zeal or enthusiasm for a special object."[18] This more active dimension has increasingly come to be emphasized in recent literature on passions and emotions.[19] What is distinctive about a passion, like fear or love, is that it is a kind of engagement or interestedness that is not simple feeling, but is constituted in part by interpretation – for example, whatever my physiological reaction (feeling), if I do not take there to be an object of danger, I am not experiencing the passion or emotion of fear. For these reasons, the category of passion does not fit neatly under either the rubric of simple passivity or of simple willpower.[20]

On the one hand, the mutual correction of leap and passion belies a purely voluntarist account of the transition to faith; on the other hand, both Climacus and Kierkegaard emphasize the freedom and responsibility of faith in ways that belie a purely passive account of the transition. Neither Kierkegaard nor Climacus falls prey to the common mistake of seeing a "divine gift" and human activity as mutually exclusive categories. Although the transition to faith is clearly a gift, it is also something *we* do – we let go, we embrace the Absolute Paradox, we leap. Climacus tries to locate and characterize that activity by excluding two descriptions: He insists that faith is neither an act of knowledge nor an act of *unconditioned* willing (*PF* 62). That leaves the possibility that it is some kind of believing short of knowledge or some kind of conditioned willing, but whatever kind of transformation it is, the transition to faith needs to be read in the light of Climacus's explicit claim that it is "a passion," an "infinite interestedness" (*CUP* 324, 326).

Climacus's appreciation of a tension – rather than dichotomy – between active and passive is illustrated in his bi-polar account of "offense" in the face of the Absolute Paradox: offense is both active and passive (*PF* 50). This suggests that such a tension, transcending dualisms between active and passive, would be a feature congenial to his account in general. On such a reading, the concept of leap would be in tension with the concept of passion, and the concept of passion itself would embody tension between active and passive.

To paraphrase Kierkegaard, then, we could say that, for Climacus, passion is the substance of the leap, the transition to the infinite consists in passion. The idea that the substance of the leap has more to do with passion or pathos (that is, with decisive interestedness or attraction, with the surrender constituted by captivating yet free engagement) than with discrete volitions or acts of willpower may strike some as counterintuitive. I suggest, however, that the mutual correction implied in the correlative attributions of leap and passion is best understood as an attempt to do justice to an activity that, even at the level of human agency, is more complex than a unilateral choice among alternatives that can be formulated independently of our engagement with them. The surrender of interestedness, of being grasped by something or decisively engaged by it, can account for both the letting-go that constitutes the leap and the passion that also constitutes it. Such interestedness seems precisely what is highlighted in Climacus's claim, noted earlier, that "To be infinitely interested and to ask about an actuality that is not one's own is to will to believe and expresses the paradoxical relation to the paradox." Climacus's understanding of the role of passion or pathos thus supports the earlier conclusion that the qualitative transition of the leap need not be seen as the result of a direct and deliberate volition.

Climacus's discussion of the difference between misfortune and suffering also reveals something about the kind of transition at work in overcoming the "qualitative dialectic [which] separates the spheres" (*CUP* 388). The "pathos-filled actuality of suffering," he insists, is not present as long as the person "understands the suffering as accidental" (as "misfortune") – that is, the "pathos-filled actuality of suffering" consists in *understanding* suffering as "essential" (445).

As long as the suffering is seen as accidental and therefore "alien," it is expected to end, and Climacus explains that when it does not end, one "despairs and the transition to another understanding of misfortune is made possible, that is, to comprehending suffering, an understanding that does not merely comprehend this or that misfortune but essentially comprehends suffering" (434). The transition thus consists in a new understanding. Indeed, Climacus's later contrast between "feeling" misfortune and "comprehending" it (443) makes it clear that the comprehension or understanding at issue is a case of seeing-as (seeing misfortune as-alien or as-essential). The qualitative transition is a shift in perspective, a new way of seeing, and such shifts, as I suggested earlier in relation to *Gestalt* shifts, need not be the result of direct and deliberate volition.

As one would expect, Climacus's understanding of decision is nuanced by its relation to passion or pathos – "essential" decisions are made differently from decisions to buy quarts of milk rather than pints. "All decision," he writes, and then specifies it more precisely, "all essential decision, is rooted in subjectivity" (*CUP* 33). Conversely, wanting "to evade some of the pain and crisis of decision" is wanting "to make the issue somewhat objective" (129). What is at stake is pathos – namely, that the reorientation be an engaged one. Moreover, "decision is designed specifically to put an end to that perpetual prattle about 'to a certain degree'" – that is, decision is equated with "what is decisive" (221). What is at stake is pathos – namely, that the reorientation be a decisive one.

Kierkegaard and Climacus distance the category of decision from that of deliberate volition in a variety of other ways as well. For example, Kierkegaard does so when he suggests that the majority of people, who "live without any real consciousness penetrating their lives" (who live "in unclarity") possibly "never come in passionate concentration to the decision whether they should cling expectantly to this possibility or give it up" (*JP* III 428). "Coming in passionate concentration to a decision" sounds like a crystallizing activity of *attending* in which we come to see that we have been decisively reoriented – passionate attention reveals that we are decided, that we already cling. This same suggestion of decision as a crystallizing gathering together is found in the equation implied in Climacus's reference to "the moment of resignation, of collecting oneself, of choice" (*CUP* 400). Likewise, when Kierkegaard writes that "A pathos-filled transition can be achieved by every one if he wills it, because the transition to the infinite, which consists in pathos, takes only courage," he highlights the possibility of a richer sense of willing than that normally thought to be involved in paradigmatic selections among options. A transition that "consists in pathos" or whose "substance" is pathos can take courage, in the way that a surrender or letting-go can take courage – without having to be thought of as a discrete act of brute willpower.

IV. PARADOX AND NONVOLITIONAL QUALITATIVE TRANSITIONS

An additional way in which passion or pathos enriches the notion of transition is found in Climacus's description of passion as "the highest pitch of subjectivity," which occurs when one is "closest to being in two places at the same time" (CUP 199). In this way, he allows the category of a pathos-filled transition to point to a transition in which a paradoxical tension is appreciated and maintained.

Paradox may not seem to be what is at issue when Kierkegaard talks about analogy and induction as paradigmatic leaps (because they are nontautological), or when he recognizes the Aristotelian enthymeme as a leap (which is not only nontautological, but also has the added dimension of persuasive argument). These generic "inferences," however, are a kind of revisioning for which involvement is a condition and in which the conclusion constitutes a qualitative shift. One could argue that a paradoxical tension is involved in any inference, or revisioning, that is not logically necessary. Indeed, Kierkegaard suggests that this is what is at stake in calling the object of our embrace a paradox: "Faith therefore cannot be proved, demonstrated, comprehended, for the link which makes a linking together possible is missing, and what else does this say than that it is a paradox."[21]

When Climacus claims that "paradox and passion fit each other perfectly" (CUP 230) and that "passion is the very tension in the contradiction" (385) he implies that the engagement and interestedness that constitute passion can also do justice to the role of paradox in religious faith. The question remains whether such an account of the leap can do justice to the obviously different category of what Climacus calls the "Absolute Paradox." Paradox as such is present even in the Socratic model of faith, but paradox "becomes even more terrible" and "manifests itself as the absolute" in the double paradox in which the message of "absolute difference" is revealed in the form of likeness (i.e., takes human form) (*PF* 47, chap. III passim). In other words, the question remains whether such an account of the leap can do justice to the radicalness of the difference between Socratic immanent religiousness (which Climacus later calls "Religiousness A") and the religion of revelation, faith in an "eminent sense," specifically Christian religiousness (which Climacus calls "Religiousness B") (*CUP* 555–6).

To answer this question we need first to consider the relation between paradox and volitionalism. The notion that we can respond appreciatively to paradox only by an act of brute and heroic willpower is based in the misunderstanding that strips the relevant paradox of all content. Given such an empty notion of mere paradoxicalness, there is little alternative to a view of acceptance through simple brute force. But it is not paradoxicalness as such that we embrace – it is a paradoxical self-understanding. In the specifically Christian realm, accepting the Paradox is not equivalent to accepting a set of teachings or propositions; nevertheless, the Teacher, who is embraced, embodies a paradoxical message. It is the message of absolute likeness and absolute unlikeness; this paradoxical self-understanding constitutes the "leap of sin-consciousness" (*JP* III 19). Granted, it is an understanding initiated from outside the self, not an immanent intellectualism, but embracing the Paradox is, nevertheless, embracing a new self-understanding and a concomitant new understanding of the world. The uniting of contradictories in the Teacher is echoed back in a new and paradoxical self-understanding, new and paradoxical because informed by the qualitatively different category of "sin." That Paradox has at least the content embodied in "the consciousness of sin" (*CUP* 583–5).[22] Embracing paradox, then, even the Absolute Paradox, need not entail a muscular "willpower" model of willing; willing can be understood more along the lines of approving affirmation than of brute creation *ex nihilo*.

The question remains whether there is any difference between the transition to Religiousness A and Religiousness B that precludes understanding the pathos-filled mechanism of transition as formally similar, or whether anything about the dialectical nature of

Religiousness B requires the operation of a different kind of (in William James's term) "superadded will force."[23] Climacus claims that "People have forgotten the qualitative dialectic and have wanted to form comparatively and quantitatively a direct transition from culture to Christianity" (CUP 606). It is important to note, however, that this is the culmination of a series of references to the notion of qualitative dialectic. The qualitative dialectic does not only refer to the "abyss" preceding Christianity – there is a qualitative dialectic even within immanence (572). Early in the discussion of existential pathos he refers to "the qualitative dialectic that separates the spheres" (388), and the reference is repeated often (399, 436, 517, 562). This suggests that there are qualitative shifts from each sphere to the next, whether they take place within immanence or are from immanence to an understanding decisively initiated from outside.[24] And this is what one would expect, given Climacus's appreciative agreement with Lessing that there is no more or less to a leap. All leaps are qualitative shifts, and *formally* all qualitative transitions are similar.

This is congruent with a distinction between two notions of dialectic that have been operating in Climacus's account: (a) "dialectic" as referring to reflection and hence to what in Christianity is against the understanding, and (b) "dialectic" as referring to the tension-filled interplay between two contrasting kinds of categories. A "qualitative dialectic" between spheres can exist before the occurrence of the "dialectical" dimension peculiar to Religiousness B. Kierkegaard makes this clear in a journal entry from 1842–3 in which he writes: "The relation between esthetics and ethics – the transition – pathos-filled, not dialectical – there a qualitatively different dialectic begins" (JP I 371). The transition from the aesthetic to the ethical and from the ethical to Religiousness A are qualitative shifts of perspective, qualitatively new and transforming realizations, and so appropriately seen as leaps.[25]

Climacus speaks of the "break," the "irruption of inwardness," through which religiousness is achieved in terms of attention and vision: "only in the inwardness of self-activity does he become aware and capable of seeing God"; "within the individual human being there is a possibility . . . that in inwardness is awakened to a God-relationship, and then it is possible to see God everywhere" (CUP 243, 246). But he also describes the Christian thought-project in terms of vision: He speaks of the "condition" in terms of the ability to "envision God," and describes how "the god gave the follower the condition to see it and opened for him the eyes of faith," for "without the condition he would have seen nothing" (*PF* 63, 65). Climacus could plausibly see both transitions as *formally* similar – the transition to Christian faith could be viewed as a *formally* similar shift in perspective, though admittedly what is seen (the God in Time and concomitantly, the sinful self) might be different.

It is crucial to stress that this formal similarity among leaps does not assimilate Religiousness B to Religiousness A. What never gets forgotten is that the condition for Religiousness B needs to be *given* – it is not (no longer?) immanent. Repeatedly stressing that crucial proviso, Climacus nonetheless reminds us that "once the condition is given, that which was valid for the Socratic is again valid" (*PF* 63). I take this to mean that once the condition is given, it is possible to view the transition as formally similar. This is all that is necessary to support the case against a volitionalist reading of the leap to faith.

A final word about the mechanism of the pathos-filled leap should be added, although it cannot be developed here at any length. Any understanding of what it is to leap requires attention to Climacus's understanding of the relation between imagination and pathos. He writes in *Postscript* that "Existence itself, existing, is a striving and is just as pathos-filled as it is comic: pathos-filled because the striving is infinite, that is, directed toward the infinite, is a process of infinitizing, which is the highest pathos" (*CUP* 92). Infinitizing is the prerogative of the imagination – only the imagination can extend something infinitely. Moreover, his description of existence involves holding elements in tension, maintaining the tension without resolving it (350); the same is true of his descriptions of passion (199, 311) and paradox. It has been claimed that this is the distinctive function of imagination, as well as that imagination transcends the dichotomy between active and passive.[26] Climacus himself gives imagination a role in passion when he explains that "In passion, the existing subject is infinitized in the eternity of imagination and yet is also most definitely himself" (197). The centrality of both the categories of passion and paradox to Climacus's account supports the concomitant centrality of imagination, and there is much that Climacus affirms that expresses a significant appreciation of the centrality of imagination to subjectivity. Although, admittedly, we find severe denunciations of its subversive and dissipating power, the centrality of imagination is expressed explicitly in Climacus's description of "all elements" of existence, where imagination ranks with thinking and feeling as equal and indispensable (and where, incidentally, "all elements" are accounted for without bringing in the category of "will") (346–8).

The preceding considerations and reminders open the way to a reconceptualization of the Climacan leap in which it can be understood by way of an alternative to volitionalism – an alternative that appreciates the idiom of will as rational *appetitus* and highlights the possibility that decisive imaginative attraction and captivation can constitute, rather than merely prepare the way for or accompany, qualitative transitions. My hope is that this will make it easier for commentators to explore more than a one-dimensional account of the leap, as well as support and further the contribution of those who have recognized in Climacus's texts a more nuanced account.

NOTES

1 Alastair MacKinnon, "Kierkegaard and the 'Leap of Faith,'" *Kierke-gaardiana* 16, pp. 107–18.

2 Its status is peculiar: On the one hand, the introduction to *Postscript* sees the promise of a sequel *already* fulfilled in *Fragments* (10), and thus fulfillable in a "postscript" (11), yet on the other hand, it claims both that "In essence there is no sequel" and that "in another sense, the sequel could become endless" (11).

3 The most plausible case for this has been made by Ronald M. Green, most fully in his recent *Kierkegaard and Kant: The Hidden Debt* (Albany: State University of New York Press, 1992).

4 It is arguable that Kant provides the proximate antecedents of the notion of the leap – for example, in works with which Kierkegaard was familiar, Kant claims that it is a "voluntary decision of our judgment to assume the existence" of God, and he uses such terms as *der Sprung*, *saltus*, *salto mortale*, and *metabasis eis allo genos*. What Kant meant by the former claim, however, is far from clear, and Kant's own possible debt to Lessing concerning the latter point must be acknowledged. Moreover, an appreciation of Kant's radical divergence from Climacus with respect to the relation between historical knowledge and faith (especially as we find it in Kant's *Religion Within the Limits of Reason Alone*) must significantly qualify the importance of Kant as a source.

Green documents Kierkegaard's familiarity (*Kierkegaard and Kant*, pp. 390–408 passim; esp. pp. 400–2, 403–5); he does not, however, note Climacus's footnote reference to the "postulate of God" (*CUP* 200n), which supports his case.

5 Michelle Stott argues that Kierkegaard used an idealized version of the historical Lessing (who was in fact less self-conscious or intentional in his lack of followers) as a pseudonym for expressing a position which focussed on "the actual embodiment of the style itself" (*Behind the Mask: Kierkegaard's Pseudonymic Treatment of Lessing in the* Concluding Unscientific Postscript [Lewisburg, Pa.: Bucknell University Press, 1993], pp. 93–4, 97, and 69). She concludes that Lessing was chosen by Kierkegaard "precisely because he did wear a mask – because the already existing ambiguity surrounding the historical Lessing was exactly suited to the Kierkegaardian needs" (96).

6 "Lessing's irony is superbly apparent" (*CUP* 102); Climacus himself admits to jest (64) while calling attention to the inexhaustibleness of Lessing's jesting (103–4).

7 Even in these cases there is ambiguity; see *CUP* 65.

8 An alternative interpretation found in commentary on Kierkegaard is that the transition is a gift of grace, a miracle that happens to us, with no describable human activity at issue (e.g., David Wisdo, "Kierkegaard on Belief, Faith and Explanation," *International Journal for Philosophy of Religion* 21 [1987]: 95–114).

9 More detail and argument can be found in my *Transforming Vision: Imagination and Will in Kierkegaardian Faith* (Oxford: Clarendon Press, Oxford University Press, 1991), chaps. 1 and 2. The remaining discussion of the leap draws and depends on the fuller account given there.

10 In *Transforming Vision*, pp. 76–81, I suggest that the model of metaphorical reconceptualization complements and corrects the *Gestalt*-shift model.

11 "This transition is manifestly a *pathos-filled* transition, not dialectical, for dialectically nothing can be derived. To me this is important" (*JP* III 15).

12 In contrast to a "dialectical" or "apodictic" syllogism.

13 The importance of implicit structure lies in the fact that retrospective justification might then account for the "continuity in reverse" mentioned earlier; indeed, Climacus seems to allow some retrospective justification of religious conclusions (*PF* 40–2).

14 This passage trades on the double use of "dialectic" to which I refer on p. 230: namely, (1) as the dynamic interplay between categories and (2) as referring simply to reflection or understanding.

15 *JP* III 427. The category of "passion, is, however, broader than that of

"pathos" – e.g., Climacus refers to "earthly passion" that inhibits subjectivity (*CUP* 312n); see also the editor's note in *JP* III 851.

16 Although Climacus says in *Postscript* that "To love is plain and simple pathos" (385), the emphasis there is on passion or pathos as the mode of appropriation (427).

17 In another sense they could also refer to the sustained struggle through time.

18 *The Rhetoric of Aristotle*, trans. Lane Cooper (Englewood Cliffs, N.J.: Prentice-Hall, 1932), 1:10, 56; *Oxford English Dictionary* (1989).

19 For example, work by Robert C. Roberts and by Robert Solomon.

20 More detail on this is found in my *Transforming Vision*.

21 *JP* III 399. Note, too, that what it means to say it is not "comprehended" is suggested in Kierkegaard's claim that "Christianity entered the world not to be understood but to be existed in. This cannot be expressed more strongly than by the fact that Christianity itself proclaims itself to be a paradox" (III 404).

22 There is every indication that Climacus agrees with Kierkegaard's claim about both content and condition: namely, that "the formal condition of being able to receive the content of Christianity" is "unconditioned passion, the passion of the unconditioned" (*JP* III 430); this notion of "content" does not, however, mean that we can explain or understand the paradox.

23 William James, *The Principles of Psychology* (New York: Dover, 1950; 1890), 2:526.

24 The implication on pp. 295 and 342 of *Postscript* is that the transition to the ethical as well as to the religious is a "leap," formally similar in being a "transition from possibility to actuality," which in concrete existence is "a halt, a leap," and a "break."

25 Kierkegaard writes in *Journals and Papers* that "The transition from eudaemonism to the concept of duty is a leap" (III 19); §2345 (p. 17) shows an apparent parallel between the transition from aesthetics to ethics and that between ethics and religiousness. In I §819 (p. 374) he suggests that "It would probably be one of the most interesting tasks to present a poet who was developed to such a degree and had come along so far that he himself really began to understand that he should make a *metabasis eis allo genos*, that is, go over into the ethical, the heroic."

26 Iris Murdoch, "The Darkness of Practical Reason," *Encounter* 27 (July 1966).

9 Arminian edification: Kierkegaard on grace and free will

Some questions are perennial, forever reemerging in textbooks when the debate is highly abstract but occasionally changing history when someone acts dramatically on conviction. Think of Socrates asking "What can we know?" and being willing to drink the hemlock, or of Jesus asking "Who should we love?" and being willing to stretch his body on a cross. A third enduring question – "Are we meaningfully free?" – is the chief focus of this essay. I do not expect to settle the ancient debate about freedom of the will, but I do hope to situate it theologically by critically examining Søren Kierkegaard's views in light of some significant precursors. Kierkegaard worries about how to balance the contingency and fallibility of human deliberation and choice with the indispensability and reliability of divine providence, but he does not treat these matters abstractly or in isolation. He is too Socratic for mere abstraction about human freedom; indeed, his fully Christian understanding is highly dramatic (even paradoxical) at times, in an effort to be true to lived complexity.

Kierkegaard often insists on radical individual responsibility before God, by suggesting, for example, that there can be little or no spiritual help or harm between human beings (*WL* 308).[1] Yet his pseudonym Johannes Climacus tells us that God "gives the learner not only the Truth, but also the condition for understanding it," and that God is thus "Teacher, Saviour, and Redeemer" (*PF* 18, 21).[2] The question is old and familiar: How can one be personally accountable for faith if God does it all? How, in particular, can it be that "[t]he error of the one doubting [*Tvivlende*] and of the one despairing [*Fortvivlende*] does not lie in cognition . . . [but] in the will?" (*EUD*

235

215). Does not the Teacher/Saviour/Redeemer heal, or even directly move, the will of the believer?

The tension here is not just between pseudonymous and non-pseudonymous works. In "The Expectancy of Eternal Salvation," Kierkegaard writes under his own name:

> . . . we are all unprofitable servants, and even our good deeds are nothing but human fabrications, fragile and very ambiguous, but every person has heaven's salvation only by the grace and mercy of God, and this is equally close to every human being in the sense that it is a matter between God and him. (EUD 271)

In his *Journals and Papers*, however, Kierkegaard allows famously:

> In order to constrain subjectivity, we are quite properly taught that no one is saved by works, but by grace – and corresponding to that – by faith. Fine.
>
> But am I therefore unable to do something myself with regard to becoming a believer? Either we must answer this with an unconditional "no," and then we have fatalistic election by grace, or we must make a little concession. The point is this – subjectivity is always under suspicion, and when it is established that we are saved by faith, there is immediately the suspicion that too much has been conceded here. So an addition is made: But no one can give himself faith; it is a gift of God I must pray for.
>
> Fine, but then I myself can pray, or must we go farther and say: No, praying (consequently praying for faith) is a gift of God which no man can give to himself; it must be given to him. And what then? Then to pray aright must again be given to me so that I may rightly pray for faith, etc.
>
> There are many, many envelopes – but there must still be one point or another where there is a halt at subjectivity. Making the scale so large, so difficult, can be commendable as a majestic expression for God's infinity, but subjectivity cannot be excluded, unless we want to have fatalism. (JP IV 352)

It would seem that human beings are *absolutely dependent* upon and yet also *equally accountable* to God. Does Kierkegaard simply contradict himself here?

Some definitions are in order before answering this question. Call "Pelagianism" the doctrine that we can have faith and earn salvation by means of our own intrinsic resources; human nature is perfectible, and no special grace is required. Call "*semi*-Pelagianism," in contrast, the doctrine that we need God's grace to be fully saved but must (and can) take the first step in God's direction; we freely make the leap, so to speak, but God must then catch us and carry us aloft. "Arminianism," in opposition to both Pelagianism and semi-Pelagianism, holds that, on our own, *we can make no move whatsoever toward God.* God must turn us and draw us. The Arminian addendum, however, is that we can say "Yes" or "No." We cannot independently reach for the gift of salvation, much less grasp it as a right, but we can either accept or refuse it. There is no merit in the acceptance, for we are merely letting God heal our abject sinfulness; but there is enough human freedom to say "Yes" or "No" to the physician.

Despite the apparent contradiction, Kierkegaard and his pseudonyms offer a consistent, and consistently Arminian, account of grace and freedom. Kierkegaard does *flirt* with the language of semi-Pelagianism, as when he writes:

The matter is quite simple. In order to have faith, there must first be existence, an existential qualification.

This is what I am never sufficiently able to emphasize – that to have faith, before there can be any question about having faith, there must be the *situation*. And this situation must be brought about by an existential step on the part of the individual. (*JP* II 20)

But the "existential step" in question is actually a patient running in place, a "dying to the world" that surrenders all hope of earthly happiness. Such a death might be called a "precondition" for the theological virtues of faith, hope, and charity, but only in the limited sense that self-surrender opens one to receive divine gifts.[3] "From the God himself everyone receives the condition who by virtue of the condition becomes the disciple," as Climacus puts it, and one can only greet this condition, the Incarnation, with "offense" or "happy passion" (*PF* 126, 67). The human role with respect to God is thus voluntary but exclusively receptive: "Man's highest achievement is to let God be able to help him" (*JP* I 22). We are fated neither to salvation nor damnation, but neither do we take an *active* step toward God on our own. (Accepting temporal death is not synonymous with finding, or even wanting, eternal life.) It is quite clear that self-righteousness and self-sufficiency are ruled out. Grace as unmerited favor is indispensable for justification before God, and only an undialectical reading can make Kierkegaard seem an advocate of the solitary "autonomy" defended by Kant and radicalized by Sartre.[4]

In calling Kierkegaard "Arminian," I do not mean to imply that he read or was directly influenced by Jacob (also known as James) Arminius, though he could hardly have been altogether ignorant of him. My point is a logical one about the content of their work and a psychological one about their habits of heart and mind, not a historical one about causal connections.

Born at Oudewater, Holland, in 1560 and ordained a pastor of the Dutch Reformed Church in Amsterdam in 1588, Arminius challenged strict Calvinist conceptions of predestination. He preached (and later lectured) that God's offer of salvation was universal and that human beings were free to accept or reject that offer. If God necessitates all human action, he argued, then God is the author of moral evil. An impious conclusion to say the least.[5] The key point of similarity between Arminius and Kierkegaard is the kenotic nature of divine grace, its self-emptying quality: True omnipotence and omnibenevolence generate freedom in creatures, not necessity or servile dependency.

A number of themes characterize Arminianism, but I want to focus on three related ones that are central to Kierkegaard's corpus: (1) a commitment to *universal access* to the highest things, over against belief in double predestination or Christ's limited atonement for the elect; (2) a commitment to *equal responsibility* before the highest things, over against strong versions of sacerdotalism or spiritual collaboration; and (3) a commitment to *human freedom*, freedom of choice, and what might be called "true" freedom, over against fatalistic doctrines of irresistible grace or an overly rationalized account of moral and religious commitment. I will treat each of these themes in turn. With respect to the third theme in particular, Saint Augustine's views on reason, will, and liberty (*liberum arbitrium* and *libertas*) will provide a useful contrast to Kierkegaard's own.

To anticipate, it is clear that Kierkegaard rejects all narrow doctrines of election and any metaphysical account that would claim compatibility between determinism and freedom of the will. Such a rejection is implicit throughout *Eighteen Upbuilding Discourses*. What is not so clear is whether this consistent position is plausible, so I will include a critical look at his views on human freedom and vulnerability, especially the limits on help and harm.[6] Kierkegaard is too sanguine, I think, about human invulnerability to communal harm. When amended, however, his defense of freedom can acknowledge profound human vulnerability without undermining individual accountability.

I. UNIVERSALITY OF ACCESS

Kierkegaard's position on the universality of access is unambiguous. "I cannot abandon the thought that every man, however simple he is, however much he may suffer, can nevertheless grasp the highest, namely religion. I cannot forget that. If that is not so, then Christianity is really nonsense."[7] I will not dwell on this claim but simply note that the Bible itself seems to be of two minds on who and how many may be saved. Undeniably, there are Scriptural passages that speak of "the elect," "vessels of wrath," and so forth, so as to imply that Christ did not die for all and hence does not offer salvation to all. But there are also passages that imply universal salvation (see, for example, John 3:16; Rom. 5:18; I Tim. 2:1–6; Col. 1:14–20 and 27:28; and Ps. 145:8–9). Although this vetust dispute cannot be settled here, it is not implausible to see the authors of the latter passages struggling to rise above archaic tribal notions of a "chosen people," laboring to see chosenness as a special vocation, a calling to be an instrument of God's gracious offer of salvation to "all nations,"[8] rather than drawing invidious contrasts between "Us the Elect" and "Them the Eternally Lost or Reprobate."

It is of paramount import, in any event, to distinguish between the *extent of God's offer* of salvation and the *extent of humanity's acceptance* of it. One might judge the empowering offer to be global but the actual acceptance to be limited. Perhaps some creatures will freely but perversely reject God's love for all eternity; to be demonic is precisely "to pray to be free from being saved" (*JP* II 77). Kierkegaard takes the human potential for faith to be general: "the only thing and the greatest – something the greatest and the lowliest of men are capable of doing for God – is to give oneself completely" (*EUD* 369). And again: "The eternal in speaking about the highest assumes calmly that every man can do it, and merely asks, therefore, whether or not he has done it" (*WL* 89).[9]

A key question remains, however, even for universalists like Kierkegaard. Does a commitment to *equal* access to the highest imply that each person, no matter his or her circumstance, will find it *equally* difficult to have faith, hope, and love? The fact that faith is a "gift of God" does not settle the issue, since one's *acceptance* of the gift may be harder or easier depending on one's personal history. Johannes Climacus asks "is it not . . . worthy of the God to make his covenant with men equally difficult for every human being in every time and place . . . equally difficult but also equally easy, since the God grants the condition?" (*PF* 134). But if Kierkegaard pushes his spiritual egalitarianism so far as to deny *any* personal variability in the task of *accepting* the covenant, that egalitarianism ceases to be credible.

Surely how one is treated, especially in the formative years, influences how readily one can, for instance, give and receive love. Having been neglected or abused as a child may leave one scarred for life, unable to trust others (including God) or able to do so only with great difficulty; whereas having a caring family that nurtures and supports one can lay a foundation for future moral and religious thriving. A loving household does not guarantee a loving child, to be sure, but it helps; even as a vicious family does not guarantee a sociopathic child, but it hurts. Peter Geach has maintained that, with God's grace, all finite persons have a *genuine* chance at Glory, though not an *identical* chance.[10] It *is* harder for some than for others to accept the offer of salvation but human nature as such carries with it the potential for saying "Yes" to grace. Geach's position is a happy alternative to Climacus's literal equality of access: It preserves universality without implausibly insisting on identity. Out of the hand of God, all creatures made in the image of God possess the wherewithal for growing into faith, hope, and love, even if lived history subsequently thwarts this "genuine chance." This brings us to our second theme.

II. EQUALITY OF RESPONSIBILITY

In "One Who Prays Aright," Kierkegaard avers that "no human being can give an eternal resolution to another or take it from him; one human being cannot be indebted to another" (*EUD* 382); in *Philosophical Fragments*, Climacus concludes that "one human being, in so far as he is a believer, owes nothing to another but everything to the God" (*PF* 127). It is tempting to think that, in matters of faith, we are free and independent (even invulnerable) with respect to other humans, yet utterly bound and dependent (even predestined) with respect to Almighty God. This picture is powerful, but, according to Kierkegaard, it must not devolve into a doctrine of irresistible grace, for "we must make a little concession. . . . [Human] subjectivity cannot be excluded, unless we want to have fatalism" and thus God be responsible for evil. As Kierkegaard puts it elsewhere, the idea of predestination is "a thoroughgoing abortion" that explains nothing (*JP* II 56).

Faith, hope, and love, for Kierkegaard, are akin to passive potentials in finite individuals. They may not be intrinsic to human nature as such, but they are obtainable by human nature aided by grace; and after the Fall they are certainly warped by sin. Yet even as divine gifts, they must be accepted and built up; faith, hope, and love cannot be necessitated – not even by God. Humans are to assume that the potential for love of God and neighbor is present in all human beings; "true greatness is equally accessible to all," as Johannes de silentio says in *Fear and Trembling* (*FT* 81). Moreover, God is owed "everything" in that God freely offers the prospective lover a necessary condition for healing his now-warped potential and coming into relation with God. The prospective lover/believer has done nothing to merit this salvation – all are equally undeserving before God's redemptive Word – but the individual remains free to accept or reject the divine invitation. One is accountable for saying either "Yes" or "No" to the grace extended to all. If this is not so, as Jacob Arminius so clearly saw, then God is responsible for evil. God does evil that "good" might come; indeed, God is the sole author of sin because He is the sole agent in history.[11] As Kierkegaard notes in his journals, better to say "I will not" in discussing one's disobedience to God than "I cannot" (*JP* II 74–5).

For Kierkegaard, then, *God's grace is indispensable but not irresistible, a necessary but not a sufficient condition, for human faith, hope, and love.* Kierkegaard grants, of course, that others can slay the body, yet in *Works of Love* he insists that *spiritual* death is always "suicide," a rushing of one's own defenses (*WL* 308). Are we, in fact, as invulnerable to *human* harm and as inaccessible to *human* help as Kierkegaard claims? There are four possible permutations; others can give us:

(1) both spiritual help and spiritual harm
(2) spiritual help but not spiritual harm

(3) spiritual harm but not spiritual help
(4) neither spiritual help nor spiritual harm

Kierkegaard often seems to opt for (4), such that in ethico-religious matters we owe no human being anything at all, positively or negatively (see, e.g., *EUD* 382). We are vulnerable to others physically, but spiritually we are radically independent. Before God, it seems, the spirit can be kept intact even in the worst of physical or psychological conditions:

Consider, for example, the woman with hemorrhages (Mt. 9:20 ff). . . . The secret she kept to herself; it was the secret of faith which saved her both for time and for eternity. This secret you can have for yourself also when you forthrightly profess the faith, and when you lie weak on your sick-bed and cannot move a limb, and when you cannot even move your tongue, you can still have this secret within you. (*WL* 44)

This is an exceptionally strong view. It makes no explicit mention of external help or harm, but it suggests an amazing durability for "the secret of faith." A view in which *all* forms of spiritual help and harm are ruled out, however, would undermine the point of Kierkegaard's authorship itself, both the direct and indirect communication. *From the Point of View of My Work as an Author* makes it clear that Kierkegaard thought others can help us remove illusions. His own edifying discourses manifestly aim at upbuilding others and thereby "helping" them in some sense, even if only to convince them of their sinfulness and to throw them back on the mercy of God. Indeed, Kierkegaard writes in *Works of Love* that *"to help another human being to love God is to love another man; to be helped by another human being to love God is to be loved"* (*WL* 113; emphasis original). But the point is to give credit where credit is due, that is, to God. As he puts it in "Every Good Gift," "the only good and perfect gift a human being can give is love, and all human beings in all ages have confessed that love has its home in heaven and comes down from above" (*EUD* 157).

To sustain and elaborate Kierkegaard's stance, we must draw at least three distinctions.[12] First, we must distinguish what obtains once one has achieved the threshold of ethico-religious agency from what obtains in one's spiritual nonage. The question of whether human beings can be classed according to spiritual maturity (e.g., strong/weak, agent/nonagent) is key to an analysis of options (1) through (4) above. Abuses of freedom, including the perversion or loss of freedom, may always be by one's own hand, but the failure ever to acquire freedom (where the spirit is "dreaming," to borrow a phrase from *The Concept of Anxiety* [*CA* 41]) may be due to outside interference. Free agents, as selves properly so-called, have equal access to the "highest," according to Kierkegaard (*JP* I 37); and, in a spiritual sense, selves are relatively invulnerable. But some, perhaps those who have never heard of the Teacher or the Word, are deprived of the occasion for faith and thus fail to achieve true self-consciousness. In some, the threshold of responsible spirit is not reached, an all or nothing affair, and freedom may indeed be permanently thwarted. Can't we make "the weak" stumble, as Saint Paul says? Consider again a child who is so sexually abused by her parents that she can never trust another human being, that she even becomes psychotic and sociopathic. Or think of Genie, the so-called wild child, who was chained to a potty-seat for months at a time by her parents and so seldom spoken to that she never learned to speak?[13] Aren't these examples of profound, even irremediable, spiritual harm? I fear so.

Second, we must distinguish between spiritual help or harm *simpliciter* and what might be called *decisive* spiritual help or harm. Decisive spiritual help would be virtue given to another even unto eternal salvation. Not just some minor character flaw is mitigated; the highest good is facilitated in, if not bequeathed to, someone. In "The Expectancy of Faith," however, Kierkegaard rules out such momentous assistance between human beings: "One person can do much for another, but he cannot give him faith" (*EUD* 12). Decisive spiritual harm, in turn, would be injury even unto permanent damnation. This too Kierkegaard denies.

Third, we must distinguish between helping and harming *partially* or *merely complicitously,* and helping and harming *decisively.* The accent here is on the adverb "decisively," *how* help is given, rather than the adjective "decisive," *what* help is given. To help another spirit decisively is to necessitate his virtue or some other moral excellence without his effort or acquiescence. In the extreme, this would amount to necessitating the salvation of another with or without her free will or consent. Call this decisive spiritual help decisively given. To harm another spirit decisively would be to necessitate vice or some other moral corruption in another with or without her free will or consent. At the abominable extreme – decisive spiritual harm decisively given – this would entail ineluctably damning someone without antecedent fault of his or her own. Kierkegaard clearly holds that, between human beings, there can be neither decisive help nor decisive harm, in the spiritual sense, and *no* form of help or harm can be decisively given. There are no demonic persons or dilemmatic circumstances that can compel vice, for example, from without; faith, hope, and love are always viable options, however difficult. Good Arminian that he is, however, Kierkegaard holds a similar position with respect to *divine*-human relations. Freedom is internal to all virtue and vice, and cannot be short-circuited, *even by God*, if responsible ethico-religious agency is to be retained. "The self is freedom" (*SUD* 29).

Saint Augustine and Kierkegaard are discussed at some length in the next section, but an anticipatory summary of their positions on grace and free will is helpful here. Augustine developed his over time, as he combatted different heresies. But the mature anti-Pelagian Augustine apparently embraced both decisive spiritual help decisively given by God to human beings and decisive spiritual harm decisively given by Adam (and Eve) to their descendants. Augustine endorsed, that is, (*a*) irresistible grace moving the wills of the elect, leaving them, in heaven, *non posse peccare* and (*b*) original sin bequeathed biologically by Adam to all future generations, leaving them, in themselves, *non posse non peccare.*[14] Kierkegaard will have none of this. God can awaken dread in innocents – as when Adam and Eve, naked in the Garden, are thrown into anxiety by God's prohibition against eating from the Tree of Knowledge – but neither God nor humanity can necessitate vice, or virtue (*CA* 44). As the pseudonym Vigilius Haufniensis says: "sin presupposes itself, obviously not before it is posited (which is predestination), but in that it is posited" (*CA* 62). All fall freely, as did Adam; we are radically individually responsible.

What are we to make of Kierkegaard's position, normatively? What are we to think of the scenario described above where another's agency is deeply wounded, if not forever blocked, through no fault of his own? Child abuse cases do come to mind, as does the "unmaking of humanity" that Elaine Scarry associates with the torture of adults.[15] Even this would not be the *necessitation of vice* in another, since vice presupposes moral responsibility, but it may be the ineluctable *deprivation of virtue.* "Freedom presupposes itself" (*CA* 112), so no one can necessitate the first free act or any subsequent free act – though freedom may be nurtured somewhat or even prompted, as by God's dreadful commandment in the Garden. But this does not preclude someone's necessitating the *absence* of the first free act. We can suspend others in an impersonal limbo, if you will, by victimizing them into moral oblivion. Do we call this decisive harm and/or harm decisively given? It is not technically decisive harm since nonagents are presumably not punished or condemned to hell; it may not even be moral harm decisively given since, again, what is compelled is not vice but the absence of virtue. But it is certainly *profound* harm, more profound than Kierkegaard usually admits. Another's personhood has been deeply frustrated, and the failure to address this possibility is a notable limitation of Kierkegaard's authorship.

Still, nothing Kierkegaard says need prevent him from endorsing the following four summary points:

1. Someone may provide the necessary and/or sufficient conditions for profound (but not decisive) spiritual harm to premoral, emergent selves (*vide* child abuse, etc.).
2. No one, other than the agents themselves, may provide necessary and/or sufficient conditions for spiritual harm to mature selves (i.e., no harm, decisive or otherwise, can be decisively given; spiritual death is always suicide).
3. Someone may provide the necessary and/or sufficient conditions for profound (but not decisive) spiritual help to premoral, emergent selves (e.g., our parents give us birth, crucial nurture, ethical education, etc.).
4. No one, other than the agents themselves, may provide sufficient conditions for spiritual help, decisive or otherwise, to mature selves (i.e., freedom is internal to virtue and not even divine grace is irresistible).

From these points, we can see how Kierkegaard might generate a plausible doctrine of social responsibility, even while preserving the strong egalitarian and individualistic theses mentioned earlier. The duty of love to our neighbor can be translated in the first instance into a duty to protect her inchoate ethico-religious freedom. Vulnerable human beings must be called into realized spirit, into personhood, by the care of others, even if we rightly assume that all are potential persons and that all actual persons are individually accountable. (Think of the Arminian free church tradition, coupled with the conviction that preventing the frustration of selfhood is the principle function of the civil law.) But this reference to freedom brings us to our third theme.

III. TWO ACCOUNTS OF CHOICE AND TWO KINDS OF FREEDOM

Let me clarify Kierkegaard's position by comparing it with Saint Augustine's – in particular, by contrasting their respective positions first on the nature of moral deliberation and choice, and then on the kinds of human freedom. In describing human faculties, Augustine largely accepts, via Plato and neo-Platonism, the classical hegemony of reason. Reason governs the soul even as the soul governs the body; reason discloses empirical, moral, and theological truths, ultimately revealing God as the final object of our fullest love: the immutable *Summum Bonum*. Unlike Plato, Augustine centers virtue and vice in the will rather than the intellect. For Augustine, wickedness, for instance, is not merely ignorance about the nature of the Good or weakness of will in pursuing it, as it was for Plato, but a defiant rejection of the True and the Good, a wrong turning of the self away from what may be known to be genuinely valuable. Sin is such a "perversion of will."[16] Even so, it remains the case for Augustine that *ideally* the will moves the individual to choose or model what reason discloses as the truly excellent. "Whatever we know, we grasp and hold to by reason."[17] Reason proposes, the will disposes. Your love defines you as your weight (*pondus*), love itself being a matter of the whole person (body and soul); but those external realities to which you *ought* to gravitate in love are determined by the governing part of the soul, reason. Mind discovers the *ordo amoris*, even if the other human faculties then conform to it.[18] In short, passion and appetite serve little or no epistemic function for Augustine: They are not valuable disclosers of moral and religious truth but (at least after the Fall) unruly faculties to blind reason and corrupt the will. If we are sinful, it is because God permits passion and desire (*cupiditas*) to have their perverse heads. When reason "rules the irrational emotions," on the other hand, "then there exists in man the very mastery which the law that we know to be eternal prescribes."[19]

Kierkegaard, in contrast, denies the hegemony of reason. He radicalizes Augustine's emphasis on inwardness by accenting the epistemic significance of passion and volition, as well as the epistemic impoverishment of reason, in ethical and religious contexts. Essential truths, Kierkegaard assures us, must be apprehended via passionate choice, free choice, rather than abstract reflection. Indeed, he turns the classical intellectualist picture of the self on its head, giving priority to passion and will (as well as imagination, when properly regulated) over objective reflection and detached control. This is the hallmark of his religious romanticism. Emotion is not vilified; it is considered an indispensable means for arriving at "existential" truths about God and oneself not available to reason alone. Although Kierkegaard admires Augustine, his verdict on him is rather harsh:

Augustine has nevertheless done incalculable harm. . . . Quite simply, Augustine has reinstated the Platonic-Aristotelian definition, the whole Greek philosophical pagan definition of faith. . . . In the Greek view, faith is a concept which belongs in the sphere of the intellectual. . . . Thus faith is related to probability, and we get the progression: faith – knowledge. Christianly, faith is at home in the existential. (JP I 71)

The frontispiece quotation to Either/Or, from the English Romantic Edward Young, raises the salient question "Is reason then alone baptized, are the passions pagans?" (EO I 1). Kierkegaard and his pseudonyms reply with a definitive "No."

For all Kierkegaard's differences with Augustine on reason and passion, it is crucial to recognize that both men speak of two senses of freedom. "Freedom of choice" (defined as the impersonal ability to do otherwise) is the formal condition of what Kierkegaard calls "true freedom" (defined as a positive capacity, a personal identity, with real material content) (EO II 174). Freedom of choice, what Augustine calls "liberum arbitrium," is a bare nonnecessitation prior to choosing: the neutral ability to do X or not to do X. True freedom, what Augustine refers to as "libertas," is the moral concreteness one acquires in and through choosing a specific alternative and subsequently binding oneself to it. True freedom is a potency, "to be able" (CA 49): a dynamic commitment to a virtuous end, rather than formal indifference as an initial means to that end.

Prior to the original sin, according to Augustine, Adam and Eve possessed both *liberum arbitrium* and *libertas*. The choice to be disobedient in the Garden, however, led to the loss of *libertas*. It destroyed that hierarchical unity of God–soul–body that makes for true human flourishing, and now all of humanity is in need of God's grace to restore right loving, to combat lust, and so on. The key question for Augustine is the extent to which *liberum arbitrium* was also lost. In some of his early writings, such as various books of *On Free Choice of the Will*, he seems to assume that individuals even now are in possession of *liberum arbitrium*. He suggests that since punishment and reward for actions are just, we have free will in this sense, even if weakened or diminished.[20] There is still some autonomy left to the will and some power left to the mind; and one can at least choose a disordered love, something that God in no way causes directly. God seems a co-causer of good choices only, as though in evil actions one merely says "No" to God's will.

In later works directed against the Pelagians and their belief in human perfectibility, however, Augustine begins to let go of even *liberum arbitrium* for postlapsarian humanity. At times, as in "On the Spirit and the Letter," there seems to be a synergistic scenario where grace and free will work together in bringing about salvation. But given that divine grace moves the will, it is unclear even here whether and how such grace can be refused. For Augustine, to call an action "voluntary" is to imply that it flows from an inner principle with some knowledge of its end or purpose. Yet God sets the conditions for faith and then awakens desire by acting through the individual's own internal agency.[21] In "On Grace and Free Will," moreover, even though "[t]here is always . . . within us a free will," it is God who empowers one to obey what God Himself commands.[22] Thus Augustine seems to let go of any doctrine of the cooperation of grace and free will. The elect are "made to will" by God such that they cannot but persevere, while the "mass of perdition" could not possibly persevere even if they wanted to.[23]

Ultimately, then, Augustine ends up with quite a strong view of predestination: Some people are moved by grace ineluctably to love God and others are not, hence there is an elect who cannot be lost and a reprobate who cannot be saved.[24] There is no human explanation for this dichotomy. God's grace is not like external coercion; it leaves human action "voluntary," in the literal sense that grace operates through one's will (*voluntas*). But one could not do otherwise than what God ordains. Augustine speaks of "the reasonable soul" giving "consent" to God's "summons," but there is, in fact, no moment of genuinely free acceptance on humanity's part, no *liberum arbitrium*, since the soul itself is fully orchestrated by God to believe and to will and to do.[25]

Kierkegaard repeatedly refers to *liberum arbitrium* as a "chimera," something "never found" in real life, a "phantasy" (*JP* II 67, 59, 73), a "nuisance for thought" (*CA* 49); but we must be careful to understand his point. If *liberum arbitrium* is defined as an utter unconditionedness that "can equally well choose the good or the evil," then it is, according to Kierkegaard, "an abrogation of the concept of freedom and a despair of any explanation of it" (*JP* II 61–2). For "[g]ood and evil exist nowhere outside freedom, since this very distinction comes into existence through freedom" (62). Nevertheless, formal freedom of choice is presupposed by true freedom. ("True freedom" quickly takes on a normative connotation in Kierkegaard, such that it would seem odd to call a vicious disposition "true freedom," even if it were self-consciously cultivated.) The mistake is in looking for, or insisting permanently upon, abstract freedom of choice *in place of* true freedom; the error, that is, is in focusing on ideal *liberum arbitrium* altogether independently of existential *libertas*. Kierkegaard does not reject *liberum arbitrium* as such, any more than he rejects truth as "identity of thought and being"; rather, he notes its abstractness when taken in isolation or out of context.[26]

Whereas Augustine eventually denies both senses of freedom for the fallen as such, Kierkegaard consistently affirms both, if taken together. Augustine saw the prelapsarian Adam and Eve as *posse peccare* and *posse non peccare*, able to sin and able not to sin, and postlapsarian humanity, all of (ungraced) humanity, as *non posse non peccare*, unable not to sin. All generations after the Fall have inherited Adam's guilt and are justly condemned by God as having "sinned with him."[27] On Kierkegaard's view, however, this draws too complete a contrast between us and the original, pre-Fall parents; it makes Adam "essentially different from the race" (*CA* 29). According to the pseudonymous Vigilius Haufniensis, sin always enters the world in qualitatively the same way, by guilty free choice; thus, every person is his or her own Adam or Eve (35–7). An

Augustinian conception of original sin is attractive to some Christian ethicists as an expression of the power of corporate sin: We are born into social structures and institutions that already embody evil, Lutherans often suggest, and our complicity in these realities means that there is no escaping dirty hands even in principle. Although raised a Lutheran, Kierkegaard thought the idea of inherited guilt explains nothing, and that a predestinating grace (or fall) that would necessitate agents and deny freedom of choice altogether is "a thoroughgoing abortion" (*JP* II 56). Predestination (and the related notion of irresistible grace) is the complementary vice of dwelling solely on libertarian freedom of choice.

The challenge of existence is to realize true freedom, historically, by moving beyond mere freedom of choice – by, as it were, binding oneself voluntarily to an integrated identity (*libertas*) such that there is no longer a question of raw choice (mere *liberum arbitrium*). Formal freedom of choice is thereby transcended or transformed in time. Kierkegaard, however, is not a compatibilist, much less a determinist.[28] *Pace* Augustine, he suggests that it is always possible for an erstwhile faithful person to fall away from virtue, to make the "leap" of sin in opposition to God's grace.[29] It is human sin that is inexplicable by reason, not merely divine grace; and a necessitated perseverance is a contradiction in terms, a denial of human historicity. The possibility of offense at God is a permanent feature of temporal life. As Anti-Climacus puts it: "The greatest possible human misery, greater even than sin, is to be offended at Christ and to continue in the offense; and Christ cannot, 'love' cannot, make this impossible" (*SUD* 126).

It is tempting to say that *liberum arbitrium* is "included in" *libertas*, just as despair is included in faith, that is, as dialectically *excluded*.[30] This reading is evocative, but it risks overstatement; freedom of choice has an ineliminable place in the stages on life's way even if it is basically "transubstantiated" by faith.

The most tremendous thing conceded to man is – choice, freedom. If you want to rescue and keep it, there is only one way – in the very same second unconditionally in full attachment give it back to God and yourself along with it. If the sight of what is conceded to you tempts you, if you surrender to the temptation and look with selfish craving at freedom of choice, then you lose your [true] freedom. And your punishment then is to go around in a kind of confusion and brag about having – freedom of choice. (*JP* II 69)

As Anti-Climacus says, "freedom is the dialectical aspect of the categories of possibility and necessity" (*SUD* 29). *Liberum arbitrium* correlates with possibility, I would suggest, and *libertas* with necessity. But the two are inseparable.

Why is being bound to God in *libertas* a source of potency? The answer is that only in this way does one participate in the life of Love that grounds and sustains one's finite being. To try to remain within pure possibility, utterly neutral and uncommitted about temporal life, is despair, a form of sin; the will always "has a history."[31] *Contra* Augustinian and Calvinist ideas of fatalistic election, however, even those espoused in the name of God's sovereignty, we must insist on *both* freedom of choice *and* true freedom – both *liberum arbitrium* and *libertas* – as essential to finite moral agency, for freedom of choice is the ontological precondition for true freedom and, properly understood, a genuine good.

Usually the freedom of being able to choose is presented as an extraordinary good. This it is, but it nevertheless depends also upon how long it is going to last. Usually one makes the mistake of thinking that this itself is the good and that this freedom of choice lasts one's entire life.

What Augustine says of true freedom (distinguished from freedom of choice) is very true and very much a part of experience – namely, that the person has a most lively sense when with completely decisive determination he impresses upon his action the inner necessity which excludes the thought of another possibility. Then freedom of choice or the "agony" of choice comes to an end. (*JP* II 74)

Note the allusion to Augustine, but note also that, on Kierkegaard's view, it is the person him- or herself who impresses the necessity on action. "[T]he opposite of [true] freedom is guilt" rather than necessity, but to think that someone *must* sin is "foolishness" (*CA* 108, 112).

We are left, then, with two major departures from Saint Augustine: (1) No external power (neither Adam's sin nor God's grace) can compel a moral choice, decisively harm or help a human being, for both senses of freedom are irreducibly present in finite moral agency; and (2) moral and religious choices are characterized chiefly by passionate commitment rather than rational assent. As Kierkegaard contends, "it is left to the individual himself whether he will or will not, whether he will or will not expose himself to sufferings and troubles and tribulations" (*JP* II 76–7). Coming to faith is not a matter of

Promethean self-creation (since grace is required), but neither is it mainly a matter of accurate cognition or preordained experience. True freedom is, for Kierkegaard, a highly individualized *libertas* in which voluntary *consent* to grace takes the form of a passionate leap, a "Yes" to a Gifted Reality that, seen objectively, looks paradoxical. This is not a crude subjectivism where "truth" is whatever feels good; Kierkegaard clearly holds that emotional allegiances can be misplaced, pathos-filled choices mistaken (see, e.g., *EO* II 167). And neither is it an irrationalism where what is known to be self-contradictory is nonetheless believed; Kierkegaard says explicitly that faith is above reason (*supra rationem*) rather than against reason (*contra rationem*).[32] But it is a consistent, if romantic, Arminianism.

Jacob Arminius asked the perennial question of freedom and came close to sparking civil war in the Netherlands; at the end of his life, Kierkegaard, too, hoped to stir individuals and shake institutions. Given Kierkegaard's disdain for most academics, Arminius's 1603 appointment as professor of theology would not have endeared him to Kierkegaard. But the fact that Arminius was hounded, and eventually condemned, by the state church made him a forerunner of the Kierkegaard who wrote "Attack on Christendom." Both Arminius and Kierkegaard had towering theological and ecclesial nemeses. As the latter railed against Hegel and Bishop Mynster, so the former wrestled with Gomar and the States General, not to mention the ghost of Calvin. (Arminius did not have to grapple, however, with tabloid journalism like *The Corsair*, which pilloried Kierkegaard.) In the end, nonetheless, Kierkegaard's legacy is more literary and theological than political and ecclesiological.

With respect to grace and freedom, Kierkegaard leaves us with three related dialectical conundrums to be appreciated as such; he is a fan of neither Kantian–Sartrean subjectivity nor Augustinian–Calvinist objectivity. Kierkegaard wants to affirm: (1) both universal access to the highest things and the rarity of individual faith before God,[33] (2) both equal accountability to the God who is Love and gracious upbuilding by that same God, and (3) both freedom of choice (*liberum arbitrium*) and true personal freedom (*libertas*). An undialectical reading of universal access leads us to think that Christianity comes to all as a brute fact of birth, while an undialectical take on the rarity of faith tempts us to believe in "chosenness" and to draw an invidious contrast between "the elect" and "the reprobate." Similarly, a too simple view of equal accountability speaks of "sheer invulnerability" and "radical autonomy," whereas a pietistic account of the graciousness of Love embraces categories like "decisive help decisively given." Finally, an un-Kierkegaardian celebration of *liberum arbitrium* translates into aesthetic arbitrariness, the pure subjectivity of some postmodernists, even as an un-Kierkegaardian perspective on *libertas* valorizes irresistible grace, the pure objectivity of some premodernists.

Kierkegaard's existential dialectic is not a rejection of God's omnipotence but an appreciation of its kenotic form. God voluntarily lets human beings act voluntarily, even in relation to the Trinity, by ceasing to be all in all. Only a truly omnipotent being could create beings with a real freedom and otherness over against God, out of which they consent to being loved and to being empowered to love others in kind. "The greatest good . . . which can be done for a being, greater than anything else that one can do for it, is to make it free. In order to do just that, omnipotence is required"(*JP* II 62). It is this insistence that we not separate divine omnipotence from divine goodness, lest we end up worshipping mere power, that marks Kierkegaard as a splendid Arminian. His authorship can still edify personal conscience, if not dramatically change human history.

NOTES

1 *Works of Love*, trans. Howard V. Hong and Edna H. Hong (New York: Harper and Row, 1962). I cite this edition.

2 *Philosophical Fragments*, trans. David F. Swenson and Howard V. Hong (Princeton: Princeton University Press, 1962). I cite this edition.

3 See Stephen N. Dunning, "Love Is Not Enough: A Kierkegaardian Phenomenology of Religious Experience," *Faith and Philosophy* 12, 1 (January 1995): 35.

4 "Kant held that man was his own law (autonomy), that is, bound himself under the law which he gave himself. In a deeper sense that means to say: lawlessness or experimentation. It is no harder than the thwacks which Sancho Panza applied to his own bottom. . . . If I am not bound by anything higher than myself, and if I am to bind myself, where am I to acquire the severity . . . ?" See *The Journals of Kierkegaard*, ed. and trans. Alexander Dru (New York: Harper and Row, 1959), p. 181.

5 Shortly after his death, in 1609, Arminius's followers composed a summary of their position entitled the *Remonstrance* and called for a synod to adjudicate the central doctrinal disputes. Although it was judged heretical by the Synod of Dort in 1618, the theology of Arminius and

the Remonstrants was highly influential on a host of Christian traditions, especially Anglicanism and Methodism. For additional biographical information and a collection of primary sources, see *The Works of James Arminius*, ed. and trans. James Nichols, 3 vols. (London: Longman, Hurst, Rees, Orme, Brown, and Green, 1825).

6 In what follows, I am especially indebted to the work of Gene Outka and Jamie Ferreira, but I also hope to mark some key points of divergence from their conclusions. See Outka, "Equality and Individuality: Thoughts on Two Themes in Kierkegaard," *The Journal of Religious Ethics* 10, 2 (Fall 1982): 171–203; Outka, "Equality and the Fate of Theism in Modern Culture," *The Journal of Religion* 67, 3 (July 1987): 275–88; and Ferreira, *Transforming Vision: Imagination and Will in Kierkegaardian Faith* (Oxford: Clarendon Press, 1991).

7 *The Journals of Søren Kierkegaard*, ed. and trans. Alexander Dru (London: Oxford University Press, 1959), p. 361. This passage is quoted by Outka in "Equality and the Fate of Theism," p. 275.

8 This Judaic drama of self-overcoming is already evident in the prophet Amos; it becomes critical in Saint Paul.

9 This passage is also cited by Outka in "Equality and the Fate of Theism," p. 275.

10 Peter Geach, *Providence and Evil* (Cambridge University Press, 1977), pp. 121–2. Outka refers to Geach's work in "Equality and Individuality," p. 198, fn 6.

11 See, for instance, "A Declaration" (1608), in *The Works of James Arminius*, 1:565–6.

12 Here I attempt to go beyond Outka's work cited in note 6 above.

13 As reported by *Nova* in an episode entitled "Secret of the Wild Child" (WGBH/Boston, 1994).

14 See, e.g., Augustine, "On Rebuke and Grace," chaps. 12, 28, and 38, and "On Grace and Free Will," chaps. 31–3, both in vol. 5 of *The Nicene and Post-Nicene Fathers*, ed. Philip Schaff, trans. Peter Holmes and Robert Ernest Wallis, rev. Benjamin B. Warfield (Grand Rapids: Eerdmans, 1978); *The Enchiridion on Faith, Hope, and Love*, trans. J. F. Shaw (Washington, D.C.: Regnery, 1961), chaps. 28–32; and *The City of God*, trans. Henry Bettenson (New York: Penguin, 1972), bk. 13, chaps. 13–14. Augustine does not use the word "irresistible" in describing God's grace, and he does in places distinguish between divine permission and divine action (e.g., *The Enchiridion*, chaps. 95–6). Nonetheless, as John Rist puts it, "salvation is independent of man's fallen will; it is a matter of God's omnipotence. God has mercy on those whom he will. . . . If God wishes a man's salvation, salvation follows *of necessity*." See Rist, "Augustine on Free Will and Predestination," in *Augustine: A Collection of Critical Essays*, ed. R. A. Markus (Garden City: Doubleday, 1972), p. 238.

15 Elaine Scarry, *The Body in Pain* (Oxford: Oxford University Press, 1985).

16 Augustine, *Confessions*, trans. R. S. Pine-Coffin (New York: Penguin, 1978), bk. 7, chap. 16, p. 150; see also *On Free Choice of the Will*, trans. Anna S. Benjamin and L. H. Hackstaff (Indianapolis: Bobbs-Merrill, 1979), bk. 2, chap. 14, p. 69. In *The Enchiridion*, Augustine does list "ignorance" and "weakness" as the "two causes that lead to sin" (chap. 81, p. 97), but here "weakness" does not refer to Platonic *akrasia* but to something more like disobedience: "we leave undone what we know we ought to do, and we do what we know we ought not to do" (chap. 81, p. 98). Augustine's equation of sin with perversity is perhaps most vivid in the famous account of his youthful theft of some pears, "not compelled by any lack" but out of "my own love of mischief" and of "my own perdition" (*Confessions*, bk. 2, chap. 4, p. 47). As much as he differs from Augustine on the stature of reason, Kierkegaard agrees that sin is not merely ignorance but rather a "polemic" attitude toward the Truth. See Climacus's *Philosophical Fragments*, p. 19.

17 Augustine, *On Free Choice of the Will*, bk. 2, chap. 3, p. 42. Reason's excellence is summarized in bk. 2, chaps. 5 and 6, pp. 46–9. Reason alone can even demonstrate God's existence; see bk. 2, chap. 15, pp. 71–2.

18 See Augustine, *Confessions*, bk. 13, chap. 9, p. 317.

19 Augustine, *On Free Choice of the Will*, bk. 1, chap. 8, pp. 18–19.

20 Augustine, *On Free Choice of the Will*, bk. 2, chap. 1, p. 36.

21 Augustine, "On the Spirit and the Letter," in vol. 5 of *The Nicene and Post-Nicene Fathers*, chap. 60, p. 110.

22 Augustine, "On Grace and Free Will," chap. 31, p. 456.

23 Augustine, "On Rebuke and Grace," chap. 31, p. 484, and chap. 16, p. 478.

24 In "On Rebuke and Grace," chap. 20, p. 480, Augustine writes: ". . . they who are truly children [of God] are foreknown and predestinated as conformed to the image of His Son, and are called according to His purpose, so as to be elected. For the son of promise does not perish, but the son of perdition." The children of God "absolutely cannot perish" (chap. 23, p. 481), to perish being to fall permanently away from the good.

25 Augustine, "On the Spirit and the Letter," chap. 60, p. 110; and "On Rebuke and Grace," chap. 4, p. 473, and chap. 38, p. 487.

26 In *Concluding Unscientific Postscript*, trans. David F. Swenson and Walter Lowrie (Princeton: Princeton University Press, 1968), the pseudonym Johannes Climacus writes:

> . . . the notion of the truth as identity of thought and being is a chimera of abstraction, in its truth only an expectation of the creature; *not because the truth is not such an identity*, but because the knower is an existing individual for whom the truth cannot be such an identity as long as he lives in time. (p. 176; emphasis added)

This point is exactly parallel to that made about *liberum arbitrium*. Both truth-as-correspondence and liberty-of-indifference must be understood existentially: They are not illusions but transcendental limits that can only be approached or presumed by finite persons. Objective truth and libertarian freedom are more like premises of pure and practical reason, respectively, than like conclusions of argument or ends of action. But it is no more accurate to call Kierkegaard a nihilist or relativist with respect to truth than it is to call him a determinist or compatibilist with respect to freedom. These "isms" cut the nerve of meaningful existence by denying the dialectic between objectivity and subjectivity, necessity and freedom, eternity and temporality that characterizes human nature. As Anti-Climacus argues (*SUD* 13–21), the two poles of human personality must be constantly "synthesized"; to deny one entirely in favor of the other or to see no tension between them is "despair."

27 Augustine, "On Rebuke and Grace," chap. 28, p. 483. Cf. *On Free Choice of the Will*, bk. 3, chaps. 18–20, pp. 126–33.

28 Jamie Ferreira sometimes talks as though Kierkegaard were a kind of compatibilist, simply hostile to freedom of choice as *liberum arbitrium*, but she is sensitive to the complexities here. See Ferreira, *Transforming Vision*, pp. 36–40. For a recent defense of the compatibility of determinism and moral responsibility, see Harry G. Frankfurt's essays in *Moral Responsibility*, ed. John Martin Fischer (Ithaca: Cornell University Press, 1986). For criticisms of Frankfurt's position, see ibid., especially the contributions by Fischer and Peter Van Inwagan. Several of Frankfurt's seminal articles are collected in *The Importance of What We Care About* (Cambridge University Press, 1988).

29 On sin being a "qualitative leap" of the individual, see *CA* 32, 47.

30 Such an "inclusive exclusion" between despair and faith was somewhat playfully asserted by Ronald L. Hall in a session on "Kierkegaard and the Poetic Imagination" in the "Kierkegaard, Religion, and Culture Group" at the 1994 American Academy of Religion conference in Chicago. Hall elaborates this view in "Kierkegaard and the Paradoxical Logic of Worldly Faith," *Faith and Philosophy* 12, 1 (January 1995): 40–53.

31 *SUD* 73. Cf. *CA* 29, where "the individual has a history."

32 *JP* III 399–400. I discuss Kierkegaard's epistemology, including the thesis that "subjectivity is truth," in my "Kierkegaard's Metatheology," *Faith and Philosophy* 4, 1 (January 1987): 71–85.

33 In spite of his commitment to equal access, Kierkegaard writes: "the majority of men never experience the spiritual life; they never experience [the] qualitative encounter with the divine." See Dru's *The Journals of Kierkegaard*, p. 172.

10 "Developing" *Fear and Trembling*

Once I am dead, *Fear and Trembling* alone will be enough for an imperishable name as an author. Then it will be read, translated into foreign languages as well.

– *Søren Kierkegaards Papirer*

Kierkegaard was prophetic in his estimate of the place *Fear and Trembling* was to have in his authorship. Although several of his pseudonymous works have also become philosophical classics, *Fear and Trembling* continues to haunt us like no other of his writings. Its defense of individual existence still resonates at the end of a century marked by horrifying mass movements, while its depiction of radical religious obedience stirs new fears as we enter a period when older political ideologies are being replaced by renewed expressions of religious absolutism.

Fear and Trembling remains so evocative partly because of its enigmatic nature. From the outset, by means of the famous epigraph drawn from Hamann, Kierkegaard signals that not everything that follows is as it seems. Beyond this, there is evidence that Kierkegaard designed *Fear and Trembling* as a text with hidden layers of meaning. In *The Point of View for My Work as an Author*, Kierkegaard tells us that the most important ethical and religious truths cannot be communicated directly, as though one were writing on a blank sheet of paper. They demand instead creative endeavor by the author and a corresponding effort by the reader that involves "bringing to light by the application of a caustic fluid a text which is hidden under another text" (*PV* 40).

Kierkegaard appears to have in mind the process by which a message written in secret ink is deciphered.[1] Although he wrote before the advent of modern photography, we can also think of his interpretative advice in terms of the process by which film is developed. Beginning with a surface material of a certain texture and color, we undertake to expose different latent images and ideas. In what follows, I want to take Kierkegaard's advice and "develop" the text of *Fear and Trembling* in this photographic sense. What we will see, I think, is that this text contains not just two, but multiple levels of meaning. Each level has its own significance. As we expose each deeper level, the messages grow more subtle. Finally, when development is complete, we have in our hands a transparent image through which we can see all the levels of meaning and which, when held to the light, reveals a religious-ethical communication of surprising richness and complexity.

I. LEVEL I: THE CALL TO CHRISTIAN COMMITMENT

At the first and most apparent level of meaning, *Fear and Trembling* is a stinging critique of both the popular and cultured Christianity of his day and a reminder of the primitive challenge of Christian faith. This critique is signaled by the choice of Abraham and the Genesis 22 episode as paradigms of faith and by the repeated use of commercial metaphors to portray the spirit of the age.

Kierkegaard believed that the cultural triumph of Christian civilization had effaced the primitive meaning of Christianity. A religious identity whose acquisition once entailed great risk had become a matter of merely being born to Christian parents in a Christian nation. Time had also transmuted the stories of the early heroes and saints of faith. Looked at with the benefit of eighteen centuries of hindsight, a false picture of historical success and well-earned veneration had replaced vivid experiences of individual risk, suffering, abandonment, or martyrdom. What Kierkegaard calls "the results" had come to overshadow the anguished choices by early Christian disciples.

As an antidote to this spiritual lethargy, Kierkegaard's pseudonym, Johannes de silentio, devises what amounts to a theological shock treatment.[2] He portrays Abraham, the "knight of faith" in the full terror of his encounter with the divine command. By following the patriarch step for step on his difficult journey to Mt. Moriah, Johannes seeks to recover aspects of faith that years of saintly veneration and familiarity with the happy ending had effaced. "What is omitted from Abraham's story is the anxiety," Johannes tells us (*FT* 28). "We are curious about the results, just as we are curious about the way a book turns out. We do not want to know anything about the anxiety, the distress, the paradox" (63).

To illustrate how far the Christianity of his day had erred from the primitive experience of faith, "The Preliminary Expectoration," portrays an imaginary churchgoer who is led by a preacher's sermon to want to imitate Abraham. Learning of this, the pastor visits the parishioner and, rising to unprecedented heights of rhetorical fervor, thunders, "You despicable man, what devil has so possessed you that you want to murder your own son?" (*FT* 28). In Johannes's view, it does this hapless fellow little good to reply, "But, after all, that was what you yourself preached about on Sunday," since the established church and its functionaries were ignorant of how thoroughly they had replaced primitive Christianity with a cliché-ridden, worldly piety.

The use of Abraham also conveys a new emphasis on faith as a way of life. This emphasis is meant to replace the centuries-old understanding of faith as merely an acceptance of dogmatic truths. Abraham is a fitting choice to communicate this lesson because his hallmark is not intellectual achievement but a prodigious ability to live trustingly and obediently. In the margin of a draft of the "Eulogy on Abraham," Kierkegaard makes this point even clearer by ending the section with a definition of faith "not as the content of a concept but as a form of the will" (*Pap.* IV B 87 p. 2). The emphasis on willing and acting rather than thinking or reasoning is also highlighted by the sheer irrationality of Abraham's faith, his belief "by virtue of the absurd" that he will get Isaac back. As Jerry Gill points out, to present a "dialectical corrective," Kierkegaard offers the story of Abraham as a *reductio ad absurdum* of all traditions that see faith as involving mental assent.[3]

These ways of evading religious-ethical commitment represent pervasive and abiding problems in Christianity, but, in Kierkegaard's day, evasion had taken a new and virulent form. Among the intellectual leadership and scholarly teachers of Christianity, a pseudo-Christianity permeated by Hegelian philosophy held full sway. Under the motto "One must go further," the Hegelians presented "faith" as a rudimentary phase of intellectual development to be transcended by their own rational philosophy. This philosophy radically subordinated matters of personal ethical and religious decision, the crucial events of *individual* history, to scholars' comprehension of the meaning of *world* history. For the Hegelians, Abraham was at best a figure of historical interest whose personal trial and response were unimportant compared to whatever historical significance he might have in the development of monotheism. It is to question this approach that Johannes takes us step by step on Abraham's arduous journey.

Jibes at the Hegelians also virtually bracket the text. The book begins, for example, with Johannes remarking that "Not only in the world of business but also in the world of ideas, our age stages *ein wirklicher Ausverkauf* [a real sale]," in which everything can be had at "a bargain price" (*FT* 5). Once, faith was a task for a whole lifetime. But now, "every speculative monitor who conscientiously signals the important trends in modern philosophy, every assistant professor, tutor, and student," is unwilling to stop even with doubting but "goes further."

Near the book's end, the epilogue returns to business matters. Johannes mentions the practice of merchants in Holland of sinking cargoes of spices in the sea to jack up declining prices. This use of the language of commerce highlights the era's (and the Hegelians') bourgeois preoccupations and mocks the age's enthusiasm for mass produced, bargain-priced faith. Translated to the realm of spirit, the Dutch merchants' practice proves instructive to Johannes. Just as they sacrificed their cargoes to raise the value of their goods, so he employs the dramatic story of Abraham's sacrifice to raise the price – and cost – of faith. Understood at this level, it is precisely the outrageousness of Abraham's conduct that makes it the fitting counterweight to cultural Christianity and Hegelian philosophy.

II. LEVEL 2: THE PSYCHOLOGY OF FAITH

Once we have assimilated *Fear and Trembling*'s deliberately shocking indictment of cultural Christianity, our encounter with the text exposes a less dramatic and more subtle level of meaning. At this level *Fear and Trembling* involves an exploration of the psychology of faith. This inquiry starts with the first level's assumption that faith is a lived commitment but seeks to understand its precise mental content for the believer. In the "Exordium," "Eulogy on Abraham," and "Preliminary Expectoration," Johannes largely sets polemic aside to focus on the psychology of various exemplars of faith, some of whom prove to be quite ordinary persons. Here, Johannes lets us know that what is important in faith is not outer deeds like Abraham's dramatic obedience, but quiet and difficult inner movements of the spirit.

The central idea here is the "double movement" of faith. The first movement, "infinite resignation," is accomplished by relinquishing one's heart's desire. For the young swain depicted by Johannes, who accepts the fact that the great love of his life lies forever beyond his reach, infinite resignation leads to the discovery of his "eternal consciousness." Like the shirt whose thread is spun in tears, infinite resignation provides "peace and rest and comfort in the pain" (*FT* 45).

The "knight of faith" embodies the second movement. He starts where the "knight of infinite resignation" ends:

He does exactly the same as the other knight did: he infinitely renounces the love that is the substance of his life, he is reconciled in pain. But then the marvel happens; he makes one more movement even more wonderful than all the others, for he says: Nevertheless, I have faith that I will get her – that is, by the virtue of absurd, by virtue of the fact that for God all things are possible. (*FT* 46)

Abraham makes these two movements. He obeys God's command and willingly relinquishes Isaac. Simultaneously, he continues to believe that God will not demand Isaac of him, and that he will again enjoy his son's presence in this life. Unlike the despairing versions of Abraham presented in the "Exordium" who manage to fulfill God's will but lose the resilience of their souls, the real Abraham retains the ability "once again to be happy in Isaac" (*FT* 35).

Johannes lets us know that the capacity for such knighthood is not confined to the older heroes and saints of faith but remains available to every human being. He imagines a knight of faith residing in the Copenhagen of his day. No outward signs reveal this person's spiritual depth. In every way he resembles a bourgeois philistine, a tax collector even. Inwardly, however, at every moment he is making "the movement of infinity." He feels the pain of renouncing everything, "yet the finite tastes just as good to him as one who never knew anything higher" (*FT* 40).

Edward Mooney argues that at this level of psychological development, *Fear and Trembling* aims at describing and commending a stance of *selfless care*.

> The knight of faith can both renounce and enjoy the finite because he sees, or knows in his bones, that renouncing all *claim* to the finite is not renouncing all *care* for it. He is at home and takes delight in the finite (witness the tax-collector) because he cares; yet this is a selfless care, for he has given up all proprietary claim.[4]

If Mooney is right, this level of meaning of *Fear and Trembling* begins to suggest to us that the text as a whole is not quite the terrifying defense of religiously commanded homicide it seems to be. Rather, it begins to appear as a more traditional defense of selfless love as a central feature of the religious life.

III. LEVEL 3: THE NORMATIVE SHAPE OF CHRISTIAN EXISTENCE

If a first level of meaning contains a call to strenuous, lived commitment to Christian faith and a second develops the psychology of faith and love, a third level of *Fear and Trembling* explores the question of the norms that should guide the conduct of a committed Christian. At this level, *Fear and Trembling* appears to be at least the beginnings of a study in ethics.

This normative inquiry comes to the fore in the three "Problemata," especially in the ideas of a "teleological suspension of the ethical" and an "absolute duty to God." These difficult conceptions have been interpreted in various ways, not all of which are consistent with one another, nor with some of Johannes de silentio's own claims and statements. Part of the problem may be due to faulty readings of the text. Others seem to reflect Johannes's complex and confusing position. As we will see, these difficulties ultimately drive us beyond ethics to a still deeper level of meaning of the book.

The first "Problema" presents Genesis 22 as involving "a teleological suspension of the ethical" in which Abraham, the knight of faith, subordinates his responsibilities as a father to the needs of his own personal relationship with God. The ethical, Johannes tells us, is the "universal" and it is one's ethical responsibility to annul one's singularity to "become the universal" (*FT* 54). Although the Kantian and Hegelian philosophies Johannes presumes develop this thought in complex ways, the idea expressed here amounts to the simple requirement that the needs of the common good take precedence over merely individual wishes. But as it is exemplified in Abraham, faith reverses this priority. Faith is "the paradox that the single individual is higher than the universal" (55).

Johannes insists that we cannot comprehend Abraham's behavior in ethical terms. From the point of view of ethics, Abraham is nothing more than the murderer of his son. At no time is he a "tragic hero" who sets aside one expression of the ethical for a still higher expression. Agamemnon, Jephtha, and Brutus are tragic heroes. They also willingly undertake to kill their children; but as responsible leaders, they do so to protect the welfare of their community and the common good. Not Abraham. "By his act he transgressed the ethical altogether and had a higher τέλος outside it in relation to which he suspended it. . . . Why, then, does Abraham do it? For God's sake and – the two are wholly identical – for his own sake" (*FT* 59).

Johannes's description of Abraham poses a sharp challenge to those who would make sense of *Fear and Trembling* as a study in ethics. On the one hand, Johannes does not shrink from depicting Abraham as fully outside the ethical – as truly the murderer of his son. Not only does his conduct violate one of our most important ethical norms, it cannot be rationally justified in any way. His conduct remains "for all eternity a paradox, impervious to thought" (*FT* 56). On the other hand, Johannes also frequently lauds the patriarch and holds him up as a model for the Christian life. "I cannot understand Abraham," he tells us, "I can only admire him" (112; cf. 57, 114). Reading *Fear and Trembling* as a work intending to offer at least a preliminary vision of the Christian moral life produces a jarring inconsistency. *Fear and Trembling* seems to hold up as exemplary and somehow worthy of imitation a kind of conduct that we cannot possibly encourage, defend, or understand in terms of general moral values.

Various interpreters have tried to reduce or eliminate this seeming contradiction. Elmer Duncan, for example, argues that the primary target of Johannes's ethical critique is a kind of Kantian ethical absolutism that makes no room for permissible exceptions. Kant, in his essay "On a Supposed Right to Lie from Altruistic Motives," had argued that one is not permitted to tell even a small lie to a criminal aggressor in order to save the life of an innocent person.[5] Duncan believes that Kierkegaard, like many other readers of Kant, found this position to be preposterous. Since he was unable to justify exceptions within the rigid theoretical framework established by Kant, he was compelled to locate their possibility in the religious domain and to argue for the superiority of the religious over the ethical sphere of life. Duncan concludes by dismissing what he takes to be the argument of *Fear and Trembling* by pointing to other, less radical ethical approaches to the problem of exceptions.[6]

This line of interpretation is interesting but it poses at least two problems. First, it is not clear that it is Kantian absolutism that Kierkegaard has in mind in framing the "teleological suspension of the ethical." The tragic hero as portrayed by Johannes is no absolutist. To fulfill a "higher" obligation to the state, Agamemnon, Jephtha, and Brutus are willing to break the moral rule against murder. Yet, according to Johannes, each is a tragic hero, not a knight of faith, and their behavior does not involve a teleological suspension of the ethical. Second, this interpretation ignores Johannes's repeated affirmations that in suspending the ethical, Abraham moved entirely outside its sphere. There is no "higher expression for the ethical that can ethically explain his behavior" (*FT* 57). In view of this, it becomes difficult to construe Abraham as seeking to break away from rigid ethical confines to express a more nuanced understanding of moral obligation.

Similar problems trouble a second interpretation of the ethical position sketched out in *Fear and Trembling*. On this view the book is a critique of ethical philistinism. As Gene Outka notes, those who hold this view understand Abraham as acting contrary to established public opinion. "He violates the canons of respectability and offends those who take as authoritative the moral opinions of their class and circumstance. The levels of dread and conflict he knows are out of reach of prosaic temperaments who are content to abide by conventional rules of their historical epoch."[7]

Outka points out that there is clearly something to this interpretation. In an impressionistic sense, it fits the general timbre of the book. It also connects well with *Fear and Trembling*'s undeniable emphasis on active, lived commitment to one's ethical or religious values. Nevertheless, by presenting Abraham as a sincere defender of genuine ethical values as opposed to mere conventionalism, this interpretation runs up against Johannes's repeated statements that Abraham's conduct is totally beyond ethical justification. This interpretation also does not fit with Johannes's important distinction between Abraham and the tragic hero. The tragic hero, Outka observes, "also requires courage and may violate conventional moral opinions."[8] Yet the tragic hero's behavior does not exemplify faith or involve a teleological suspension of the ethical.

A third interpretation sees Johannes's argument as sharpening the book's broad critique of Hegelian philosophy. Now the focus is on Hegel's ethics, especially the primacy he places on the public morality and social roles embodied in his idea of *Sittlichkeit.* For Hegel, as for Kant, ethics involves subordinating individual inclinations to the demands of the universal. Hegel further insists that the universal in ethics must take form in the concrete public life of a people, institutionalized in family, civil society, and the state. The state itself, he proclaims, is an earthly deity (*Irdisch-Göttliches*) that commands our highest loyalties.[9]

It is easy to read *Fear and Trembling* as a critique of this Hegelian ethical position. At the opening of the first Problema, Johannes refers to Hegel and asks whether "social morality" in the Hegelian sense really is the highest (*FT* 55). As presented by Johannes, Abraham clearly violates his two principal social role responsibilities: as a father and leader of his people. Indeed, since Isaac's life represents the promised continuance of the people, both these roles are simultaneously violated by Abraham's conduct. As Johannes tells us, "Insofar as the universal was present," for Abraham, "it was cryptically in Isaac, hidden so to speak, in Isaac's loins" (59). By subordinating these compelling communal responsibilities to his own spiritual salvation, Abraham takes a step beyond any social definition of the self.

Taken as a critique of Hegel's ethics, *Fear and Trembling* can be read in two different ways that reduce the apparent inconsistency between Johannes's moral condemnation and praise of Abraham. One the one hand, we can see *Fear and Trembling* as an *ethical* statement rejecting Hegel's nearly total subordination of the individual to the nation state and as a prophetic defense of the rights of the individual in the face of oppressive social collectivities. Those who read the book in this way see it as an incipient protest against the horrendous totalitarian movements that nineteenth-century mass philosophies were to produce, some of which, like Marxism, were based on Hegel's thought. By affirming the priority of the individual, *Fear and Trembling* is seen as offering an important corrective to this dangerous loss of self. Unfortunately, this very common reading of *Fear and Trembling* draws its force from the implicit idea that Abraham's conduct somehow represents a higher ethical possibility than Hegel's nationalism. As such, it runs directly up against Johannes's repeated statements that Abraham cannot be ethically "mediated" or understood. The importance of the individual and prophetic resistance to the mass are major themes certainly present in abundance elsewhere in Kierkegaard's writings. But unless we assume, as some interpreters have done, that Johannes has merely resorted to hyperbole in denying the moral justifiability of Abraham's conduct,[10] it violates the spirit of *Fear and Trembling* to read Johannes's defense of Abraham primarily in these terms.

Some who read the book as a rejection of Hegel's ethics take it not so much as a thesis on moral rules and appropriate forms of conduct as a call for personal individuation. Jerome Gellman puts this well when he states that the "voice of God," for Kierkegaard, is not literally a command to do a specific act. Rather, it is

a "call" out of the "infinity" of the self, for self-definition as an individual, as opposed to self-definition from within the institutions of society, specifically the family. . . . The story is not about Abraham's daring to kill his son, but is about Abraham's having the courage to be *willing* to see himself not as a father, but as an individual.[11]

This interpretation has the advantage of squaring well with the text's obvious critique of bourgeois complacency and with the Hegelians' own repeated tendencies to smooth down the hard edges of faith and ethics. It has the disadvantage of leaving the normative ethical import of *Fear and Trembling* in doubt and of leaving us wondering why, apart from its shock value, Genesis 22, of all Biblical texts, was chosen to make this point.

A final major interpretation of the normative level of *Fear and Trembling* sees Johannes (and perhaps Kierkegaard) as unabashedly defending a "divine command" view of ethics. Those who read the book in this way maintain that the lesson of Abraham's conduct is that every committed religious person must remain open to the possibility of a direct command from God that takes precedence over any rational ethical duties. Supporting this interpretation is Johannes's clear repudiation at the outset of the second Problema of the Kantian ethical position that denies there are any direct duties to God and that sees all relationship to God as contained within obedience to the rational moral law (*FT* 68). Also supporting it are several explicit statements in *Fear and Trembling* that for Abraham "duty is simply the expression for God's will" (60; cf. 70).

Some who defend this view of the book's ethical message see it as solving the puzzle of how Johannes can both paint Abraham in the starkest ethical terms and laud him as a model of religious behavior. The solution lies in Kierkegaard's/Johannes's assumptions about God's nature. Johannes tells us early on, for example, that he is convinced that "God is love" (*FT* 34). Within the context of such a belief, unstinting obedience to God makes sense even when he appears to require horrific deeds or sacrifices, as in the case of Genesis 22.

C. Stephen Evans develops an interpretation of this sort when he argues that it is Abraham's "special relationship with God" that explains his inability to offer reasons for his conduct while still maintaining his ethical integrity and moral resolve. Because of this special relationship, says Evans,

Abraham knows God as an individual; he knows God is good, and he loves and trusts God. Although he does not understand God's command in the sense that he understands why God has asked him to do this or what purpose it will serve, he does understand that it is indeed God who has asked him to do this. As a result of his special relationship, Abraham's trust in God is supreme. This trust expresses itself cognitively in an interpretive framework by which he concludes, all appearances to the contrary, that this act really is the right thing to do in this particular case. God would not in fact require Isaac of him. . . or even if God did do this thing, he would nonetheless receive Isaac back. . . . Abraham's willingness to sacrifice Isaac might be compared with the confidence of a knife-thrower's assistant in the accuracy of a knife-thrower's aim.[12]

This type of divine command position – one combining what Outka calls "general trust with specific perplexity"[13] – has a venerable place in the traditions of commentary on Genesis 22.[14] It certainly corresponds well with Kierkegaard's own personal religious position. In various writings, he unites a firm insistence on God's unwavering goodness with an aversion to autonomous Kantian ethics and a preference for a divine command position.[15] At several points, Kierkegaard tells us that to view moral requirements as self-imposed can only lead to moral laxity. For our moral obligations to elicit our full respect, we must regard them as emanating from an authoritative lawgiver who issues and upholds his commands (*Pap.* X² A 396; *JP* §188).

It may be that this is the ethical position Kierkegaard wished to present in *Fear and Trembling* and for which he has Johannes employ the example of Abraham's conduct in Genesis 22. But if so, *Fear and Trembling* is strangely lacking in the development of such a view. Johannes places great emphasis throughout on the horrifying nature of Abraham's conduct and the willingness of a knight of faith to go beyond ethics. But there is very little mention of the theological beliefs needed to render this view ethically comprehensible or compelling. Apart from the one fleeting remark about God's love in the "Preliminary Expectoration" (*FT* 34), there is no discussion of the divine nature, nor even of the special qualities of Abraham's relationship to God that would render his obedience more intelligible morally. Instead, all attention is given to the horrific command itself and to the definitive way in which it leads Abraham outside any conceivable realm of ethical justifiability. If *Fear and Trembling* defends a divine command ethic, therefore, it is a forbidding and frightening ethic, indeed. Johannes's use of Genesis 22 suggests that the god of *Fear and Trembling* and his loyal devotee, Abraham, are more "beyond good and evil" than most commentators have wanted to admit.[16]

Read as an ethical treatise, *Fear and Trembling* leaves us strangely disturbed. Once we put aside the compulsion to ethicalize Abraham's conduct in the ways that violate the clear sense of the text, we are left with a book whose exemplar borders on the psychopathic. Of course, this may be part of Kierkegaard's purpose in troubling his contemporaries' religious complacency. In that case, without really intending to offer Abraham in Genesis 22 as a model of behavior, Kierkegaard/Johannes would deliberately use this provocative and troubling episode to reinforce the book's call to personal religious engagement and commitment.

Before we conclude that *Fear and Trembling*'s treatment of ethics exists only for its shock value, it is worth considering whether it may point to another, and still deeper, level of meaning in the text.

This would be in keeping with Kierkegaard's program of writing a book in such a way that it forces the reader to probe beneath its surface utterances. The presence of this still deeper level will have to be shown on the basis of textual evidence despite the author's attempt to conceal it. This further level might help solve the puzzle of why Johannes repeatedly commends a figure so dramatically "beyond ethics" as Abraham.

IV. LEVEL 4: SIN AND FORGIVENESS

I believe this further level of meaning exists. At this level, we can read *Fear and Trembling* as addressing an abiding question of Christian faith: How can the individual believer be saved from sin? At this level, *Fear and Trembling* involves an exploration of each individual's inevitable encounter with the problems of moral self-condemnation and sin, and the possibility of God's overcoming these through an act of divine grace. From the perspective of this level, all the other levels of *Fear and Trembling* – the focus on Abraham, the investigation of the psychology of faith, and the lengthy discussion of the "teleological suspension of the ethical" – have as their latent meaning the themes of sin and forgiveness.[17]

Questions related to soteriology are obviously important ones for Kierkegaard. The religious discourses that bracket *Fear and Trembling* in his authorship address them, and they are central themes in adjacent pseudonymous works like *The Concept of Anxiety*, *Philosophical Fragments*, and *Concluding Unscientific Postscript*. Ordinarily, however, issues of sin and salvation are not seen to be a major preoccupation of *Fear and Trembling* itself. Its central figure, after all, is Abraham; and Abraham, as Johannes repeatedly tells us, "is not a sinner."

To perceive the importance of the themes of sin and grace in this book, we must invoke three different areas relevant to the text: (1) the tradition of interpretative commentary on Genesis 22; (2) the text of *Fear and Trembling* itself; and (3) aspects of Kierkegaard's biography.

The interpretative tradition

As David Lerch has shown, a long tradition of commentary existed that had already appropriated Genesis 22 for Christological purposes.[18] This tradition has its start in Galatians (3:13–14) with Paul's identification of Isaac with Christ as the "child of promise." It is picked up in Hebrews (11:17–19), whose author, presumably drawing on Jewish sources that held Isaac actually to have been sacrificed,[19] alludes to the Genesis episode as proof of the resurrection of the dead. Among the early Church fathers, these scriptural beginnings led to a standard view of Abraham as a type or figure of God whose willing sacrifice of his son symbolizes God's involvement in the crucifixion.

We know that Kierkegaard was familiar with this tradition well before writing *Fear and Trembling* since he refers to it in a journal entry for 1839 (*Pap.* A 569; *JP* §298). Equally important, this tradition was also familiar to Kant, whose treatment of Abraham in his *Religion within the Limits of Reason Alone* and *The Conflict of the Faculties* may have provided the stimulus for *Fear and Trembling*.[20] Among other things, Kant's aim in these treatises is to deny the value of relying on historically mediated salvation as a solution to the problem of sin. Any such reliance, Kant maintains, threatens to usurp the place of rational conscience and moral striving in our redemption and to degenerate into immoral "superstition."[21] In keeping with this theme, Kant offers Abraham as the negative example of someone who placed alleged divine commands above the clear dictates of rational conscience. Lest the reader miss the link between this criticism of Abraham and orthodox Christian ideas of salvation, Kant refers in a footnote of the *Conflict* to the tradition of viewing Abraham's willingness to offer his son as "a symbol of the world-savior's own sacrifice."[22]

There is considerable evidence that Kierkegaard's specific defense of the importance of a historical savior in *Fragments* and *Postscript* was a response to Kant's position in both these writings.[23] If so, we can regard *Fear and Trembling* as an opening salvo in this intense battle with Kant – and by extension with any rationalist philosophy (including Hegel's) that underestimates the seriousness of sin and the radical measures needed to overcome it. To introduce these issues, Kierkegaard employs the figure of Abraham in a limited and purely symbolic way. Abraham is not a sinner. *Fear and Trembling* offers none of the analysis of sin and its psychology found in works like *The Concept of Anxiety* or *The Sickness unto Death*. Instead, the text uses Genesis 22 to establish the possibility of a realm of faith above the realm of rational morality. Through Abraham's experience on Mt. Moriah, we learn that God can transcend the ethical and enter directly into the lives of those who themselves have transcended the ethical (for whatever reason). Without God, we are told, Abraham is "lost" (*FT* 81). With God, Abraham the murderer becomes Abraham the father of faith. What Kierkegaard has done, in other words, is to establish an analogy between Abraham and God, on the one hand, and the rest of us and God, on the other. Some features of this analogy (the possibility of an absolute relationship to God that suspends the ethical) are relevant to both sides of the analogy, while others (the precise way in which Abraham and we suspend the ethical) are not.

This use of a biblical figure in a purely symbolic and typological way is not unique to *Fear and Trembling*. It occurs also in *Repetition*, with which *Fear and Trembling* was simultaneously published. Here it is Job who is used to explore the possibility of loss beyond "every *thinkable* human certainty and probability" of recovery (*R* 212). Like Abraham, Job gets everything back, including the family he had lost. Both men are undeniably innocent – Abraham because his deed results from a divine command, and Job by virtue of information given us in the prologue to the book. Yet Kierkegaard provides clues suggesting that each figure is a "type" for the loss and recovery represented by sin and forgiveness. In comments in his papers and in a draft for the manuscript of *Fear and Trembling*, Kierkegaard considers presenting Abraham's previous life "as not devoid of guilt," with the result that the patriarch is led to "perceive the divine command as God's punishment" (*Pap.* IV A 77; *JP* §5641; cf. *Pap.* IV B 66). In *Repetition*, Job's righteousness is said to include "being proved to be in the wrong *before God*." This important theme is familiar from the "Ultimatum" of *Either/Or*, where it introduces the idea of sin.[24] Thus, in both *Fear and Trembling* and *Repetition* the suffering and redemption of innocent Biblical prototypes is used to hint at the experience of ordinary mortals. If God's commands can imperil such paragons of virtue, what must these commands do to people like you and me caught up in frailty and sin? And if a personal relationship with God can redeem these men – returning to each the descendants he appeared to have lost – what wonders can God's grace do in our lives? Shortly we will see that the familial aspect of the Abraham and Job narratives adds yet another dimension to the complex analogy Kierkegaard is constructing.

Themes of sin and grace

It is common to deny that sin forms much of a theme in *Fear and Trembling*.[25] Certainly, psychological and ethical issues capture most of the attention. Nevertheless, once we entertain the possibility that sin and forgiveness form an important deeper level of meaning in the text, these themes become far more apparent. The book's title, for example, hearkens back to Paul's discussion of sin, grace, and redemption in Philippians 2:12 with its reminder that "God is at work in you, both to will and to work for his good pleasure." The "Exordium" obliquely refers to God's creation of free beings and their painful separation from him,[26] and there are numerous smaller references to sin throughout the text (*FT* 13).

Although sin and forgiveness are only touched on early in the book, they suddenly spring up before us in the story of Agnes and the merman that dominates the third Problema. Examining the painful choices facing the merman who has seduced and then fallen in love with an innocent young woman, Johannes now embarks on an extended discussion of the problems of sin and repentance. "When the single individual by his guilt has come outside the universal," Johannes tells us, "he can return only by virtue of having come as the single individual into an absolute relation to the absolute" (*FT* 98).

The discussion continues in the text and a footnote with a critique of Hegel's concept of sin, with an observation on how sin takes the individual demonically higher than the universal, and with a statement that an ethics that ignores sin is a futile discipline while one that acknowledges it has exceeded itself. These observations are all prefaced by the remark, "Now here I would like to make a comment that says more than has been said at any point previously" (*FT* 98), and they close abruptly with the reminder that "nothing of what has been said here explains Abraham, for Abraham did not become the single individual by way of sin" (99).

It is no accident that Kierkegaard's choice of words in this discussion, especially his remarks about the repentant individual having to come "as the single individual into an absolute relation to the absolute" are identical with those Johannes uses earlier to describe Abraham's movement of faith. What Kierkegaard is here letting us know is that Abraham and the merman are counterparts, positive and negative expressions of the same problem. Both have suspended the ethical, one by obedience and one by sin, and both are saved only by a direct, supraethical relationship to God. Once we understand that Abraham functions as a figure for the problem of sin and atonement, I think we also can see that this discussion of sin is not a chance aside but a window into *Fear and Trembling*'s deepest concerns.

Repetition provides confirming insight into Kierkegaard's authorial strategy in both these works. Like *Fear and Trembling*, most of *Repetition* ignores the problem of sin as it develops its special concern, the possibility of repetition in life. The focus is on the psychology of repetition and the experience of the young man who wishes to recover his alienated love. Job is introduced to expand the idea of loss and recovery, and near the end of this discussion, we find brief mention of Job as sinner (*R* 212). Yet in his papers, Kierkegaard repeatedly informs us that the true repetition involves a return to the integrity lost by sin. In a lengthy unpublished reply to Heiberg's review of *Repetition*, he dismisses Heiberg's vague appeal to repetition as involving "spiritual development of a self-conscious free will." Remarking that repetition "cannot be left in this nebulous way," he tells us that "it is a question of nullifying the repetition in which evil recurs and of bringing forth the repetition in which good recurs" (*Pap.* IV B 111 p. 267). In its highest sense, he states, repetition is atonement.[27] In a long entry signed by the pseudonym Constantin Constantius, we are offered insight into the deeper intention of the book.

Repetition was insignificant, without any philosophical pretension, a droll little book, dashed off as an oddity, and curiously enough, written in such a way that, if possible, the heretics would not be able to understand it. . . . [T]he true repetition is eternity; however, that repetition (by being psychologically pursued so far that it vanishes for psychology as transcendent, as a religious movement by virtue of the absurd, which commences when a person has come to the border of the wondrous), as soon as the issue is posed dogmatically will come to mean atonement.[28]

The themes in this comment should by now be familiar to us from *Fear and Trembling*: a text with a deliberately hidden message; the movement from psychology to dogmatics; and the intensification of religious consciousness "by virtue of the absurd." The considerable parallelism between these two works provides confirming evidence that themes of sin and grace are far more salient at this point in Kierkegaard's authorship than they are commonly assumed to be.

Biographical correspondences

The ordinary cautions against using the facts of an author's life to interpret his writings have special relevance to a writer like Kierkegaard. As the Hongs observe, "no writer has so painstakingly tried to preclude his readers' collapsing writer and works together and thereby transmogrifying the works into autobiography or memoir."[29] Despite this, there can be no doubt that *Fear and Trembling* is among the most personal of Kierkegaard's writings. The events of his broken engagement to Regine Olsen provided an immediate stimulus for the book, and tales of frustrated love and marriages blocked by fate abound.[30] In his papers Kierkegaard states boldly, "He who has explained this riddle has explained my life" (*Pap.* IV A 76; *JP* §5640).

Most commonly, the biographical correspondences here are linked to the ethical themes of the text. In his selection of Genesis 22, Kierkegaard is seen as providing Regine – his secret reader – an explanation of their broken relationship. Just as Abraham received a divine command to sacrifice what was dearest in his life, so Kierkegaard was compelled to obey the divine "governance" and set aside his worldly hopes of happiness in order to undertake his solitary vocation as a religious author. Regine herself contributed to this reading in later statements that cast the breach in these terms.[31] This focus on conflicting ethical responsibilities and priorities also fits nicely with the view that the Problemata are primarily a rejection of Hegelian *Sittlichkeit* with its preference for social role responsibilities over the individual existence.

In all his discussions of the biographical events that underlay the book, however, Kierkegaard offers a very different explanation. God, he tells us, had issued a "no" to the marriage. The reasons for this lay not in any call to a religious vocation but in Kierkegaard's own melancholy and sense of perdition – what he called "the eternal night brooding within me" (*Pap.* IV A 107 p. 43; *JP* §5664). This melancholy was itself the fruit of a familial tradition of sin begun by his father, Michael Pedersen Kierkegaard. The elder Kierkegaard's youthful curse of God from a hillock on Jutland heath and his sexual sins, including his extramarital relationship with Kierkegaard's mother, the handmaid Ane Lund, following his first wife's death, had led him to see himself as fated to lose his children as a punishment.[32] Indeed, he did live to bury five of the seven Kierkegaard children. If there is a link between the Abraham story and Kierkegaard's life, therefore, it is the peril to which the elder Kierkegaard's acts had exposed the family. In this context, it is not Regine who plays the role of Isaac but Søren himself.[33]

Abundant textual evidence supports the claim that the father's conduct forms a major biographical substratum to the book. Father-child themes abound, from the epigraph's opening mention of Tarquinius Superbus's secret message to his son, through the numerous tragic heroes whose conduct imperils their offspring, to the choice of Abraham. (In *Repetition* it is again a father, Job, whose relationship to God threatens his family.) The book's several tales of frustrated marriages – including Aristotle's story of the young man whose marriage threatens to "destroy a whole family"; and the stories of Sarah and Tobias and Agnes and the merman (*Pap.* IV B III p. 267) – all either assume family lines bearing a curse or unions blocked by a sinful past. *Fear and Trembling* may be a message to Regine, but it is not simply about Kierkegaard's call to a religious vocation. Rather, it is an explanation of why Søren, himself both sacrificer and sacrificial victim, Abraham and Isaac, had acted to spare her involvement in his family's melancholy fate.

Not that *Fear and Trembling* is wholly negative in this regard. Read as an examination of faith and grace, its larger message, whether directed to Kierkegaard's deceased father, to Regine, or to Kierkegaard himself, is one of hope. God's command imposes on Abraham a grueling ordeal. But in the end, God's sovereignty over ethics triumphs. Not only can he command murder, but he can make a murderer the father of faith. As Abraham discovered, God's last word is not death and condemnation. God can effect a teleological suspension of his justice to renew his relationship with an individual. With this anguished religious hope in mind, we can also perhaps better understand Johannes's repeated expressions of doubt that he could exhibit the kind of faith shown by Abraham. A sense of inescapable sin and familial disaster had blocked Kierkegaard's marriage. Perhaps, in faith, one could make the absurd leap that Abraham did, believing that God could snatch life from the jaws of death and somehow continue a family line otherwise doomed to extinction. However, neither Kierkegaard nor his pseudonym is sure he possesses Abraham's faith. Against the background of these difficult beliefs we can better understand Kierkegaard's remark in his journal: "If I had had faith, I would have stayed with Regine" (*Pap.* IV A 107; *JP* §5664).[34]

V. TOWARD A TRANSPARENT TEXT

I have argued that as we proceed through *Fear and Trembling* we come across new themes and ever deeper levels of meaning. Beginning as an impassioned call to lived Christianity, the text leads through discussions of the psychology of faith and the ethical outlines of the Christian life and finally to themes of salvation, grace, and forgiveness.

Kierkegaard proposes a metaphor of the text as progressively disclosed by a caustic fluid. I want to close with the suggestion that a comprehensive reading of *Fear and Trembling* aims at a text that is a fully developed and transparent image. Although each level of meaning preserves its independent significance, the cumulative meaning grows with each new level of disclosure until we arrive at a penetrating view where each level of meaning is superimposed on and enhances the others.

The meaning of the call to lived commitment, for example, deepens as we encounter the demanding psychology of faith. Here the text not only challenges bourgeois complacency but uses a consummately bourgeois knight of faith to hint at the depths of suffering and interiority that mark true Christian faith. As we turn to the Problemata, both the call to commitment and the psychology of faith receive new significance from an outline of the normative demands of Christian life. With the suggestion that Christians may be required to go beyond the confines of family or nation to establish their own relation to the absolute, the themes of commitment, loss, infinite resignation, and faith are amplified and made concrete. Christian love emerges as selfless care rooted in the psychic renunciation of all proprietary claims.

Finally, we reach the level where themes of sin and grace predominate. Looked back on from here, the call to commitment is now seen to involve repentance: the awareness that one's life, however accomplished and successful by outward measures, stands under judgment. Applied to culture, this also becomes a critique of Hegelianized Christian civilization for its superficiality, pride, and obliviousness to sin. At the level of psychology, the two movements of faith also take on new meaning. Infinite resignation is now seen to require an abandonment of one's sense of moral integrity and an acknowledgment of the reality of sin (a movement the merman can make), whereas faith, the second movement, becomes an absurd hope of redemption and renewal beyond all one's reasoned claims or expectations (a movement beyond the merman's powers).

The awareness of sin and grace also permeates the specifically ethical level of the text with new significance. The radicalness of the Christian ethic – the possibility that one may be called to individual existence beyond family or state – sharpens obligations to the breaking point and eliminates any false sense of one's ability to comply with God's commands. Acceptance of Jesus's life as the pattern for one's own – including the command to "hate" one's father and mother (Luke 14:26) – establishes an ethic requiring virtually inhuman commitment. One who is aware of these ethical demands must conclude that "Before God, we are always in the wrong." At the same time, an appreciation of the depth of even our mundane human sins, our greed, lusts, and anger, renders naive any merely social definition of the self. Hegelian *Sittlichkeit* runs aground on its own spiritual shallowness. Here *Fear and Trembling* tells us that relationship to God, as judge and redeemer, takes primacy – and must precede – any social integration of the self. Seen in this way, as the acknowledgment of sin and acceptance of grace, the teleological suspension of the ethical becomes just that: a *suspension* of ethics rather than its annulment. Grace aims at one's full moral renovation.[35] An awareness of God's gracious forgiveness ends self-obsession and pride, and elicits the selfless care that is morality's highest telos.

Earlier, we noted a deep tension at the ethical level of *Fear and Trembling* between the admiration repeatedly voiced for Abraham and the equally clear assertions that, ethically speaking, what he does amounts to murder. We saw that some commentators have tried to overcome this tension by inappropriately ethicalizing Abraham's conduct. Viewed in relation to the themes of sin and grace, however, these seemingly opposed aspects of *Fear and Trembling* can be seen to reside comfortably beside one another. Like Paul and Luther before him, Kierkegaard can celebrate Abraham's transcendence of the moral law – in the sense that nothing whatsoever in his ethical conduct warrants his election or renown – while simultaneously holding him up as a model for all to emulate. Precisely because he is justified by grace alone, Abraham is deservedly the "father of faith." He is also a beacon to all those who knowingly "suspend the ethical" in a frank admission of sin and look to God alone for their salvation.

VI. CONCLUSION

Fear and Trembling has earned renown as a provocative statement of challenge. But it is far more than that. *Fear and Trembling* is an introduction or propaedeutic to Kierkegaard's authorship as a whole. Read at all the levels of its meaning, *Fear and Trembling* contains the major themes of Christian faith and ethics that will emerge in the ensuing pseudonymous works and many of the religious discourses. *Fear and Trembling* deserves the fame that Kierkegaard predicted for it, but that very fame may have obscured the fact that this is no eccentric statement by a youthful poet. It is a profound theological treatise firmly rooted in the Pauline and Lutheran tradition to which Kierkegaard belonged.

NOTES

1 For an analysis of *Fear and Trembling* in terms of this image, see my "Deciphering *Fear and Trembling*'s Secret Message," *Religious Studies* 22 (1986): 95–111. The choice here of the metaphor of photographic development signals my more recent view that *Fear and Trembling* contains not one but a series of interrelated manifest and latent meanings.
2 Paul Dietrichson, "Kierkegaard's Concept of the Self," *Inquiry* 8, 1 (Spring 1965): 2.
3 Jerry H. Gill, "Faith Is as Faith Does," in *Kierkegaard's* Fear and Trembling: *Critical Appraisals*, ed. Robert L. Perkins (Tuscaloosa: University of Alabama Press, 1981), p. 204.
4 Understanding Abraham: Care, Faith, and the Absurd," in *Kierkegaard's* Fear and Trembling, ed. Perkins, p. 108.

5 In *Critique of Practical Reason and Other Writings in Moral Philosophy*, trans. and ed. Lewis White Beck (Chicago: University of Chicago Press, 1949), pp. 346–50.

6 A similar reading is offered by Geoffrey Clive, who argues that the ethical that is transcended or suspended here is the morality of general rules. "The Teleological Suspension of the Ethical in Nineteenth-Century Literature," *The Journal of Religion* 34 (April 1954): 75–87.

7 "Religious and Moral Duty: Notes on *Fear and Trembling*," in *Religion and Morality*, ed. Gene Outka and John P. Reeder (Garden City, N.Y.: Anchor Press and Doubleday, 1973), p. 212.

8 Ibid., p. 212.

9 G. W. F. Hegel, *Elements of the Philosophy of Right*, ed. Allen W. Wood (Cambridge University Press, 1991), §272, p. 307.

10 George D. Chryssides, "Abraham's Faith," *Sophia* 12 (April 1973): 10–16.

11 "Kierkegaard's *Fear and Trembling*," *Man and World* 23 (1990): 297.

12 "Is the Concept of an Absolute Duty toward God Morally Unintelligible?" in *Kierkegaard's* Fear and Trembling, ed. Perkins, p. 145.

13 Outka, "Religious and Moral Duty: Notes on *Fear and Trembling*," p. 243.

14 See my *Religion and Moral Reason* (New York: Oxford University Press, 1988), chaps. 4–5 and David A. Pailin, "Abraham and Isaac: A Hermeneutical Problem before Kierkegaard," in *Kierkegaard's* Fear and Trembling, ed. Perkins, 10–42.

15 Witness the importance of James 1:17–22, "Every good gift and every perfect gift is from above," in his religious discourses.

16 Philip Quinn has argued that the biblical Abraham faces a genuine and tragic moral dilemma: a conflict between two equally indefeasible requirements from which the agent "cannot escape wrongdoing and guilt." "Agamemnon and Abraham: The Tragic Dilemma of Kierkegaard's Knight of Faith," *Journal of Literature and Theology* 4, 2 (July 1990): 183. See also his "Moral Obligation, Religious Demand, and Practical Conflict," in *Rationality, Religious Belief, and Moral Commitment*, ed. Robert Audi and William J. Wainwright (Ithaca: Cornell University Press, 1986), pp. 195–212.

17 Within the interpretative tradition, this understanding of *Fear and Trembling* has been offered by Louis Mackey in "The View from Pisgah: A Reading of *Fear and Trembling*," in *Kierkegaard: A Collection of Critical Essays*, ed. Josiah Thompson (New York: Doubleday, 1972), pp. 394–428 and Gregor Malantschuk, *Kierkegaard's Thought*, ed. and trans. Howard V. Hong and Edna H. Hong (Princeton: Princeton University Press, 1971), p. 238.

18 *Isaaks Opferung christlich gedeutet* (Tübingen: J. C. B. Mohr, 1950).

19 Shalom Spiegel, *The Last Trial* (New York: Pantheon Books, 1967).

20 *Religion within the Limits of Reason Alone,* trans. Theodore M. Green and Hoyt H. Hudson (New York: Harper and Row, 1960), pp. 81, 175; *The Conflict of the Faculties,* trans. Mary J. Gregor (New York: Abaris Books, 1979), pp. 115n, 119.

21 *The Conflict of the Faculties,* p. 119n.

22 Ibid., p. 121n.

23 See my, *Kierkegaard and Kant: The Hidden Debt* (Albany, New York: State University of New York Press, 1992).

24 In the Supplement to *Repetition,* the Hongs' footnote at this point adds: "In a copy of *Enten/Eller,* II (*SV* II 306), Kierkegaard wrote: 'If a person is most fully in the right, before God he ought always have an even higher expression: that he is in the wrong, for no human being can penetrate his consciousness absolutely' (*Papirer* IV A 256)."

25 Gene Outka, "God as the Subject of Unique Veneration: A Response to Ronald M. Green," *Journal of Religious Ethics* 21, 2 (Fall 1993): 211–15.

26 Edward F. Mooney describes these sections of *Fear and Trembling* as presenting ordeals of love and separation, and he notes that in *Postscript* Kierkegaard relates these same ideas to God, whose creation of free beings involves an act of resignation in granting such beings independence *over against himself. Knights of Faith and Resignation: Reading Kierkegaard's* Fear and Trembling (Albany: State University of New York Press, 1990), p. 30.

27 This remark is in a preliminary draft of *Pap.* IV B 117 that appears in *Pap.* IV B 118 p. 300. This passage is translated in the Supplement to *Repetition,* p. 320.

28 *Pap.* IV B 120 p. 306. This passage is translated in the Supplement to *Repetition,* p. 324.

29 "Historical Introduction," in *Fear and Trembling* and *Repetition,* p. xi.

30 These include mention of the young swain and princess (*FT* 41–5); a young girl forced by her parents to marry someone other than the one she loves (85); a young swain blocked from possessing his beloved because doing so will "destroy a whole family" (85); a bridegroom "to whom the augurs prophesied a calamity that would have its origin in his marriage" (89–92); Queen Elizabeth's sacrifice of her love, Essex, for the state (93–4); the tale of Agnes and the merman (94–9); and the story of Sarah and Tobias (102–6).

31 Steen Johansen, *Erindringer om Søren Kierkegaard* (Copenhagen: C. A. Reitzels Boghandel, 1980), pp. 32–44.

32 Sylviane Agacinski argues that the unmentioned sin that underlay the elder Kierkegaard's sense of perdition was the rape of the handmaid, Ane Lund. See her *Aparté: Conceptions and Deaths of Søren Kierke-*

gaard, trans. Kevin Newmark (Tallahassee: Florida State University Press, 1988).

33 Malantschuk, *Kierkegaard's Thought*, p. 238.

34 *Pap.* IV A 107 p. 41; *JP* §5664. See George Pattison, "A Drama of Love and Death: Michael Pedersen Kierkegaard and Regine Olsen Revisited," *History of European Ideas* 12, 1 (1990): 79–91 for a discussion of the complexity of the relationship between Kierkegaard's biography and his writings and for a treatment of the intricate ties between Kierkegaard's relationship to his father and his relationship to Regine. For a more traditional view of Kierkegaard's remark as relating primarily to his choice of a religious vocation over marriage to Regine, see Sylvia Fleming Crocker, "Sacrifice in Kierkegaard's *Fear and Trembling*," *Harvard Theological Review* 68 (April 1975): 125–39.

35 This conforms to the text's insistence that only a *suspension* of ethics is being implied; *FT* 54.

11   *Repetition:* Getting the world back

Kierkegaard's slim book *Repetition* was published in 1843 on the same day as *Fear and Trembling.* Six weeks later he published a discourse on *The Book of Job.*[1] The theme of sudden loss and wondrous restoration recurs: Abraham must release Isaac and then he gets him back; Job is stripped of his world and then he gets it back. The book *Repetition* alludes to Job's yearning for his world's return and also depicts the suffering of a young man who has lost his love and yearns for her return. These motifs provide a clue to the concept of repetition. The question posed by *Repetition* is whether repetition is possible, whether a world or loved one, now lost, can be restored. But unraveling either the text or the concept is not a straightforward task.

I. PRELIMINARIES

Repetition is written under the pseudonym Constantin Constantius. It gives ample grist for dialectical mills: repetition is paired with *kinesis,* the Aristotelian "motion" of becoming, and it is marked as "the task of freedom."[2] We learn that repetition is (paradoxically) both "the *interest* of metaphysics and the interest on which all metaphysics comes to grief" (R 149). But these remarks are largely undeveloped, and to complicate matters, they are inserted casually, perhaps even ironically, within a book that reads as a puzzling romantic roman à clef or novella. Theoretical insights float precariously on a complex literary surface. However serious the idea of repetition is for Kierkegaard, in this book it often seems to flicker merely as an artifice or entertainment. Walter Lowrie confesses that of all the Kierkegaardian terms of art, none "is more important and none so baffling" as repetition.[3] And the same might be said of the novella. In his journals, Kierkegaard calls it "insignificant, without any philosophical pretension, a droll little book, dashed off as an oddity."[4] But this jest itself is meant to throw us off the scent.

Why are Kierkegaard's intentions so concealed? At least three factors motivate his indirections and disguises. First, there is the autobiographical factor. Kierkegaard was immersed in the stories of Job and Abraham, writing the "Job Discourse," *Fear and Trembling,* and *Repetition,* precisely as he was breaking off his engagement to Regine Olsen, and then, belatedly, wishing for a reconciliation.[5] Both Job and Abraham were beneficiaries of a wondrous repetition or return. If they were candidates for divine restorations, then Kierkegaard too might be eligible for repetition – if only he could attain exemplary faith. But it would be embarrassing, to say the least, for his regret that he had abandoned Regine to become public knowledge.

A second and more philosophical factor bringing Kierkegaard to strategies of irony and indirection springs from his awareness that his "enlightened" Copenhagen was in fact deceived about its spiritual condition. He aimed for a social critique of bourgeois Christendom, yet realized that a direct attack would not do – at least not as a *beginning.*[6] Repetition might work its renewals at this more inclusive, social level, but if so, what discursive resources could Kierkegaard rely on? He adopts a familiar literary form, the novella or roman à clef, to capture the interest of his readers while evading or disarming their defenses. An otherwise disquieting critique thus becomes less threatening. But there is more at work here than a matter of convenience or diplomacy, the advantage of soft pedaling an otherwise brutal social or personal judgment. The conceptual resources available for Kierkegaard's critique are embedded in the very languages and traditions he finds corrupt. He wants to push the revisionary – or revolutionary – potential of the idea he calls repetition through the various ethical, aesthetic, political, and religious strata of the world he inherits. Yet if he is to be heard, he must speak in the flawed language, evoking the flawed perceptions and understandings, of the very world he wishes to undo. In this light, irony and disguise are unavoidable strategic devices, devices that necessarily mimic the defenses Kierkegaard wishes to penetrate. At first glance, what do we have in *Repetition?* It seems we're handed a casual novella that recounts the yearnings of a love-sick youth and delivers offhand asides about Greek philosophy and the sufferings of Job. But beneath this facade, *Repetition* becomes a Trojan horse from which a critique of its apparently casual aesthetic musing can enter the cultural stronghold undercover.

Third, Kierkegaard's concepts are fluid and elusive because they develop through the course of his authorship. Indirection and disguise allow him the authorial distance to alter, complicate, or revise his views without having to go on record spelling out the exact nature of the change. Often he may himself be uncertain of the precise extent of a concept's development or complication, an overview becoming available only in considerable retrospect.[7] For example, the faith of Judge William in *Either/Or* is not Abraham's faith, and neither William's nor Abraham's faith is Socratic or strictly Christian. Similarly, repetition may have one meaning in the context of an aesthetic or ethical way of life and quite another even *contrary* meaning as one approaches a Christian life. Concepts change as the context of their elucidation changes, and as Kierkegaard's literary, moral, and philosophical intentions change. An obviously perverse "repetition" appears in the discussion of Mozart's *Don Giovanni* in *Either/Or, Part I.*[8] A respectable but still inadequate repetition-like movement is proposed by Judge William, who warns the aesthete to "choose himself," to choose the ethical.[9] The anticipated "metamorphosis" of self is a retaking or restoration of the detail of one's life, reviving and thus repeating it under an ethical frame.[10] But these early descriptions of a need of repetition, or even of its ethical necessity, in the long run are false leads.[11] The judge's view of self-choice as repetition fails because it assumes that self-consolidation can be achieved as a matter of effort or willpower. It becomes corrected (or reversed) in Kierkegaard's later discussions of Job and Abraham. True repetition, what Kierkegaard calls "repetition in the pregnant sense," is something received, a grant of life and world, not an outcome that can be cornered.[12] It is the restoration Johannes de silentio, in *Fear and Trembling*, calls faith's "second movement," the return of Isaac, the beloved, or worldly life.[13] We will consider the details of this religious repetition and its seductive counterfeits in sections III and IV.

II REPETITION: THE NARRATIVE

Kierkegaard dubs the author of *Repetition* "Constantin Constantius." The name, take note, is itself a repetition. It recreates eponymously the tension between something *constant* (an element to be repeated) and *motion* (something repeated). And if we probe further, there are several more clues to repetition contained in Kierkegaard's choice of pseudonym.

The name can call to mind, second, someone who is steadfast, a pillar of strength on whom a friend might rely. In fact, as the novella unfolds, Constantin does appear as a steady object – at least to a young man shaken by an unhappy love who turns to him in a series of confidential letters collected in the second part of *Repetition.* Contrasted with his more volatile young counterpart, Constantin appears constant. But there is a third possibility. The name might also call to mind one who *seeks* constancy, has this as his goal – not one who has in fact achieved it. And indeed Constantin finds himself on a "psychological experiment" seeking constancy through repetition (or constantly seeking repetition). He would corner repetition, intellectually and theoretically; he sets about the task of reproducing it experientially. If the notion of repetition has substance, he ought to be able to relive the experience of a fondly recalled trip to Berlin. Hence portions of *Repetition*'s first half concern Constantin's comical attempt to get things back the way they were on an earlier outing.

Fourth, the constancy of Constantin may be in fact an existential *complacency.* Although his young friend may lean on him, to a disinterested observer he seems a rather hollow figure, a questionable friend with all too glib advice. Furthermore, Constantin's "interest" in repetition is at most halfhearted. His complacency is unmistakable if we compare his idle play with repetition to the terrifying, gripping *need* of repetition overwhelming Abraham or Job. Constantin's facile counsel for his friend, his philosophical flourishes, and his side trip to Berlin are little more than aesthetic diversions. In a novella of many fits and starts, Kierkegaard's invention of Constantin Constantius as his pseudonym is just the beginning of a complex and sometimes nearly indecipherable string of ambiguities.

Repetition opens with Constantin's lectures on pagan versus Christian views, and his confident announcement that repetition is "the new category that will be discovered" (R 148). He predicts it will supplant or defeat the fashionable Hegelian reliance on "mediation" and will be found superior to Greek "recollection" – these being repetition's two metaphysical competitors.

Repetition, mediation, and recollection are offered as alternative solutions to the problem of transition or motion, especially the transitions of self-development. How does one move, for example, from an aesthetic to an ethical way of life? If Hegelian mediation were the key to motion or development, we would expect a pattern of "immanent negations." A quite simplified sequence of such negations could be described as follows.[14] Begin with an initial state where an infant and its surroundings are largely undifferentiated. In the course of time, this initial state gets "negated": an individual emerges through opposition to its context. (We might picture here the rebellions of an adolescent against family and society.) In this hypothetical scenario, differentiation could lead to an increasing sense of alienation and isolation. But with increasing maturity, this lonely rootlessness itself may be negated as the social matrix of civic morality supervenes. Notice that this pattern of development is general or universal; its goal is "moral," construed in this case as the assimilation of modes of cultural and civic decency or propriety; it is exclusively natural or immanent; and it proceeds entirely by negations.

Constantin mocks this progression as the "1, 2, 3," dance step of Hegelian dialectic (R 226). Perfectly general or universal schemes of moral advance bury the crucial factor of individual choice, of personal decision in moral progress; the goal of assimilation is a tawdry substitute for the proper goal of continuing individuation; a purely immanent natural process excludes the "transcendent" interventions and bestowals familiar even in secular experience (say, in moments of falling in love, in awe or insight, in encountering the sublime); such transcendent interventions are obviously essential to any Christian perspective where revelation plays a role; and finally, to characterize personal "motion" or advance as powered exclusively through "negation" is distorting.

Consider the contrasting model of transitions in development provided by Judge William in *Either/Or*. A self, an *individual* self, will choose or receive itself. This occurs one by one, not as a collective or general movement. As the judge describes the development of personality, the place of such decision and responsibility becomes preeminent. Furthermore, the self choosing itself does not advance exclusively through negations. Choice is positive. And the self receiving itself (Judge William's second picture of the self in motion) explicitly draws on powers higher than itself, powers that can confer a self.[15] Here transcendence (nonimmanence) is explicit. Development is not just a natural historical process, but one intertwined with transcendent spirit.

If we go along with Kierkegaard in assuming that this disposes of the Hegelian account of movement in terms of a series of mediations, alternatives to this account nevertheless remain. Constantin avers that "If one does not have the category of recollection or of repetition, all life dissolves into an empty meaningless noise" (R 149). If mediation fails, why not consider Platonic recollection? To avoid the disintegration of life into a meaningless hubbub, do we need a "new category" of repetition?

For Plato, we move toward the Good by "recollection," by contact with a Form, a meaning source that already exists in some static "past eternity," a good that becomes accessible to us in memory through Socratic questioning. This escape from a meaningless life of noise would be "backward" into a timeless past. In contrast, Kierkegaard offers a forward future-oriented move toward a God or Good of open possibilities, not fixed finalities.[16] Repetition is not just a grant of one's familiar life as it was previously possessed – now devoid of noise and chatter (although it is partially this). It is also, paradoxically, the delivery of new and surprising meaning. God will appear to Job in an extraordinary Whirlwind, in violation of all natural expectations; and in the context of Abraham's crisis, what could be less anticipated than God's demand for Isaac or Isaac's subsequent return?

Still courting paradox, Constantin claims that repetition and recollection are the *same* movement, but in opposite directions; and he characterizes repetition as "recollection forward." This formulation is not exactly transparent, but neither is it a piece of diversionary nonsense.[17] If it is an oxymoron, it can be unpacked.

Take the movement at issue to be a movement toward meaning or value, a gathering of meaning, say, into the present. If this gathering is faced backward we have a Platonic collection (or recollection) of meaning; if this gathering is faced forward toward the future, then we have a repetition, a reception of meaning that is radiating not from one's past but from one's *future* – toward one's present, offering to receptive agents open fields of possibility.

Constantin waxes professorial on recollection, mediation, and repetition. He declares that "repetition is the *interest* of all metaphysics and the interest on which it founders" (R 149). But this theoretical vein soon runs dry. His attention wanders. He shifts from unveiling his "new category" to wondering if the whole business of repetition might be illusory. The question What *is* repetition? is replaced by the question Is repetition *possible?*

Ironically, Constantin is quite inconstant in his aims. Furthermore, having changed his question, he also changes his approach entirely. On a whim, he sets off to find his answer not by continuing his philosophical and poetic reflections but by embarking on a journey. His task will be to replicate, to try to repeat, the experiences of an earlier journey.

His return to Berlin in search of repetition is rendered in finegrained detail. There is a jolting coach ride to the city, a visit to the theater and a fondly remembered café. We meet the now-married German hotel manager, his previous host. As Constantin shows off his literary talent, the project of an experimental test of repetition recedes in importance, overshadowed by his story-telling magic. Perhaps we should have expected this inconstancy, for just as he shifts gear from his professorial exegesis to his mesmerizing travelogue, Constantin warns us that his whole interest in repetition may be a trick, a farce. Quoting Hamann with approval, he says

[I] express myself in various tongues and speak the language of sophists, of puns, of Cretans and Arabians, of whites and Moors and Creoles, and babble a confusion of criticism, mythology, *rebus*, and axioms, and argue now in a human way and now in an extraordinary way. (R 149)

(Yet he also asks us to assume that what he says "is not a mere lie" [R 149]. Reader beware!)

Perhaps Constantin is like a soldier returning nostalgically to a scene of battle, or like a lover returning to old haunts, hoping for a glimpse of the beloved. If so, we would expect his trip to show a yearning, a wish for roots and the familiar where one could be the self one once was, and thus relieve the ache of exile or aimless wandering. But for Constantin there is no ache, no longing. There is no drama or suffering in his search for the familiar. Nothing deeper than curiosity moves him to try the coffee across town at a favorite shop (*R* 170).

In *Fear and Trembling* repetition is much more sharply pitched. Abraham's belief that Isaac will be restored, his expectation of repetition, is more than curiosity about *whether* Isaac can be restored. Abraham's ordeal is not a casual "experiment" to validate an hypothesis. Even to say that Abraham *needs* Isaac returned, though true, is massive understatement. Or consider Job's grief, his need for repetition. Constantin neither needs Berlin nor grieves its loss. The Berlin experiment is childish whimsy.

In the opening pages of *Repetition,* Constantin seemed serious about his "new category" of repetition that would replace recollection or mediation, and that had potential for restoring passion, life, to a dull and dampened world. But now the scene has changed. His talk of repetition may be only puns, babble, sophism. He embarks on a misguided and trivial experiment, and comes up with negative results: he declares that everything in Berlin has changed, which proves that repetition is impossible. But as ever, we should be cautious drawing conclusions. The Berlin experiment is only a partial test, and empirical tests, however complete, are inappropriate for proof or disproof of a metaphysical theory. Kierkegaard is surely aware that his concept can't be so easily dismissed. In the same tenor as his experimental side-trip, Constantin's withdrawal of belief in repetition is mainly theater. *Fear and Trembling* and the "Job Discourse" take the category seriously, providing *Repetition's* required counterpoint.

Apart from illustrating Constantin's literary-dialectical prowess, and the inconstancy, complacency and indifference of his character, the zig-zag course of *Repetition's* opening narrative raises two larger questions. The first is whether repetition is the master-element in a metaphysical theory, or is instead a critical, antimetaphysical device. The second is whether repetition is something humans can achieve by work or effort. Let me consider the second here, reserving the question of metaphysics and antimetaphysics for later.

Constantin decides that repetition is impossible, but behind the curtain of his conclusion lies a more serious point. Seeking repetition may be like shoving on a door that opens only inward or pushing one that only someone else can open. If Job or Abraham provide our pattern for a successful repetition, their success is surely not the outcome of a specific effort to *get* repetition. Job does not labor furiously to repossess his world; Abraham does not labor to retrieve his son. In fact, attempts to regain what they had lost would backfire.

Sometimes value lost is reacquired precisely when we stop trying to regain it. We may need a stance of receptivity, willingness, rather than the narrow focus of willed achievement. We are told in Kierkegaard's papers that at its highest, repetition gives up the idea of self-sufficiency.[18] Realizing that the outcome of our search for roots or love or world is not under our control may be a necessary condition of openness toward emerging roots or love or world, and hence the satisfaction of the need. Giving up on repetition as an explicit task is preparation for repetition as world-bestowal. Whatever one's need of repetition, one cannot be bent on forcing its appearance.

III. *REPETITION:* THE LETTERS

We should not neglect the young man who suffers unrequited love. The second part of *Repetition* includes a collection of letters written to Constantin from this nameless youth who has come to Constantin for counsel. This story of unrequited love provides the third angle in *Repetition's* triangulation of the concept "repetition." There is the lab experiment, repetition as the attempt to duplicate results experientially; there is a metaphysical or antimetaphysical task, the attempt to unravel dialectically the concept; and there is an existential challenge, the hope for repetition as support or faith in weathering an ordeal where life itself may be at risk. *Repetition*, however, does not complete this third angle of approach. If we want a figure who actually *meets* repetition's existential challenge, who undergoes the ebb and flow of a higher ethico-religious repetition, we must turn to Job or Abraham: neither Constantin nor his companion will do.[19]

This nameless young man's suffering reminds us of the young man in *Fear and Trembling*, not quite a "knight of faith," but one who advances above the "slaves of misery, the frogs in life's swamp." Johannes de silentio describes a lad who resigns his love and all his hope for worldly happiness, but as a "knight of infinite resignation" steadfastly cherishes her eternal image (*FT* 41–6; *FT*[h] 70–5). To be a knight of faith, he would have to sustain a hope of repetition, of her return, even as he acknowledges her loss. But this, we are told, is a "movement" the lad cannot perform. He has given up all hope for her return.

Repetition's young man is neither a knight of faith nor a knight of resignation, as we will see, though his stance is a charming mimic of a knight of faith. In his favor, he craves repetition, a return of his beloved, which shows that his relationship to repetition is deeper than Constantin's idle curiosity. Like Job, to whom he woefully appeals as a companion in suffering, he hopes his world, his love, will be returned. But he is not prepared, morally or religiously, for the sort of repetition granted to Job or Abraham.

Consider the young friend's cry for help. He calls out to Job for comfort. This resembles Johannes de silentio in *Fear and Trembling* calling out to "Father Abraham" for help in understanding the painful enigma that Abraham represents (*FT* 23; *FT*[h] 56). But in both cases, the lyrical invocation of a biblical figure may seem contrived and sentimental. Could Abraham or Job really aid these wayward poets? *Repetition's* young man, like the poet Johannes de silentio, values the effect the biblical allusion will create and the importance cast on his *own* plight through this grandiose association. Imitating Job, he "awaits his thunderstorm," a storm he hopes will restore his world (*R* 214). But is it really credible that he suffers as Job does, or that appealing to Job might help, or that a world-restoring Whirlwind might appear again, in particular to *him?*

There are other grounds to suspect these calls for help. Why would the youth expect that *Constantin* could give him solace in his pain? Are we to believe Constantin is capable, through word, deed, or silent presence, of compassionate response to another's concrete suffering? Finally, there is a hint that Constantin has *staged* this existential crisis, that the young man does not exist apart from Constantin's literary contrivance. He boasts to have "brought the poet into existence" (*R* 228). After all, is it beneath Constantin's power of invention to produce letters (apparently from a young man) as a foil, as part of a purely narrative exercise?

Constantin sets himself lower than his creation, averring that his friend is now a "poet whose soul has taken on a religious resonance" (*R* 228). But why take this characterization at face value? On reading the young man's letters, do *we* find that his voice conveys a religious sheen – as opposed, say, to a shallow sentimental one?

Without Constantin's aside, I think we'd see that neither he nor his friend are qualified to be recipients of truly deep repetition – what Kierkegaard elsewhere calls "repetition in the pregnant sense."[20] For each of them, theatricality seems a stronger element of personality than responsibility.

Both Constantin and his friend lack the moral-religious serious-ness requisite for the sort of religious repetition we find in Job or Abraham. As Constantin avers, the youth may be "born to himself" as a poet (R 221). And it's true that both can experience momentary aesthetic bliss. But neither seems prepared for the repetitions of self-choice that Judge William counsels, let alone a more strenu-ously religious repetition. As Constantin frankly puts it, "the de-lights of conception" are to be valued over "the pains of childbirth" (141).[21] Being entertained by seductive ideas is preferred to the labor of bringing oneself to birth, or to the further steps of resigning the world, preparing for what Johannes de silentio would call faith's sec-ond movement.[22]

IV. THEORY AND ANTITHEORY

Stepping back from the narrative texture of *Repetition*, I'd like to test the more abstract characterizations of the "new category" that Constantin provides. Is repetition the keystone of a metaphysical arch?

Kierkegaard was pleased that his idea of repetition could be ex-pressed in simple Danish (R 149).[23] His master-concept travels al-most anonymously without philosophical pretensions. It is the linguistic equivalent of *Fear and Trembling*'s unassuming shop-keeper knight of faith.[24] Repetition is explicitly connected with a host of other metaphysical concepts (freedom, consciousness, *kine-sis*, and so forth); and Constantin characterizes repetition as the *in-terest* of metaphysics, as if it were theory's crowning goal. But the case is not straightforward. He also says that repetition will bring metaphysics to grief. So its main work might be deflationary, a tool to counter recollection or mediation. Or given Constantin's whim-sical detachment from theory, it might be projected as a literary or academic toy.

Given these possibilities, I suggest that we proceed by granting Kierkegaard (and Constantin) an intermediate "parametaphysical" or "critical" Kantian position. That is, we'll assume that the field of metaphysical concepts surrounding repetition is intended seriously by Kierkegaard, but also that the theory we pursue is explicitly self-critical, metaphysics in battle with its own limits. Thus it is less than settled positive doctrine but more than Constantin's bluff, bluster, and deflationary feints.[25]

It may come as a surprise that Kierkegaard's critical approach can be characterized as broadly Kantian – Kantian, insofar as we enter metaphysics largely to press toward and define its limits.[26] Kant is simultaneously the champion of enlightenment reason and the critic of "pure" metaphysical reason. Without hesitation or reserve Kierkegaard adopts Kant's critique of speculative reason. It is more surprising, however, that the general thrust of Kierkegaard's category of repetition itself can be sketched by a Kantian analogy (and contrast). Alastair Hannay puts the matter this way:

It is as though the structuring of the world of experience were to be seen in a Kantian way as taking shape in the form of inner intuition, and the psycho-temporal pair of recollection and repetition give you two ways of understanding the temporal constitution in consciousness of the only kind of reality that can save you from boredom and nihilism. But there is a sharp opposition to Kant, too, for in order to achieve that kind of reality your relation to a transcendent God plays an essential part. There is no way of "returning" to the universal [a shared reality that matters] within the limits of reason alone.[27]

Kierkegaard holds that our initial, premoral and prereligious connection with the world and others is insufficient, a first or aesthetic immediacy, bound to end in "boredom and nihilism." With the world-conferral of repetition, we are granted a "second immediacy," a vital connection through which things and persons matter, a connection more adequate to our human and spiritual needs. Setting aside this intriguing parallel (and contrast) with Kant, let us turn to Kierkegaard's own sketch of "the constitution in consciousness" of a reality worth having.

There are numerous metaphysical remarks about repetition scattered throughout *Repetition.*[28] In a page from Kierkegaard's journals, written just after the text's publication, we find these gathered in a single compact passage, part of a letter addressed to "My dear Reader." The intent is precisely to address a reader needing some assistance in deciphering the metaphysical import of "repetition." This unpublished (and undelivered) letter, unlike the published novella, nests repetition in its theoretical context.

[We should know] . . . that repetition is a task for freedom, that it signifies freedom itself, consciousness raised to the second power, that it is the *interest* of metaphysics and also the interest upon which metaphysics comes to grief, the watchword in every ethical view, the *conditio sine qua non* for every issue of dogmatics, that true repetition is eternity, that repetition . . . will come to mean atonement.[29]

Let us consider these drastically abbreviated claims in sequence. First, how is repetition a task for freedom?

Approached from the side of a self becoming itself, a task for freedom is a task for self. A self's task is increasing its freedom, increasing its openness toward the possibility of repetition. Being closed off from the world of existential possibilities (where one could find oneself) is to be cast into aesthetic indifference and despair:

. . . get me possibility, get me possibility, the only thing that can save me is possibility! A possibility and the despairer breathes again, he revives; for without possibility it is as though a person cannot draw a breath.[30]

The Sickness unto Death defines the self as freedom (*SUD* 29; *SUD*[h] 59). As we have seen from the examples of Job and Abraham, repetition is not attained by willpower alone, by making plans and taking steps to secure its possession. Nevertheless, there is labor involved in remaining open, in the midst of a devastating loss, to the possibility of repetition. In that sense, repetition is a task, a job for freedom.[31]

To picture the contrast between repetition as a task and repetition as a reception, consider the difference between musicians *taking* a repeat (playing a section again with appropriate variation) and the attentive *hearing*, the "reception," of that repeat by an awakened audience. Individuals assume, or are placed in, both roles: they are both "performers" and "audience" in the music of creation and self development. But as one moves toward the religious or wondrous, one becomes less an actor than an alert receptor. Here the job of freedom is sustaining receptivity. A nondespairing self is ready at every instant both to resign the world (as target of one's interventions) and get it back again (as gift).[32] The world one gets is in part a function of the self one is: a self tempered, alert, and open; and the self one gets is in part a function of the world one has: a world stocked with worth that calls on and stills the business of mobile selves. Self and world become reciprocally articulate.

Approached from the side of world-conferral, repetition is a transcendental task performed in the bestowal of a world to Job, an Isaac to Abraham, or a beloved to a lover. It is a task performed in the name of freedom. If, as Johannes de silentio has it in *Fear and Trembling,* God is that all things are possible, then we might say that insofar as God has tasks, these are also the tasks of opening possibilities "at the border of the wondrous."[33] A task in the name of freedom is accomplished as world and self become revived *in toto* – as in the wonder of Job's encounter with the Whirlwind, or as Abraham receives a new Isaac. Repetition signifies freedom's possibilities bequeathed to otherwise despairing individuals. A nondespairing self depends on the resources of repetition to sustain its freedom; and the freedom of a self is expressed in terms of its receptivity to the bestowal of such resources.[34]

Repetition is also "consciousness raised to the second power."[35] Consciousness can turn on itself, and this process can be repeated. We can have worries, and worries about our worries – and that's worth worrying about! For any given datum of consciousness, we are free to reflect on it and free to take up a stance toward it. This dual capacity, to reflect and to "take up," might be called the core of human freedom.

I may be bound in some respects, but I am free both to reflect on this fact from various perspectives (some strongly evaluative, some relatively indifferent) and also to take up one of those perspectives as the one that is mine. Humans who have moved beyond brute response to the given or beyond a sophisticated aesthetic indifference will have the capacity to respond in their worlds with the intensity of second-order reflection, second-order care, or as Kierkegaard has it, "consciousness raised to the second power (*R* 149).[36]

Constantin calls repetition a modern view in contrast to an "ethnical" view (*R* 149).[37] In this tribal or traditionalist view, self-identity is secured by successful assimilation into prevailing cultural currents. In contrast, repetition requires for identity that we step back from these common currents to a stance ready for *individual* evaluations and individual self-choice. This flows naturally from the idea that "repetition is a task for freedom."

Moving through the items in Kierkegaard's letter, we are told next that "repetition is the *interest* of metaphysics" (*R* 149). What could this mean? We might think of metaphysics as whatever scheme confers meaning on the largest range of things. In that case, we certainly have an interest in achieving such an integrated global picture. And repetition may be the keystone in such a scheme. Humans seek wholeness and completion as well as difference, and in the largest scheme of things. This pursuit is a matter of individual initiative and, when vigorous, laden with subjective passion.[38] Seeking repetition can be construed as a quasi-metaphysical quest. But we must beware, for Constantin goes on to claim that repetition is what brings metaphysics to grief.

Perhaps repetition is the sort of limiting or totalizing concept we can aspire to possess, to aim at, but which we nevertheless can never hope to fully grasp. If so our efforts come to grief in the way that Kant suggests all our metaphysical endeavors must ultimately founder. In a famous passage from the *Critique of Pure Reason*, Kant confesses that we are fated to pursue metaphysical inquiries "that [we] can never abandon and yet [are] unable to carry to completion."[39] And there may be a more specific, existential reason why "repetition" will defy a satisfactory intellectual completion or explication.

Presumably, we are seekers, not as some abstract general mind but as singular, interested *individuals.* Yet metaphysics is a perfectly general theory of the meaning of things, geared to satisfy any and all interested parties, and so does not provide a *special* purchase for the needs of anyone in *particular.* Thus its structure must itself frustrate our understanding of the personal or existential nature of its quest. We seek to get out of the world to get a better view of it; but then we find we're not part of the world we've escaped. In fact, we're to be found nowhere in particular and hence nowhere period. Constantin's friend turns to Job, not to metaphysics, for comfort in his pain. So our metaphysics comes to grief. It cannot give *me* meaning if it remains bound to a universality that excludes my particularity and to an objectivity that excludes my passions.[40]

Why should repetition be "the watchword (or password) in every ethical view"? Why does "every ethical view" *need* a password – the sort of sign sentries exchange in the dark?[41] From the standpoint of *Fear and Trembling,* ethics as a conventional code of requirements and prohibitions is insufficient. The crisis-ridden world of Abraham is a not-so-subtle critique of the complacent world of Judge William, just as the "Job Discourse" is a critique of Constantin Constantius's superficial interest in repetition. We need a password to escape the temptations of Constantin's aesthetic playground or Judge William's world of civic propriety. The municipal and family ethics of the judge needs a supplement. Repetition is the password that provides relief when the radical insufficiency of bourgeois ethics becomes inescapably apparent.

An ethics of Judge William's variety founders on its own requirements. It requires a responsibility for self and others that outstrips what moral agents can deliver on their own. As the burden of moral suffering caused by awareness of this inability inevitably grows, ethics will reach an impasse. It would be a shameful capitulation to relieve the accumulated moral debt by slackening moral demands. And relief through forgiveness is also outside the provenance of ethics. The forgiveness we need cannot be *required* of any friend or acquaintance or moral judge; hence ethics cannot secure it for us.[42] In Kierkegaard's view, if forgiveness arrives it must come from a more-than-moral or transcendental source. Repetition becomes atonement or forgiveness "from above," a transcendental gift of world-renewal in which our moral tasks can be resumed. Repetition is the "password," providing escape from an otherwise intolerable moral burden, in every ethical view. Our watch is relieved. In addition, repetition is the *sine qua non* of all dogmatics (forgiveness of sin cannot be other than a matter of faith).[43] As the "dogma" of forgiveness, repetition grants relief from otherwise unbearable moral pain.

Next is the enigmatic claim that "eternity is the true repetition" (*R* 221). Perhaps the idea is this, that the source of world-bestowal will hover "outside of time," arching over those worldly, temporal things on which repetition bestows meaning, sense, and worth. Eternity would be the domain from which true repetition flows – or so we might suppose. Pursuit of repetition, then, is pursuit of eternity, the answer to a metaphysical, personal, and existential interest.[44] One gets the world, the finite and familiar, back again, repeated, but now under the aegis of infinite value, limitless importance.

Finally, as we have seen, "repetition will come to mean atonement." But in the letter to "My dear Reader" this claim is interrupted by a long parenthetical remark that I excised in my original quotation. Here is the passage with parentheses restored:

repetition (by being pursued so far that it vanishes for psychology as transcendent, as a religious movement by virtue of the absurd, which commences when a person has come to the border of the wondrous) will come to mean atonement.[45]

Let us work through this parenthesis.

Repetition can be an object of psychological reflection or it can ascend to a status far too grand or uncanny for psychology to encompass. When we desire the return of something loved and lost, we desire repetition. Both this desire and its hoped-for fulfillment are comprehensible in terms of our ordinary psychology. Perhaps the person we loved is only temporarily removed, and there are clear reasons to believe that she or he may be returned. If we, however, desire the return of someone for all intents and purposes unavailable, then comprehension in terms of natural expectations starts to falter.

If like Abraham we both desire to obey God in his demand that Isaac be sacrificed and equally desire that Isaac be restored, the subject "vanishes for psychology." It vanishes in the sense that we can give no intelligible account of how two incompatible beliefs can be held with equal fervor. It is impossible, we might say, to believe a contradiction – at least from the standpoint of commonsense psychology. And if Isaac is returned, that event also shatters or transcends psychological comprehension. Witnessing the return of Isaac or the return of Job's world, we stand in awe, beyond the urge – or *capacity* – to offer explanation. So both the religious desire for Isaac's return (or for the return of Job's world) and the religious fulfillment of those desires will be "movement[s] by virtue [or on the strength] of the absurd."[46] They defy psychology. Job and Abraham receive religious repetition at "the border of the wondrous," or "the marvelous" – at the threshold of the sublime (*R* 185).[47]

The story of Job is a story that the young man in *Repetition* knows by heart and repeats every night during his affliction. Several of his letters attempt an interpretation that parallels the pattern of discussion in the "Job Discourse." Job exemplifies a "boundary situation." To be, as Job is, at the limit of human (or perhaps ethical) understanding amounts to Job's discovery that he can be denied the sort of justice or account that he demands yet nevertheless be granted a value-laden world through the Whirlwind despite the reality of his suffering.[48]

Job works at "the border of the marvelous" because in his straits *any* bestowal will seem wondrous, given his deprivation, bleak prospects, and nearness to despair. And secondly, this bestowal is wondrous because he's not granted just any ordinary world. The world delivered through the Whirlwind's voice is filled with magnificence and power, the wonder of the heavens, the stars, the sea and all its creatures – things the same yet born anew. Third, Job is at "the border of the marvelous" because this world-conferral or repetition successfully outstrips or bypasses his ethical demands – *without thereby defeating him:* as his world is renewed, so is he.[49]

Repetition is characterized here as a movement "by virtue of the absurd."[50] Isaac was in his father's care, was lost, then restored; this second grant is itself a repetition of his initial marvelous delivery to Abraham and Sarah in their old age. Repetition signals the wondrous conferral of Isaac, against all worldly expectation and independently of Abraham's efforts to *achieve* his end directly. He does not set out to get Isaac back, but to sacrifice him. Isaac's return marks a religious repetition "on the strength of the absurd," not a psychologically comprehensible outcome of Abraham's *work* for repetition. And ultimately, repetition is linked with Christian doctrine in which saving value is first wondrously embodied, then lost or stripped away, and finally faithfully expected to return: not on the strength of a rational prediction, and not on the basis of a metaphysical axiom known to be true, but on the strength of faith that baffles reason. Hence, once more, repetition becomes a *sine qua non* of dogmatics.

These last parenthetical remarks from the passage to "My dear Reader" reinforce the view that faith occurs on the other side of theory, where "the wondrous" marks the edge of viable metaphysics or moral psychology. Whether as a task for freedom, as consciousness raised to the second power, or as a password for ethics, repetition gives us a cluster of navigational points in a theoretical or metaphysical field; simultaneously, Constantin (and Kierkegaard) charts the limits of this field, catching the spots where metaphysics comes to grief.

V. IS REPETITION POSSIBLE?

In keeping with our theme, we can conclude by starting over, reviewing the pivots on which repetition turns. We can pitch these lessons midway between Constantin's dense and abbreviated para-metaphysical feints and parries and the enigmatic self-deconstruct-ing indirections of his novella.

1. Repetition is not a self-initiated project but an other-initiated grant. Experience cannot be brought back to life simply by willing it to happen and taking steps. Concepts cannot animate the soul simply by dint of our dialectical finesse – defeating the opponents, writing up a plausible alternative. My existential crisis cannot be wiped away by simple rote advice or coaching. Nevertheless experi-ence, meaning, or value can be restored to those for whom it has be-come lost.

If we take our cue from Job or Abraham, repetition is possible. Job has his world restored; Abraham gets Isaac back. Their wounds are healed. But it is not by their own power or by their setting out to achieve the goal that they win repetition. Paradoxically, they gain repetition while their hearts are set on something else. Job does not demand or work to get his world restored: he asks *why* it has been taken, he demands *reasons*. Abraham does not demand or set out to get Isaac back: he sets out to give Isaac up. Both are beneficiaries of repetition, but neither makes the attainment of repetition his ex-plicit project.

Repetition can be desired, and when attained, shore up an other-wise demoralized self. But just as a resignation or despair of the search for some sorts of worldly satisfaction may be a necessary condition for their subsequent attainment, so getting the world back may require first that we give up all attempts to get it back. This means that conceived as a human task or as an outcome an-ticipated on the basis of reasonable expectations, repetition is im-possible. Its essence is the shock of knowing its impossibility, resigning its possibility – as a strategic *human* goal.

2. Repetition is not to be confused with recollection. Platonic rec-ollection in Kierkegaard's view should provide such continuity and content as could save a soul. The self would become true, good, beautiful through contemplation or recollection of enduring forms of truth or good or beauty. It would gain eternity. Despite the at-tractions of this view, which include Christian overtones of a soul's ascent toward the Good, Kierkegaard still holds that "recollection" is a pagan view. Meaning or value is not in the "past-eternity" of finished knowledge – as if we were looking for a mislaid set of keys

that will be where we left them, once we remember where that is. It's to be found or received through the faith that the future will *provide* keys, perhaps not exactly the same keys, but welcome nevertheless. The divine may confer a value-laden world appropriate to our needs in ways hitherto unforeseen – in ways that have *not* always existed. Repetition returns what was lost on new and unexpected terms. A self or world renewed streams forth as new day's light from an open future.

3. Repetition is based on a need for world, for global value, and completes itself as world or value is transcendentally provided.[51] Insofar as one confronts the "meaningless" repetition of "merely natural" cycles, one falls short.[52] Here is a lament from *Fear and Trembling:*

if one generation succeeded the other as the songs of birds in the woods, if the human race passed through the world as a ship through the sea or the wind through the desert, a thoughtless and fruitless whim . . . how empty and devoid of comfort would life be! (*FT* 15; *FT*[h] 49)[53]

But Kierkegaardian repetition is not "merely natural" senseless flux. For the knight of faith, the cycles of loss and attainment are not just fixed in nature or poetically repeated in speech, but are lived through, celebrated in the concrete tenor of his life, embraced by his receptive soul. To see through natural or aesthetic recurrences, to know in one's bones, as Abraham does, the giving up and getting back that is faith is to acknowledge transcendental world-bestowal. To hold a faith that value will surely dawn, that there are worlds to be conferred is to hold out for full-fledged repetition.

4. Finally, we have the contrast between doctrine or theory and lived experience. For Kierkegaard, human fulfillment does not rest on a comprehensive grasp of intellectual contrasts, say, between objectivity and subjectivity or between recollection and repetition or between pagan and Christian lives. Nor is it sufficient to ardently endorse the (putatively) superior term in each of these contrasts. Fulfillment rests on receiving repetition. This is not grasping a theory, not even grasping it in utmost passion. It is having a concrete encounter appropriate to one's specific need. Abraham gets Isaac back – he needn't care about Johannes de silentio's "double movements." Job gets back his world transformed – he needn't care about the philosopher's "problem of evil." What is "repeated," restored, is

a world infused with objects of sustaining value, an enigmatic, value-saturated world whose power, allure, and potential for support far exceeds whatever muffled thoughts or passing theory might arise about the ground or source of that world bequeathed. Too much theory is a threat. Gemma Corradi Fuimara puts the danger this way:

at the very moment in which we "arm" ourselves with a cognitive model we are, paradoxically, justified in losing interest in the object. We no longer consider it as enigmatic since it is our turn to speak. . . . It is almost as though a dense cloud of theory, interpretation, and explanation formed around the object, blunting *its* prospective eloquence.[54]

Horizons, worlds, and things embraced therein can be lost or put at risk – as we find in Job's case. Thus, the stage is set for their restoration being wondrous. Repetition becomes enablement, allowing life whatever significance it may have, despite our failure to ground that significance in terms of some explicit all-inclusive theory.[55] Kierkegaard brings us back to sustaining values that are concrete, particular, and pretheoretical. He portrays the importance of repetition for life while batting away our attempts to box up an all-purpose theory of the "mechanism" or "structure" or "metaphysics" of repetition that we presume will allow us to acquire and manipulate meaning and value at will. If Kierkegaard could revive an alertness to the unmasterable particulars of action, reception, situation, and understanding whose strands can crystallize to form a habitable world, he would have prepared us for a grant of life.

NOTES

1 What I call the "Discourse on Job" (or "Job Discourse") is the first of Kierkegaard's *Four Upbuilding Discourses,* originally published 6 December 1843; the given title is the biblical heading from Job, "The Lord Gave and The Lord Took Away." This discourse is collected in *EUD* 109–24.

2 *Pap.* IV B 108. Portions are collected in "Selected Entries from Kierkegaard's Journals and Papers Pertaining to *Repetition,*" in *R* 324. (Hereafter, Supplement).

3 See Walter Lowrie, *Kierkegaard* (London and New York: Oxford University Press, 1938), p. 630. David Cain provides a revealing list of the ways "repetition" (*Gjentagelse*) has been characterized by Kierkegaard schol-

ars: "a burning bush that is not consumed"; "the Christian idea of a 'new creature'"; "in the act of repetition [the existing individual] becomes what he is"; "Repetition is to give thanks always." See David Cain, "Notes on a Coach Horn: 'Going Further,' 'Revocation,' and *Repetition*," in *International Kierkegaard Commentary*, Fear and Trembling *and* Repetition, ed. Robert L. Perkins (Macon, Ga.: Mercer University Press, 1993), p. 338f.

4 *Pap.* IV B 120, Supplement, p. 324.

5 While page-proofs for *Repetition* were being set, Kierkegaard learned that Regine had become engaged to someone else. Realizing that there was now no way for him to undo his "sacrifice" or to regain her, he ripped out the final pages of *Repetition* and rewrote them.

6 Kierkegaard dropped his strategies of concealment in the last phase of his critique, in what has been called his "attack" literature. See, for example, *Attack on Christendom*, trans. Walter Lowrie (Princeton: Princeton University Press, 1968), and *For Self-Examination and Judge for Yourselves*, trans. Walter Lowrie (Princeton: Princeton University Press, 1944).

7 See Alastair Hannay's useful discussion of alternative ways of construing Kierkegaard's complex vacillation in how he himself should assess *Either/Or* in the light of his later work and life-decisions: "The Judge in the Light of Kierkegaard's Own Either/Or: Some Hermeneutical Crochets," in *International Kierkegaard Commentary*, Either/Or, Part II, ed. Robert L. Perkins (Macon, Ga.: Mercer University Press, 1995), pp. 183–205.

8 *EO* I 75ff, 302ff; see also *EO^h* 60–135, 247–376. The discussion of *Don Giovanni* is found in the section titled "The Musical Erotic."

9 "The Balance Between the Esthetic and the Ethical in the Development of the Personality," *EO* II 155ff. See also "Equilibrium between the Aesthetic and the Ethical in the Development of Personality," *EO^h* 247ff.

10 See my "Self-Choice or Self-Reception: Judge William's Admonition," in *International Kierkegaard Commentary*, Either/Or, Part II, ed. Robert L. Perkins (Macon, Ga: Mercer University Press, 1995), pp. 5–31.

11 In his papers, Kierkegaard distinguishes different stages in the development of the concept of repetition, corresponding roughly to aesthetic, ethical, and religious versions; he admits that the earlier versions distract us from the authentic religious sense, introduced later. See *Pap.* IV B 117, Supplement, pp. 301f. Roger Poole correctly challenges Thulstrup's oversimplified contrast between a "merely poetic" and a "religious" repetition, but he goes too far in his claim that the text of *Repetition* does not itself give us internal grounds for distinguishing quasi-religious from trivially nonreligious versions of the concept. For

example, we are surely justified in ranking Constantin's frivolous trip to Berlin as a "lower" interest in repetition than the young man's "higher" tormented interest in the return of his beloved. Furthermore, the text of *Repetition* may not give us all we need to understand the concept "repetition": "The Job Discourse" and *Fear and Trembling* are surely central here, as well as Kierkegaard's papers. (See, e.g., *Pap.* IV A 178, Supplement, p. 336, where Constantin's Berlin journey is characterized as a farce.) For his critique of attempts to make sense of "repetition," see Roger Poole, *Kierkegaard: The Indirect Communication* (Charlottesville: The University Press of Virginia, 1993), pp. 72f. Also, see my "Kierkegaard's Job Discourse: Get-ting Back the World," *International Journal for the Philosophy of Religion* 34 (1993): 151–69.

12 See *Pap.* IV B 111, Supplement, p. 294.

13 Of course, the *concept* of repetition, although not named as such, is central to *Fear and Trembling* as well as to the "Job Discourse." A connection, and contrast, between *Fear and Trembling* and *Repetition* could be put schematically in this way. By challenging both conventional and rational accounts of ethical value, *Fear and Trembling* raises an ontology of value, launching it above and beyond conventional, Hegelian, Kantian, or utilitarian accounts. *Repetition* raises the question of human access *to* that realm of special, saving value.

14 Constantin Constantius is not a completely reliable guide to Hegel. For a good discussion of the (disputed) character of Hegelian dialectic, see Michael Forster, "Hegel's Dialectic Method," in *The Cambridge Companion to Hegel*, ed. Frederick C. Beiser (Cambridge University Press, 1993), pp. 130–70.

15 See my "Self Choice or Self-Reception."

16 For an excellent discussion of types of repetition, see Stephen Crites, "'The Blissful Security of the Moment': Recollection, Repetition, and Eternal Recurrence," in *International Kierkegaard Commentary:* Fear and Trembling *and* Repetition, ed. Robert L. Perkins (Macon, Ga.: Mercer University Press, 1993), p. 225–46.

17 Hence Roger Poole's dismissal of "recollection forward" is premature. See *Kierkegaard: The Indirect Communication,* p. 63.

18 *Pap.* IV A 169, Supplement, p. 326.

19 See, e.g., *Pap.* IV A 178, Supplement, p. 336, where Constantin's Berlin journey is characterized as a farce (see note 11 above).

20 *Pap.* IV B 111, Supplement, p. 294. Also, see note 12 above.

21 Constantin is here quoting Lessing with approval.

22 See my *Knights of Faith and Resignation: Reading Kierkegaard's* Fear and Trembling (Albany: State University of New York Press, 1991), chap. 6.

23 *Gjentagelse* can mean "taking again" or "retake," as well as "repetition" or "a repeat."

24 Johannes de silentio, the pseudonymous author of *Fear and Trembling*, introduces a knight of faith so ordinary that he might be mistaken for a shopkeeper. *FT* 39; *FT*[h] 68.

25 Constantin claims he has "given up theory," *R* 216. Roger Poole concludes his discussion of *Repetition* with the claim that there is "no Kierkegaardian doctrine of repetition." (*Kierkegaard: The Indirect Communication*, p. 82.) That Constantin Constantius makes a bewildering variety of claims about repetition is indisputable. It does not follow, however, that there is no pattern to the discussion of "repetition" other than a perverse intention to undermine all pattern to the concept. Whether or not a stable *doctrine* emerges, clearly much can be – and is – said about repetition that is illuminating and instructive. A dialectical concept may be subversive of doctrine without being self-subversive.

26 I discuss connections between Kant's critical project and Kierkegaard's lyrical-dialectical productions in *Selves in Discord and Resolve: Kierkegaard's Moral-Religious Psychology from Either/Or to Sickness unto Death* (New York: Routledge, 1996), chap. 1. On the Kant-Kierkegaard connection more generally, see Ronald M. Green, *Kierkegaard and Kant: The Hidden Debt* (Albany: State University of New York Press, 1992).

27 Alastair Hannay, "The 'Impossibilities' of Repetition," unpublished ms., 1995, final paragraph. The interpolation is mine.

28 In discussing repetition, John D. Caputo equates metaphysics quite narrowly with *stasis*. On this basis, he believes that repetition, which concerns flux, motion, or personal becoming, must undermine all metaphysics. But Hegel's mediation, Aristotle's *kinesis*, and Spinoza's *conatus* are familiar metaphysical concepts that grapple with "motion." Caputo's construal of metaphysics is unnecessarily narrow. See John D. Caputo, "Kierkegaard, Heidegger, and the Foundering of Metaphysics," in *International Kierkegaard Commentary:* Fear and Trembling *and* Repetition, ed. Perkins, pp. 201–24.

29 Supplement, p. 324.

30 *SUD* 38–9; *SUD*[h] 69. I thank Steve Webb for reminding me of this passage.

31 See my *Selves in Discord and Resolve*, chap. 8.

32 In *Fear and Trembling* the knight of faith will have a dancer's leap, a movement made over and over, every moment. *FT* 40f; *FT*[h] 70.

33 For God, "all things are possible." *FT* 46; *FT*[h] 75. The concept of the divine appearing "at the borders of the wondrous" is discussed on pp. 298–9.

34 The connections between freedom and stages of repetition are spelled out in detail in *Pap.* IV B 117, Supplement, pp. 301f.

35 *R* 229; Supplement, pp. 274f.

36 See Harry Frankfurt on "second-order" desire and care in *The Impor-
    tance of What We Care About* (Cambridge University Press, 1988); also
    Charles Taylor, "What Is Human Agency?" *Human Agency and Lan-
    guage* (Cambridge University Press, 1985), chap. 1, pp. 15–44.

37 The concept resembles Hegel's *Sittlichkeit*. See Crites, "The Blissful
    Security of the Moment," p. 231.

38 In *The Concept of Anxiety* Kierkegaard points out that reflection is not
    a disinterested pursuit but a passionate or "subjective" one – intending
    a contrast with Kant, who characterizes the aesthetic stance as "disin-
    terested"; see *CA* 18n. But Kierkegaard has oversimplified the ques-
    tion. In fact, Kant does not neglect the factor of "interest." In *The
    Critique of Judgment* his phrase for the aesthetic stance is "disinter-
    ested *interest*."

39 Kant, *Critique of Pure Reason* (London: St. Martin's Press, 1965), p. 295
    (A 235–6; B 294–5). See note 25 above.

40 See Thomas Nagel, *The View From Nowhere* (Oxford: Oxford Univers-
    ity Press, 1986) and my discussion in *Selves in Discord and Resolve*,
    chap. 7.

41 In personal correspondence, Alastair Hannay has suggested "password"
    or "countersign" (as between sentries) as an alternative to the Hongs'
    "watchword."

42 Even to permit forgiveness as a general virtue may be problematic eth-
    ically, for there may be faults so vicious that forgiving them would it-
    self be ethically mistaken.

43 See my *Knights of Faith and Resignation*, pp. 120–3.

44 Again, see Crites, "The Blissful Security of the Moment."

45 *Pap.* IV B 120, Supplement, p. 324.

46 Hannay's version of this term of art from *Fear and Trembling* is "on the
    strength of the absurd," while the Hongs offer "by virtue of the absurd."

47 The paradoxical blend of pleasure and pain, of dread and attraction in
    encounter with the wondrous or sublime is discussed in the context of
    Kant's *Third Critique* in J. M. Bernstein, *The Fate of Art: Aesthetic
    Alienation from Kant to Derrida and Adorno* (University Park: The
    Pennsylvania State University Press, 1992), esp. chap. 1.

48 See my "Kierkegaard's Job Discourse."

49 As the young man puts it, Job "avoids all cunning ethical evasions and
    wily devices" (*R* 214). That is, he knows that his suffering is ethically
    undeserved and will not give in to the "wily devices" his "friends" ad-
    vance for twisting his suffering into punishment that is justly deserved.

50 See *Pap.* IV B 118, Supplement, p. 321: "repetition is . . . transcendent,
    religious, a movement by virtue of the absurd."

51 Repetition as transcendental bestowal and its relation to sectors of imagination and bending of the will are discussed in my "Kierkegaard's Job Discourse"; see also note 55 below.

52 See Kierkegaard's letter to Heiberg, Supplement, p. 306.

53 See also my discussion in *Knights of Faith and Resignation*, pp. 32f. The contrast between Nietzsche's eternal recurrence and Kierkegaard's repetition is developed in Giles Deleuze, *Repetition and Difference*, trans. Paul Patton (New York: Columbia University Press, 1994). For Nietzsche, the test is whether one can face the possibility that the past will be repeated. For Kierkegaard, the test is whether one can face the possibility that a world now lost will be restored.

54 Gemma Corradi Fuimara, *The Other Side of Language: A Philosophy of Listening* (New York: Routledge, 1990), pp. 106–7.

55 World-conferral establishes what Charles Taylor calls "horizons of significance," background frames that set parameters of meaning and value independent of our desire or choice, which let our desires or choices *be* meaningful because they are thereby addressed to issues *already* significant. Choice and desire operate *within* a frame that already differentiates between options that can carry a given weight of meaning and other options that cannot. Frames that determine ethical options and salience, for example, set a scale of significance incommensurable with aesthetic options, differently framed – say those one confronts at a hairdresser's. In the normal course of things, matters of hairstyle cannot fall under the same horizon of significance as ethics, and my will cannot alter this fact. See Charles Taylor, *The Ethics of Authenticity* (Cambridge: Harvard University Press, 1992), chaps. 4 and 6, and *Philosophical Arguments* (Cambridge: Harvard University Press, 1995), chaps. 2 and 3.

12 Anxiety in *The Concept of Anxiety*

I. PRELIMINARIES

The Concept of Anxiety is a maddeningly difficult book. In one of the most lucid commentaries on this short tract, Arne Grøn[1] has suggested that the book is too difficult; in other words, it could have profited from another rewrite. In one of the central images of *The Concept of Anxiety*, anxiety is likened to dizziness. One reader of Kierkegaard has commented that the book attempts to evoke the very dizziness that it describes. Another prominent Kierkegaard scholar insists that the book is simply a spoof, devoid of any serious psychological insight.[2] While I disagree with this scholar's assessment, I sympathize with his judgment that *The Concept of Anxiety* has elements of farce.

If someone were to articulate a Kierkegaardian ethic, one of the dictums would certainly be – be honest about what you know and do not know. In all honesty, I must confess that there are many passages in *The Concept of Anxiety* the meaning of which completely escapes me. Worse yet, Kierkegaard scholars are silent on most of these passages. Nevertheless, exasperating as it is, *The Concept of Anxiety* is a wise book. It is also a book that has exercised an enormous influence on philosophers such as Heidegger and Sartre and theologians such as Tillich, Barth, and Niebuhr. Moreover, if a single text needed to be chosen as the source book of existential psychology and psychoanalysis, it would most certainly be *The Concept of Anxiety*. But never minding Kierkegaard's influence on intellectual luminaries and the history of twentieth-century thought, *The Concept of Anxiety* and a number of Kierkegaard's other pseudonymous writings have attracted a multitude of readers by sheer force of the fact that the titles of his books suggest he is a kindred soul to that household of millions who find themselves troubled by feelings that answer to the names "anxiety" and "despair."³

One of Kierkegaard's central insights, an insight inscribed in various forms throughout this text and, I believe, the entire authorship is that the struggle to lead a good and true life is a struggle against, or if not against then with, anxiety. Even in our own psychological age, an age in which the god-terms, "comfortable and uncomfortable" have superseded good and evil, we, psychologized men and women, have learned to appreciate to the point of obsession the power of the mysterious force that is anxiety. It was, I think, part of Kierkegaard's psychological genius to recognize the connection between anxiety and sin, or, if you would prefer, between anxiety and evil. Less than fifty years later, Freud would learn to acknowledge the same connection.

In the essay that follows, I will summarize some of the major themes of *The Concept of Anxiety.* Subsequently, I will double back and more closely examine Kierkegaard's, or as it were, Haufniensis's definition of anxiety and the promise that he tenders at the end of the book, namely, that anxiety is a primary resource for our spiritual education, as opposed to something that should be taken to the physician and if necessary suppressed with medication.

Before proceeding there is, so far as Kierkegaard studies go, the perennial question of how to approach Kierkegaard's pseudonymous works. Should we follow Walter Lowrie's hermeneutical counsel and regard the entire authorship as the work of Søren Kierkegaard? Or should we follow the poststructuralists and treat the entire authorship, signed works and journals included, as though it were all the work of pseudonyms? In his "First and Last Declaration," appended to *Concluding Unscientific Postscript,* Kierkegaard wrote:

My wish, my prayer, is that, if it might occur to anyone to quote a particular saying from the books, he would do me the favor to cite the name of the respective pseudonymous author. . . . From the beginning I perceived very clearly and do still perceive that my personal reality is an embarrassment which the pseudonyms with pathetic self-assertion might wish to be rid of, the sooner the better, or to have reduced to the least possible significance, and yet again with ironic courtesy might wish to have in their company as a repellent contrast. (*CUP* 551)

For reasons that I will not go into, which is by no means to pretend that they are definitive, I am inclined to respect Kierkegaard's wishes and refer the views expressed in his pseudonymous works to the corresponding pseudonyms. However, where the position stated by a pseudonymous author such as Vigilius Haufniensis is nearly the same as one expressed in the journals, I will assume that the position is Kierkegaard's.

Under the nom de plume Vigilius Haufniensis, Kierkegaard published *The Concept of Anxiety* on 17 June 1844. Four days earlier, Johannes Climacus's lapidary *Philosophical Fragments* had gone on sale at Copenhagen's Reitzel's bookstore. At the time, Kierkegaard was thirty-one years old. His pseudonymous authorship was already in full stride. Behind him were the masterworks *Either/Or, Repetition*, and *Fear and Trembling*. By 1831, Kierkegaard was in the habit of publishing an "upbuilding discourse" in his own name for every book he published pseudonymously. The books to which he signed his name were to represent the religious point of view, whereas those to which he did not were to be expressions of an aesthetic or ethical orientation. To put it another way, with every indirect communique, Kierkegaard produced a direct communication – at least up until *The Concept of Anxiety*. This book must have seemed direct and religious enough since he did not proffer an accompanying set of upbuilding discourses. Just the opposite. Along with the somber and sometimes ponderous *Concept of Anxiety*, he published the relatively airy *Prefaces*, the official author of which is none other than Nicolaus Notabene.

Unlike Johannes Climacus and Anti-Climacus, Vigilius Haufniensis writes only one book and then disappears from the literary scene. However, as Reidar Thomte has noted (*CA* xiii–xiv), the psychological concerns that earmark Haufniensis's perspective run back to *Either/Or* and *Repetition* and forward to *Stages on Life's Way*, and most especially to *The Sickness unto Death*, a book, which like *The Concept of Anxiety* is deeply engaged in the psychology of sin and the psycho-spiritual vicissitudes of sinfulness.

II. HAUFNIENSIS ON THE RELATION BETWEEN CONCEPT AND MOOD

In the rich introduction to *The Concept of Anxiety,* Haufniensis complains about the sloppiness of contemporary thinking. With

Hegel and his epigones clearly in mind, Haufniensis charges that the thinkers of his time are forever committing acts of intellectual hubris, stepping outside the boundaries of their particular disciplines:

Thus when an author entitles the last section of the *Logic* "Actuality," he thereby gains the advantage of making it appear that in logic the highest has already been achieved, or if one prefers, the lowest. In the meantime, the loss is obvious, for neither logic nor actuality is served by placing actuality in the *Logic*. Actuality is not served thereby, for contingency, which is an essential part of the actual, cannot be admitted within the realm of logic. Logic is not served, for if logic has thought actuality, it has included something that it cannot assimilate. (*CA* xiii–xiv)

Unlike the Hegelians, Haufniensis thought that contingent or actual existence falls outside the science of logic. Logic is the province of necessity. In *Philosophical Fragments*, Johannes Climacus argues that the actual is that which has come to be. What comes to be, changes, and whatever changes does not exist of necessity (*PF* 71f). Therefore, it is a mistake of category to treat actuality as though it were a subject matter for logic.

According to Haufniensis, there is a science appropriate to every object of thought, and it is of the utmost importance that the sciences remain within their boundaries. To take a much more pertinent example than actuality and logic, Haufniensis observes that thinkers have approached the idea of sin from metaphysical, ethical, and aesthetical points of view. In every case the result is a confusion of the most dangerous kind, namely, the kind that "gives birth to its own enemy" (*CA* 14n), that is, a confusion one never becomes aware of being enmeshed in.

Psychologist that he professes to be, Haufniensis footnotes the following remark:

That science, just as much as poetry and art, presupposes a mood in the creator as well as in the observer, and that an error in modulation is just as disturbing as an error in the development of thought, have been entirely forgotten in our time. (*CA* 14n)

For every object of thought there is an appropriate mood, and where the mood is wrong the concept of it is falsified (*CA* 14–15). When this reasoning is universalized it seems problematic. In what sense might I falsify a concept in, for example, metaphysics by thinking about it in the earnest mood that is the subjective signature of the ethical point of view? Nevertheless, when applied to certain subject matter, Haufniensis's observation is a light. It could, for instance, be argued that when someone thinks about the Holocaust with curiosity, he fails to grasp the significance of the ovens. Or, again, when someone "does ethics" in a crossword-puzzling mood, as though ethics were a hobby or a way of advancing his career, we might surmise that he has not really understood his subject matter. It is as though Haufniensis were saying that one cannot understand certain subject matter without feeling a certain way. Throughout the authorship, Kierkegaard places enormous emphasis on the importance of appropriating what we think. Indeed, he often gives the impression that you cannot understand what you think unless you try to live according to what you think. The underscoring of appropriation takes different forms in different works. For instance, in *Postscript* it is expressed rather straightforwardly in Climacus's long and wide-ranging discourse on subjectivity. In *The Concept of Anxiety* the significance of appropriation is mirrored in the importance that Haufniensis attributes to moods.

As applied to sin, Haufniensis comes right out and declares, "Whenever the issue of sin is dealt with, one can observe by the very mood whether the concept is the correct one" (*CA* 15). According to Haufniensis, when we think about sin in any mood other than that of earnestness, we are not so much grappling with the idea of sin as we are expressing and ultimately intensifying our own sinfulness.

III. ON SIN-CONSCIOUSNESS AS A RECURRENT THEME IN KIERKEGAARD'S WORKS

Anti-Climacus offers the profound observation that what we really need a revelation for is not to understand that we are saved but rather to understand that we are sinners.[4] If you cannot begin to understand that you are a sinner, then what motivation could there be for thinking that you need to be saved? None of Kierkegaard's writings leave the impression that contemplating theories of sin could be of any spiritual use. In *The Point of View of My Work as an Author*, Kierkegaard reveals that right from the start the whole of his authorship was driven by a religious purpose. Whether or not Kierkegaard was kidding himself or perhaps trying to kid his readers, it is a fact that in many of his writings he seems devoted to the task of enhancing our receptiveness to the idea that we are sinners. Kierkegaard maintained that his age was engaged in producing fire sale standards of faith. Inasmuch as he strove to retrieve some sense of what it really means to believe in God, Kierkegaard can be understood as trying to make faith possible again.[5] Judging from the text, the author of *The Concept of Anxiety* believed that at the time of his writing there were circulating a number of self-serving ideas of sin, ideas that could easily serve as vehicles for the repression of sin-consciousness. In *Postscript*, Johannes Climacus offers a brief review of *The Concept of Anxiety*:

The Concept of Anxiety differs essentially from the other pseudonymous writings in having a direct form, and in being even a little bit objectively dogmatic. Perhaps the author has thought that on this point a communication of knowledge might be needful, before going on to engender inwardness; which latter task is relative to one who may be presumed essentially to have knowledge, and hence not in need of having this conveyed to him, but rather needing to be personally affected. (*CUP* 269–70)

As Climacus understands him, Vigilius Haufniensis is engaged in the task of trying to disarm some rather inviting forms of confusion about sinfulness and, most especially, about original sin or, as it is expressed in the Danish, *arvesynd* (inherited sin). According to Haufniensis, some accounts of original sin suggest that unlike the first human we, the descendants of Adam, are innately corrupt and hence cannot resist sinning. And so, why try? Others, such as Hegel, read Genesis as a mythical account of the necessary evolution of self-consciousness.

We find in the Bible a well-known story abstractly termed the Fall. This representation is very profound and is not just a contingent history but the eternal and necessary history of humanity – though it is expressed here in an external and mythical mode. For this reason there are bound to be inconsistencies in this representation.[6]

Haufniensis does not agree that Genesis is just an important myth with a number of unavoidable inconsistencies. As Niels Thulstrup observes, Haufniensis reads Hegel's interpretation as putting the notion of individual responsibility for sin to sleep.[7] Although there are a number of points on which Haufniensis seems sympathetic to Hegel, for example, in his insistence that there is a "quantitative something" that is passed along from generation to generation,

Thulstrup is, by and large, correct in his verdict that Kierkegaard and Hegel are opposed in their readings of the Fall.

IV. VIGILIUS HAUFNIENSIS'S INTERPRETATION OF THE FALL

Before offering his version of *Paradise Lost*,[8] Haufniensis acknowledges that for most of his nominally Christian readership, the story of the Fall is a myth to be placed alongside the myths of the Greeks. Haufniensis invites us to shrug off our smug sense of superiority and take the Genesis account as though it were telling us the truth about ourselves – the truth that sin comes into being for each of us by our sinning. Sometimes Haufniensis writes as though the problem we face is not so much in treating the story as a myth as it is in a benighted understanding of myth. At other points, he seems to take the story of the Fall as history. *Contra* Hegel, he proclaims, "The Genesis story presents the only dialectically consistent view" (*CA* 32). And then a few pages later he calls upon his reader:

Let us now examine the narrative in Genesis more carefully as we attempt to dismiss the fixed idea that it is a myth, and as we remind ourselves that no age has been more skillful than our own in producing myths of the understanding, an age that produces myths and at the same time wants to eradicate all myths. (*CA* 46)

On the question as to whether Haufniensis understands the Genesis story as history, it is important to acknowledge that he goes to rather bizarre lengths to argue that though we do not inherit our sinfulness from Adam, we do inherit a quantitative something, which telegraphically speaking is none other than "objective anxiety."[9]

From the beginning, Haufniensis rejects accounts of the first sin that "places Adam outside the race." As the first human being, Adam must not differ in any essential way from us, his descendants. Thus, the author dismisses any reading of the Fall in which Adam is represented as having sinned freely but we, his descendants, are understood as having been born with a nature so corrupt that we are predestined to sin. Such accounts not only transform Adam into something fantastic, they volatilize the concept of sin; for on Haufniensis's reckoning, if we are compelled to sin, we are not sinners and there is no need for Christ or the atonement. Equally telling, Haufniensis argues that contemplation of the very idea that Adam is the only one who has ever freely sinned engenders a mood that is antithetical to the development of sin-consciousness.

As *Fear and Trembling, Philosophical Fragments,* and other texts evince, Kierkegaard and his pseudonyms try to make their accounts of religious phenomena square with the Scriptures. Scripture tells us that prior to his sin Adam was ignorant of the difference between good and evil. In the first movement of his rendition of the Fall, Haufniensis writes:

Innocence is ignorance. In innocence, man is not qualified as spirit but is psychically qualified in immediate unity with his natural condition. (*CA* 41)

Prior to the positing of sin and the categories of good and evil, Adam is psychically qualified as a unity of body and soul, but not as spirit.

For Haufniensis and a related pseudonym, Anti-Climacus, human beings are best understood as a synthesis of body and soul. In their respective books, both pseudonyms elaborate upon this claim by somewhat inexplicably adding one of the most important lines in the Kierkegaardian oeuvre, "a synthesis is unthinkable if the two are not united in a third. This third is spirit" (*CA* 43). Plato believed that human beings are a synthesis of body and soul, as did Aristotle, Descartes, and others, yet none of these thinkers argued that there was something else that related body and soul to each other and then, as is expressed in *The Sickness unto Death,* related the relation to itself (*SUD*[h] 43 passim). Whether or not the term "spirit" raises spectres of ghosts, holy and otherwise, Kierkegaard repeats, in this text and others, that human beings are spirit. Over and over, he reminds us that were it not for the fact that we are spirit, anxiety, despair, sin, and faith would be impossible. But exactly what it means to say that we are spirit, Haufniensis, unlike Anti-Climacus, never tries to make clear, perhaps for the same reason that he resists offering a definition of sin or the self.

Haufneinsis's reading of the Fall is much closer to poetry than it is to a psycho-philosophical treatise. Once again, there are a number of logical counterthrusts but very little in the way of positive arguments. The author who considered himself a kind of poet and whom we consider more a philosopher than anything writes that in innocence spirit is present "as immediate, as dreaming." Perhaps he means that in innocence the synthesizing activity of spirit is unreflective or unselfconscious. Haufniensis continues:

In this state there is peace and repose, but there is simultaneously something else that is not contention and strife, for there is indeed nothing against which to strive. What, then, is it? Nothing. But what effect does nothing have? It begets anxiety. This is the profound secret of innocence, that it is at the same time anxiety. Dreamily the spirit projects its own actuality, but this actuality is nothing, and innocence always sees this nothing outside itself. . . . Awake, the difference between myself and my other is posited, sleeping it is suspended; dreaming, it is an intimated nothing. (CA 41–2)

At the outset, I noted that there are knots in this text that some Kierkegaard scholars insist only mock the attempt to unravel them. This is one such koan. Haufniensis proclaims that before good and evil are posited, there is a peace and repose that is not entirely peace and repose but not strife either. Prior to the Fall in which spirit and freedom are posited, spirit projects itself, through, I suspect, the imagination. However, at this point, spirit is not yet anything actual and thus it projects itself as a nothing. Whether it bespeaks an affinity with Hegel or a caricature of him, this text is thick with hypostatized terms. In this case, "Innocence sees" the nothing that is projected spirit as outside itself. These shadowgraphs of spirit, which are experienced as an external something, are an intimation of a pregnant distinction between self and other, but the salient point is that while innocence may be ignorance, it is also anxiety.

Spirit dreaming, as opposed to spirit dead asleep, feels a presentiment of the powers of spirit but as something external.[10] When God prohibits Adam to eat from the tree or else surely die, Adam cannot, in a sense, understand Him, for he knows neither good and evil nor death:

Because Adam has not understood what was spoken, there is nothing but the ambiguity of anxiety. The infinite possibility of being able that was awakened by the prohibition now draws closer, because this possibility points to a possibility as its sequence. (CA 45)

With God's dictum, Adam's anxiety as a feeling of being able is both concretized and intensified, "in this way, innocence is brought to its uttermost. In anxiety it is related to the forbidden and to the punishment. Innocence is not guilty, yet there is anxiety as though it were lost" (*CA* 45). Anxiety, understood as the vague experience of being able and forbidden, is the last stop before the first sin. Haufniensis adds, "further than this psychology cannot go, but so far it can go, and above all, in its observation of human life, it can point to this again and again" (45). In other words, psychology can reflect upon and point to the state that immediately precedes sin, but it cannot and should not try to explain the fact that we sin.

Philip Quinn has convincingly argued[11] that the advance in Kierkegaard's account of the Fall over others, notably those of Kant and Schleiermacher, is in providing Adam with a motivation for his transgression. Not that Haufniensis encourages such speculation, but why the deuce would Adam disobey God? In his journals (e.g., *JP* I 41; *Pap.* X[2] A 22), Kierkegaard notes that what is needed is a middle term that will explain how Adam and the rest of us get from innocence to guilt. The middle term in a syllogism is of course that through which the minor and major premises combine into something new. Anxiety has elements of both innocence and guilt:

But he who becomes guilty through anxiety is indeed innocent, for it was not he himself but anxiety, a foreign power that laid hold of him, a power that he did not love but about which he was anxious. And yet he is guilty for he sank in anxiety, which he nevertheless loved even as he feared it. (*CA* 43)

Repetitiously, Haufniensis reminds us that it is impossible to explain the fact that we are sinners; however, in what amounts to a transcendental argument, Haufniensis explains the possibility of sin. Anxiety makes sin possible. But what, according to Haufniensis, is anxiety?

V. THE CONCEPT OF ANXIETY IN *THE CONCEPT OF ANXIETY*

There are very few straight lines in *The Concept of Anxiety*, but two points are fixed, anxiety is virtually synonymous with possibility, and more specifically with the possibility of freedom. "Anxiety is the possibility of freedom" (*CA* 155). And again, anxiety is "defined as freedom's disclosure to itself in possibility." And yet very early on, Haufniensis offers this aside, "freedom is never possible, as soon as it is, it is actual" (22). And so, while anxiety is freedom's disclosure to itself in possibility, freedom, like God, is never possible – it simply is.

Throughout *The Concept of Anxiety* Haufniensis frequently comments, "every contradiction is a task." Is the task here to resolve the apparent contradiction: anxiety is the possibility of freedom and freedom is never possible but "arises out of nothing"? Although Haufniensis does not have the authority to dictate our reading of his work, I doubt that his "dear reader" would be the one who, after perusing this book, slams it shut and sets to work on solving the above-mentioned philosophical Rubic's Cube. The whirlwind of his own abstractions notwithstanding, there are three objects of inquiry that Haufniensis does not encourage our theorizing about, namely, self-consciousness, freedom, and sin. Obsessing about this kind of academic puzzle is against both the letter and the spirit of *The Concept of Anxiety*. Nevertheless, a few comments do not constitute an obsession.

It could, I think, be argued that although anxiety is the experience of the possibility of freedom, it is the disclosure of freedom actualized in a less than perfect form; that is, as freedom "entangled in itself." Haufniensis declares:

Anxiety is neither a category of necessity nor a category of freedom; it is entangled freedom, where freedom is not free in itself but entangled, not by necessity, but in itself. (CA 49)[12]

In anxiety, we use our freedom to make ourselves feel powerless or unfree. But in order for freedom to become entangled in itself, it must be actual. On the other hand, one could contend that though anxiety is the "possibility of freedom" or "the possibility of the possibility of freedom" (CA 44), it is only with the renunciation of anxiety (faith) that freedom is actualized. Freedom exists only inasmuch as we are freed from the bondage of sin and freed from the anxiety out of which sin leaps forth. Without turning this into a scholastic debate, one could here reply that, according to Haufniensis, we sin out of anxiety. But if freedom is only actualized after we have overcome anxiety, the un-Kierkegaardian conclusion will follow that we do not sin freely, since anxiety will, on this account, be an indication that for the sinner, freedom is not yet actual. And how can someone sin freely, if the freedom that they have or are, is not yet actual?

As Heidegger, Sartre, Tillich, and others have taken careful note,

Haufniensis held that it is in anxiety that we come to understand, feelingly, that we are free. If we abide by the cognition/affect dichotomy, so firmly entrenched in the Western tradition, then we should certainly say that for Haufniensis, anxiety is an affect with cognitive content.

Anticipating the modern psychiatric conception of anxiety, Haufniensis insists that anxiety is almost always about nothing. I say "almost" because in charting the variety of forms that anxiety can take, Haufniensis notes that with anxiety about sin "the object of anxiety is a determinate something and its nothing is an actual something . . . and anxiety therefore loses it dialectical ambiguity" (*CA* 110–11). Just the same, whereas other thinkers such as Kant and Hegel classified anxiety as a kind of fear, Kierkegaard was the first to note that anxiety differs from fear in that the object of anxiety is usually indeterminate.[13]

Gregory Beabout has observed that for Haufniensis,[14] the nothing around which anxiety forms itself is usually the future. Inasmuch as the future is fraught with possibility, our relationship to the future is fraught with anxiety. Very late in the day of his authorship, the individual who gave us the Byzantine *Concept of Anxiety* summarized, "anxiety is about tomorrow" (*CD* 80) and, again, "anxiety is simply impatience (see *JP* I 41; *Pap.* V B 55 p. 10 and X² A 384).

The link between anxiety and the future is underscored by the fact that the experience with which Kierkegaard/Haufniensis most closely connects anxiety is, strangely enough, the experience of presentiment. Some six years before he wrote *The Concept of Anxiety*, Kierkegaard expressed the less than intuitive idea that "A certain presentiment [*anelse*] seems to precede everything that is to happen, but just as it can have a strong deterring effect, it can also tempt a person to think that he is, as it were, predestined" (*JP* I 38; *Pap.* II A 18). Kierkegaard and his pseudonyms refer to the magic pictures that anxiety can conjure up, and especially for someone anxiously thinking about anxiety. Perhaps the notion of presentiments, of having an inkling of what one is to do or of what is to happen, is just one of these magic pictures, these deceptions conjured up by the sophistry of anxiety. Perhaps it was Kierkegaard's way of compromising with the doctrine of predestination, which his father tried to impress upon him and which Haufniensis rejects. While he argues that it is a sin of sorts to pretend that you are on track to sin,

Kierkegaard did believe that we receive signs or cues from God (see *SUD*[h] 114). In fact, he put off the publication of *The Sickness unto Death* for a fortnight while he waited to see whether or not an apparently chance meeting with Regine's father was a message from on High. But once again, anxiety is in part, or seen from one perspective, an inkling that, like so many aspects of the spirit, is dialectical in the sense that it can either move us toward or away from that which we have an inkling about. However, for obvious theological reasons, it is important to remember that under no circumstances can this presentiment, which is anxiety, determine sin.

In the philosophical literature on Kierkegaard, there is a great deal of emphasis legitimately placed on considering anxiety as a structure of the self. To briefly summarize, anxiety is a manifestation of the fact that we are free. Anxiety is a shining forth of our spiritual nature. It reflects our relationship to possibility and the future. Anxiety predisposes us to sin and is the consequence of sin. Although the history of modern philosophy will attest that these are important claims, I would argue, as though it needed to be argued, that Kierkegaard/Haufniensis also has something to contribute to our understanding of anxiety as a feeling, as a psychological phenomenon.[15] In a famous journal entry Kierkegaard scribbles, "all existence makes me nervous" (*JP* V 131; *Pap.* II A 420). In some other well-traveled lines he all but sighs.

Deep within every human being there still lives the anxiety over the possibility of being alone in the world, forgotten by God, overlooked among the millions and millions in this enormous household. (*JP* I 40; *Pap.* VIII[1] A 363)

These passages and others are proof positive that the thinker who cried out for a more human, more realistic psychology would not have been perplexed by our own medico-psychological understanding of anxiety as a rather inexplicable life-constricting force.

Anti-Climacus notes that "there is a certain sophistry in despair" just as there is in sin. By this he at least means that the despairing individual is prone to deceive himself about his despair. Similarly, Haufniensis refers to the "ingenious sophistry of anxiety." Like Freud, but with a very different set of categories up his sleeve, that is, like Freud but with a different account of the origins of repression, Haufniensis recognized that we often respond to anxiety with conscious and unconscious attempts to deflect our anxiety. Deep inside, Everyman is afraid of being alone, unrecognized, invisible. One tries to keep this anxiety "at a distance by looking at the many round who are related to him as kin and friends, but the anxiety is still there, nevertheless, and he hardly dares to think how he would feel if all this were taken away" (*JP* I 40). Haufniensis and a number of other writers who worked at Søren Kierkegaard's desk held that anxiety is often unconscious. Haufniensis recognized that some would read *The Concept of Anxiety*, shake their heads, and wonder who the devil the author was talking about. In a rather violent condemnation repeated throughout the canon, Haufniensis asserts that if anyone is a stranger to anxiety it is only because "he is very spiritless." Having stated this verdict, he proceeds to discuss the anxiety of spiritlessness at chapter length.

Under the chapter title, "The Concept of Anxiety," Haufniensis proclaims that psychologically understood "anxiety is a *sympathetic antipathy* and an *antipathetic sympathy*" (*CA* 42). Anxiety is a paradoxical form of desire, or if you will, a paradoxical form of fear. In his journals, Kierkegaard explains:

Anxiety is a desire for what one fears, a sympathetic antipathy, anxiety is an alien power which grips the individual, and yet one cannot tear himself free from it and does not want to, for one fears, but what he fears he desires. Anxiety makes the individual powerless. (*JP* I 39; *Pap.* III A 233)

At the risk of seeming reductionistic, I suggest that sensuous desire combined with the belief that sensuousness is sinfulness is the Platonic form of anxiety framed as it is here, an approach/avoidance conflict. While I am reluctant to indulge in psychological intellectual history, it would be careless to ignore the fact that Kierkegaard was very familiar with this kind of internal strife.[16] Witness the hundreds of journal entries discussing his love, break, and lifelong devotion to Regine. Kierkegaard's personal life aside, Haufniensis, no less than his twentieth-century colleagues draws the connection between anxiety and sensuousness. In a musical, almost fugue-like style, Haufniensis repeatedly reminds us, "By sin, sensuousness became sinfulness." He elaborates, "After Christianity had come into the world and redemption was posited, sensuousness was placed in a light of opposition such as was not found in paganism" (*CA* 74). In a phrase that will reverberate through the final stages of Kierkegaard's life and works, Haufniensis announces, "In Christianity, the religious has suspended the erotic" (70). For those who have not tried to close themselves off from the good, which is to say, for those who have not taken what Haufniensis considers the well-t odden path of the demonic, the consequence of sin is, among other things, anxiety about sin. Understandably, the psychic tug of war between sensuousness and the fear of sensuousness as sinfulness culminates in a feeling of powerlessness.[17]

Kierkegaard and Haufniensis agree that the first sin for every individual – whatever that might mean – is a product of weakness, as opposed to defiance. It could not be defiance for it is only with the first sin that the categories of good and evil are posited. This, however, is not to say that we are not responsible for the weakness. The feeling of being unable to rise above our desires is a trap door conjured up by the cunning of desire to give us leave to do what we desire. To put it in terms of *The Sickness unto Death*, the powerlessness that leads to sin is self-intensified weakness. Part of Kierkegaard's psychological genius and a blindspot for Freud and his followers, conscious and otherwise, is Kierkegaard's recognition that many of the states that we feel we are suffering from are in fact states that we have either conjured up or amplified.[18] Following an inordinately crabbed line of thought, Haufniensis concludes that every generation is more sensuous than the one before. And yet in a voice that will find an echo in many of Kierkegaard's later works, Haufniensis the psychologist declaims that Christianity teaches the individual "to lift himself above this 'more,' and it judges him who does not do so as being unwilling," not unable (CA 73).

Long before Freud, Kierkegaard discovered the pit of desire in the fruit of anxiety. Haufniensis tells us that there are two kinds of sinners: those who are anxious about the good and those who are anxious about sin. Hidden in the anxiety over sin, which, Kierkegaard insists, often leads to sin, is the desire to sin. Likewise, inherent in the demonic's anxiety about the good is a desire for the good.

Continuing with the theme of the paradoxical nature of anxiety, Haufniensis oddly, if not perversely, insists that anxiety is something that we want to flee from and yet love, "really love." For anyone who has suffered from anxiety, the suggestion that he or she loves their anxiety will seem callous. After all, anxiety in all its variegated forms is today listed as a "mental disorder" and no one loves having a mental disorder. One could, I suppose, defend Haufniensis by claiming that inasmuch as anxiety contains an element of desire, albeit for something we fear, it is still about something we desire; hence, we must desire our anxiety. But while anxiety itself may have an element of desire, it does not follow that we must therefore desire, much less love, our anxiety.

In one of his most compelling images, an image reworked many times over by Sartre,[19] Haufniensis writes:

Anxiety may be compared with dizziness. He whose eye happens to look down into the yawning abyss becomes dizzy. But what is the reason for this? It is just as much in his own eye as in the abyss, for suppose he had not looked down. Hence anxiety is the dizziness of freedom, which emerges when the spirit wants to posit the synthesis and freedom looks down into its own possibility, laying hold of finiteness to support itself. (*CA* 61)

The dizziness, elsewhere represented as a feeling of powerlessness, is something that we bring upon ourselves. Interestingly enough, we lay hold of the finite to steady ourselves, and this laying hold of the finite is sin for "Freedom succumbs in this dizziness . . . freedom, when it again rises, sees that it is guilty" (*CA* 61). In depth psychological terms, we have the reasonable conclusion that anxiety is the last stop before transgression. But again, where is the love of anxiety that Haufniensis insists upon? Perhaps it inheres in the simple fact that we love our freedom, just as we fear it, and loving it we can scarcely take our mind's eye off it.

There is, however, another suggestion. Here and there throughout this text and *The Sickness unto Death*, Kierkegaard insists that people cleave to their anxieties and other internal wounds. After all, while we may experience anxiety as a foreign power, it emanates from us. We produce it and, with God's help, we can renounce it. In a footnote, Haufniensis makes the astute observation that melancholy or depression develops out of the culture of anxiety. By his own diagnosis, Kierkegaard and his whole family suffered melancholy, and yet Kierkegaard confessed that he loved his melancholy, truly loved it. Religiously speaking, he took this love to be a near fatal flaw. While the cure for his melancholy was there, Kierkegaard would not let himself be cured of it, so identified was he with his sorrow that he could not imagine himself without it. Or again, so invested was he in the poetry of his sorrow that he would not give it up. But to return to more normal and mortal creatures, we may be said to love our anxiety in the sense that, *pace* Haufniensis, we could renounce our anxiety and yet we refuse to. Judging from the coda to *The Concept of Anxiety* ("Anxiety as Saving Through Faith"), Haufniensis believes that the seas of our lives can be calmed.

VI. BEING EDUCATED BY ANXIETY AND POSSIBILITY

In *The Sickness unto Death* Anti-Climacus offers a series of pictures of the different forms of despair, or when viewed under another set of assumptions, of the different forms of sin.[20] These spiritual daguerreotypes are strung on a continuum from the more passive to the more active or defiant forms of despair/sin. Having insisted that anxiety is both the predisposition to sin and the consequence of sin – to say nothing of a mark of man's perfection – Haufniensis provides a psychological showcase of the different shapes that anxiety can take when considered as a consequence of sin. Once again, presaging the weakness/defiance continuum of *The Sickness unto Death*, Haufniensis proclaims that post-Fall anxiety is of two basic kinds – anxiety about sin and anxiety about the good (*CA* 61). After walking us through a veritable hothouse of specimens of anxiety, Haufniensis argues that there is a way of relating to anxiety that can either prompt our self-destruction or enable us to "overcome anxiety" to "renounce anxiety without anxiety."

Like one of the Stoics, Haufniensis instructs us that we must learn to be anxious in the proper way, lest "we perish by never having been in anxiety or by succumbing to anxiety" (*CA* 155). The first death refers to the spiritless denial of the tasks of the spirit and the latter to more active forms of sinfulness. Against the wisdom of our own brave new world, Haufniensis promises that "whoever has learned to be anxious in the right way has learned the ultimate" (155).

But what is the right way to be anxious? Or, again, what is the proper object of our anxiety? Haufniensis makes it plain that the individual who is anxious over externals is in the wrong school. Similarly, he contrasts the kind of anxiety that he is bidding us to study with, with anxiety about "finiteness and finite relations." The individual who has mettle enough to ride through life with his eyes open will soon come to understand that "he can demand absolutely nothing of life and that the terrible, perdition, and annihilation live next door to everyman" (*CA* 156). But the person who refuses to be examined by possibility, who frets over finiteness and finite relations will graduate with a degree in finite wisdom:

... finiteness and the finite relations in which every individual is assigned a place, whether they be small, or everyday, or world historical, educate only finitely, and a person can always persuade them, always coax something else out of them, always bargain, always escape from them tolerably well, always keep himself a little on the outside, always prevent himself from learning absolutely something from them. (*CA* 157)

A page later, Haufniensis explains that with actuality, things never get so bad that we can't find some hope, some breath of possibility. Let the roof cave in and still "common sense says quite correctly that if one is cunning, one knows how to make the best of things" (*CA* 158).

The anxiety that prepares us to renounce anxiety is anxiety about "freedom's possibility." Haufniensis announces that the more profoundly one is in anxiety, the greater the individual one is. He then explains that the individual whose greatness glows in his anxiety is anxious "in the sense that he himself produces the anxiety" (*CA* 155). In other words, the anxiety that will lead us where we do and yet do not want to go is anxiety about oneself.

Four years after the publication of *The Concept of Anxiety*, Anti-Climacus remarks that while the Christian knows that earthly life is rich in horrors, he has the courage to keep finite things in their proper perspective:

As a Christian he has acquired a courage unknown to the natural man, a courage he acquired by learning to fear something even more horrifying. That is always how a person acquires courage: when he fears a greater danger he always has the courage to face a lesser. When one fears a danger infinitely, it is as if the others weren't there at all. (*SUD*[h] 39)

Once again, to be anxious about freedom's possibility is to be anxious about what one will do with one's freedom: it is to be anxious about being in sin. In *The Sickness unto Death*, Anti-Climacus presses the cruel thought, What is a person to do when his worst nightmare has come true? Haufniensis replies that inasmuch as our worst nightmare refers to something external, something that does not come from us, the actualization of our personal apocalypse should not be nearly as anxiety provoking as the anxiety about being in sin.

For once, Haufniensis is straightforward enough, "in order that an individual may thus be educated absolutely and infinitely by the possibility, he must be honest toward possibility and have faith" (*CA* 157). Oddly enough, Haufniensis goes on to use Hegel to qualify his understanding of faith, so that faith is cast as "the inner certainty that anticipates infinity" (157). Haufniensis continues, "When the discoveries of possibility are honestly administered, possibility will discover all the finitudes, but will idealize them in the form of infinity and in anxiety overwhelm the individual until he again overcomes them in the anticipation of faith" (157).

The doctor of anxiety is honest both with himself and possibility. Haufniensis recounts the story of an Indian ascetic "who for two years lived on dew that he once came to the city, tasted wine, and became addicted to drink" (*CA* 158). Some will find this vignette comic, others tragic; but the true student of possibility will immediately see himself in the story, for he, better than anyone, understands that under the right conditions he is capable of anything.

Haufniensis warns us about what Kierkegaard apparently learned from experience, namely, that just as the fear of illness can produce illness, so can anxiety about sin lead to sin. And one of the sins that anxiety about sin can lead to is the sin of being dishonest with ourselves about our sinfulness. But the individual who has been educated by anxiety "does not permit himself to be deceived by its countless falsifications." He, quite simply, "accurately remembers the past" (*CA* 159). Being honest about his past, he knows that he is guilty. But note well: "Whoever learns to know his guilt only by analogy to judgments of the police court and the supreme court never really understands that he is guilty, for if a man is guilty, he is infinitely guilty" (161). As Anti-Climacus describes it, our sins of action are but the puffs of smoke whereas the engine of sin is the will. The person who has learned to be anxious in the right way looks at his finite sins and grasps that he is infinitely guilty.

In the denouement of *The Concept of Anxiety*, Haufniensis preaches that one does not need to go to Paris or London to become a "pupil of possibility." One need only to place the aspirant "in the middle of the Jutland heath, where no event takes place" (159) and where Kierkegaard's father as a boy once cursed God. In an addendum to *Either/Or*, Judge William shares a sermon with his anxiety-ridden friend. The sermon, written by a pastor "stuck out in a little parish on the heath in Jutland" (*EO* II 337), is entitled "The Upbuilding That Lies in the Thought that We are Always in the Wrong" (always in the wrong before God).

Kierkegaard seems to work with an algorithm of the spirit. The more profound the individual, the stronger the spirit, the graver the danger is of a fall. Haufniensis notes that the individual who lets himself be searched out by anxiety, who understands that he can demand nothing of the world, and who, as a sinner, has no grounds at all for demanding anything of God is "in danger of a fall, namely, suicide" (*CA* 159). That is why education by anxiety and possibility requires that the student not only be honest with himself but that he also have faith. And yet it is only the person who knows that he is infinitely guilty who will look in the right direction for rest. In the penultimate sentence of *The Concept of Anxiety*, Haufniensis comes full circle from the Fall, writing "he who in relation to guilt is educated by anxiety will rest only in the Atonement" (162). And when, after having been searched out by anxiety, we rest in the atonement, anxiety can be said "to eradicate precisely what it brings forth itself" (159), namely, anxiety, which is the predisposition to sin: to reject the promise of the atonement.

NOTES

I would like to extend my profound thanks to Alastair Hannay and Begonya Saez Tajafuerce for their helpful comments on this essay.

1 See Arne's Grøn, *Begrebet angst hos Søren Kierkegaard* (Copenhagen: Gyldendal, 1993), pp. 10f.

2 See Roger Poole, *Kierkegaard: The Indirect Communication* (Charlottesville: University of Virginia Press, 1993), pp. 107ff.

3 The protagonist of David Lodge's *Therapy* (London: Penquin, 1996) expresses a similar view. See pp. 64–5.

4 *SUD*ʰ 127–8; see also David Gouwens' superb *Kierkegaard as a Religious Thinker* (Cambridge University Press, 1996), pp. 124–8.

5 See my "Making Faith Possible," *The Atlantic Monthly*, July 1993, pp. 109–13.

6 Hegel, G. W. F, *Lectures on the Philosophy of Religion*, trans. R. F. Brown, P. C. Hodgson, and J. M. Stewart (Berkeley and Los Angeles: University of California Press, 1988), p. 215.

7 See Niels Thulstrup's *Kierkegaard's Relation to Hegel*, trans. George Stengren (Princeton: Princeton University Press, 1980), pp. 356–65.

8 For an exquisite comparison of Milton and Kierkegaard on the Fall, see John S. Tanner, *Anxiety in Eden: A Kierkegaardian Reading of Paradise Lost* (New York and Oxford: Oxford University Press, 1992).

9 See, *CA* 56–60. Also for an informative discussion of Haufniensis's rather peculiar theory of objective anxiety, see Gregory Beabout's *Freedom and Its Misuses* (Milwaukee: Marquette University Press, 1996), pp. 52–5.

10 Haufniensis develops the idea of spirit experienced as other into a very interesting interpretation of the notion of fate. See, e.g., *CA* 96–108.

11 Philip Quinn, "Does Anxiety Explain Original Sin?" *Nous* 24 (1990): 227–44.

12 Also see Arnold Come, *Trendelenburg's Influence on Kierkegaard's Modal Categories* (Montreal: Inter Editions, 1991).

13 See John M. Hoberman's "Kierkegaard on Vertigo," in *International Kierkegaard Commentary:* The Sickness unto Death, ed. Robert L. Perkins (Macon, Ga: Mercer University Press, 1987), pp. 185–208.

14 Beabout, *Freedom and Its Misuses*, pp. 63ff.

15 For two very important studies of Kierkegaard's Psychology, see Vincent McCarthy, *The Phenomenology of Moods in Kierkegaard* (The Hague: Martinus Nijhoff, 1978) and Kresten Nordentoft's *Kierkegaard's Psychology*, trans. Bruce Kirmmse (Pittsburgh: Duquesne University Press, 1972).

16 For a very useful commentary on Kierkegaard's personal life, see Bruce Kirmmse's *Kierkegaard in Golden Age Denmark* (Bloomington and Indianapolis: Indiana University Press, 1990), *Encounters with Kierkegaard* (Princeton: Princeton University Press, 1996), and his contribution to this volume, "Out with It!: The Modern Breakthrough, Kierkegaard and Denmark." Roger Poole, *Kierkegaard: The Indirect Communication*, also offers a valuable perspective on Kierkegaard.

17 Hoberman, "Kierkegaard on Vertigo," pp. 190–200.

18 Robert C. Roberts speaks to a similar point. See his "Existence, Emotion, and Virtue: Classical Themes in Kierkegaard," in this volume.

19 For an evaluation of Sartre's debt to Kierkegaard, see William McBride's "Sartre's Debts to Kierkegaard: A Partial Reckoning," in *Kierkegaard in Post/Modernity*, ed. Martin Matuštík and Merold Westphal (Bloomington and Indianapolis: Indiana University Press 1995), pp. 18–42.

20 See Alastair Hannay's contribution to the present volume, "Kierkegaard and the Variety of Despair."

13 Kierkegaard and the variety of despair

You are always hovering above yourself, but the higher ether, the more refined sublimate into which you are vaporized, is the nothing of despair, and you see below you a multitude of areas of learning, insight, study, observation which for you, though, have no reality but which you quite randomly exploit and combine so as to adorn as tastefully as possible the palace of mental profusion in which you occasionally reside.

– Either/Or

When are we in despair? Is it when we find ourselves powerless to grasp or retain some salient good? Or when it seems nothing can be done to prevent our world collapsing? Or when the running out of possibilities has left us now paralyzed? What exactly *is* despair? Is it the experience itself, the sheer sense of hopelessness? Or is despair what our lives are thenceforth "in" once what we so "desperately" want proves beyond reach? Habits or rules of language give us no clear answers here, but psychology may help. It seems clear that any lingering sense of frustration and hopelessness assumes some continued but problematic interest in the salient good once hoped for, or now lost.

Despair is a central concept in several of Kierkegaard's works and there are many passing references to it. The Danish *Fortvivlelse*, like the German *Verzweiflung*, bears "two" (*tvi*) on its face, so the suggestion of complexity is conveyed here even more directly than in the case of "despair" and its cognates. In *Purity of Heart*, a signed work, Kierkegaard asks whether despair isn't "simply double-mindedness."[1] While in some works the notion occurs only *en passant*, as, for example, in *Concluding Unscientific Postscript*, in others, such as *Works of Love*,[2] it enters integrally into the discourse. But the most comprehensive treatments appear in two works that virtually span the authorship, *Either/Or* and *The Sickness unto Death*. It is to these two works that we turn in an attempt to make clear how, and with what consistency, Kierkegaard uses the term "despair."

The texts do not yield their concept, or concepts, easily. So little so that there is significant disagreement, perhaps even confusion, on how to read them. Some have gone so far as to dismiss *The Sickness unto Death* as a joke at the expense of Hegelians. And many of those who take it seriously are nevertheless inclined to blame the author rather than themselves for any unclarity about "despair." Still others may chide readers for their search for clarity, seeing this as merely an obstruction to the creative powers of a reader's subjective fantasy. Each of these responses offers, however, an excellent illustration of just that complexity already hinted at and about which, in referring to "the cunning and sophistry present in all despair" (*SUD*[h] 143–4), the author of *The Sickness unto Death* shows himself to be very clear indeed. The presumptions that there is no sense to look for, that an author must be to blame for what a reader finds obscure, or that obscurity may be a virtue can all express that premature hopelessness one finds in people whose real hope is that there is nothing of the kind in question to hope for. This idea, it will be argued, is the core of Kierkegaard's concept of despair, not just in *The Sickness unto Death* but in the other texts mentioned too.

Anti-Climacus, its pseudonymous author, says at one point in *The Sickness unto Death* that every human being is "primitively organized as a self." Everyone is "characteristically determined to become himself" (*SUD*[h] 63). This sounds like an anthropological claim, to be tested by examining the structure of human being. It suggests that it would be useless to try to prevent oneself becoming a self, whatever "self" turns out to mean in this claim. One might suppose from this that the general notion of despair that Kierkegaard appeals to is one that implies the "vanity" of trying to do something. He would then be claiming that despair is trying to prevent something, namely, being or becoming oneself, when either "deep down" or quite consciously we know that this is impossible.

Anti-Climacus also makes a theological claim. From his Christian point of view he asserts that the self is established by "something

else," a "power" (SUD^h 43, 44), and that "ultimately no one can resist that power . . . [d]espite all . . . despairing efforts, that power is
the stronger." This is not the same claim but it is not immediately
clear how or whether it is related to the former. In terms of what
"despair" means, however, the point would be the same. Selfhood,
we seem to have to understand, is some salient good toward which,
if only the difficulties involved in appropriating it were less, everyone would be on course. If a person, due to the difficulties, does not
want to be this self, the power nevertheless "compels him to be the
self he does not want to be" (50).

But there are footholds for other notions of despair in Anti-
Climacus's claims. Let us therefore look first at some alternatives.
In one sense, despair, or doing something despairingly, is knowing
or suspecting that one is powerless to achieve some cherished goal
but continuing, against the odds or all reason, to attempt to achieve
it. The drowning swimmer clutches "despairingly" at the rope because she knows it is too short, or that even if she could grasp it she
lacks the strength to hang on. The distinctions here are not necessarily altogether sharp, but one could say that this contrasted in one
direction with saying that she clutched at the rope "desperately,"
where to say this implies she might still succeed. The former notion
engages, one might say, the idea that all (relevant) possibilities have
on the contrary run out, but instead of the paralysis referred to in
our opening paragraph we have "despairing" activity. To say that it
is despairing is partly to point out that it is inappropriate to the
facts.

In quite another and opposite direction, to "despair" is precisely
to act in accordance with the facts, to give up the attempt *because*
the goal is impossible. Despairing of something in this sense is
abandoning the project of achieving the salient good because one
finds oneself powerless to achieve it. One could put this by saying
that, unlike the previous example, the activity here, or rather ces-
sation of activity, was appropriate to the facts. But we must be careful. We might be failing to take proper account of the "cunning and
sophistry" that lurk behind our beliefs. Might it not be the case, for
example, that one's "finding" oneself powerless was the outcome of
a strategy that conveniently absolves one from responsibility for
having to make further efforts?

This idea of strategy, which is central to much of the account in

The Sickness unto Death, will be pursued later. First we must be clear what Anti-Climacus means by despair. At the very outset he makes a threefold distinction between an inauthentic or nongenuine form of despair and two genuine forms. They are:

[B]eing unconscious in despair of having a self (inauthentic despair), not wanting in despair to be oneself, and wanting in despair to be oneself. (*SUD*[h] 51)

Neither of the expressions "despairingly" or "desperately" seems to fit comfortably here. How could one be *un*conscious in a despairing or desperate way of having something? One might, as indicated above, talk of despairingly not wanting to be oneself in this sense, that is, because one knows it is not possible to be rid of oneself. The same might be said for the third form, since being oneself might be something one cannot do either if, as indeed the text says, the "oneself" in this kind of case is something other than the self one ineluctably is but wants to be rid of, is indeed a self one tries to interpose in the vain attempt to avoid being oneself. If we read Anti-Climacus carefully, however, it becomes obvious that the idea of futility is no part of his concept of despair. The formula for all despair, says Anti-Climacus is "to want to be rid of oneself" (*SUD*[h] 50), it is a response to whatever it is about one's "self" that makes one unhappy being it, its particular defects, its contingent historical situation, the human condition as such, or certain demands implicit in the notion of selfhood.[3] Despair, for Anti-Climacus, just *is* wanting rid of the self. Consequently, "despair"-expressions do not qualify this project but simply refer to it. In the passage just quoted, "in despair" should be read appositively, as saying that what all three descriptions describe are despair, because they are all ways of, in some sense or other, trying (though in vain) to be rid of oneself.

There is something distinctive about this notion of despair that does not appear in other texts. In *Postscript,* for example, "despair" comes close to the idea of paralysis due to loss of possibility mentioned earlier. Johannes Climacus says "despair is despair because it does not know the way out" (*CUP* 520). What is especially interesting is that this is also Hegel's concept. Since what is claimed here is that, at least in *The Sickness unto Death,* this is not Kierkegaard's concept, it will be useful to have Hegel's concept in mind. In outline Hegel's idea is this: Consciousness is on course for knowledge of the truth about itself, roughly speaking, the truth that it itself *is* knowledge. On the way to that destination, however, it (that is to say consciousness, for we are talking here in the typical Hegelian vein) makes a succession of progressively better stabs at what real knowledge is, and therefore, because of the assumed identification, at what it itself is. For instance, it identifies itself with "phenomenal knowledge," knowledge of the world as it appears. But this identification proves inadequate, and the recognition that it is so is experienced as "loss of its own self." Hegel actually says that the road can therefore be regarded as the pathway of doubt (*Zweifel*), or more precisely as the way of despair (*Verzweiflung*). "Despair" is here distinguished from doubt – "shilly-shallying about this or that presumed truth, followed by a return to that truth again, after the doubt has been appropriately dispelled" – as "the conscious insight into the untruth of phenomenal knowledge."[4] Despair, in other words, is the realization that one is not the self one assumed. But since no alternative has yet been envisaged, the despair, one might say, is total, the running out of all possibility leaves one paralyzed. But because despair resolves into a healthy skepticism about "all the so-called natural ideas, thoughts, and opinions" that have "hampered" progress so far, it leaves the way open to examine further "what truth is."[5]

It isn't hard to transfer this idea to Kierkegaard,[6] particularly since the "stages" offer a plausible parallel both to the "road" along which Hegel has consciousness travel and to the "series of configurations" which he has it go through in its "education . . . to the standpoint of Science."[7] Take the notion of "the nothing of despair" in our epigraph above. The passage is from Part II of *Either/Or*, where Judge William, defending the ethical life-view he personifies, tries to persuade his young friend the aesthete, author of the papers comprising Part I, that any aesthetic life-view "is despair" (*EO*[h] 502). Of his friend's mature aesthetic life-view, William remarks that "it has to an extent admitted to itself a consciousness of the nothingness of such a life-view" (502). One might take the nothingness here to mean the futility of the aesthetic life-view on its own terms, its failure, say, through some internal inconsistency to apply in practice. Recognition of this nothingness would be a case of "loss of self" because it involves the realization that what was entered upon as *the* way to become, or be, oneself proves to be "untruth." But then, and to exploit further the parallel with Hegel, the recognition gives way to an initially disconcerting but in principle healthy skepticism about this way of conceiving life, which then allows room for a competency to seek further. As confirmation, one can see a parallel between Hegel's explicitly calling this skepticism a "state of despair"[8] and Judge William's otherwise rather enigmatic injunction to his friend to *choose* "despair" as the way to choose himself (*EO*[h] 511) – though the parallel limps a little at the idea of the choice of a state of mind. Apart from that, however, despair opens the way to truth by ridding one's self-conception of what was no doubt a necessary station "on" the way but is now clearly "in" the way. To despair is to negate, or "lose," the self that saw itself wrongly in this way. It is a kind of solvent-cum-propellent necessary for keeping the journey going.

The notion of despair as a solvent is certainly present in Kierkegaard. In *Postscript* there is a reference to despair as the response to misfortune that brings one out of immediacy, so that "the transition to another understanding of misfortune is made possible" (*CUP* 434). What could sound more Hegelian? And yet there is a crucial difference in the "journeys" Hegel and Climacus describe. In Hegel despair is the necessary preliminary to a better standpoint for grasping one's oneness with the world. The sense of hopelessness here is really just a sign that one has reached a point where the goal of oneness must, but also can, be reconceived in a way that offers new hope of grasping it. In Kierkegaard, however, in the case of the person who despairs due to misfortune, the new standpoint is one that enables him to "comprehend suffering" (434), in the sense of accepting it as an essential part of life rather than as an in-principle avoidable intrusion. On Kierkegaard's journey selfhood becomes increasingly strenuous as the gap between life as it is given "immediately" and what fulfillment requires widens. Despair, because it knows no way out, Climacus also says, "wants to withdraw" from the "pain," and a little later he describes it as "a kind of irascibility" (*en Art Arrigskab*).[9] In this respect despair contrasts with humor (which together with irony one may think of as functional equivalents of Hegel's skepticism) as having its apprehension of "the infinite, the eternal, the totality in the moment of impatience" (544; translation amended).

Impatience with the eternal is the link we need to Anti-Climacus's "despair." What prompts despair, in *The Sickness unto Death*, is the (at first only dawning) realization that there is "something eternal" in the self (see, e.g., *SUD*[h] 77). One may think therefore of Anti-Climacus's despair as impatience with the self, with oneself, with the demands selfhood imposes. Put succinctly, Anti-Climacus's despair is not the idea of a propellent but of a retardant. It is not the loss of one "self" inadequately conceived, the losing of which then makes room constructively for another and more adequately conceived "self." It is, on the contrary, *not* wanting to be a self otherwise conceived than the self one finds it more congenial to be. Or, recalling once more the sophistry and cunning of despair, it is not wanting there to *be* any more adequate conception, even refusing to entertain the very notion of such a conception. If we were to apply *The Sickness unto Death*'s account of despair, as not wanting to be oneself, to the stages – a very risky thing to do, and which has no basis in the texts – each of the successive stages would be in itself a case of despair, whether or not its project proved to be futile. The stages prior to Religiousness B would be classified in *The Sickness unto Death's* terms as ways of avoiding the path to truth, not ways of improving one's awareness of what truth is. Certainly, and this is where the Hegelian model might also be applied to *The Sickness unto Death*, there is a "negative" development of the kind in which the nature of what one is aiming at becomes ever clearer, but the crucial difference is that in Kierkegaard what becomes clearer is not that we *are* the truth but how much more is needed if we are to *be* it – to be the selves we are.

Either/Or and *The Sickness unto Death* use almost identical terms in defining "self." And yet a crucial distinction is made in the latter that is not made, at least so explicitly, in the former. In *Either/Or* it sounds at first as if our selves were merely the selves we commonsensically take ourselves to be, the identities we inherit, adopt, or accept. The self is a "diversely determined concretion" (*EO*[h] 543). One who "chooses oneself" (543) "concretely" is "aware of this self as this definite individual, with these aptitudes, these tendencies, these instincts, these passions, influenced by these definite surroundings, as this definite product of a definite outside world" (542). Leaving aside here what "choice" of self amounts to, we can note that *The Sickness unto Death* repeats this definition of the self in terms of "this quite definite thing [*dette ganske Bestemte*], with these aptitudes, predispositions, etc." and "aptitudes and talent" (*SUD*[h] 99, 86;

*SV*³ XV 122, 112). But the quotation here is from a passage in which a clear distinction is made between the self that a person "takes possession" of in a merely "outward direction" ("what he calls his self") and the self in a "deeper sense" that one can possess only by taking an "inward direction." This indicates that the "self," at least in Anti-Climacus's formula, is not the commonsensically grasped self. How far the notions of self differ in the two works is a topic for some other study, but one important difference between the works is that while selfhood in *Either/Or* is that of an ethically disclosed self, a self visible in its deliberately adopted social roles, *The Sickness unto Death* draws attention to a vast range of undeliberately adopted facade-"selves," selves of a kind the aesthete would never aspire to because he would see through them so quickly (but among which he might also with some justification claim to locate something very like the self that Judge William urges him to choose).

This need not imply, however, that the two works employ distinct concepts of despair. To examine this question let us ask what William means when he says to the aesthete, "Take note, then, my young friend, this life is despair" (*EO*ʰ 509). The last of the aesthetic life-views outlined by Judge William in the second of the three letters forming Part II of *Either/Or* is that of a reflected and highly organized person. But in some important sense the aesthete has not "chosen himself," so his organization is not a *self*-organization. The control this aesthete aims to preserve is only so much as to preserve an interplay between the world and human nature that maximizes enjoyment and the avoidance of pain. William says that "every aesthetic life-view is despair" (502; cf. 521–2). He might mean by this that the aesthetic life is by its very dependence on contingencies of nature prone to feelings of what the aesthete will himself call "despair," frustrations of all kinds and feelings of hopelessness, what one might call "everyday" despair. But despair of this piecemeal and random kind is "finite" and partial, while what William seems to mean by the term is something that pervades a whole life. Certainly, to suffer a serious setback can make one despair over "oneself" in what seems an all-encompassing way. But, it does so only in the sense that the self in this respect is conceived as "a finitude as every other finite thing" (520). One simply wishes one were better able to live according to the principle upon which one currently bases one's life. This is not the despair William refers to.

Alternatively, William might mean that insofar as setbacks become more frequent, and it becomes increasingly evident that the aesthetic project is nonsustainable, the aesthete will despair in the Hegelian sense of finding himself at a dead end. There is also perhaps some foothold here for the notion of desperation: as one becomes more anxious about failure, one also becomes increasingly "desperate" for success. It is clear, however, that a "last-ditch" concern for success of this kind, typical of the life-view William attributes to *Either/Or*'s mature aesthete, cannot be what he means when he says that *all* aesthetic life-views are despair. For some aesthetic life-views this ditch is still out of sight. Nor, by the same token, can the despair ascribed to "every" aesthetic life-view be the sense of not knowing where to go. Not having come to the point of having to defend their life-views to destruction, "early" aesthetes may still be happy with their aesthetic lives and may not even have come to the point of thinking that an aesthetic life-view is what they are enacting.

Yet, basing one's life explicitly on an ideal or principle, a principle that one may of course enact without as yet having made it explicit, is to suppose that doing so successfully is to bring out the inherent value of that life. But if basing one's life on an aesthetic principle proves to be no more than the attempt to make finite goals "eternally" satisfying when reflection shows that they can have no bearing on the eternal question of the value-in-itself of one's life as a whole, clarity about this shortcoming should prompt the admission that the aesthetic life is in a crucial sense an empty one. Further, in respect of the project of bringing out the inherent value of one's life, persistent dedication to an aesthetic principle should be recognizable for what it is – a failure to face the challenge of realizing the inherent value of one's life.

Significantly, *Either/Or*'s aesthete has suffered no setbacks that would cause him to despair in an everyday sense. As a "complete" aesthete, with "all the requirements of an aesthetic life-view" (*EO*[h] 502; cf. 511), he has managed to keep misfortune at bay. But for that very reason everyday, piecemeal despair does not hamper his grasp of the real thing. He is not able, as most people are, to confuse what Anti-Climacus in *The Sickness unto Death* calls "despair over the earthly or over something earthly" (*SUD*[h] 80) with "despair of the eternal or over oneself" (91). He is closer to the ironical vantage point (corresponding to the solvent of skepticism in Hegel's account) that makes that grasp possible but is by the same token more openly defensive about his current life-view and is on, if not actually over, the threshold from which he can admit that his life is despair. He refuses to "admit despair" (EO^h 501), but that is just what makes his despair a defense.

Addressing the aesthete directly, Judge William says, "[E]veryone who lives aesthetically is in despair whether he knows it or not. But if one does know it, and you indeed do, then a higher form of existence is an inescapable requirement" (EO^h 501). This suggests that the "despair" that the aesthetic life-view itself *is* is a reluctance to meet the demands of a higher standard of selfhood. Despair, on this reading, is relational. The despair proper to one life-view is due to its being a failure to measure up to the standards of another, higher view. If so, then *Either/Or*'s conception of despair conforms with Anti-Climacus's formula: "to want to be rid of oneself." Although this may look unpromising for the less reflected forms of the aesthetic life-view, at least we can see how exponents of what William calls the "last" aesthetic life-view can want *not* to be some higher self than the one they currently conceive themselves as being.

If the parallel is vindicated, then we can say quite generally that despair in Kierkegaard's pseudonyms is unwillingness to live up to an expectation of selfhood. In *The Sickness unto Death* this notion is put forward quite explicitly. In the opening pages of Part II we read: "Everything is qualitatively what it is measured by" and, applied to the self, its "standard . . . is always that directly in the face of which it is a self" (SUD^h 111). The child, who first has its parents' standard, "becomes a self through acquiring, as an adult, the State as its standard," but then an "infinite accent is laid upon the self when it acquires God as its standard" (111). This tells us also that the notion of self in Kierkegaard is linked with that of a goal or telos that is the "measure" of what it means to become a self. There is this sense then, again made more explicitly in this later work, that selfhood is a project: "[t]he self is the conscious synthesis of infinitude and finitude, which relates to itself, whose task is to become itself, which can only be done in the relationship to God" (87). Judge William saw the task rather differently but that is because quite soon afterwards in the authorship the standard of selfhood had been raised. For William one becomes oneself by a choice but in *The Sickness unto Death* "oneself" is no longer something one can simply *choose* to be. A metaphorically abbreviated reason is given in the half-humorous rehearsal of the pseudonymous series to date in *Postscript*. There Johannes Climacus says that immediately subsequent to *Either/Or* (the first in the series) exception was already taken in the pseudonymous writings to Judge William's too complacent assumption that one can "win oneself" by choosing despair (*SV*³ IX 213; cf. *CUP* 258). Climacus puts the objection by saying that once having used your *self* to despair you have no self left to come back with and therefore need divine help. "Coming back," for William, means "repenting [one]self back into [one]self, back into [one's] family, back into the race, until [one] finds [one]self in God" (*EO*ʰ 518). For Anti-Climacus, being "before God" is not an outcome of the return but its precondition.

The crucial difference between the despairs of *Either/Or* and *The Sickness unto Death* is therefore that where the former work's account culminates in the advanced aesthetic life-view as exemplifying the "nothing of despair," the latter offers a typology intended to identify whole ranges of life-*styles* (rather than life-views) and attitudes – indeed, practically any way of life recognizable to us at all – as doing exactly the same but in a wide variety of ways. As we saw at the beginning, despair is divided into three categories: one in which the relevant notion of selfhood is not yet in place and the other two in which it is but is either resisted ("not wanting in despair to be oneself") or shelved in favor of an alternative version adopted deliberately as *not* resting in the "power" that "established it." The latter categories are called respectively "weakness" and "defiance."

The crux in the analysis in *The Sickness unto Death* is the idea of a weakness that one might describe as addiction to the world. The analysis involves the strategies with which despair with "cunning and sophistry" deals with the dawning consciousness of this weakness and of the fact that it is indeed a weakness to be addicted to the world. It is a premise of the analysis that human beings are peculiar among other beings by not being exhaustively identified by finite properties. There is an irreducible particularity, an "I," for which each "definite" collection of properties is its own collection. At the level of singularity we have to be our own selves. This does not mean that what we really are is no more than this unspecified singularity. To suppose that we were merely bare particulars would be to ignore personality, something quite concrete and essential to selfhood. Personality, or concrete selfhood, is the specific, discernible way our collection of dispositions and abilities functions or works in society. According to Judge William the aesthete can only become himself, a self at all, by "repenting," looking back at the collection's past from a vantage point in the present occupied by what one is willing to accept is the *same* self, a self for which one is responsible for having become. Accepting this personal identity must be part of what it means to "choose" to be the definite thing one is. Choosing oneself is therefore, for William, in part the choice of this vantage point, with the self that ocupies it and the pain and grief it has experienced and caused. But there is also a forward-looking dimension, having a future that is also determined by this vantage point, the possibilities of this self circumscribed by what it is able to do and able to envisage for itself.

The analysis in *The Sickness unto Death*, in brief outline, goes as follows. Despair as "weakness" is anything that counts as failure to adopt the position of one's singularity. This might be because it has not yet occurred to one that one is singular in this way, but the analysis focuses on the thought that much of human behavior is an attempt to escape this position or obscure the thought that it is there to be claimed. At the level of experience, this despair is experienced as loss of earthly things or of the earthly as such. What underlies this response, however, on Anti-Climacus's account, is the opposite: an attempt to "lose" the "eternal," which amounts on this account to wanting to be rid of oneself, the "formula for all despair" (*SUD^h* 50). But in the transitional case the individual recognizes his concern for the earthly (his touchiness about despair over finite losses) as the weakness it is. In the first instance, however, there is an attempt to cancel this unwelcome recognition of weakness by repressing the very notion of what it is an unwillingness to appropriate. After all, the less salient some prospect one is too weak to face, the less topical the idea one is too weak to face it. Because this form of despair, which goes by the name of "reserve" (*Indesluttethed*) (*SV^3* XV 118; cf. *SUD^h* 94), still expresses resistance to the appropriation of singularity, it still counts as "weakness." Defiant despair, which comes in two forms, active and passive in that order, ensues when the idea that one is singular can no longer be held at bay. Active despair exploits the consciousness of being singular – Anti-Climacus calls it the negative form of the self – "experimentally" (SUD^h 123). Despair here takes the form of making one's own mark on the world, putting one's talents to one's own use, totally turning one's back on the idea that dedication to the world can be a weakness. This is correct in a way, the world is indeed where personality belongs, but it is not how a self "transparently grounded in the power that established it" is dedicated to the world, and the latter is Anti-Climacus's formula for the unrooting of despair (44). Here the relation to that power is put aside and the negative form of the infinite self treated as though it were an absolute beginning from which selves can be fashioned perpetually *de novo*.

It is crucial to understanding Kierkegaard here that any such exploitation of the negative form of the self is still a form of weakness rather than of (e.g., Nietzschean) strength. It is the weakness of a conveniently presumed inability to free oneself from the pull of the world when we know that what we really aim for cannot find its fulfillment there. But note that despair is now not the weakness itself; it is one's trying not to see the weakness. Instead of eliminating it and going on to faith, or hope ("humbling himself before God under his weakness"), which would be the progressive development and what it means to accept or want oneself, the despairer is one who backs off from the notion that there is anything "eternal" to measure up to. The passively defiant despairer, for his part, instead of putting the weakness out of mind, makes a point of being weak. He parades weakness as a decisive reason for claiming that the project of selfhood in any nonimmanent sense is not worth the candle, at least for him, and in the extreme case as proof that there is no such project.

But Part II of *The Sickness unto Death* then tells us that the task of selfhood as Part I has described it is only from the human point of view, with "man" the measure. Part II presents another measure: God, and toward the end of *The Sickness unto Death* this measure becomes more concretely Christ, through whom God has revealed "what stupendous reality a self has" (SUD^h 147). Now does this, in accordance with the principle that the self's standard is "always: that directly in the face of which it is a self" (SUD^h 111), give us at last the full account of the project of selfhood? Or does Part II's "measure" introduce a similar but new task, to be faced even if the first has been accomplished? And if the latter, does the distinction between "weak" and "defiant" despair apply here all over again, from *this* higher level of existence?

The truth seems to be somewhere in between. The second "measure" only comes into the reckoning once the first has been fully appreciated for what it is. That means that the theology does not apply in any adequate way until consciousness of self has reached the point of the negative form of the infinite self. Many have observed that theology has been more or less scrupulously expunged from Part I. The "formula" just mentioned for the state of the self "when despair is completely eradicated" does not identify the power in which the self is transparently grounded with God, nor is the "grounding" said to be something that can only be done "before God." One might try to read Part II as a kind of template to be added to Part I in order to provide the full account. That would mean making the appropriate substitutions, for instance, "before God" for the notion of there being "something eternal in the self." Against this one must note that the proposal would clearly destroy much of the phenomenological appeal of the account. The self's singularity, the negative form of the infinite self, is – at least it may be argued – something structural to mankind. But being before God is not as arguably structural; it is at best a notion of which one can have no adequate conception, grasp, or existential appreciation until the latter notion is in place, which then supports the Hegelian reading suggested here. Besides that, there is a point where the template does not fit: weakness and defiance become "the converse of what they normally are," not wanting to be oneself (at this level of expectation a sinner) is now defiance (*SUD*[h] 146). So there are good negative grounds for the Hegelian reading, which says, roughly, that you do not appreciate the need of a renewed specification of the task until, reaching the stage of the negative form of the infinite self, there would be nowhere to go from the point of view of the purely negative "self" except back to the world on the world's terms. Part II does not provide a supplement to Part I, it exploits the analysis in Part I to add one further dimension. The missing specifications apply only when the self becomes conscious of having the "stupendous reality" that standing before God admits.

It is not sufficient for the unrooting of despair that you merely have some notion or other of oneself as God-grounded. On the other hand, it is at least necessary to have some notion of yourself as particular, and of there being "something eternal" in the self. Only then can the task acquire its additional dimension, but it does have to acquire this dimension before despair can be unrooted. This is indeed anticipated in Part I, where the self is said to be "the conscious synthesis of infinitude and finitude, which relates to itself," and whose task is to "become itself," which, the passage goes on to say, "can only be done in the relationship to God" (*SUD^h* 59). And the earlier formula for the eradication of despair reappears already in Part I in an expanded context with "God" clearly in place:

Every human existence not conscious of itself as spirit, or not personally conscious of itself before God as spirit, every human existence which is not grounded transparently in God, but opaquely rests or merges in some abstract universal (state, nation, etc.) or, in the dark about its self, simply takes its capacities to be natural powers, unconscious in a deeper sense of where it has them from, takes its self to be an inexplicable something [*et uforklarligt Noget*]. (*SUD^h* 76; see *SV³* XV 102).

The aesthete, it will be remembered, was content to be nothing, even if he might resist that appellation, or at least its negative connotation. On the other hand, he would resist even more strongly an identification as a "something" of this murky kind. Had he read *The Sickness unto Death* it might even with some justice have occurred to him to accuse Judge William of being just such a murky self. For according to *The Sickness unto Death* the self we become when preferring the worldly option, the self that develops in an outward rather than inward direction and whose outward direction does not express an inward direction, must be "broken down" in order to become itself (*SUD^h* 96). But of course, in William's defense one can say that he does not conceive the ethical self as worldly. But in that case, not seeing the distinction between the inward and the outward direction, and the way in which the outward direction can deceive with the appearance of selfhood, he has simply underestimated the extent of the task of selfhood.

These murky selves that see themselves in abstract universal terms are not selves standing before God. They are not selves at all in Kierkegaard's sense. In the kind of despair Anti-Climacus calls weakness, they are pseudo-"selves" who assume they adopt a relation to God by standing in certain relations to one another. On the other hand, in the kind of despair Anti-Climacus calls defiance, they do indeed see themselves as alone, singular; but then they deny they are related to God. They "want to be themselves," but this wanting is a form of despair precisely because it excludes the thought of being established by a "power." True, they are not obfuscated in the above way; but until they gain an idea of what it means to stand before God, they are not yet "clarified." They still lack the idea of standing before God.

This suggests that, as they stand, they have indeed no alternative to despair, for anything short of grounding oneself transparently in God while before God counts as despair; there can be no nondespairing alternative outside that relationship. One may even wonder how far that is possible even within the relationship. In Part I, Anti-Climacus, at the beginning of his account of the development of the consciousness of despair, pegs the development's end with a limiting case, the devil, a "pure" spirit. There being in this case no "obscurity which might serve as a mitigating excuse," the devil's defiance is "absolute" (SUD^h 72); standing before God, and knowing exactly that this is what he is doing, the devil turns his back on God. But human beings are not pure spirit, their self-knowledge is never pure, they are exposed always to that "cunning and sophistry" (of their own) with which despair exploits the fatal gap between "understanding" what is to be done and "doing" it (125). So even when they understand that the task of becoming themselves requires that they are "conscious of themselves before God as spirit" (76) and that only when the task is conceived in that way can they free themselves from despair, they still face the prior "task" of mastering their own susceptibility to self-deceit.

There is a clear autobiographical reference. It is a remarkable feature of The Sickness unto Death that while in Part II it brings Kierkegaard's own personal dilemma into focus, it tries in Part I to see this dilemma against a background that brings it conceptually into continuity with what Kierkegaard saw as the malaise of Danish (and any other relevantly similar) society. The problem facing Kierkegaard himself was that even when the "measure" is God, one still does not know whether one is in despair or not. Such knowledge is always suspect. The "calling" that requires one to be "extraordinary" may from this elevated standard simply be just one more easy way out, a way of avoiding the truth rather than witnessing to it.

One treats "the thorn in the flesh" as if it had been specially implanted by eternity to equip one for some divine purpose (SUD^h 109). But if God is the standard, perhaps the thorn in the flesh should be accepted as part of the "definite thing" that is oneself? If so, one should "humble oneself under this weakness" before God, for whom, after all, everything is possible (110). Maybe the only convincing proof that one did that and was not still in despair would be martyrdom, for to lose everything, even life itself, would *show* to the world that the "calling" was not an easy way out and therefore not despair. Perhaps from the point of view of the theological self, losing one's life in the cause of the universal might be a way of realizing it (something that according to the "human" standard would be quite unintelligible). But conceivably, even this thought might be a despairing one, still an example of "before God in despair not wanting to be oneself" (113; cf. 111).

Apparently, very far from these personal dilemmas we have the claim in Part I of *The Sickness unto Death* that the most common forms of despair "in the world" are those in which people are as yet not conscious of themselves "as spirit" (SUD^h 75). A person lacking "consciousness of an infinite self" (100) cannot yet see the task of selfhood for what it is. But nevertheless the young girl who finds life unsupportable unless she can be "another's" (50), in the sense in which she understands this, manifests, knowingly or not, some grasp of the negative form of the infinite self. For her, we might guess, an intuitive access to this negative form is barred much less effectively than in the case of people more easily satisfied with their worldly personae. Maybe Anti-Climacus's account could be glossed in a way of which Kierkegaard would have approved. We might say that the Borgia figure with "Caesar or nothing" as his motto (49), just because he represses the "weakness" that is his addiction to the world, is further removed from this grasp than the young girl with the fragile self-image. The point is that flight and evasion take many forms and society itself is a rich provider of ready-made "identities" for those too weak to be "spirit," as well as of opportunities for those bent on being their own selves. One might gloss *The Sickness unto Death* further by talking of "objective" despair, as Vigilius Haufniensis does of objective anxiety, despair as a malaise embedded in society and its forms (*CA* 56ff).

There is one further "local" reference to note in *The Sickness unto Death.* We saw that the task to be accomplished in "the relationship to God" is that of "becoming oneself." The expression used to describe the self that has the task included "synthesis." The self is "the conscious synthesis of infinitude and finitude," a conscious synthesis that "relates to itself" (*SUD*[h] 59). Kierkegaard's notion of a synthesis is never explicated in depth. But the reader may find it rewarding to consider two relevant senses of "synthesis." In one, and here we may again think of Kierkegaard writing under the shadow of Hegel, this "synthesis" could refer to the completed task of selfhood, or perhaps (and this is a distinction that needs working out) to the form the task of continuing to be, and in this other sense becoming oneself, takes when despair is overcome (though again, do we ever know whether it is overcome?). That is, being oneself is sustaining the synthesis of finite and infinite, bringing off the synthesis in intellectually ungroundable ethical activity. Becoming oneself would be successfully grounding oneself in God, going on doing that in one's allotted time and place, not being engaged in the struggle to *be* doing that. On the other hand, once put in this way, it seems more likely that the struggling and the continuing go together, that one must always be resisting the resistance of despair.

Negatively, the synthesis can be understood simply as a juxtaposition of opposites, the task being to get them together *as* opposites. What the reader is being expressly told is that it can only be carried out with God's help. The development toward self-consciousness that Kierkegaard has Anti-Climacus trace is one in which the opposition becomes ever clearer, assuming in the moral and practical plane a status analogous to what Hegel called an "either/or" of the understanding. The opposition is not metaphysical dualism or mind-body dualism or the like. The idea of a synthesis in this negative sense has to do with what Kierkegaard refers to in his journals as the human being's "double nature" and has to be understood in an ethical context. Kierkegaard is here criticizing his contemporaries, especially the Grundtvigians, for not admitting this double nature. They believe human fulfillment to be the fruition of a natural development. Anti-Climacus's "theological self," even more so the Christological self, though he doesn't use that expression, is in direct rebuttal of this (in more than one sense) popular conception. By making the God-man the model and the relationship to God the sense of the "eternal" in oneself, Kierkegaard pushes fulfillment beyond the reach of our natural capacities. Some would agree but deny that this can be the measure; "ought" implies "can," and it is simply cheating to say that everything is possible for God. For Anti-Climacus, however, a veritable Christian, such denial is the ultimate sin. To despair is to give up the hope of this good. But then on these terms, the Grundtvigians too would be sinners.[10]

NOTES

1 *Purity of Heart is to Will One Thing: Spiritual Preparation for the Office of Confession,* trans. with introductory essay by Douglas V. Steere (New York: Harper and Brothers, 1958), p. 61; *SV³* XI 35.

2 See, e.g., Philip L. Quinn, "Kierkegaard's Christian Ethics," in the present volume.

3 A cogent proponent of this reading is Michael Theunissen. See *Der Begriff Verzweiflung. Korrekturen an Kierkegaard* (Frankfurt am Main: Suhrkamp, 1993); see also Theunissen, "Für einen rationaleren Kierkegaard: Zu Einwänden von Arne Grøn und Alastair Hannay," in *Kierkegaard Studies/Yearbook 1996,* ed. Niels Jørgen Cappelørn and Hermann Deuser (Berlin and New York: Walter de Gruyter, 1996), pp. 61–90. The volume contains several further essays on *The Sickness unto Death* relevant to the present one, including the present author's "Basic Despair in *The Sickness unto Death*" and "Paradigmatic Despair and the Quest for a Kierkegaardian Anthropology."

4 See *EOᴴ* 502, where the same distinction is made between two levels of despair. Kierkegaard also distinguishes doubt from despair as merely intellectual (see 514).

5 Hegel, *Phenomenology of Spirit,* trans. A. V. Miller (Oxford: Clarendon Press, 1977), §78, pp. 49, 50.

6 See, most recently, Michael Weston, *Kierkegaard and Modern Continental Philosophy: An Introduction* (London and New York: Routledge, 1994), p. 168, if I read him correctly.

7 Hegel, *Phenomenology of Spirit,* §78, pp. 49, 50.

8 Ibid.

9 *SV³* X 224; cf. *CUP* 554. The relation of irascibility to despair has a source in St. Thomas Aquinas (*Truth,* trans. from the definitive Leonine text by Robert W. Schmidt, S. J. [Chicago: Henry Regnery Co., 1954], vol. 3, questions 21–9):

> A passion in the irascible power can . . . regard either good or evil. If it regards good, this can be a good possessed or one not possessed. Regarding a good possessed there can be no passion in the

irascible power, because once a good is possessed it causes no difficulty to the possessor. Consequently the notion of the arduous is
not verified in it. But regarding a good not yet possessed, in which
the notion of the arduous can be verified because of the difficulty
of obtaining it, if that good is judged to exceed the capacity of the
one seeking it, despair ensues; but if it is judged not to exceed that
capacity, hope arises. (264)

The concept of "irascibility" stems from Plato's discussion of the "spirited" (not "spiritual") aspects of irrational nature that are superior to
"mere" appetite ("concupiscence") (see *Republic* 4:396). For more on
the parallel with Aquinas, see my "Kierkegaardian Despair and the
Irascible Soul," *Kierkegaard Studies/Yearbook 1997*, ed. Niels Jørgen
Cappelørn and Hermann Deuser (Berlin and New York: Walter de
Gruyter, 1997).

10 There are several things this essay has not done. One is to spell out the
comparison with Hegel. Others have discussed it more thoroughly elsewhere (most recently Judith Butler, "Kierkegaard's Speculative Despair,"
in the *Routledge History of Philosophy*, vol. 6, *The Age of German
Idealism*, ed. by Robert C. Solomon and Kathleen M. Higgins [London
and New York: Routledge, 1993], pp. 363–9). *Either/Or*'s despair might
turn out to be closer to Hegel than I have suggested, although I suspect
that the claim that all aesthetic life-views are despair is harder to make
sense of in terms of Hegel's concept of despair. But there might well be
less continuity than the reading offered here claims. Then again, the relation of Kierkegaardian despair to corresponding discussions in other
philosophers ancient and modern, not to say postmodern, offers a potentially inexhaustible topic, which raises the question of what we should
make of Kierkegaard's concept once we feel justified in claiming that we
have grasped it. Will we decide, as many quickly assume, that it is obsolete? Or is there perhaps an existential core in the concept that must and
can be rescued from the Christian framework within which Anti-
Climacus writes? May the relation to religion be discussed profitably in
terms of some alternative theology, one which will allow Kierkegaardian
insights to throw light on and enrich our grasp of human being? Perhaps
we should say not everything but quite a lot is possible.

14 Kierkegaard's Christian ethics

The ethics whose teleological suspension is at issue in Kierkegaard's *Fear and Trembling* is the secular ethics of his own time. This secular ethics is the ethical that is contrasted with the aesthetic in his *Either/Or*. Scholars disagree about the relative importance of the Kantian and Hegelian strands in ethics thus conceived.[1] This is also the first ethics spoken of in the introduction to *The Concept of Anxiety*. Vigilius Haufniensis, the pseudonymous author of that work, tells us that "the first ethics was shipwrecked on the sinfulness of the single individual" (*CA* 20). It is only the second ethics, he goes on to say, that can deal with the manifestation of sin (*CA* 21). For Kierkegaard, the second ethics is a distinctively Christian ethics. His most thorough treatment of this ethics occurs in *Works of Love*. According to Bruce Kirmmse, this book is Kierkegaard's "major ethical work and one of the most important works in his entire authorship," and it contains "his clearest and starkest formulation of a Christian ethics."[2] Hence most of this essay will be devoted to a discussion of *Works of Love*. Kierkegaard, however, writing under the pseudonym of Anti-Climacus, also treats Christian ethics from a somewhat different perspective in *Practice in Christianity*, and this essay will have something to say about that book as well.

Before turning to Kierkegaard's Christian ethics, however, we need to understand how the first ethics came to be shipwrecked on the sinfulness of the single individual. Even the first ethics is sufficiently stringent to open up what John E. Hare characterizes as the moral gap, "the gap between the moral demand on us and our natural capacities to live by it."[3] As he sees it, for those who are unwilling to invoke divine assistance in bridging the moral gap, there

349

are three strategies for dealing with it, none of which has succeeded. The first is to keep the moral demand high and to puff up our natural capacities to live by it. The second is to reduce the demand. The third is to acknowledge the gap and to look for a naturalistic substitute for divine assistance. Those who are willing to invoke divine assistance, as Kierkegaard is, will deal with the moral gap in other ways.

In *Religion within the Limits of Reason Alone*, Kant accounts for the moral gap by arguing that there is radical evil in human nature. There is in each of us, Kant thinks, a propensity to evil that ought to be regarded as *"brought* by man *upon himself."*[4] Since it is to be so regarded, we are accountable for it, and so it is a product of our freedom. Hence it is morally evil. It is the subjective ground of the possibility of the deviation of the maxims we use to determine our actions from the moral law. According to Kant,

this evil is *radical,* because it corrupts the ground of all maxims; it is, moreover, as a natural propensity, *inextirpable* by human powers, since extirpation could occur only through good maxims, and cannot take place when the ultimate subjective ground of all maxims is postulated as corrupt; yet at the same time it must be possible to *overcome* it, since it is found in man, a being whose actions are free.[5]

In our struggles to overcome it, "we cannot start from an innocence natural to us but must begin with the assumption of a wickedness of the will in adopting its maxims contrary to the original moral predisposition," and "we must begin with the incessant counteraction against it."[6] But, at best, this leads only to progress from bad to better. We can, at best, only narrow the moral gap; we can never close it.

How can we even begin to narrow the moral gap if the ultimate subjective ground of all our maxims is corrupt? Kant is sure that "when the moral law commands that we *ought* now to be better men, it follows inevitably that we must *be able* to be better men."[7] He supposes that "if a man reverses, by a single unchangeable decision, that highest ground of his maxims whereby he was an evil man (and thus puts on the new man), he is, so far as his principle and cast of mind are concerned, a subject susceptible of goodness, but only in continuous labor and growth is he a good man."[8] Such a reversal would be, Kant tells us, a moral revolution in one's disposition. But further questions now arise. Can anyone become even a subject susceptible of goodness if the ultimate subjective ground of all his or her maxims is corrupt? And can it be done without divine assistance?

Kant takes it to be a basic principle that "each must do as much as lies in his power to become a better man," and he thinks that only when this much has been done "can he hope that what is not within his power will be supplied through cooperation from above."[9] On Kant's view, it is hard to reconcile the idea of such cooperation from above with the idea that "man *himself* must make or have made himself into whatever, in a moral sense, whether good or evil, he is or is to become."[10] Yet Kant insists that the impossibility of cooperation between freedom and grace cannot be proved "because freedom itself, though containing nothing supernatural in its conception, remains, as regards its possibility, just as incomprehensible to us as is the supernatural factor that we would like to regard as a supplement to the spontaneous but deficient determination of freedom."[11] So we are to do whatever we can to make ourselves subjects susceptible of goodness, and we may then hope for a divine supplement to our efforts if one is needed.

Kant defines sin as "the transgressing of the moral law as a divine command."[12] He thinks we have a *sui generis* duty to form an ethical commonwealth whose highest lawgiver can only be thought of as someone "with respect to whom all *true duties*, hence also the ethical, must be represented as *at the same time* his commands."[13] He concludes that "an ethical commonwealth can be thought of only as a people under divine commands, i.e., as a *people of God*, and indeed *under laws of virtue*."[14] Kant will therefore allow us to represent the moral law, which is a deliverance of our own practical reason, as a divine command and thus to represent transgressions of it as sins. Using this system of representation, we may say that each of us becomes sinful by bringing upon himself or herself the morally evil propensity to evil. By doing so, we create the moral gap. Having done so, we in our fallen state lack the natural capacities to live up to the demands of the moral law. Thus, on Kant's view, we ourselves are responsible for the shipwreck of first ethics, for getting ourselves, by becoming sinful, into a situation in which we cannot live up to its demands. Having become sinful, we can at best narrow the moral gap by trying to make progress from bad to better.

Whether our efforts to make moral progress succeed may depend on whether we receive divine assistance, and only when we have done our best to make such progress may we hope for a divine supplement to our efforts.

The Christian ethics set forth in Kierkegaard's *Works of Love* is at least as demanding as Kantian ethics. Its demands are, he thinks, specified by genuine divine commands and not merely by a moral law that can also be thought of as a divine command. How can such an ethics avoid being shipwrecked on sinfulness? How can it be the second ethics that can deal with the manifestation of sin? In other words, how can it deal with the moral gap?

I. WORKS OF LOVE

The ethics of love set forth in the Gospels portrays love as the subject of a command. In Matthew's Gospel, Jesus states the command in response to a question from a lawyer about which commandment of the law is the greatest.

You shall love the Lord your God with your whole heart, with your whole soul, and with all your mind. This is the greatest and first commandment. The second is like it: You shall love your neighbor as yourself. On these two commandments the whole law is based, and the prophets as well. (22:37-40)[15]

Mark 12:29-31 and Luke 10:27-8 contain similar accounts of the promulgation of the Great Commandment. And in his last discourse, recorded in John's Gospel, Jesus tells his followers that "the command I give you is this, that you love one another" (John 15:17). So the authors of those documents concur in thinking that Jesus expressed his ethics of love in the form of a demand upon his followers, a command that they love one another and their neighbors as themselves. In *Works of Love*, Kierkegaard follows these authors in speaking of Christian love as "*commanded* love" (WL 19). Can love be commanded?

Works of Love is, as its subtitle indicates, "Some Christian Deliberations in the Form of Discourses." In the second discourse of the first series, Kierkegaard comments on Matthew 22:39, "You shall love your neighbor as yourself." The first section of this discourse is entitled "You *Shall* Love." Kierkegaard addresses this topic because "this is the very mark of Christian love and its distinctive characteristic – that it contains this apparent contradiction: to love is a duty" (WL 24). As Alastair Hannay has pointed out, it is plausible to suppose that the apparent contradiction arises from the fact that Kierkegaard's slogan that to love is a duty seems to contradict Kant's claim that there is no such thing as a duty to love.[16] The apparent contradiction will not, however, be a real contradiction if the kind of love Kierkegaard takes to be a duty differs from that Kant has in mind when he denies that love is a duty. The kind of love Kant has in mind is love that is a matter of feeling. Since Kant thinks feelings are not subject to the will, he denies that such love can be brought about at will. He then applies *modus tollens* to the ought-implies-can principle to conclude to the denial that such love ought to be brought about at will. There is, therefore, no duty to have such love, and it cannot be the proper object of a moral command. But it remains to be seen whether the kind of love Kierkegaard takes to be commanded, and hence a duty, is this kind of love.

Even if it is supposed that Christian love is not a matter of feeling, a question arises about why it needs to be commanded. As I see it, to a first approximation, the answer is that the love of neighbor of which Jesus speaks is unnatural for humans in their present sinful condition. It does not spontaneously engage their affections. For most of us most of the time, love of neighbor is not an attractive goal, and, if it were supererogatory or above and beyond the call of duty, most of us simply would not pursue it. Such love must be presented to us, at least in the first instance, as an obligatory love with the feel of something that can curb or check natural desires and inclinations. In the religious tradition of Jesus and his hearers, it is taken for granted that divine commands impose obligations, and so an obligatory love would in that tradition naturally be represented as commanded by a divine lawgiver. Indeed, in the Christian development of that tradition, which Kierkegaard accepts, Jesus himself, who is also God the Son, is a divine lawgiver.

What is more, like the requirements of Kantian morality, the demands of Christian love open up the moral gap. In the first section of the third discourse in the first series, Kierkegaard speaks of Paul's remark that "love is the fulfillment of the law" (Rom. 13:10). He concludes this section as follows:

> Is there any more accurate expression for how infinitely far a person is from fulfilling the requirement than this, that the distance is so great that he cannot begin to calculate it, cannot total up the account! Not only is so much neglected every day, to say nothing of what guilt is incurred, but when some time has passed, one is not even able to state accurately the guilt as it once appeared to oneself, because time changes and mitigates one's judgment of the past – but, alas, no amount of time changes the requirement, eternity's requirement – that love is the fulfilling of the Law. (WL 134)

According to Kirmmse, when we read passages such as this about the Law's demand, "we are compelled to confront the radical absoluteness of Christian ethics and our inability to live accordingly."[17] Or, to be more precise, we are compelled to confront our inability to live up to the Law's demand without divine assistance. Kierkegaard insists that "you *shall* love – this, then, is the word of the *royal law*" (WL 24). But how are we to love?

Kierkegaard begins to answer this question by distinguishing three kinds of love. It is a commonplace of Christian thought that there is a distinctively Christian form of love (*agape, caritas*) that stands in sharp contrast to both erotic love (*eros, amor*) and friendship. The aim of both erotic love and friendship is to love this single human being above all others and in distinction from all others. Both kinds of love are preferential, while agapeistic love is not.

> Therefore, the object of both erotic love and of friendship has preference's name, "the beloved," "the friend," who is loved in contrast to the whole world. The Christian doctrine, on the contrary, is to love the neighbor, to love the whole human race, all people, even the enemy, and not to make exceptions, neither of preference nor of aversion. (WL 19)

The Christian doctrine, moreover, is that love of neighbor is a duty. And being a duty is, Kierkegaard thinks, a necessary condition for securing love of neighbor against the kinds of mutability that destroy erotic love and friendship. As he puts the point, "*only when it is a duty to love, only then is love eternally secured against every change, eternally made free in blessed independence, eternally and happily secured against despair*" (WL 29). How does loving dutifully provide such security?

When Kierkegaard speaks of securing love against change, he is thinking of changes in the desires or feelings that are in part constitutive of erotic love and friendship, desires and feelings that sometimes spontaneously alter even when there is no change in the object of love or in the lover's beliefs about that object. As Robert Brown has observed,

a woman's love for her husband can change into dislike even though her appraisal of his character or personality is unaltered. She can simply become bored with him for displaying the same familiar characteristics, each of which she still values but no longer wishes to observe at such close quarters.[18]

Only if love of neighbor is a duty, Kierkegaard supposes, can it be rendered invulnerable to changes in the lover's emotions, moods, and tastes in virtue of being motivated by a stable sense of duty. A love thus motivated, however, would not be a matter of feeling. It could exist and persist independent of feelings, though it need not do so.

When Kierkegaard speaks of making love free in blessed independence, he has in mind independence of mutable characteristics of the loved one. The dependence of erotic love and friendship on mutable characteristics of the beloved and the friend make them vulnerable to alterations in their objects. If the beloved loses the traits that made her or him erotically attractive, then erotic love without illusion dies. If the friend who was cherished for virtue turns vicious, the friendship will not survive unless one is corrupted and turns vicious too. But Christian love of neighbor is invulnerable to alterations in its object. Kierkegaard says:

To be sure, you can also continue to love the beloved and the friend no matter how they treat you, but you cannot truly continue to call them the beloved and friend if they, sorry to say, have really changed. No change, however, can take the neighbor from you, because it is not the neighbor who holds you fast, but it is your love that holds the neighbor fast. If your love for the neighbor remains unchanged, then the neighbor also remains unchanged by existing. (WL 65)

If there is to be such a love that, in Shakespeare's words, alters not where it alteration finds, it cannot be held fast by or depend on mutable features of the neighbor. According to Kierkegaard, it will have the requisite independence of such features only if it is a duty, for only then can it be motivated by a sense of duty instead of by affections or preferences that change in response to alterations in the loved one. "Such a love," he tells us, "stands and does not fall with the contingency of its object but stands and falls with the Law of eternity – but then, of course, it never falls" (WL 39). Or at least it need never fall provided we assume that we can always obey the Law of eternity because we ought to do so.

When Kierkegaard speaks of securing love against despair, he is pointing, in the first instance, to the unhappiness the lover feels in response to misfortunes such as the loss of the beloved or the friend. However, he takes despairing unhappiness to be only a symptom of the underlying state of being in despair, which is a misrelation in a person's innermost being. Being in despair, Kierkegaard tells us, is due to "relating oneself with infinite passion to a particular something, for one can relate oneself with infinite passion – unless one is in despair – only to the eternal" (WL 40). In other words, one who is in despair cleaves to a particular finite and temporal good with an infinite passion only properly directed to an eternal good. The only security against being in despair is to undergo the change of eternity by investing infinite passion in the eternal and in obedience to the Law of eternity.

Despair is to lack the eternal; despair is not to have undergone the change of eternity through duty's *shall*. Despair is not, therefore, the loss of the beloved – that is unhappiness, pain, suffering – but despair is the lack of the eternal. (WL 40–1)

Of course the change of eternity is by itself no cure for unhappiness. It does not remove the pain and suffering involved in the loss of a loved one. But the command to love makes it a duty to love despite unhappiness, pain, and suffering. Of course, not giving up on love in such circumstances requires great courage, and it may seem impossible for humans to muster up such courage when pain and suffering are extreme. Kierkegaard asks: "Who would have this courage except eternity; who has the right to say this *shall* except eternity, which at the very moment love wants to despair over its unhappiness commands it to love; where can this command have its home except in eternity?" (WL 41). However, if eternity does say this *shall* by right, humans must be able to act with the requisite courage, even if they cannot do so without assistance. Thus Kierkegaard insists that "when eternity says, 'You shall love,' it is responsible for making sure that this can be done" (41). We can be confident, I think, that eternity will have to assist many of us if we are to be kept secure from despair in the face of extraordinary unhappiness, pain, and suffering.

According to Kierkegaard, then, three things threaten to destroy our loves: changes in our inclinations and feelings, changes in the objects we love, and the unhappiness, pain, and suffering that can lead to despair. Such things often do destroy erotic loves and friendships. Love of neighbor will not be vulnerable to the first two of them only if it is a duty and so compliance is motivated by a sense of duty independent of inclinations, feelings, and mutable characteristics of the neighbor. It will not be vulnerable to the third of them, Kierkegaard suggests, only if it is a duty whose source is eternity, a duty imposed by a divine command, so that divine assistance can be relied upon if needed to make compliance a real possibility. In short, only the love that is obedient to the divine command is immutable.

We can in some cases test our love for immutability. In the ninth discourse of the second series, titled "The Work of Love in Recollecting One Who Is Dead," Kierkegaard tells us that we have duties to the dead. One of them is to "recollect the dead, weep softly, but weep long" (WL 348). If we too quickly forget the dead, our love for them lacks the requisite independence of changes in ourselves. The dead do not change. "If, then, any change takes place between one living and one dead," Kierkegaard argues, "it is indeed clear that it must be the one living who has changed" (358). When such a change occurs, our love for the dead lacks the immutability required by duty and so fails in obedience to the divine command. As Kierkegaard sees it, "in the relationship to one who is dead, you have the criterion by which you can test yourself" (358). Judged by this criterion, many of us fail the test.

Christian love of neighbor differs from erotic love and friendship in another important way. In the second section of the second discourse of the first series, entitled "You Shall Love *the Neighbor*," Kierkegaard contends that erotic love and friendship are both infected with partiality because they rest on exclusive preferences. The poets praise them because of their exclusivity. Kierkegaard tells us:

In the poetic sense, it is a stroke of good fortune (and certainly the poet is an excellent judge of good fortune), the best of good fortune, to fall in love, to find this one and only beloved. It is a stroke of good fortune, almost as great, to find this one and only friend. (WL 51)

Because finding the one and only beloved or the one and only friend is a matter of luck rather than choice, one is never obliged to find the beloved or the friend. The one and only beloved or the one and only friend is the object of a passionate preference that Kierkegaard considers akin to self-love. "Just as self-love selfishly embraces this one and only *self* that makes it self-love," he says, "so also erotic love's passionate preference selfishly encircles this one and only beloved, and friendship's passionate preference encircles this one and only friend" (WL 53). Moreover, exclusive love cherishes traits that differentiate the beloved or the friend from other people. According to Kierkegaard, "in erotic love and friendship, the two love each other by virtue of the dissimilarity or by virtue of the similarity that is based on dissimilarity (as when two friends love each other by virtue of similar customs, characters, occupations, education, etc., that is, on the basis of the similarity by which they are different from other people, or in which they are like each other as different from other people)" (56). Confirmation for the view that erotic love and friendship are exclusive loves comes from Aristotle. He restricts the best kind of friendship to good people who are equal in virtue and maintains that we must be content with only a few friends of this kind. "One cannot be a friend to many people in the sense of having friendship of the perfect type with them," Aristotle says, "just as one cannot be in love with many people at once."[19] The view that erotic love and friendship are exclusive is not a Kierkegaardian idiosyncrasy.

By contrast, Christian love of neighbor involves self-denial, does not play favorites, and is all-inclusive. For Kierkegaard, the disagreement between the poet, an aesthetic figure, and Christianity is simple, sharp, and deep:

The issue between the poet and Christianity can be defined very precisely as follows: *Erotic love and friendship are preferential love [Forkjerlighed] and the passion of preferential love*; Christian love [Kjerlighed] is self-denial's love, for which this *shall* vouches. To deprive these passions of their strength is the confusion. But preferential love's most passionate boundlessness in excluding means to love only one single person; self-denial's boundlessness in giving itself means not to exclude a single one. (WL 52)

But passionate preference is rooted in our natural inclinations and predilections. In order to counteract it, Christianity needs something that can win a struggle against natural inclinations. Only thus armed, can Christianity "thrust erotic love and friendship from the throne" (WL 44). On Kierkegaard's view, Christianity proposes for this role dutiful obedience to the divine command, this *shall*, to love God and the neighbor. Motivated by a sense of duty that goes contrary to natural inclinations, the Christian makes God rather than preference the middle term in love of neighbor. Kierkegaard holds that "in erotic love and friendship, preferential love is the middle term; in love for the neighbor, God is the middle term" (57–8).

Love God above all else; then you also love the neighbor and in the neighbor every human being. Only by loving God above all else can one love the neighbor in the other human being. The other human being, this is the neighbor who is the other human being in the sense that the other human being is every other human being. (WL 58)

In short, only if it is mediated by the commanded love of God can the commanded love of neighbor reach out to every other human being, excluding no one on preferential grounds.

Because it is to be all-inclusive, commanded Christian love of neighbor cannot rest on differences among persons or on likenesses grounded in differences. It demands instead, Kierkegaard observes, an eternal equality in loving, which is just the opposite of exclusive love or preference.

Equality is simply not to make distinctions, and eternal equality is unconditionally not to make the slightest distinction, unqualifiedly not to make the slightest distinction. Preference on the other hand is to make distinctions; passionate preference is unqualifiedly to make distinctions. (WL 58)

The demand for eternal equality in loving is a remarkable and unnatural demand.

Up to this point, however, what Kierkegaard has said about erotic love and friendship seems plausible. They are mutable and exclusive loves. But he has more to say. He also claims that passionate preferential love is another form of self-love. He notes that "the beloved and the friend are called, remarkably and profoundly, to be sure, the *other self*, the *other I*" (WL 53) and then argues that "The one whom self-love, in the strictest sense, loves is basically the *other I*, because the *other I* is he himself. Yet this certainly is still self-love. But in the same sense it is self-love to love the *other I*, who is the beloved or the friend" (57). This is, needless to say, not a persuasive argument. It is far from clear that love for the *other I* who is myself is self-love in the same sense as love for the *other I* who is the beloved or the friend. To be sure, erotic love is often selfish. In addition, the two lower forms of Aristotelian friendship are selfish because, as Aristotle says, "those who love for the sake of utility love for the sake of what is good for *themselves,* and those who love for the sake of pleasure do so for the sake of what is pleasant to *themselves.*"[20] However, it does not follow from these considerations that erotic love is always selfish or that all forms of friendship are selfish.

Yet even here, if we make allowances for his rhetorical exaggeration, Kierkegaard has a serious point to make. As he indicates, the Christian command does not require self-hatred; it only requires that a person love her neighbor as herself, that is, as she ought to love herself. Properly understood, says Kierkegaard, the love commandment also says this: *"You shall love yourself in the right way"* (WL 22). Similarly, commanded Christian love is to dethrone erotic love and friendship but is not to abolish either of them. Because love of neighbor excludes no one, the beloved or the friend is also the neighbor. Hence, Kierkegaard urges:

No, love the beloved faithfully and tenderly, but let love for the neighbor be the sanctifying element in your union's covenant with God. Love your friend honestly and devotedly, but let love for the neighbor be what you learn from each other in your friendship's confidential relationship with God! (WL 62)

What is more, when both erotic love and love of neighbor focus on a single person, priority must be given to love of neighbor. For Kierkegaard, "your wife must first and foremost be to you your neighbor; that she is your wife is then a more precise specification of your particular relationship to each other" (WL 141). Similarly, when both friendship and love of neighbor focus on a single person, your friend must first and foremost be to you your neighbor. But subordinating erotic love and friendship to love of neighbor may carry with it a very great price. From the Christian perspective, Kierkegaard thinks, "truly to love another person is with every sacrifice (also the sacrifice of becoming hated oneself) to help the other person to love God or in loving God" (114). So if one can help the beloved or the friend to love God by breaking off the relationship, love of neighbor demands that one make this sacrifice, even if one becomes hated as a result. Unless one is prepared to pay this price, one's erotic love or friendship is not wholly free of selfishness or self-love, and one has not completely subordinated these other loves to love of neighbor.

Christian love of neighbor, as Kierkegaard portrays it, gives rise to many questions. Is it even possible to love without making distinctions? And if it is possible, is such undiscriminating love desirable? Is it desirable to be willing to sacrifice erotic love or friendship for the sake of the loved one's God-relationship? Can things that go so much against the grain of our natural inclinations and predilections really be duties? Kierkegaard knows perfectly well that such questions are bound to arise. He insists that the command to love one's neighbor, interpreted in this way, will be, like much else in Christianity, an offense to many. As he puts it, "the Christian world is still continually offended by the actual Christian" (WL 201). Nonetheless, he urges us to become actual Christians and to try to obey the command. "Only confess it," he pleads, "or if it is disturbing to you to have it put this way, well, I myself will confess that many times this has thrust me back and that I am yet very far from the delusion that I fulfill this commandment, which to flesh and blood is an offense and to wisdom foolishness" (59). When we consider it in a cool hour, we too are apt to be thrust back by the command and at least tempted to find it offensive.

Throughout the second series of discourses Kierkegaard depicts works of love in ways that make the Christian who performs them seem foolish by worldly standards. In the discourse called "Love Builds Up," he tells us that *the one who loves presupposes that love is in the other person's heart and by this very presupposition builds up love in him – from the ground up, provided, of course, that in love he presupposes its presence in the ground"* (WL 216–17). Unless we presuppose at least a seed of love in the heart of the neighbor, Kierkegaard thinks, we will not try to bring the seed to fruition by building up love in the neighbor. However, the neighbor is everyone, and so we must presuppose at least a seed of love in the heart of everyone. Yet, from a worldly point of view, it seems foolish to presuppose that even a seed of love remains in the heart of a serial killer such as Jeffrey Dahmer. In the discourse titled "Love Hides a Multitude of Sins," to give a second example, Kierkegaard says: "Let the judge appointed by the state, let the servant of justice work at discovering guilt and crime; the rest of us are called to be neither judges nor servants of justice, but on the contrary are called by God to love, that is, with the aid of a mitigating explanation to hide a multitude of sins" (293). It seems foolish to suppose, however, that only public officials are or should be concerned about criminal justice; it is a matter of concern to all citizens. It seems equally foolish to suppose that all crimes occur in circumstances that provide the basis for a correct mitigating explanation. To be sure, we are enjoined by a Mishnaic dictum to "judge every human with a bias in his favor [lechaf zechut]."[21] But worldly wisdom would seem to teach us that such a bias, like the legal presumption of innocence, is often overturned on the basis of good evidence.

Yet there is worse to come. Not only will the Christian who performs works of love look foolish in the eyes of the world, such a Christian can expect to be persecuted by the world. As Kierkegaard sees it, "Christianity cannot keep anything other than what it promised at the beginning: the world's ingratitude, opposition, and derision, and continually to a higher degree the more earnest a Christian one becomes" (WL 194). The reward a Christian who obeys the divine command to love the neighbor can expect to receive from the world is not praise for great virtue or gratitude for heroic sacrifice but vilification. Kierkegaard says: "the merely human idea of self-denial is this: give up your self-loving desires, cravings, and plans – then you will be esteemed and honored and loved as righteous and wise" (194). By contrast, "the Christian idea of self-denial is: give up your self-loving desires and cravings, give up your self-seeking plans and purposes so that you truly work unselfishly for the good – and then, for that very reason, put up with being abominated almost as a criminal, insulted and ridiculed" (194). Or, at least, a practitioner of Christian self-denial must be willing to put up with such treatment at the hands of the world, which makes such a practice look especially foolish from the point of view of the world.

So Christian love is, according to Kierkegaard, "an offense to worldliness" (*WL* 146). Yet Christianity offers people a choice, he thinks, and "terrifyingly compels them to choose: either to be offended or to accept Christianity" (200–1). If one chooses to accept Christianity, one chooses to accept the divine command to love the neighbor and the duties it imposes, despite the apparent foolishness of performing the works of love they specify. But is it possible for humans to perform works of love? If so, how is it possible? The possibility of doing such things as giving alms is, of course, not in doubt. As Kierkegaard is well aware, however, "even giving to charity, visiting the widow, and clothing the naked do not truly demonstrate or make known a person's love, inasmuch as one can do works of love in an unloving, yes, even in a self-loving way, and if this is so the work of love is no work of love at all" (13). Whether or not such things as giving alms are genuine works of love depends on how they are done. Hence the question to be asked is whether sinful humans have the capacity to perform works of love in the right way.

The key to Kierkegaard's answer, I believe, is to be found in his claim that in Christian love of neighbor God is the middle term. One thing this means, as Kirmmse points out, is that "we owe all our love to God, but that he commands us to express this in loving our Neighbor; one loves God by loving one's Neighbor."[22] Another, I suggest, is that God assists us in loving the neighbor in the right way. Kierkegaard provides an account of the form such assistance might take.

In the third section of the second discourse in the first series, called "*You* Shall Love the Neighbor," Kierkegaard connects love of one's enemies to love of neighbor by means of a polemic against making distinctions. One's enemies are, after all, among one's neighbors.

Therefore the one who truly loves the neighbor loves also his enemy. The distinction *friend* or *enemy* is a difference in the object of love, but love for the neighbor has the object that is without difference. The neighbor is the utterly unrecognizable dissimilarity between persons or is the eternal equality before God – the enemy, too, has this equality. People think that it is impossible for a human being to love his enemy, because, alas, enemies are hardly able to endure the sight of one another. Well, then, shut your eyes – then the enemy looks just like the neighbor. Shut your eyes and remember the commandment that *you* shall love; then you love – your enemy – no, then you love the neighbor, because you do not see that he is your enemy. (*WL* 68)

The enemy, however, provides only a special case of a general truth. According to Kierkegaard, "one sees the neighbor only with closed eyes, or by looking *away from* the dissimilarities" (*WL* 68). Yet the failure to mark distinctions among persons does not render love of neighbor blind or evasive; it is not a defective form of love. On the contrary, Kierkegaard's view is that "because the neighbor has none of the perfections that the beloved, the friend, the admired one, the cultured person, the rare, the extraordinary person have to such a high degree, for that very reason love for the neighbor has all the perfections that the love for the beloved, the friend, the cultured person, the admired one, the rare, the extraordinary person does not have" (66). So Kierkegaard takes it to be a virtue, or even a perfection, in love of neighbor that it shuts its eyes to, or averts them from, excellences in the loved one that other kinds of love cherish. This seems only to heighten the offense of commanded Christian love.

But Kierkegaard also gives us something to mitigate the offense. As he develops the apparently paradoxical metaphor of seeing with closed eyes, he suggests that something positive may become evident when and only when ordinary faculties of discernment are switched off. Closing one's eyes to dissimilarities among persons may enable one to envisage something in them hidden from ordinary sight, something discerned only with divine assistance.

When someone goes with God, he does indeed go without danger; but he is also compelled to see and to see in a unique way. When you go with God, you need to see only one single miserable person and you will be unable to escape what Christianity wants you to understand – human similarity. (*WL* 77)

What does this unique way of seeing reveal in the person in misery? Using scriptural language, we might describe it as the image of God in the miserable person. For Kierkegaard, it is a question of seeing every other human person as a neighbor, perceiving neighbor as eternity's mark on every human person one encounters. Such discernment calls for both special effort and the aid of special spiritual lighting conditions. Kierkegaard offers this analogy:

Take many sheets of paper, write something different on each one; then no one will be like another. But then again take each single sheet; do not let yourself be confused by the diverse inscriptions, hold it up to the light, and you will see a common watermark on all of them. In the same way the neighbor is the common watermark, but you see it only by means of eternity's light when it shines through the dissimilarity. (WL 89)

But the image of God, who is perfectly good, is presumably a mark that renders all who bear it lovable. If one can discern it in another, one will be motivated to some extent to love the other in whom it is perceived.

Kierkegaard provides an extended simile to drive his point home. Looking at the ordinary world of dissimilarities and distinctions is like looking at a play. "But when the curtain falls on the stage," he reminds us, "then the one who played the king and the one who played the beggar etc. are all alike; all are one and the same – actors" (WL 87). Similarly, when at death the curtain falls on life, we are all alike; we are all just human beings. Moreover, there is an equality within life that corresponds to equality in death. Like the actors' costumes, the dissimilarities that appear on the stage of life are really disguises. Kierkegaard tells us that "if someone is truly to love his neighbor, it must be kept in mind at all times that his dissimilarity is a disguise" (88). Christianity takes dissimilarities to be garments that hang loosely on people. "When the dissimilarity hangs loosely in this way," Kierkegaard affirms, "then in each individual there continually glimmers that essential other, which is common to all, the eternal resemblance, the likeness" (88). Loosely hanging garments can be transparent to this glimmer, and so they are penetrable disguises. When one penetrates them, what is to be seen through both the king's magnificent raiment and the beggar's wretched rags Kierkegaard calls "the inner glory, the equality of the glory" (88). As he sees it, then, there shines equally in each human being an inner glory that is invisible to the eye focused exclusively on dissimilarities and distinctions but visible to the eye that with divine assistance penetrates these disguises. It is this glory that makes each human being lovable quite apart from any distinguishing excellences. This is eternity's mark on the neighbor. If with divine assistance we discern it and are motivated by that discernment to perform the works specified by the divine command, we perform them in the right way and they are works of love.

It should, however, be emphasized that, even if there is an inner glory in each of us, many will still be thrust back by the command to love the neighbor. Some will think it foolish even to look for the image of God in all those they encounter; some will look but fail to see it. Others will write off ostensible discernments of inner glory as illusions fostered by religious sentimentality. Such people will typically not perform works of love in the right way. It must also be admitted that eternity's light shines at best dimly and fitfully in the lives of most people. All too often we can see nothing of the image of God in our enemies and in those who lack the qualities we cherish in the beloved or the friend. Frequently enough the dissimilarities that preoccupy or even obsess our ordinary affections remain opaque to any common mark of glory that lies behind them. So the moral demand of the love command is too high to be something we can expect to satisfy completely. In other words, we cannot expect to close the moral gap; we can only expect to bridge it sometimes with divine assistance. We can also anticipate continuing to sin by violating the love command and hence continuing to need forgiveness. And even when we do bridge the gap, we should not make too much of our successes. We should not think that even the works of love we do in the right way are meritorious, for, according to Kierkegaard, God "is too sublimely transcendent ever to think that to him a human being's effort should have meritoriousness. Yet he requires it, and then one thing more, that the human being himself not dare to think that he has some meritoriousness" (WL 379). Kierkegaard's God is the Lutheran God from whom salvation comes through faith alone (sola fide). We do not earn righteousness through the merits of our works of love.

For Kierkegaard, as for Kant, the moral life is at its best a progress from bad to better. In the presence of the command to love the neighbor, one can initially perform works of love for a particular person from a sense of duty, even when it is far from apparent that there is anything lovable about that person. Absent the command, there would be no such incentive for even trying to love those who do not appear to be lovable. Perhaps only those who are well advanced in the practice of works of love should hope to be blessed with a growth in the brightness of eternity's light that will enable them to see steadily what makes some of their neighbors lovable. If this is so, only those who first perform works of love because they are commanded should hope eventually to be able to perform them because they have come to be motivated and hence empowered by a perception of the neighbor's inner glory. In other words, we may hope to perfect our love of our less attractive neighbors to the point at which we practice works of love in the right way only if we begin by practicing such works of love for duty's sake in response to the divine command. On this view, dutiful obedience to the divine command is an essential part of practice in Christianity. Practice in Christianity is, of course, hard work. According to Kierkegaard, God requires each of us to live an "essentially strenuous life" (WL 370). How far can strenuous effort get any of us? Even with divine assistance, can anyone get to the point at which he or she is, as Kierkegaard thinks we all should be, "completely and wholly transformed into simply being an active power in the hands of God?" (279). Is it possible for sinful humans to do better, with divine assistance, than occasionally bridging the moral gap?

Kierkegaard begins the conclusion of *Works of Love* by introducing the Apostle John, who says, "Beloved, let us love one another" (I John 4:7). He observes that "you do not hear the rigorousness of duty in these words; the apostle does not say, 'You *shall* love one another'" (WL 375). But Kierkegaard insists that the command to love is not altered in the slightest way, least of all by an apostle. So he infers that "the change then can be only that the person who loves becomes more and more intimate with the commandment, becomes as one with the commandment, which he loves" (375–6). To be sure, the apostle speaks so gently that it is almost as if it had been forgotten that Christianity commands love. "If, however, you forget that it is the apostle of love who is speaking, you misunderstand him," Kierkegaard warns us, "because such words are not the beginning of the discourse about love but are the completion." He concludes:

Therefore, we do not dare to speak this way. That which is truth on the lips of the veteran and perfected apostle could in the mouth of a beginner very easily be a philandering by which he would leave the school of the commandment much too soon and escape the "school-yoke." (WL 376)

With the possible exception of the greatest saints and other holy people, all of us are, I think, to be included in the "we" who should listen to the apostle's words but not dare to make them our own.

The reason we would go astray if we tried to escape the school-yoke of the love command is not hard to understand. We are sinful; we cannot expect to close the moral gap even with divine assistance. In our lives eternity does not cast its light on everyone at all times. We cannot rest assured that all those for whom we are called upon to perform works of love will appear lovable to us; we may never discern the inner glory in our worst enemies or in the wretched of the earth. Nor can we have confidence that our perception of the image of God in others will be continuous rather than intermittent, and so we cannot count on this perception being present whenever it is needed to motivate works of love performed for those in whom we fitfully see the inner glory. The image of God, moreover, is all too often too faintly discerned to be motivationally sufficient for those works of love that demand great self-denial, and so we need to be able to rely on the "You *shall*" of the love command for strong and steady backup motivation. We will have to mobilize the motive of duty on many occasions as a substitute for or a supplement to the motive provided by perceived inner glory if we are to obey the love command to the best of our abilities. Unlike the perfected apostle, we are not as one with the love commandment; even if we respect its demands, we do not love them.

I think Kierkegaard assesses with sober realism the responses human beings in their sinful condition are apt to make to the radical demands of his agapeistic Christian ethics. He does not puff up their natural capacities or overestimate what they are likely to achieve even with divine assistance. I see cause, however, for melancholy in the fact that most of us cannot count on getting beyond the elementary grades in the love command's school during our earthly lives.

II. PRACTICE IN CHRISTIANITY

The only place in *Practice in Christianity* where Kierkegaard speaks in his own name is in the editor's preface. There he tells us that "the requirement for being a Christian is forced up by the pseudonymous author to a supreme ideality" (*PC* 7). Anti-Climacus, the pseudonymous author, ratchets up Christianity's moral demand by spelling out what we would have to do in order to imitate Christ.

There is, of course, nothing new in the general idea that the life a Christian is called upon to lead is a life that imitates the life of Christ. As Kierkegaard was well aware, Thomas à Kempis's *The Imitation of Christ* presents the life of Christ as a pattern for the lives of his followers to imitate. So Anti-Climacus is speaking from within an important tradition in Christian ethical thought when he tells us that "Christ's life here on earth is the paradigm; I and every Christian are to strive to model our lives in likeness to it" (107). Likeness, however, is a matter of degree, and it would not be very difficult to lead a life that is only a little like Christ's life. The demand becomes more stringent as the degree of likeness increases. According to Anti-Climacus, the imitator of Christ leads a life that is as much like his life as possible, and so "to be an imitator means that your life has as much similarity to his as is possible for a human life to have" (106). Hence, to require that Christians be imitators of Christ is indeed to raise the requirement for being a Christian to the highest level of stringency or ideality. Forcing the requirement up to this level can only widen the gap between what is demanded of a Christian and what a Christian can achieve by the exercise of natural capacities. Yet Anti-Climacus insists that "only the imitator is the true Christian" (254).

The true Christian has become a contemporary of Christ. According to Anti-Climacus, "as long as there is a believer, this person, in order to have become that, must have been and as a believer must be just as contemporary with Christ's presence as his contemporaries were" (*PC* 9). He tells us that contemporaneity with Christ is the condition of faith and, more sharply defined, is faith. The Christ with whom the Christian is to become contemporaneous is not the glorious Christ of the Second Coming but the crucified Christ of history. This Christ is, Anti-Climacus claims, "the sign of offense and the object of faith, the lowly man, yet the Savior and Redeemer of the human race" (9–10). But Christ should not be judged by the results of his life in history. We know from history that Christ taught a moral doctrine that has had a great impact on Western civilization and that he founded one of the world's great religions. Even those of us who are not Christians can admire him for leading a life that had such historical results. Christ's actual contemporaries, however, had no such knowledge, and so the believer who has become his contemporary does not use such knowledge in judging him. As Anti-Climacus puts it, "he does not want to be judged humanly by the results of his life, that is, he is and wants to be the sign of offense and the object of faith; to judge him according to the results of his life is blasphemy" (23). Becoming a contemporary of Christ is thus a way for the Christian to filter out historical knowledge that should not form the basis of one's response to him.

Anyone who becomes a contemporary of Christ will have to come to grips with Christ in his lowliness and abasement. This is meant to teach a lesson. "Christ freely willed to be the lowly one," Anti-Climacus says, "and although his purpose was to save mankind, yet he also wanted to express what *the truth* would have to suffer and what the truth must suffer in every generation" (PC 34–5). Hence imitators of Christ must be prepared and willing to suffer. If their lives are to be as similar to the life of Christ as is humanly possible, they will suffer in a way akin to his suffering. Anti-Climacus explains: "To suffer in a way akin to Christ's suffering is not to put up patiently with the inescapable, but it is to suffer evil at the hands of people because as a Christian or in being a Christian one wills and endeavors to do the good: thus one could avoid this suffering by giving up willing the good" (173). To be sure, not every Christian who persists in endeavoring to do good will be killed for it as Christ was, but every Christian should anticipate ill treatment from the world. "If you become contemporary with him in his abasement and this sight moves you to want to suffer with him," Anti-Climacus maintains, "there will be opportunity enough for you to be able to suffer in a way akin to his suffering – that he will guarantee you – and even if the opportunity is not given, it is in any case not so much a question of opportunity as of the willingness to want to suffer in a way akin to his suffering" (172). At the very least, then, imitators of Christ must be willing, as he was, to suffer for trying to do good, even if many of them may, as it happens, endure little or no suffering on that account.

Coming to grips with Christ in his lowliness and abasement also involves being "halted by the possibility of offense" (PC 39). Anti-Climacus describes with considerable wit how typical people of various sorts from Kierkegaard's age might have been offended if they had actually been Christ's contemporaries. The sagacious and sensible person might say: "What has he done about his future? Nothing. Does he have a permanent job? No. What are his prospects? None"

(43). The clergyman might denounce him as "an impostor and dem-
agogue" (46). The philosopher might criticize him for lacking a system and having only "a few aphorisms, some maxims, and a couple
of parables, which he goes on repeating or revising, whereby he
blinds the masses" (48). The sagacious statesman, the solid citizen,
and the scoffer might revile him in other ways; but no one can arrive at mature Christian faith without first confronting the possibility of offense. "The possibility of offense is the crossroad, or it is like
standing at the crossroad. From the possibility of offense, one turns
either to offense or to faith, but one never comes to faith except
from the possibility of offense" (81). Thus imitators of Christ can
also count on being found offensive by those who have chosen to
turn to offense rather than faith.

Imitators of Christ should, therefore, anticipate suffering for trying to do good and expect to be found offensive. Nonetheless, the
Christian ethical demand is that we be imitators and not mere admirers of Christ. What is the difference between an admirer and an
imitator? "An imitator *is* or strives *to be* what he admires," Anti-
Climacus says, "and an admirer keeps himself personally detached,
consciously or unconsciously does not discover that what is admired
involves a claim upon him, to be or at least to strive to be what is admired" (*PC* 241). There are circumstances in which mere admiration
is entirely proper. For Anti-Climacus, mere admiration is appropriate "whenever it is true that I am prevented by a condition beyond
my control from being able to resemble that which is admired even
if I would like to" (241). Had Christ come into the world in the lofti-
ness of his glory, we could have done nothing but admire him; he
would in that case have had no claim on us to be or strive to
be like him. However, Christ came into the world, Anti-Climacus
thinks, with the purpose "of being *the prototype,* of leaving foot-
prints for the person who wanted to join him, who then might become an imitator" (238). For this reason, he came into the world in
lowliness and abasement. What is more, Christ had only those conditions to offer anyone who joined him, and they are conditions on
which no mere admirer would want to join him. For Anti-Climacus,
the exact conditions offered are these: "to become just as poor, despised, insulted, mocked, and if possible even a little more, considering that in addition one was an adherent of such a despised individual, whom every sensible person shunned" (241). The imitator

must be ready and willing to join Christ even on those conditions. Kirmmse takes Anti-Climacus to be committed to the claim that imitation "will certainly (or almost certainly) call forth persecution, suffering, or even martyrdom at the hands of society's protectors of 'reality.'"[23] At any rate, imitators must be willing to endure such things, even if it is not certain that they will occur to all those who choose to be imitators.

Two further contrasts between mere admiration and imitation deserve some attention. One concerns the way in which admiration can undermine an adequate response to the moral demand that we imitate Christ. For Anti-Climacus, the moral demand is a matter of "the universally human or that which every human being, unconditionally every human being, is capable of, that which is not linked to any condition save that which is in everyone's power, the universally human, that is, the ethical, that which every human being shall and therefore also presumably can do" (PC 242). Confronted with the moral demand, we are to act promptly to satisfy it; pausing for admiration is inappropriately evasive. Anti-Climacus says: "If I know a man whom I must esteem because of his unselfishness, self-sacrifice, magnanimity, etc., then I am not to admire but am supposed to be like him; I am not to deceive myself into thinking that it [admiration] is something meritorious on my part, but on the contrary I am to understand that it is merely the invention of my sloth and spinelessness; I am to resemble him and immediately begin my effort to resemble him" (242). One who stops to admire Christ in personal detachment is really hanging back from beginning the immense task of imitating Christ.

The other contrast focuses on the way in which the admirer refuses the Christian moral demand. According to Anti-Climacus, "the admirer will make no sacrifices, renounce nothing, give up nothing earthly, will not transform his life, will not be what is admired, will not let his life express it – but in words, phrases, assurances he is inexhaustible about how highly he prizes Christianity" (PC 252). Unlike the admirer, the imitator, who also acknowledges in words the truth of Christianity, acts decisively to obey "Christian teaching about ethics and obligation, Christianity's requirement to die to the world, to surrender the earthly, its requirement of self-denial" (252). And, Anti-Climacus adds, mere admirers are sure to become exasperated with an imitator.

Practice in Christianity certainly does not narrow the moral gap. In comparison to *Works of Love*, perhaps it even widens the gap. All or almost all of us will fail to imitate the life of Christ as fully as is possible in the circumstances of our own lives. Some will be content to remain mere admirers of Christ. Others will imitate Christ only when it does not cost them too much. There will be those who are unwilling to offend or exasperate their friends and acquaintances. Some will draw the line beyond which they will not go in imitating Christ at the point where they would be insulted and mocked for doing so; others will draw it at the point where they would be poor and despised; yet others will draw it at the point where they would be persecuted and martyred. Few if any of us will draw no line at all.

Like Kant's moral law, Kierkegaard's interpretation of the love commandment and Anti-Climacus's understanding of the imitation of Christ set the moral standard so high that it is almost inevitable that we will fail to live up to it. In this respect, they do what St. Paul thought the Mosaic Law did. As Kierkegaard puts this point, "the Law with its requirement became everyone's downfall because they were not what it required and through it only learned to know sin" (*WL* 99). It is this feature of Kant's moral theory, I think, that is being alluded to when Kirmmse claims Kierkegaard "indicates that what Moses was to St. Paul, Kant can be to us."[24] To this astute remark, I would only add that Kierkegaard and Anti-Climacus can play the same role.

When one reflects hard on the stringency of the accounts of morality proposed by Kant, Kierkegaard, and Anti-Climacus, one becomes tempted to reduce the demand. One way of doing so in response to Anti-Climacus would be to deny that the requirement to imitate Christ as fully as possible in one's own life is universally human. Maybe it would make sense to think of it as binding only on religious virtuosi with special vocations to saintliness. Another way would be to insist that the highest level of ideality is the realm of the supererogatory and lies beyond the domain of the obligatory. There is, however, another alternative open to the Kierkegaardian. As Gregor Malantschuk has pointed out, the Kierkegaardian might acknowledge that this is the requirement and then have recourse to grace.[25] If we are required to imitate Christ as fully as possible in our own lives, recourse to grace may be needed twice. Perhaps gracious divine assistance will be needed, at least sometimes, to help us bridge the moral gap when imitating Christ is particularly difficult. Certainly gracious divine forgiveness and mercy will be needed in response to our many failures to imitate Christ as we should. It seems to me that what makes Kierkegaard's ethics of commanded love and Anti-Climacus's ethics of required imitation of Christ forms of the second ethics that can deal with the manifestation of sin is precisely that they allow for the propriety of having recourse to grace because they are embedded in a larger Christian worldview.

Both these forms of Christian ethics are likely to look harsh and inhuman if viewed from outside a Christian worldview or if recourse to grace is disallowed. I believe this only shows that they contain within themselves the possibility of offense. Kierkegaard, I am sure, would regard this as confirmation of the view that they are authentic forms of Christian ethics. I agree with this view. My conclusion is that Kierkegaard's ethics of commanded love and Anti-Climacus's ethics of required imitation of Christ are two authentic forms of Christian ethics, powerfully and sometimes movingly presented either in Kierkegaard's own voice or through the pseudonymous author whose voice was closest to his own.[26]

NOTES

1 An interesting recent contribution to the scholarly debate is Ronald M. Green, *Kierkegaard and Kant; The Hidden Debt* (Albany, N.Y.: State University of New York Press, 1992).

2 Bruce H. Kirmmse, *Kierkegaard in Golden Age Denmark* (Bloomington and Indianapolis: Indiana University Press, 1990), p. 306.

3 John E. Hare, *The Moral Gap: Kantian Ethics, Human Limits, and God's Assistance* (Oxford: Clarendon Press, 1996), p. 1.

4 Immanuel Kant, *Religion within the Limits of Reason Alone*, trans. Theodore M. Greene and Hoyt H. Hudson (New York: Harper and Row, 1960), p. 24.

5 Ibid., p. 32.

6 Ibid., p. 46.

7 Ibid.

8 Ibid., p. 43.

9 Ibid., p. 47.

10 Ibid., p. 40.

11 Ibid., p. 179.

12 Ibid., p. 37.

13 Ibid., p. 90–1.

14 Ibid., p. 91.

15 I use *The New American Bible*.

16 Alastair Hannay, *Kierkegaard: The Arguments of the Philosophers* (London: Routledge and Kegan Paul, 1982), pp. 242, 254.

17 Kirmmse, *Kierkegaard in Golden Age Denmark*, p. 312.

18 Robert Brown, *Analyzing Love* (Cambridge University Press, 1987), p. 6.

19 Aristotle *Nicomachean Ethics* 1058a10–11.

20 Aristotle *Nicomachean Ethics* 1056a14–16.

21 Quoted in L. E. Goodman, *God of Abraham* (New York and Oxford: Oxford University Press, 1996), p. 109.

22 Kirmmse, *Kierkegaard in Golden Age Denmark*, p. 308.

23 Ibid., p. 396.

24 Ibid., p. 309.

25 Gregor Malantschuk, *Kierkegaard's Thought*, ed. and trans. Howard V. Hong and Edna H. Hong (Princeton: Princeton University Press, 1971), p. 365.

26 In my discussion of *Works of Love* in this essay I make use, with significant revisions, of some material from my "The Divine Command Ethics in Kierkegaard's *Works of Love*," in *Faith, Freedom, and Responsibility*, ed. Daniel Howard-Snyder and Jeffrey Jordon (Lanham, Md.: Rowman and Littlefield, 1996).

15 Religious dialectics and Christology

It is frequently said that if Christ came to the world now he would once again be crucified. This is not entirely true. The world has changed; it is now immersed in "understanding." Therefore Christ would be ridiculed, treated as a mad man, but a mad man at whom one laughs. . . . I now understand better and better the original and profound relationship I have with the comic, and this will be useful to me in illuminating Christianity.

–*Journals and Papers* (*Pap.* X^1 A 187)

I. HISTORICAL SITUATION

At the beginning of the nineteenth century, lived religiousness and piety were no longer a matter of course in the intellectual circles of Europe. Schleiermacher's early work, *On Religion: Speeches to Its Cultured Despisers*, signals this shift, as does the religion that is at once criticized and philosophically defended in Hegel's concept of Absolute Spirit.[1] The opposition of rational enlightenment to non-conceptual (religious) revelation such as Kant and Lessing had carried out with exemplary success at the end of the eighteenth century lay like a long shadow over every effort of the subsequent period to present faith in God and religion – or even the core of Christianity, reconciliation – at all *argumentatively*.

Kierkegaard's own epoch, the middle of the nineteenth century, escalates the problem yet again, this time in opposition to the stamp that Romanticism and Idealism had given to apologetics. Feuerbach

Translated by Dennis Beach

and Marx made explicit an implicit and inevitably atheistic separation from traditional, orthodox Christian dogma and applied it to the practical realm, rendering the critique of (Christian) religion politically and socially effective. But the signature of the spirit of the age that distinguishes Kierkegaard's epoch from all preceding ones is its impulse to probe assiduously in the present the *post*-Romantic and *post*-Idealist crisis, and to carry out this inquiry not only in academic fields and intellectual conceptions. This characteristic allows Kierkegaard's epoch to be a model not only for modernity but also for the postmodern situation that persists today. Consciousness of the crisis in religion was refined and dispersed by various fluctuations in the intellectual and social frameworks; it was sometimes exacerbated and sometimes inhibited by the force of epochal developments, but confrontation with it was unavoidable. In any case, these processes made the conscious motives and implications of human thought increasingly explicit in the spheres of both practical and theoretical knowledge. The incisive dilemma of the crisis, however, remained the question of how this knowledge could be harmonized with the circumstances in which people sought to live responsibly, and, again, how all of this could be integrated with the conceptual and experiential capabilities of these same people. The impetus and focus – both for modernity and afterward – lay in the critical coordination of science, morality, and religion.

From this point on, however, religion had to be understood in two ways. On the one hand, it is the historical and communal expression of the worldview and orientation of a given time (and thus a concept valid for all religions with such a tradition and function). On the other hand, starting with Kierkegaard, it is more importantly the always personal (*existential*) appropriation and obligation of the human condition in humankind's *self-relation*, which, as the destiny of this relation, presupposes relation to God in principle. This latter meaning is more exactly expressed by the term "religiousness."

II. RELIGIOUSNESS

Kierkegaard did not develop his conception of religiousness with a historical, theological, or dogmatic intention. However, he always places this dimension of the problem foremost in the presuppositions of thinking that characterize his age when he wants to highlight with fullest fidelity the urgency of the existential appropriation and obligation of personal religiousness. This sought-after fidelity quickly becomes dialectical in the process of appropriation. On the one hand, a merely personal event stands opposed to its universalized presentation, just as the systematically elusive concretion of individual life stands opposed to the abstraction of propositions about human life in general. On the other hand, this universalization in thought and language can in no way be avoided – else the existential personality would be wholly impossible to understand and cut off from all communication. Kierkegaard is compelled by this necessity to use the indirect means of access afforded by the literary disguise of the "religious author," an artifice that is intentionally misleading on the surface but at the same time conducive to true understanding (*SV*¹ XIII 524ff).[2]

The (existential) concretization of religion that always emanates from the biographical details of Kierkegaard's life and toward which his entire work ultimately aims is the Christian piety drawn from Lutheran theology and Pietism: the paradoxical experience – at once tormenting and liberating – of sin and forgiveness in the image of the crucified Christ. In order to shield this basic configuration from all the misunderstandings of his age – from romantic, idealist, atheistic, political, ecclesiastical, missionary, and so on – Kierkegaard erected above this foundation the divergent and thus complementary complex of the pseudonymous polemical texts addressed to intellectuals and *Upbuilding Discourses* appealing directly to human proximity.

Johannes Climacus's famous distinction in *Concluding Unscientific Postscript* (cf. *SV*¹ VII, 485ff) between Religiousness A and B, that is, between the universal religious dialectic of a person's relationship to his or her eternal destiny (A) and the specifically Christian (paradoxical) dialectic based on the connection of this relational destiny with the historical contingency of the New Testament Jesus (B), is a consequence of Kierkegaard's strategy as a religious author of both safeguarding Christianity and providing an exacting delineation of what it means to be Christian. Talk about Christianity in the strict sense must first focus on the extremity of the impassioned struggle for genuine, ineluctable self-examination in one's relation to life and to God. This struggle is especially characterized as *paradoxical* because of the polemical separation of

Christology (of God in history [cf. *Philosophical Fragments, SV*¹ IV
250ff, 271]) from literally *all* other approaches: from the religious
and societal (civic) approaches of contemporary "Christendom," as
well as from the intellectual trends of historical or speculative academic theology. Moreover, despite Religiousness A's marked differentiation from Religiousness B, it is nevertheless the necessary presupposition of the latter! This condition does not contravene the
just-mentioned rupture with all other avenues of approach, for
Kierkegaard does not maintain that there is a smooth transition between them, but only wants to note consistently a necessary condition of every existential understanding: impassioned self-relation
without any external constraint.

It is *Upbuilding Discourses* that explicitly tread the path of Religiousness A, and in so doing, at first consciously avoid Christological categories – omitting even to speak the name of Christ. At
their center stands the eloquent endeavor to focus sympathetically,
with full cognizance of human nature, on that which can be said to
count generally as the phenomenological realm of Religiousness A
(and therefore also as its definition): That what we seek most of all
in life, what we seek with all passion of feeling, thought and action,
can in no way be either brought under the control or placed at the
disposal of any human being.

A perfect example of Religiousness A is the 1845 discourse, "On
the Occasion of a Confession."³

1. The discourse invites one to confession, and the proper situational mood of confession is that of "stillness," in which the external world with all its distinctions and intentions disappears, so that
the differences between the human and the world are canceled *sub
specie aeternitatis:* "Whoever says that this stillness does not exist
is merely making noise" (179). "Seek God," the theme of the discourse (183), becomes identical with unreserved self-surrender to
this stillness. An argument or desire to excuse oneself from this situation must perforce appear as a suppression of its inexorable
power, drowning out its stillness with doubt. This circularity in the
perspective of God does not offer itself explicitly as an argument for
the reality of God; yet ultimately, in the pathos of the discourse, the
insistent defense of this structure of the confessional experience
amounts to this: There is a perspective (that of God), and a situation coupled with it (that of confession), in which rich and poor,

guilty and innocent, fortunate and unfortunate, and so on, are rela-
tivized and neutralized to the point of a reciprocal inversion: "The
injured party possesses the most" of something – namely, "forgiveness" – that "someone else needs" (180). The "emptiness" that
here appears to the worldly, human perspective, "the infinite nothing" (181) marks the very turning point that was sought: Standing
before God in stillness and purity is "becoming a sinner" (182). In
this way the decisive reversal takes place – in the situation of stillness and the perspective of God: The person who seeks God is the
one who is transformed, "so that he himself can become the place
where God in truth is" (189).

The Lutheran doctrine of justification – *simul iustus et pecca-
tor* – is renewed in the existential situational mood and its eloquent
insistence on precisely this "moment" (189). The simultaneity of
"fearing" and "finding" God in this moment becomes the condition
of the only acceptable experience of God, an experience here illustrated. This grounding of the basic situation of religion echoes
Luther's oft-repeated guiding question for the interpretation of the
Ten Commandments in the *Small Catechism* of 1529: "We should
fear and love God!" Only here, under the conditions of the nineteenth century, God and "nothingness" have a situationally intensive correspondence: the "nothingness" of self-feeling becomes a
"sign" of the proximity of God (194). In contrast, all universal, objective, philosophical, or ecclesiastical frameworks, which in
Kierkegaard's time could no longer safeguard either the divine or religiousness, retreat completely into the background.

2. The experiential situation *sub specie aeternitatis* sought in this
manner has to become at the same time a human-religious basis, a
point of departure – although it is hardly possible, in keeping with
its nature, to conceive of this as such with full precision. Kierkegaard specifies a triple step: first, adoration as "sighing without
words," unclear and ambiguous; second, the increasing awareness of
God in adventitious "thought"; and third, the thought that "[finds]
the words" (183). But Kierkegaard's discourse in no way thus en-
dorses the preeminence of words, the preeminence of rationality and
concepts in opposition to the emotionally stronger imprecision of
"sighs." The invoked absurdity of the Zeitgeist consists precisely in
this: That without deliberation, it sought to draw forth rational communication – as the "highest" communication – from the "still-

ness" (185ff). This stillness begins, however, with the conceptually ambiguous and elusive "sighs of adoration"! Hegel's critique of the "beautiful soul"[4] testifies to the philosophical disparagement of "religion of feeling" and its objectless and conceptless "yearning." Kierkegaard's discourses, however, seek human proximity also *prior to* its conceptual and systematic evaluation, namely, in "a sigh . . . , if the thought of God is only to shed a twilight glow over existence" (183). It is precisely here that the discourse unfolds its own aesthetic and religious power.

3. If the next level of understanding is to make explicit where human seeking – under the condition of *stillness* – ultimately finds its object, it is clear that the "highest" goods among conceivable goods is not determinate and is thus not something to be aimed at. Instead, fully in accord with the mode of seeking and desiring, it is "the unknown – and this good is God" (185). The response to this unknown is fulfilled then not with any being or having, but rather in the mode of "wonder, and wonder is immediacy's sense of God and . . . the beginning of all deeper understanding" (185). The discourse intends to sketch in due course how such "deeper understanding" can be effected and how it is structured, so that here such conceptual labor remains better hidden for the sake of presenting the value of the universal human experience with greater imaginative power. The human-religious universality of this experiential value is in a sense presupposed; it can be verified only in the individual experience of a concretely lived life. This is the crux of the whole discourse; its address to the individual "listener" who, before God, becomes an individual "alone in the whole world" (190) demonstrates the hermeneutic turn of the religious dialectic. The presupposition of God is not controlled by humankind, but shines forth in the conditions of the experience of confession, in its stillness, individualization, and "wonder" in the face of the authentically "unknown."

In referring to the "object" of impassioned seeking, the discourse consciously avoids the concept that the pseudonymous author of *Philosophical Fragments*, Johannes Climacus, had employed: the *absolute paradox* (cf. *SV*[1] IV 204ff). The discourse is not concerned with concept and object as such, but only with the human relation to the unknown *summum bonum:* whether a person "is getting closer . . . or further away" from this unknown good (185). How is such a relation to be more closely determined? Kierkegaard gives two answers: first a basic description of religious wonder itself, and then its development in the three stages of the dialectic.

3.1. The basic description of an indeterminate immediacy can be undertaken in two directions. First, in the direction of deepening its immediacy, that is, in taking advantage of its independence from precise knowledge and fixed practical goals in the sense that it is a unitary, qualitative state, a *feeling*. Schleiermacher's definition of *piety* fits with this approach, insofar as he generally highlights the legitimacy of "feeling" in opposition to metaphysics ("knowing") and ethics ("acting").[5] Furthermore, he understands the specific "determination" of religious feeling – "simply being subject to . . . awareness of God"[6] – in no way as an object-related consciousness, but rather as a "pure dependence,"[7] that is, as a qualitative emotional state. Kierkegaard's theology, by contrast, consciously avoids the concept of *feeling*, and thus strikes out in the other direction appropriate to a fundamental description of religiousness. It does not seek to deepen the originary circumstance of religion, but to grasp its relationality immediately in its ambivalence: "Wonder is an ambivalent state of mind containing both fear and blessedness" (185; cf. 189). This means that Kierkegaard agrees with Schleiermacher in the strict differentiation between religious wonder and "knowing" (cf. 187f); however, in opposition to Schleiermacher, he does not want to begin with the unity of a basic (religious) feeling, but with the ambivalence of "blessedness in fear and trembling" (185; cf. Phil. 2:12) that stems from Lutheran piety. Two questions will return later: Why cannot this starting point (again in contrast to Schleiermacher), for its purity's sake, be conceived primarily as a community feeling? Why is another relation to "action" (cf. 201) implied in the existential situation of such individuation?

3.2. The developmental forms of religious immediacy or wonder proceed in three stages. The first of these stages will be described as a pagan-religious nature relation (185f), in that the zeal for the unknown becomes confused with the unknown itself without being able to see through this confusion. Religion and poetry are two sides of the same appearance: "Idolatry purified is the poetic." In other words, the emotional world of wonder itself becomes, in the medium of feeling, quasi-objective – as polytheism in the history of religion, and as poetry in the epoch of Enlightenment. For both, a definition of God as "the inexplicable all of existence" (186) would suffice.

In the second stage the subjective and the objective sides of wonder separate from one another, exactly as in Hegel's phenomenological dialectic. The impassioned relationship is like a *striving* toward the ever-retreating unknown (187); the freedom of this striving is directed toward the infinite, which, however, does not allow of comprehension and withdraws as "fate" (187). The analyses of the pseudonymous author Vigilius Haufniensis (cf. *CA* III 2; *SV*^{1} IV, 366ff) bring to greater precision than the discourse does the idea that the anxiety-producing obscurity of the concept of fate can only be surmounted if the categories of guilt and sin, which are related to individual persons, intervene. In the face of God, *striving* by itself can never secure a return; it can neither reach God nor founder on him.

The third stage escalates the ambivalence of the possibility of insight into religious wonder to confuse the subjective and objective sides on still higher levels. Since the goal of wonder would be attained when "what is sought" is found, when "the enchantment is gone" (187), the passion of relation to the unknown would also vanish. Because the relation as such, in the sense of the human-religious foundation, cannot diminish to nothing, its appearance as "nothing" (187) must be either a misunderstanding or an expression of despair. This appearance is misunderstanding if the knower erroneously supplants the relation to the unknown with quantitative definitions of "knowledge" (187f): The unambiguous world of one who thinks all is known already or can be known leaves no room for either wonder or the unknown. In the second case – and in the design of the discourse, this is, no matter how hidden, the unique enlightenment *sub specie aeternitatis* – the appearance that the relation diminishes to nothing is an expression of despair if, in being "deceived" by knowledge, the actual human process of *appropriation* (187f) falls apart. The confusion arises from classification of the unknown as alien when the individual nevertheless "has what is sought" in the sense that he is in danger of "losing" it and thus in his "despair" suffers from this loss (189). In turn, this suffering is the best sign of the renewed wonder at wonder itself (188f). The dialectic of destiny and loss, the "ambivalent state of mind" of "fear and blessedness" (cf. 185) is thus taken up into the third stage describing the basis of human religion. One reaches again the religious

dialectic, in which, from the perspective of God, "the seeker himself is changed" (189). The reversal of recognition from fraudulent
"knowledge" to existential transformation in "fear and blessedness" is the sign of relation to God: the sinner before God (193).
Here it ought to be simply acknowledged, not considered an objection, that "understanding" meets its limit insofar as it cannot comprehend the abiding wonder and the ongoing action of appropriation
(191). Only thus will the path be cleared for heightened wonder.

3.3. If in its renunciation of *knowledge* this religious dialectic remains close to Schleiermacher's definition of *piety*, the clear difference lies nevertheless in what Kierkegaard always sees as the fundamental ambivalence of possible forms of renunciation,
misunderstanding, anxiety, and doubt. Kierkegaard emphasizes the
unconditionality of the irreplaceable individual expressly to protect
this fundamental situation of "fear and blessedness" that is founded
upon "fear and trembling" (185, 192). It is not simply that the religious situation concerns the "individual human being" in contrast
to "humanity in general" (194); rather, Kierkegaard, in his perception of the sociocultural and political crisis of his time, is able to regard and reject social forms decisively as mere externals. They are
seen as a "crowd," the homogenized "common harmony of equals,"
the anonymous "course of world-history" (195ff), and the "diversions of others" (200). In other words, social forms are to be avoided
as purely quantitative, unhelpful reproductions that dissipate the
existential gravity of the individual's primordial experience of relation to God in *stillness*.

The theological rationale for this restriction of human social
forms to mass phenomena is again that Kierkegaard does not start (as
does Schleiermacher) with the fundamental human-religious phenomenon of "wonder" as the unitary ground or transcendental condition of possibility for all further differentiations and determinations, but with it as an intensification of experience situated directly
in the conflict between the human and the world. On the other hand,
the fundamental experience of "fear and blessedness" must be freed
from its worldly perspective (poor and rich, happy and unfortunate,
young and old, etc.) so that it can discover at the same time, in the
same experience, the perspective of God. Because both positions are
to be valid – the conscious proximity to everyday experience as well
as the perspectival distantiation from this – the relevant religious-

ness must be concentrated on the impassioned self-experience of the individual, and only on this. For Kierkegaard, everything else would signify an inappropriate slackening of the existential situation.

Upbuilding Discourses before 1846/47 address this strategic duality of external world and existential seriousness with evenhandedness and stylistic charm, while the early pseudonymous texts and especially the later *Christian Discourses* and the writings of Anti-Climacus shift to open and harsh polemic. For this reason it is fitting – and here is the further point of differentiation from Schleiermacher – that the immediate ambivalence of the existential situation evoked by the discourse is always pursued with a view to the decisiveness and the seriousness of a practical situation in which the basic religious feeling of "wonder" before the "unknown" is not only encountered but has to guarantee its own significance. *Not* to define abstractly the relation between God and self means for Kierkegaard that he must conceive of it solely as a practical situation of decision. This is what human religiousness enjoins in the dialectic it exhibits: "In regard to what is essential *to be able* essentially means *to be able to do* it" (200). *Appropriation* thus means that one "essentially appropriates the essential only by doing it" (201). The significance of *knowledge* and intellectual decisions is thereby neutralized, and the significance of *ethics* is taken up into the self-relation as the defining perspective for action.

III. CHRISTOLOGY

Kierkegaard's particular conception of Religiousness B in *Concluding Unscientific Postscript* responds in a new way to both basic problems of modern Christology: (1) How, with the patristic and scholastic (Aristotelian-Thomistic) ontology of substances no longer at our disposal, can we still speak in any meaningful way of *one* divine-human *person* with two *natures*?[8] (2) How, presupposing historical investigation, at least as it was developed as standard by Protestant theology, can the authority of biblical texts, from, for example, the miracle stories to the resurrection of Jesus, be in any way still effectively represented?[9]

Kierkegaard does not provide a direct scholarly discussion of these two questions, but his entire work should be read as a beacon lighting the way to a response. If Religiousness A must be conceived solely as an impassioned relationship and not as somehow "objective," this is even more true for the paradoxical Religiousness B, and not only in regard to the crucial dogmatic question of the doctrine of reconciliation, but even in regard to the historical aspect of the New Testament. Kierkegaard solves this problem by undermining its legitimation: there is no "objective" means of access, in the sense of modern historical "objectivity," to an adequate understanding of Jesus Christ, not even of his crucifixion. Johannes Climacus expresses it thus: "One wants to consider objectively – that the God was crucified – an event that, when it occurred, did not permit even the temple to be objective, for its curtain tore, did not even permit the dead to remain objective, for they rose up from their graves" (CUP; cf. SV¹ VII 238). Both the difficulty and the interest of this argument derive from the fact that historical objectivity is immediately obstructed by the dogmatic presupposition of the "God-man," yet this presupposition itself is not advanced as quasi-objective but by referring back to the narrative of the New Testament: "And the curtain of the temple was torn in two from top to bottom" (Mk 15:38). While Kierkegaard balked at the historical research of his time, he anticipated and made use of one of its twentieth-century conclusions: the testimony of the gospels is to be understood as a literary form, and therein lies its power. The meaning of the "God-man" can therefore only be reached and rediscovered in this way, namely, in opposition to historicizing and objectivizing misunderstandings.

It is to this task of a reconceptualized Christology that the programmatic concerns of Johannes Climacus are dedicated, as well as the ever more explicitly Christologically elaborated discourses. *Upbuilding Discourses in Various Spirits* (1847) contain in their third part "The Gospel of Sufferings," characterized as a "Christian Discourse." Here Kierkegaard for the first time in a discourse goes beyond the foundational human-religious experience and invokes the authority of the New Testament (cf. *Pap.* VIII¹ A 6f; *JP* §638). What does this shift to the sharper "pathos" of Religiousness B (cf. *SV*¹ VII 485ff.) signify? This shift to the Christian paradox of reconciliation in Christ as a category invested with authority (*Pap.* VIII¹ A 11; *JP* §3089)? The fourth of the *Christian Discourses* offers an exemplary response to the Christological questions.[10]

1. That religious passion becomes "care" is a motif already contained in the discourse on confession of 1845 (*SV*ᴵ V 192). For in the moment when the individual before God is transformed, the person, without changing place, shifts position: From the one who seeks, wondering in the face of the unknown, the person is transformed into the one who is found – who is, before God, estranged, guilty, a sinner – and thus attains the heightened level of wonder (*SV*ᴵ V 188, 191f, 195). However, *Christian Discourses* do not speak of concern and care, but turn without hesitation to "suffering." In other words, the condition of suffering is consistently inscribed into the religious dialectic. And here first do we find direct reference to Christ: The sharpening of scandal, the authority of God, and the exemplary suffering of Christ mark the passage to Religiousness B. In this, Kierkegaard is careful to employ theological thematics and terminology as traditionally as possible, not wanting to promote anything at all new, original, or purportedly modern. But why then introduce this manifestly deliberate and innovative difference between two basic forms of religiousness?

The dialectic *sub specie aeternitatis* developed in Religiousness A has a decisive weakness: Its experience of contingency is always only on one side, the human. The divine perspective *makes* the human side dialectic, rendering it incapable of controlling the unknown that it seeks. Instead, the human side finds itself always facing the divine in ever-intensified wonder. In Religiousness B, by contrast, the divine side is itself exposed to the contingency of the human side. It is subject to time, to the historical moment, to the most extreme human suffering, and precisely here are found the title and tidings of reconciliation. Kierkegaard's own response to the historical investigations of the New Testament and dogmatic Christology's loss of authority is to use the literary form of the discourses to sharpen and intensify the scandal of the crucified God-man. Kierkegaard radically transforms the medium: For the philosophical-historical argumentation employed by the current theology, he substitutes the poetically imaginative power of discourses; for conceptual-dogmatic propositions, he substitutes analysis of the existential situation of guilt and suffering, with the (Christian) paradox as the limit-concept. These two transformations are inspired by one and the same reaction to the powerful experience of contingency, an experience sharpened both historically and dogmatically in the nineteenth century. And this re-action is obligatory if God is to be perceived not merely *sub specie aeternitatis* but also *sub specie crucis.*

2. In this discourse on "The Joy of It That in Relation to God a Person Always Suffers as Guilty," themes and biblical texts are in-troduced both narratively and by means of a progressive argument: If one must place trust in the words of King Solomon by virtue of his royal position and experience, how much more ultimate is the authority to be attributed to the words of a thief on the cross, words spoken in the face of death: "We are receiving what our deeds have deserved, but this one has done nothing wrong" (Lk 23: 41; cf. 350). The conversion of king to thief and the shift from life to death endow the scene, the word, and the theme with the impression that here every merely historical reference would fail.

In the next stage, first the human-religious passion (following Religiousness A) must be traced through the situation familiar from the discourse on confession with regard for "concern about oneself" (350), the pain of "unhappy love" (350f), and finally the love of God (351), so that doubt as to whether or not God is really love can be seen to rest upon an unexamined and ultimately despairing misun-derstanding, namely, that one has lost impassioned love altogether (351f). Or, alternatively, so that the "becoming guilty" of impas-sioned (human) love must be understood in the context of *"God's love,* which always surpasses it and is its vindication. Doubt is con-quered only when the roles are assigned as follows: on the human side, guilt; on God's side, true love. Such an arrangement integrates the experience of shipwreck into the conception of one's relation to God, and this is "the joy" beyond all worldly limitations (352).

However, the transition to Religiousness B is only fully effected when the discourse lets the situation of being before God appear con-tradictory from God's side as well as from the human side. In other words, the contingency must be duplicated theologically. Kierke-gaard acknowledges two conditions in regard to Religiousness A that still permit one to doubt God's love. (1) If a person were wholly free from guilt (353), the whole dialectic of "joy" would be fruitless; God could hardly function as the vindication of "becoming guilty." Such a scenario can here be disregarded insofar as it always takes place in the misunderstanding and the evaporation of passion mentioned above.[11] (2) If one should enter into "the depth of this horror" (354), which stands in radical contradiction to "the idea that God is love" (353), the situation would no longer admit of a human solution. The latter is, however, precisely the crux of Christology: The only one who was without sin before God is he who must suffer this death for sinfulness. The God-forsakenness of the crucified Christ (354) is thus the most extreme conception of human contingency possible – embracing subjection to worldly and historical conditions, corporeality, the assumption of guilt, and the struggle with death – for it inscribes this human condition into the very idea of God.

Kierkegaard does not expound this train of thought as such, but rather uses a double criterion to guard it from invalid expropriation: Contingency in God cannot be "grasped" but only "believed" (354).

3. This opposition of "conceive" and "believe," coupled with the fact that the remainder of the discourse is wholly motivated by the Christological question concerning "doubt"[12] as to whether "God is love," makes it clear that this is a discourse *against theoretical doubt*. What *Upbuilding Discourses* achieved by the delimitation of knowledge can here succeed only by laying bare the existential devastation that would ensue were the theoretical doubt at all indulged. The project of asking what grounds there are that God should actually be love is flawed from its inception; it is "presumptuousness" (357, 362) because it wants to "demonstrate" that which is inherently contradictory (362). Whoever undertakes such a project is already finished with God (365ff). For, since it begins with an artificial abstraction that endlessly perpetuates itself, the existential situation falls apart, and thus neither logically nor existentially can the "conclusion" that is actually sought be found (369). It is clear, however, that the concerns of dogmatic theology completely displace such vain processes as are necessarily produced in the sphere of knowledge, thought, and doubt. Although the discourse does not state this in so many words, it nevertheless expresses it quite clearly. To be inherently "guilty" before God – this alone effectively destroys doubt (cf. 357, 368), and only the destruction of doubt casts the suffering individual without illusions back on him- or herself, but now as one *in relation to God*. This cannot be completely grasped, known, or theorized in terms of proof, but faith "grasps" it (357). Still, how is this mode of understanding to be understood?

4. What faith "grasps" is manifestly something double: (1) If the human being is always guilty – not just guilty here and there and

in this or that respect – then the question of guilt is decided once and for all, and it cannot and must not be as if this question were yet to be decided by reference to God. (2) What is "joyful" (358), what faith understands, lies in the living possibilities that open up, lies in the fact that, in the light of one's own guilt, *there must always be something to do.*" In place of hopelessness and anxiety for the future appear hope and activity (358ff; cf. 362). The ethical theme for the discourse on confession is resumed and amplified: the ethical is to be taken up into one's self-relation not only as the defining perspective for action but also as the "joyful" perspective. And, seen from within the religious dialectic of relation to God, it makes for joy precisely on the basis of inherent guilt before God. There is therefore no situation that cannot be overcome, for failure and guilt do not need to be repressed and God's love is no longer in question.

5. Moreover, a decisive intensification of the impassioned self-relation now becomes apparent because the repression of guilt or doubt concerning one's own situation (cf. 361f) is no longer a concern. Now an appropriate situational analogue is available: the humanly incomprehensible comparison with the "superhuman" suffering of the innocent crucified one (363). Thus does Christianity ground its "clarity" on this question: Although it may not be able to understand extreme and unfathomable suffering, nevertheless, in the image of the crucified one it can stand thoughtfully in the presence of such suffering. For one thing, there is certainly an "ever-yawning gap" between the (innocent) crucified one forsaken by God and all other (guilty) human suffering, even though it cannot be made transparent to human intelligence. At the same time, it must be acknowledged that Christ's suffering is at once "human" and "superhuman." In this existential differentiation and correlation at the limits of comparability, Kierkegaard repeats and substantiates the Christological doctrine of Jesus' double nature and its soteriological function: *Sub specie crucis* there is an image of God-forsakenness that cannot and must not remain a human model. If God himself takes up the God-forsakenness that only the crucified one experienced, all doubts and questioning beyond this come to an end, so long as it is clear that the human side stands in guilt – and God is love. This thought – that God is love – "contains all the blessed persuasion of eternity" (364).

6. The final conceptual differentiations offered by Kierkegaard in this discourse – God and human, and "being in the wrong" and "being guilty" – indicate once again the heightened Christology of the relation to God addressed here. (1) From the human perspective *guilty* signifies guilty before humankind as well as guilty before God. (2) From the human perspective *innocent* suffering must be judged ambivalently: Humanly speaking, "injustice" before God remains warranted, but to assert guilt from this external perspective would be cynical. The example from Job (366ff; cf. *Pap.* X¹ A 196; *JP* §1386) shows that although it is really inadmissable to label him guilty, (3) everyone is *sub specie crucis*, that is, in one's basic relationship, guilty before God (368). Furthermore, this has been revealed Christologically in God himself as what is "joyful": There is simply no longer any quarreling or grounds for doubt with God; whoever persists in this direction attacks only himself (368)! What this means is that here, under the rhetorical conditions of the discourse, Kierkegaard views the opposition of God's love and guilt as a complete disjunction that is similarly divided in the unequal relation between God and the human. Either God is love, in which case guilt falls to the human side (and this is for Christians precisely the conclusion that is "joyful"), or God is potentially (in terms of doubt, knowledge, proof) not love, in which case not only would God himself be quasi-guilty, but on the human side there would loom the horror of the loss of self. The passion of relation with God would be rendered a vain illusion about either oneself or God.

This train of thought is persuasive only because it starts from the impassioned human seeking of Religiousness A, then sharpens this Christologically by means of the double contingency of Religiousness B in order to make the God's love–guilt alternative inescapable. Every conclusion other than the joyful one must disqualify itself, lest one opt for a solution that would be either passionless or horrific. But such would only improperly reiterate and misconstrue the existential problem of guilt in self-relation, as it would reopen the question of theological doubting of God's love. Neither the passionless nor the horrific solution need be entertained, because "there is one" that has introduced the horror of innocent suffering to God himself, so that the loss of God is worked out within the relation to God itself: Religiousness B.

IV. CRITIQUE

In the years after 1848, Kierkegaard elaborated the Christological dialectic even more essentially by giving an increasingly polemical shape to the narrative form of the discourse (cf. *Christian Discourses* [1848]) and by allowing both aspects to be fused with the theological and conceptual literary expression of the late pseudonym, Anti-Climacus, above all in *Practice in Christianity* (1850). The critical highpoint of this literary form, which integrated the religious author's preceding approaches, is presented in the sarcastic tract *The Moment* (1854/55). These late presentations of the paradoxical Religiousness B, while strongly New-Testamental in many of the specific ways they conceptualize the dogmatic tradition, are always and essentially presented as narrative, persuasion and exhortation. By way of conclusion, they will here be summarily presented and employed for critical evaluation by focusing on three key themes.

1. *Historical knowledge* about Christ, writes Anti-Climacus in the first part of *Practice in Christianity*, "is not worth a pickled herring."[13] For, from the religious point of view or under the presupposition of Religiousness A and in Anti-Climacus's perspective of Religiousness B, there is only a "contemporaneous," passionate relationship to Christ, which immediately excludes a distant relationship to something in the past. As the God-man who suffers both humanly and superhumanly, Christ is "an extremely unhistorical person" in the "situation of contemporaneity" (60f). Kierkegaard does not therefore argue with historical investigation and scholarship as such and in general, nor does he ever endorse an irrationality inherently devoid of concepts. But, in matters of religiousness, the historical and scientific approach cannot serve as the path to personal belief. The Christian doctrine of the God-man and reconciliation is not accessible by means of knowledge, but rather solely in the existential seriousness of belief.

In this way, Kierkegaard shifts the compelling power of Christianity into the textual narrative's ability to "make present," or, more precisely, into the existential proximity of all content of the Christian tradition. To effect this proximity is Kierkegaard's task as a religious author. Kierkegaard also sees that his contemporaries, stamped as they are by the cultural and social situation of the mid-nineteenth century, are hardly in a position to make this turn in the understanding of Christianity with him. But he refuses to accede to either scientific apologetics or the simple traditional acceptance of Christianity as the state religion. It were best, in direct attack upon Christianity, to come to a kind of *contemporaneity* with its message – namely, "offense" – the dark side of belief (cf. Part II of *Practice in Christianity*).

Here too there occurs a Christological escalation of his thought insofar as Christ himself was obliged to become this *offense* in his suffering for others (cf. 93f). In this tension inherent to Christian contemporaneity, Kierkegaard sees more than ever that his age and his society are far removed from any religious insight. Compelled to view passionless detachment as religion's fundamental affliction and most catastrophic misunderstanding, he polemically attacked the state religion of Christianity by directing his characterization of Christian religiousness outward: The banality of the Zeitgeist misunderstood Christianity's synthesis of the most sublime and the most lowly – the suffering of the God-man – as either barren sentimentality or pointless comedy (*SV*^{I} XII 56). The disappearance of impassioned seriousness, obligation, and resolution, which reduces Christ to a merely traditional or comic figure, is the chief target of Kierkegaard's late writings.

The one-sidedness of the literary battles Kierkegaard undertook in his last years is not a reason to reject them, for such ventures in learned exaggeration represent one of the stylistic genres he consciously brought to bear in his work. The self-appointed role of the *corrective* (cf. *Pap.* X^I A 640, *JP* §6467) is to be taken seriously. But this does not mean that the polemicism of Kierkegaard's distinction between historical knowledge and narrative-existential appropriation must be obligatory for the twentieth and twenty-first centuries as well. Historical mediations and contemporary appropriation are not identical, but neither must they reciprocally fear one another. What Kierkegaard pointed out with regard to the medium of contemporary understanding in the conflict over the application of the historical-critical method to Christology was that the desire to understand oneself as somehow distanced would be a manifest misunderstanding.

2. The *image of Christ and the aesthetic work* of the religious author become the preeminent and decisive argument of the discourses of Kierkegaard, and they do so paradoxically because he desires to separate the *poetical* strictly from the *Christian* (since, by

definition, the poetical is not existentially serious).[14] For the allusion to what is no longer assimilable in purely human terms, to the crucified one, requires the utmost effort and application of aesthetic resources if it is to be effective. This occurs paradigmatically in the representation of the suffering of the God-man, in the "gripping sight" of the image of Christ (cf. 162; also *Pap.* IX A 395, *JP* §270). The power of this representation, carried out through several pages, is heard in the innocent response of a child viewing a gallery of children's pictures among which has been surreptitiously placed a picture of the crucified Christ: "But why were they so mean to him, why?" (164). Ought innocence, God's love for humankind, be so tortured?

The power of reconciliation arises from the image of suffering, which discloses human guilt and sympathy, and brings the passion of the religious to its highest pitch, to belief in the God-man, belief embodied in the relationship of sin and guilt. Kierkegaard wishes to put Christology in play only through the disclosure and appropriation aroused by literary and aesthetic experience, and decidedly not by dogmatic or historical warrant. This does not mean that Kierkegaard had grown indifferent to the Lutheran dogma of his religious origins, nor that he ignored or wanted to abjure it. The meaning of the corrective signifies here too. The premises of the tradition are to be brought critically to bear in such a way that only their appropriation is emphasized, since tradition as such is virtually irrelevant to this appropriation: The present "telling" of the story of the crucified Christ must be made so aesthetically independent that its tradition can and should be "forgotten" in the actual telling (164)!

Metacritically, one must also keep in mind here that this primacy of appropriation can only bear the burden it is charged with so long as its correlate, the textual and conceptual tradition, remains culturally viable. An appropriation sundered from its religious tradition would dissolve itself. In this precise respect Kierkegaard's initiatives presuppose very specifically the circumstances of his age, while the twentieth and twenty-first centuries find themselves increasingly in circumstances that must be defined as reversed: In the interests of appropriation, they must first make the genuine objects, concepts, and texts again accessible.

3. From Kierkegaard's posture as a corrective there proceeds, with regard to politics and cultural critique, a *Christian critique of ideol-*

ogy, which he, on the basis of his radical demands for a contemporaneous and impassioned Christianity, directed against the emerging mass and mass-communication society. Under the complex conditions described for Religiousness B, the Christian truth cannot be safeguarded by institutions. Kierkegaard relied upon Reformation theology and developed it further in his critique of church and society: Truth can only lie in striving for truth, in *becoming Christian:* "A Church triumphant in this world is an illusion" (193). In this respect Kierkegaard had counted subsisting Christendom the worst enemy of Christianity and also strictly rejected church participation in the civil political reforms. Conservative and revolutionary agendas are mixed here; and here, too, the role of the corrective is not to be overlooked. Kierkegaard's concentration on the impassioned appropriation of Christianity does not in any way exclude reforms, social development, participation in politics, a Christian social ethic, and so on, and the anarchist demand for destruction of all social forms is nowhere to be found. Instead, Kierkegaard fought against the – on his view – false value placed on the social. Reforms, societies, political participation – without individuals capable of making judgments – quickly deteriorate into mere power games played for group interests, into a caricature of the community as a whole. As its fundamental criterion, a Christian social ethic requires individual persons and relations of personal trust. Kierkegaard has not only been justified in harboring the suspicion that the collectivity would always be favored over the individual, but this suspicion has proved a prophetic analysis at the onset of the industrial society of the nineteenth century. In the twentieth and twenty-first centuries, however, those ethically responsible for the direction of these industrial societies must not renounce the questions of social organization if they are to take charge of or effect changes for the better.

Kierkegaard's entire work – and ultimately his own self as religious author – was an outcry: a fervent protest against the disappearance of human and religious individuality, against the leveling of the Christian doctrine of reconciliation. Stated positively, Kierkegaard proclaimed the existential truth that, in the figure of the crucified Christ, salvation has become visible, believable, and ethically binding. That Kierkegaard, in order to sharpen the edge of this existential religiousness, undertook a massive critique of all the social structures of his age does not in any way mean that it is not our task at the end of the twentieth century, and in the name of Religiousness A and B, to work to make these social structures succeed.

NOTES

1 F. D. E. Schleiermacher, *On Religion* (1799); G. W. F. Hegel, *Encyclopedia* [1830], §§384, 573.
2 *The Point of View of My Work as an Author: A Report to History*, trans. W. Lowrie; ed. B. Nelson. (New York: Harper, 1962), section 1.B: "Religious Author."
3 *Three Discourses on Imagined Occasions* (trans. Hongs, 1993), *SV*¹ V 177ff. In this section of the article, further references to this work will be made with simple parenthetical citation of the page number from *SV*¹ V.
4 *Phenomenology of Spirit*, trans. A. V. Miller (Oxford: Oxford University Press, 1977), pp. 406ff.
5 F. Schleiermacher, *The Christian Faith*, trans. H. R. Mackintosh and J. S. Stewart (New York: Harper and Row, 1963), §3.
6 Ibid., §4.
7 Ibid., §4/4.
8 Cf. W. Härle, *Dogmatik* (Berlin and New York: W. de Gruyter, 1995), chap. 9.4.1; R. C. Neville, *A Theology Primer* (Albany: State University of New York Press, 1991), chap. 12/II.
9 Cf. Härle, *Dogmatik*, chap. 9.2; Neville, *A Theology Primer*, chaps. 11/III, 12/IV.
10 *Upbuilding Discourses in Various Spirits* (trans. Hongs, 1993) "Part Three: The Gospel of Sufferings. Christian Discourses," no. IV: "The Joy of It That in Relation to God a Person Always Suffers as Guilty," *SV*¹ VIII 348ff. Further citations in this section refer to the *SV*¹ VIII page number in parentheses.
11 In two places the discourse itself makes slight reference to this first condition: it is an "impossibility" (358) and therefore destructive of relationship to God, from which follows in turn the fact of "hopelessness" (360).
12 Cf. *SV*¹ VIII 356, 357, 362, 365, 367, 368, 369.
13 *Practice in Christianity* (trans. Hongs, 1991), *SV*¹ XII 39. Further citations in this section refer to the *SV*¹ XII page number in parentheses.
14 Cf. Anti-Climacus in *The Sickness unto Death* (1849; trans. Hongs, 1980): "Christianly speaking, every poet-existence (esthetics notwithstanding) is sin," *SV*¹ XI 189.

16 The utilitarian self and the "useless" passion of faith

I.

A constant theme in Kierkegaard is what might be called the presence of the Absolute, though Kierkegaard does not often use this Hegelian term. He talks instead of God's unchangeableness, of the infinite, the unconditioned, or the absolute good. What can unchangeableness in the presence of change mean to us today? More than a limited scientific rationality would allow, no doubt. But within the so-called postmodern context, indifference and skepticism to such an idea have as their counterpart nothing but an escalation of irrational religious needs.

The dizzying speed of change in highly industrialized societies has given wide currency to talk of "crises of meaning" and with that ample scope for the expression of religious needs. But we should prevent such talk or needs from entering into theoretical discourse as a way of bolstering argument; pressure emanating from a need can substantially distort discussion in matters of truth. Today, it is only by skeptically insisting on even greater caution, and minimizing as best we may (for we can never altogether eliminate) the powerful dynamic of wishful thinking that we can keep the ideological function of religion separate from its absolute truth claim. The *functions* of religion can of course be analyzed from sociological and psychological points of view, but it is impossible in principle to reduce the *meaning* of absolute spiritual presence to these functions and they themselves contain hints of something more. Certainly, religion may be indispensable for the stabilizing of societies caught up in rapid social change, but a skeptical theology will be very

Translated by Frederick S. Gardiner

397

much aware of the radical critique of religious needs as presented, for example, by dialectical theology. And perhaps the areas illuminated by the Feuerbach- and Marx-inspired critique of the need for religion – namely, compensation and projection – are symptomatic of a thoroughgoing misunderstanding of the God-relationship, on the part of the self.

After this word of caution the main thesis may be formulated thus: The God-relationship should no longer be made to serve life's purposes. Or, to put it more drastically: The Absolute is pointless.

This is not to disvalue individual and collective needs, hopes, and desires; these are the proper subject matter of the strategies we devise for providing humane solutions to human problems. But such needs should be freed of all entanglement with the idea of God. The Absolute is "absolute" in a pregnant sense precisely to the extent that it is conceived to be absolved from whatever teleology lies, or is thought to lie, in living processes, as well as from all instrumental rationality immanent in human society. The interlocking of instrumental rationality with considerations of ethical and cultural value and of human salvation (which Max Weber, among others, brought to our attention) fails to hold up under critical scrutiny. Whereas the reasoning that judges means in relation to finite ends suggests that what is superfluous in this regard lacks "meaning," life in its fullness has its highest form of freedom in an abundance – even overabundance; the expressive possibilities of the self triumph over the calculations of expansive self-assertion. Absolute truth as freedom is at one with the "intentionlessness" so much stressed by Walter Benjamin. In this freedom the Absolute is absolved from any need to provide justification, from all exploitation as a "meaning resource."

No one adopting Kierkegaard's skeptical theological approach imagines nowadays that it is possible, just by providing reasons, that is to say, by making statements claiming to be universally true, to point conclusively to what makes some particular situation or event "good." That would require ascertaining the proper place of such a good within the total scheme of things, but all belief in the human being's ability to determine such an onto-theological state of affairs "by its own powers" has vanished. For what "one's own powers" never fail to do is assert *them*selves, thus introducing into discourse an egoistic distortion – as will be discussed more fully below under the theme of power. If there really were an ability to appreciate the value of some significant occurrence, that could only be by virtue of a suspension of all desire for direct mastery over things. Such a suspension, or abstention, is itself a confession of the need to be forgiven for one's own insurmountable particularity and for the self-assertion inherent in that.

All this is in fundamental opposition to the embodied dynamic of wishing that infiltrates and infects all our thinking and runs counter to the various strategies people adopt in their attempts to suppress the idea of their finitude. Lack of purpose – or existential dysfunctionality, as the mirror image of the absolute meaning of freedom – transports one into a state of wonder and dread; it is only by traversing this abyss of uncertainty hard by the edge of despair that the self can acquire that fathomless lightheartedness (Johannes Climacus's "humor") that is the courage required of the leap into the absolute sovereignty of God. Kierkegaard, who occasionally draws on the metaphor of the tightrope dancer for this particular configuration of human existence, says: "whoever has truly learned how to be anxious will dance when the anxieties of finitude strike up the music" (CA 161).

In a time when the apathy, religious indifference, and frivolousness characteristic of the "last man" (so vividly portrayed by Nietzsche) prevail, it becomes clear why for Kierkegaard faith is primarily passion. Even decisive opposition to religion is preferable to a lukewarm Christianity:

The iron resolve to have no religion already has an element of the passionate and is therefore not the most dangerous kind of indifference. That is why it seldom occurs. No, the most dangerous, and thoroughly ordinary, kind of indifference is the following: to have a certain religion, but one that has been watered down and vulgarized to pure twaddle.[1]

Ignorance and indifference habitually betray themselves in the stock phrase "to a certain degree" (CUP 229).

The kind of thinking that arises in Kierkegaardian faith, passionately relinquishing imperial intentionality and the reduction of reason to instrumentality, challenges the self to understand itself as absolute over against the "general" (Almene, often misleadingly translated "universal"), living as an exception to the rule, if that is what is called for. Freedom in this sense remains untouched by the widespread accusation of infantilism directed at religion particularly by Freud. However, the fact that the constellation of faith and freedom in this sense has become so distinct and accessible is the result of the historical unfolding of a thoroughly instrumentalized form of life. Secularization as a condition to be desired (at least in retrospect) was a necessary preliminary to the progressive debunking of the manifold secondary functions of religion, as well as of their metaphysical presuppositions. It was this that first made it possible for faith finally to understand and express itself, authentically, as that purpose-free exposition in which the person accepts the glorious gift of grace freely granted and becomes a "gestalt" of the sovereign presence of God. In particular, this type of thinking takes the ground from under speculations on what goals history might possibly have – whether they be religious or atheistic. A new relationship between absoluteness and contingency has been brought to light in Christology. In order to experience infinite, transient facticity as meaningful in spite of the inevitability of its passing, to "know" that even the failures and evil of one's own existence are forgiven, it is no longer necessary for the self to insist upon the transparency of the underlying causes of the occurrences in question, as if they could be "coped with" only by ascribing to them some ultimate aim. An end is thus put to those compulsive theological rationalizations that with the help of "providence" explain away the horrors of history, tracing events back to an ultimate will manipulating our fates behind our backs. The new Kierkegaardian way of thinking and the freedom that comes from it leave the traditional view of God behind, that is, God as an omnipotent being ruling in the mode of domination. God rejects rule by despotism "because He communicates creatively in such a way that in creating he *gives* independence *vis-à-vis* himself" (*CUP* 260; emphasis original). Omnipotence on Kierkegaard's understanding proves itself in the granting of autonomous freedom to finite existence. In order to explicate this Kierkegaard makes use of the notion of the *contractio Dei*, which is of course also found in the cabbalistic tradition. The free and independent finite being emerges as such from the continuity of God's omnipotence only to the extent that God holds himself back or withdraws. The nothing of the *creatio ex nihilo* is the sphere of finite freedom, in the all-encompassing being of God made available by this withdrawal.

All finite power creates dependence. Omnipotence alone is able to make independent, to bring forth out of nothing that which receives its inner being by virtue of the fact that omnipotence constantly withholds itself.

Omnipotence is not intent on a relationship with the other, for there is no other to which it could relate. No: it is able to give without thereby relinquishing its power in the slightest, which is to say that it is able to make independent.

This is what is incomprehensible, that omnipotence is not only able to bring forth that which is most imposing, the visible totality of the cosmos, but also that which is most delicate and fragile: a being independent vis-à-vis omnipotence. . . . It is indeed an impoverished and worldly notion of the dialectic of power that it steadily augments itself to the extent that it can coerce and make dependent. (*JP* §1251; translation mine)

As stated above, on Kierkegaard's view it is only through passion that the person is elevated to the spiritual existence of faith; the correlative determination of God is one of the passion of almighty love – an understanding that has transcended once and for all the old ideas of an overbearing sovereignty, these now exposed as unserious products of the imagination (*JP* §2452). Intense spiritual self-relatedness manifests itself concretely in the courage to be powerless. This is true in a preeminent sense of almighty love, which in a changeless act of condescension places itself at the mercy of man and his freedom and, by so doing, manifests itself concretely in the suffering of God on man's account. "From a religious point of view, the greatest impotence is the greatest power. Therefore Christ has no sceptre in his hand, only a reed, the symbol of impotence – and yet at that very moment he is the greatest power" (*JP* §4214).

Nothing in the Gospels is as striking as Jesus' abstaining from the exercise of the power to which he at the same time lays full claim: According to Scripture, to him "has been given all power." The renunciation of this power is indeed the decisive offense, and offense was taken by his contemporaries from the very start. A perfect fullness of power, which refrains from asserting itself out of respect for the freedom of the weak and the guilty, is a stance that flies in the face of all expectations and wishes. The powerful acceptance of powerlessness in the life of Jesus should provide us with the occasion radically to question our own desires. Whoever takes the risk of breaking away from the fixation on his own power, and from anxiety about the deficits of this power, to him it will no longer seem plausible to use or, rather, to abuse God as a symbol of his own wish-fulfilling fantasies. And what is more, he will stop interpreting the Incarnation as a means to an end, for instance, the tallying up of guilt and sin. Within the horizon of an absolute, purpose-free spiritual presence, finite reflection understands the provisional nature of all its concepts, including its theological speculations.

II.

Within this postmetaphysical horizon a logically compelling demonstration of the certainty of the belief in God becomes superfluous in any case. This is especially so in view of the fact that instrumental science, with its steady production of reasons, is quite willing, for every position in public discourse, to meet society's needs for the provision of grounds. It is nevertheless a worthwhile enterprise to present the good grounds of faith, and the power of metaphor to convince on the periphery of that silence in which the strictly logical demonstration ends "speaks for itself" – each time in a different way to each single individual. A "verbalization of the sacred" adequate in the sense of forming a set of intersubjectively verifiable and controllable statements is neither desirable nor possible, for the sacred is a truly luxuriating dimension of our freedom in which the will to power over one's own existence has been renounced. For each person this embarkation on a purpose-free existence under the aegis of overabundant divine being takes on a different form. One will recall the *Mémorial* of Pascal, who wrote down a dated testimony of his conversion and sewed it into the lining of his frock. This act is highly significant: the existential center of the individual remains a mystery, kept intentionally from the inquisitive looks of others. Making it communicable would jeopardize the possibility of the absolute individuality of the other, who has the task of finding his own unique path. There is nothing here that can serve as a model. Pascal is certainly the most apt example of the refusal to make the center of one's own existence the material of a narrative that can be imparted, and Kierkegaard with his "theory of indirect communication" has said the final word on the matter. To be sure, if in our lives we actually experience an encounter of unconditional concern, then our hearts abound and we wish to communicate this to others. There is an intense desire to hold fast to what has transpired and make it accessible. Hence it is a personal, theologically grounded resolve not to impart the facticity of such events, to withhold one's *kairos* from communication and from the possibility of its becoming an object of idle talk. The decision not to go about spreading the news of one's own fundamental experience and making it "intelligible" to everyone is a conscious decision. It is precisely the center of one's own existence that remains the exclusive province of the incognito, for otherwise the temptation that lies in public acclamation and in putting one's inwardness to use as a beacon for the half-hearted and insipid would be too great. Discovering one's own integrity is a task for and the responsibility of the individual alone. And besides, it is not possible in one's own life to reproduce the life of another, not even that of the Saviour. The story of Jesus is not intended to explain everything once and for all but to encourage living a life that no longer seeks, or requires, a derivation from an overarching principle or an explanation in terms of such.

The irreducible particularity of each individual's movement of transcendence cannot be made compatible with the communicative processes with which human beings reach understanding among themselves. From the point of view of what is of unconditional concern to me, this kind of "intersubjective exchange" appears as the avoidance tactic of one who shrinks from the annihilation (*Zu-Grund-Gehen*) of being taken up (*Eingehen*) into the power of God (*JP* §1960). A radical theological reflection on freedom shows "that one person cannot help another at all," for "the terms of salvation differ for every individual, for every single solitary human being" (*JP* §4922). The ineffable nature of the concrete act of becoming a self is accomplished in the flicker of an eye – no postponing, no opportunistic weighing of pros and cons. Above all, no sideways glances in search of others' approval. It is certainly more comfortable to abstain from such a way of acting in favor of standardized ethical norms; most individuals content themselves with the simple reproduction of life, with life at second hand. The life context within the framework of science and technology mechanizes life's decisions and eliminates the primordiality that actualizes itself in the sharp outlines of a clearly focused decision: "There is nothing to live through, nothing to experience, everything is finished" (*CUP* 344).

Knowledge replaces experience and becomes a substitute for action: "One does not love, does not have faith, does not act; but one knows what erotic love is, what faith is" (*CUP* 344), and "limited and busy people fancy that they are acting and acting and acting," while on the other hand, continues Kierkegaard, intellectuals of a particular type can be said to cultivate a "virtuosity in knowing how to avoid acting" (*CUP* 604). According to Kierkegaard it can be appropriate, even mandatory, to refuse to enter into discourse. It is of course inadmissible to dispense with the notion of universalizability when weighing the acceptability of maxims for acting, and even the passionate existential decision should possess relevance for the universal. But there is no leveling of the absolute difference between the universal and the individual. Withdrawal into subjectivity could well draw the attention of the prevailing normativity to certain fissures out of which a new historical constellation of order could arise. The silence of nonconformity can be both a demonic, self-destructive manifestation of total refusal and rejection and a manifestation of an authentic possibility that can provide an important impulse for others. This inspiration must not, however, become the occasion for mere imitation.[2]

Judged in terms of standardized thinking and the unreflected normality of our attention to everyday problems, the contrariness of such Christian existence represents a breach. Whoever attempts to live in accordance with the impulse of absolute purposelessness becomes in some way suspect, for such a person by undermining the fixation on self-preservation is to some extent a destabilizing factor. It means, after all, a refusal to take part in that market of possibilities with its offers to satisfy the need for meaning, where religion is prepared and served up as an elixir for coping with extreme situations.

III.

A key role is played in these processes by the fixation upon one's own vital powers. The self does to a limited extent have power. It manifests itself in the striving for self-realization. The rarely acknowledged awareness of the limits of its finite power is a source of unrest in the self. One must strive for more power in order not to sink into oblivion. This striving for ever more power is born of the anxiety one has for one's own self-preservation, the inner mechanisms of which have been lucidly depicted by Hobbes.

Kierkegaard describes the impulse of Christian faith as the unnatural suspension of creaturely self-assertion: "The tragedy of the majority of men is by no means that they are weak but that they are too strong – genuinely to be aware of God" (*JP* §4453). The danger lies in becoming aware of one's own strength, the illusion of being able to stay the process of one's own transitoriness, or at least of being able to circumvent or defy time. One historical variation of this transcending of the frailty and limitation of individual power is self-dissolution in the "mortal" god of the collective ego. For human beings have an enormous anxiety about becoming "solitary individuals"; they are constantly casting about for excuses to hide behind others (people, institutions, ideas) in order to avoid being called upon to assume a risk-laden responsibility in which the risk of failing one's self is greater (*JP* §2166). It is true that the alienation and anonymity of power in mass action is not infrequently experienced by the individual in an illusionary manner as a pleasurable sensation of enhanced power. Where mass activity predominates, the individual sense of responsibility dissipates in the process. This being so, Kierkegaard observes: "Everything that is mass is *eo ipso* perdition" (*JP* §2970).

Anxiety in the face of the risky odyssey of becoming a self is only one motivating factor behind the secret lust for collectivization. The other lies in our fallen nature itself, the dynamic structure of our rationality with its virtually inherent tendency to dominate. Closed systems of meaning, be they of traditional or recent vintage, help to cope with the precariousness of existence by suggesting a totality of explanatory connections, for the self derives a feeling of security from the notion of having real mastery over a given state of affairs. This dynamic of reason is simply the counterpart of a sensual impulse infecting reason. The human being "continually feels an urge to have something finished, but this urge is of evil and must be renounced" (*CUP* 86). For anyone who opens himself to God, the daunting nature of becoming a self becomes clear by the very contrast: In faith the self should bring itself "to think infinitely the uncertainty of all things" (*CUP* 87). What makes this proposal extraordinary is the fact that reason on Kierkegaard's understanding cannot help but continue to integrate in its holistic (re)constructions of the totality of sensible reality every phenomenon with any claim to meaning. Reason has "always already" fallen prey, as it were, to the utilitarian temptation that helps to patch over and disguise the fragmentary nature of the human being's existential constitution. In this manner reason is a victim of the "most subtle of all deceptions" (CUP 253). Therefore, the first step of letting oneself in for the venture of faith means to mobilize the "distrust of infinity" against oneself. Arguments from finality, which confine theological speculation within a teleological framework, are deprived of their claim to validity: "The divine passion is present right here in the most decisive hatred of everything which even in the remotest manner resembles human probability and calculation" (JP §2096).

The theology of sacrifice is thereby removed from the center of theological theory: "The thought: to do this or that, to offer this or that, to venture this or that – in order to serve the cause of God – this thought has never moved me" (JP §1431). It is the infantilism of the grown-up that creates the fantasy of God's pursuing some sort of activity. One probably comes closest to imagining the God-relationship if one pictures it in terms of the well-known situation in which an older person really joins in a child's game in order to make the child happy (JP §1431). Thus, Kierkegaard's existential earnestness ultimately culminates in divine-playful humorousness.

But God has put sweat and tears in the way of the humorous side. The antiutilitarian dimension of meaning in the God-relationship is disclosed only to a mode of thought that does not shy away from the absurd effort of thinking against the grain of the quasi-inborn mechanisms of reason and its manifest or hidden instrumental constructions: "The believer derives no benefit whatever from his [understanding]" (CUP 226).

This sovereign freedom is betrayed by conformity – by adapting to, and fitting into, absolutized constructs of totality. Of course it is only natural for people to slink off into ideologized worldviews, for the Christian challenge to live an unsheltered existence is an imposition that produces malaise. It would seem that the human being has an innate tendency toward paternalism and authoritarianism, and a corresponding distaste for the mobility of the spirit, as well as for the mobility in real historical existence, and gladly succumbs to the sweet poison of an unconsciously desired captivity.

Of course if we wish to grasp reality, we must construct totalities.

There is also no reason why we should not project utopias in order to reach a common understanding of our history. But we know that these constructions are merely provisional, and we also know that the ground of freedom, God, eludes every fixation in terms of any concept of reality as a whole. What is expected of us is to live and act in a world that no longer enjoys the status of a divine prefabrication. For this absolute esteem the solitary individual has to pay a high price: he becomes acquainted in his own soul with the loneliness of the God who suffers on account of mankind.

IV.

It is the intention of paradoxical Christianity so to express the crossroads where the Absolute encounters contingent, historical existence that all projections of historical continuity and a "gentle" entry of the divine into history are shattered. The volitional dynamic of the desire to subjugate meaning is hurled back upon itself by the roadblock of the absurd. Kierkegaard speaks of a crucifixion of reason – of a reason, that is, that strives to subjugate every form of reality, including the fountainhead of all meaning, and conform it to its own hermeneutical project. Pierced and thrown back by the paradoxical, it dawns on the self that this specific reality can truly not be its own enterprise of thought. For as long as the self is capable of enduring this repelling alienation in the no man's land on the borderline of reason, just so long is it able to endure the absolute intensification of uncertainty in the paradox of the God-relationship. Where the paradox takes hold in truth, there thought must relinquish its attempt to subjugate this reality by comprehending it. And only this derailment can be referred to as a paradox. This is the meaning behind the remark that "nonsense" cannot be believed "against the understanding"; you cannot believe what to the understanding by itself is transparently nonsensical (*CUP* 568). So "believing against the understanding" is not a matter of being religiously inspired by what a positivistically constricted understanding concludes is nonsense – "just as if Christianity were a tidbit for dunces because it cannot be thought" (*CUP* 557). On the contrary, the task with the paradox is to grasp its unthinkableness and that requires full use of the categorical power of reason.

In the passionate leap of faith the suspicion against which, if left to its own devices, the understanding has no defenses is dispelled, the suspicion, namely, that even in the most deeply felt, godly fear of the "Wholly Other," the self confesses a god of its own making.[3] For the idea of the absolute difference is itself a distinction inherent in reason. What is meant by "paradox," then, is a clearly distinguished negative concept demarcating the borderline of human reason. What reason recognizes as paradoxical "is composed in such a way that reason has no power at all to dissolve it into nonsense and prove that it is nonsense; no, it is a symbol, a riddle" (*JP* §7). That is to say, the paradoxical is a riddle precisely for reason. The power of reflection, as the pole opposite to passion, strengthens inwardness. Reflection is the instrument with which "to reset the trigger springs for the essentially Christian so that it may stand its ground – against reflection" (*JP* §3704). In order that faith's "simplicity armed with reflection" be attained at all, the battle "must of course be waged within the keenest qualifications of reflection" (*CUP* 607). The passion of faith draws reason into its infinite movement and brings it up against its limit – the very place where passion continually regenerates itself. At this limit the self experiences the provocative and evocative power of that which for reason is the absurd. In the at once attracting and repelling action of the absurd a fullness of being is disclosed to which there is no transition from the functionality of reason with its instinct of self-preservation.

Even in his most intricately theoretical moments Kierkegaard cannot suppress his sarcasm: "But let us never forget that not everyone who has not lost his reason thereby proves incontestably that he has it" (*JP* §2290).

The goal of this process of self-transformation is the successfully accomplished surrender of the self, the fortunate "loss of self" as a movement of transcendence to pure, that is to say, unmotivated communication with God. In the tension-laden strivings of our empirical existence, however, this movement means letting oneself in for "unintelligible" suffering. "To see yourself is to die, to die to all illusions and all hypocrisy – it takes great courage to dare look at yourself" (*JP* §3902). In the ordeal undergone in this struggle against the self, the person is implanted in the *memoria dei*. Not to have known this existential suffering is for Kierkegaard evidence of distance from God (*JP* §4681). To suffer in such a manner means having a secret with God. This secret is emblematic of the blessedness of being in agreement with God as the sovereign ground of existence, in which the omnipotence of love encompasses also the abyss of suffering.

A caveat must be attached to this explicit reminder that suffering is unavoidable: Its inevitability is no justification for thinking of suffering instrumentally as having some purpose within an economy of salvation! Religious masochism is subject to the same critical verdict as religious heroism and a readiness for sacrifice. Otherwise martyrdom could degenerate into an existential test of courage or be made into a tool for the self-satisfaction of the pious.[4] It takes genuine courage to devote oneself to an idea and, in the extreme case, to let oneself be put to death for it. But that can also be a matter of lack of inwardness. The God-relationship also puts the readiness for self-sacrifice in question. Suffering may indeed be "the negative form of the highest," but in itself it brings no assurance of the authenticity of the God-relationship. No one should imagine "that sorrow is more meritorious than joy" (*JP* §2178). Here again the self goes astray on a utilitarian path; whoever is of the opinion that one must suffer in order to arrive at one's goal has already wandered into a blind alley.

In the leap of faith, finite ties are put at risk and cultivated capacities and dispositions are suspended along with allegedly ultimate commitments. What is known to faith as "eternal salvation" is disclosed only in a movement that runs counter to utilitarianism. The path of passionate discipleship, unflinching at the prospect of suffering, is what is decisive here – in contradistinction to every other good that can be "acquired" (*CUP* 427). As Kierkegaard puts it: "The absolute difficulty of this [appropriation] is the only sign that one is relating oneself to the absolute good" (*CUP* 428). "In the unconditioned all teleology vanishes. . . . Only when every 'Why?' vanishes in the night of the unconditioned and becomes silent in the silence of the unconditioned, only then can a man venture everything; if he dimly glimpses one 'Why?' something is impaired" (*JP* §4901). Inasmuch as faith delivers itself up to uncertainty in such a radical manner, it can no longer be unmasked as a pious form of barter (*CUP* 425). Hence the content of faith is not constituted by communicative behavior patterns such as care and comfort projected along an eternal trajectory. The content of faith is the almighty sovereignty itself. Faith is a process in which the self pierces through the inherent utilitarian structure of its ontological constitution by virtue of the sublimity of the infinite, thereby becoming transformed by the reality of God. To this extent what is essentially Christian is not a specific content but rather a certain form of intensity of individual self-becoming whose spiritual enthusiasm is revealed precisely by the unconditionality of an ethical commitment that on *pragmatic* grounds would be wholly inexplicable (*JP* §4224).

The Being-of-God-for-me is my own God-relationship as self-relationship, hence the freedom of God is my own freedom in the strenuous exertion of the spirit. Kierkegaard can therefore say, "It is really the God-relationship that makes a human being human" (*CUP* 244). For in this process of transformation "God" is nothing external, "but rather infinity itself" or, as Kierkegaard also puts it, "infinite selfhood" (*JP* §532).

At the pinnacle of intensity of the struggle, at the point where the "likeness with God" manifests itself (*CUP* 178). existential earnestness becomes transformed into the lightheartedness of effortless discipleship. The self, however, is not capable of sustaining the concentration of this moment and therefore sinks once again into the distance from God, thereby according *humor* an eminent theological significance.

NOTES

1 *Der Augenblick* (*The Moment* [or *Instant*]), Ger. eds., *Aufsätze und Schriften des letzten Streits,* vol. 34 of *Gesammelte Werke* (Düsseldorf and Köln: Diederichs, 1959), p. 206.
2 Kierkegaard, *Das Buch über Adler,* vol. 36 of *Gesammelte Werke* (Düsseldorf and Köln 1962), pp. 40ff (*Nutidens religieuse forvirring: Bogen om Adler* [Copenhagen: C. A. Reitzel Boghandel, 1984].
3 *Philosophical Fragments or a Fragment of Philosophy,* trans. David F. Swenson, rev. trans. Howard V. Hong (Princeton: Princeton University Press, 1962), p. 55; cf. p. 57. The translation has "absolute unlikeness."
4 *Einübing in Christentum,* vol. 26 of *Gesammelte Werke* (Düsseldorf and Köln 1961), pp. 293f (*Indøvelse i Christendom, SV³* XVI).

BIBLIOGRAPHY

WORKS IN DANISH

Breve og Aktstykker vedrørende Søren Kierkegaard. Ed. Niels Thulstrup. 2 vols. Copenhagen: Munksgaard, 1953–4.
Samlede Værker. Ed. A. B. Drachmann, J. L. Heiberg, and H. O. Lange. 3rd ed. 20 vols. Copenhagen: Gyldendalske Boghandel, 1962. 4th ed. forthcoming.
Søren Kierkegaards Papirer. Ed. P. A. Heiberg, V. Kuhr, and E. Torsting. 16 vols. in 25 tomes. 2nd ed., edited by N. Thulstrup, with an Index by N. J. Cappelørn. Copenhagen: Gyldendal, 1968–78.

ENGLISH TRANSLATIONS

Hannay

Either/Or: A Fragment of Life. Trans. Alastair Hannay. Harmondsworth: Penguin Press, 1992.
Fear and Trembling. Trans. Alastair Hannay. Harmondsworth: Penguin Press, 1985.
Papers and Journals: A Selection. Trans. Alastair Hannay. Harmondsworth: Penguin Press, 1996.
The Sickness unto Death. Trans. Alastair Hannay. Harmondsworth: Penguin Press, 1989.

Hong

Journals and Papers. 7 vols. Ed. and trans. Howard V. Hong and Edna H. Hong, assisted by Gregor Malantschuk. Bloomington and Indianapolis: Indiana University Press, 1967–78.
Kierkegaard's Writings. Ed. and trans. Howard V. Hong, Edna H. Hong, Henrik Rosenmeier, Reidar Thomte, et al. 26 vols. projected (20 vols. published as of August 1997). Princeton: Princeton University Press, 1978.

Volume 1   *Early Polemical Writings: From the Papers of One Still Living; Articles from Student Days; The Battle between the Old and the New Cellars* (1990)

Volume 2   *The Concept of Irony; Schelling Lecture Notes* (1989)

Volume 3   *Either/Or* I (1987)

Volume 4   *Either/Or* II (1987)

Volume 5   *Eighteen Upbuilding Discourses* (1990)

Volume 6   *Fear and Trembling; Repetition* (1983)

Volume 7   *Philosophical Fragments; Johannes Climacus* (1985)

Volume 8   *The Concept of Anxiety* (1980)

Volume 9   *Prefaces* (not yet published)

Volume 10   *Three Discourses on Imagined Occasions* (1993)

Volume 11   *Stages on Life's Way* (1988)

Volume 12   *Concluding Unscientific Postscript* (2 volumes; 1992)

Volume 13   *The Corsair Affair* (1982)

Volume 14   *Two Ages* (1978)

Volume 15   *Upbuilding Discourses in Various Spirits* (1993)

Volume 16   *Works of Love* (1995)

Volume 17   *Christian Discourses; Crisis [and a Crisis] in the Life of an Actress* (forthcoming 1997)

Volume 18   *Without Authority; The Lily in the Field and the Bird of the Air; Two Ethical-Religious Essays; Three Discourses at the Communion on Fridays; An Upbuilding Disourse; Two Discourses at the Communion on Fridays* (1997)

Volume 19   *The Sickness unto Death* (1980)

Volume 20   *Practice in Christianity* (1991)

Volume 21   *For Self-Examination; Judge for Yourself* (1990)

Volume 22   *The Point of View: The Point of View for My Work as an Author; Armed Neutrality; On My Work as an Author* (not yet published)

Volume 23   *The Moment and Late Writings; Articles from* Faedrelandet*; The Moment; This Must Be Said, So Let It Be Said; Christ's Judgement on Official Christianity; The Changelessness of God* (not yet published)

Volume 24   *The Book on Alder* (not yet published)

Volume 25   *Kierkegaard: Letters and Documents* (1978)

Volume 26   *Cumulative Index* (not yet published)

Other

Attack upon "Christendom" 1854–1855. Trans. Walter Lowrie. Princeton: Princeton University Press, 1968.

Christian Discourses. Trans. Walter Lowrie. London and New York: Oxford University Press, 1940.

The Concept of Dread. Trans. Walter Lowrie. Princeton: Princeton University Press, 1957.

Concluding Unscientific Postscript. Trans. David F. Swenson and Walter Lowrie. Princeton: Princeton University Press, 1968.

The Crisis [and a Crisis] in the Life of an Actress. Trans. Stephen Crites. New York: Harper and Row, 1967.

For Self-Examination and Judge for Yourselves. Trans. Walter Lowrie. Princeton: Princeton University Press, 1944.

The Journals of Soren Kierkegaard. Ed. and trans. Alexander Dru. London: Oxford University Press, 1951.

Kierkegaard's Attack upon "Christendom." Trans. Walter Lowrie. Princeton: Princeton University Press, 1944.

On Authority and Revelation, The Book on Alder. Trans. Walter Lowrie. Princeton: Princeton University Press, 1955.

Philosophical Fragments. Trans. David F. Swenson and Howard V. Hong. Princeton: Princeton University Press, 1962.

Prefaces: *Light Reading for Certain Classes as the Occasion May Require, by Nicolaus Notabene.* Ed. and trans. William McDonald. Tallahassee: Florida State University Press, 1989.

The Point of View for My Work as an Author: A Report to History. Trans. Walter Lowrie. London and New York: Oxford University Press, 1939; rev. ed., edited by B. Nelson, New York: Harper and Row, 1962.

The Present Age. Trans. Alexander Dru. London: Collins, 1962.

Works of Love. Trans. Howard V. Hong. New York: Harper and Row, 1962.

BOOKS ON KIERKEGAARD

Adorno, Theodor W. *Kierkegaard: Construction of the Aesthetic.* Ed. and trans. Robert Hullot-Kentor. Minneapolis: University of Minnesota Press, 1989.

Agacinski, Sylviane. *Aparté: Conceptions and Deaths of Søren Kierkegaard.* Trans. Kevin Newmark. Tallahassee: Florida State University Press, 1988.

Beabout, Gregory R. *Freedom and Its Misuses: Kierkegaard on Anxiety and Despair.* Milwaukee: Marquette University Press, 1996.

Bell, Richard H., ed. *The Grammar of the Heart: Thinking with Kierkegaard and Wittgenstein. New Essays in Moral Philosophy and Theology.* San Francisco: Harper and Row, 1988.

Bertung, Birgit, ed. *Kierkegaard – Poet of Existence. Kierkegaard Conferences.* Copenhagen: C. A. Reitzel Boghandel, 1989.

Bigelow, Pat. *Kierkegaard and the Problem of Writing.* Tallahassee: Florida State University Press, 1987.

The Cunning, The Cunning of Being. Tallahassee: Florida State University Press, 1991.

Bohlin, Torsten. *Kierkegaards dogmatiska åskådning*. Stockholm: Svenska Kyrkans Diakonistyrelses, 1925.

Kierkegaards dogmatische Anschauung. Trans. Ilse Meyer-Lüne. Gütersloh: Bertelsmann, 1927.

Brandt, Frithiof. *Den Unge Søren Kierkegaard*. Copenhagen: Levin og Munksgaard, 1929.

Brandt, Frithiof, and Else Rammel. *Kierkegaard og pengene*. Copenhagen: Levin og Munksgaard, 1935.

Bretall, Robert, ed. *A Kierkegaard Anthology*. New York: The Modern Library, 1959.

Cappelørn, Niels Jørgen, and Hermann Deuser, eds. *Kierkegaard Studies/Yearbook 1996*. Berlin and New York: Walter de Gruyter, 1996.

Collins, James. *The Mind of Kierkegaard*. Princeton: Princeton University Press, 1983.

Come, Arnold B. *Kierkegaard as Humanist: Discovering My Self*. Montreal and Buffalo: McGill-Queen's University Press, 1995.

Trendelenberg's Influence on Kierkegaard's Modal Categories. Montreal: Inter Editions, 1991.

Connell, George B. *To Be One Thing: Personal Unity in Kierkegaard's Thought*. Macon, Ga.: Mercer University Press, 1985.

Connell, George B., and C. Stephen Evans, eds. *Foundations of Kierkegaard's Vision of Community*. Atlantic Highlands, N.J.: Humanities Press International, 1992.

Creegan, Charles L. *Wittgenstein and Kierkegaard: Religion, Individuality, and Philosophical Method*. London and New York: Routledge, 1989.

Crites, Stephen. *In the Twilight of Christendom: Hegel vs. Kierkegaard on Faith and History*. Camersbury, Pa.: American Academy of Religion, 1972.

Croxall, Thomas H. *Kierkegaard Studies*. London: Lutterworth Press, 1948.

Derrida, Jacques. *The Gift of Death*. Trans. David Wills. Chicago: University of Chicago Press, 1995.

Dewey, Bradley R. *The New Obedience: Kierkegaard on Imitating Christ*. Foreword by Paul L. Holmer. Washington and Cleveland: Corpus, 1968.

Diem, Hermann. *Kierkegaard's Dialectic of Existence*. Trans. Harold Knight. London: Oliver and Boyd, 1959.

Dunning, Stephen N. *Kierkegaard's Dialectic of Inwardness: A Structural Analysis of the Theory of Stages*. Princeton: Princeton University Press, 1985.

Dupré, Louis. *Kierkegaard as Theologian: The Dialectic of Christian Existence*. New York: Sheed and Ward, 1963.

Elrod, John W. *Being and Existence in Kierkegaard's Pseuodonymous Works*. Princeton: Princeton University Press, 1975.

Emmanuel, Steven M. *Kierkegaard and the Concept of Revelation*. Albany: State University of New York Press, 1996.

Evans, C. Stephen. *Kierkegaard's "Fragments" and "Postscript": The Religious Philosophy of Johannes Climacus*. Atlantic Highlands, N.J.: Humanities Press International, 1983.

Passionate Reason: Making Sense of Kierkegaard's Philosophical Fragments. Bloomington and Indianapolis: Indiana University Press, 1992.

Søren Kierkegaard's Christian Psychology: Insight for Counseling and Pastoral Care. Grand Rapids, Mich.: Zondervan Publishing House, 1990.

Fenger, Henning. *Kierkegaard: The Myths and Their Origins*. Trans. George C. Schoolfield. New Haven: Yale University Press, 1980.

Fenves, Peter. *Chatter: Language and History in Kierkegaard*. Stanford: Stanford University Press, 1993.

Ferguson, Harvie. *Melancholy and the Critique of Modernity: Søren Kierkegaard's Religious Psychology*. London and New York: Routledge, 1995.

Ferreira, M. Jamie. *Transforming Vision: Imagination and Will in Kierkegaardian Faith*. Oxford: Clarendon Press, 1991.

Fowler, James W. *Stages of Faith: The Psychology of Human Development and the Quest for Meaning*. San Francisco: Harper and Row, 1981.

Gardiner, Patrick. *Kierkegaard*. Oxford Past Masters. Oxford and New York: Oxford University Press, 1988.

Garff, Joakim. *"Den Søvnløse" Kierkegaard*. Copenhagen: C. A. Reitzels Boghandel, 1995.

Golomb, Jacob. *In Search of Authenticity: From Kierkegaard to Camus*. London and New York: Routledge and Kegan Paul, 1995.

Gouwens, David J. *Kierkegaard's Dialectic of the Imagination*. New York: Peter Lang, 1989.

Kierkegaard as a Religious Thinker. Cambridge University Press, 1996.

Green, Ronald M. *Kierkegaard and Kant: The Hidden Debt*. Albany: State University of New York Press, 1992.

Grøn, Arne. *Begrebet angst hos Søren Kierkegaard*. Copenhagen: Gyldendal, 1993.

Hannay, Alastair. *Kierkegaard*. The Arguments of the Philosophers. Ed. Ted Honderich. London and New York: Routledge and Kegan Paul, 1982; rev. ed. (Routledge), 1991.

Hendriksen, Aage. *Kierkegaard's Romaner*. Copenhagen: Glydendal, 1954.

Holmer, Paul L. *The Grammar of Faith*. San Francisco: Harper and Row, 1978.

Johansen, Steen. *Erindringer om Søren Kierkegaard*. Copenhagen: C. A. Reitzels Boghandel, 1980.

Johnson, Howard A., and Niels Thulstrup, eds. *A Kierkegaard Critique.* New York: Harper and Brothers, 1962.

Khan, Abrahim H. *Salighed as Happiness? Kierkegaard on the Concept Salighed.* Waterloo, Ont.: Wilfrid Laurier University Press, 1985.

King, G. Heath. *Existence, Thought, Style: Perspectives of a Primary Relation Portrayed through the Work of Søren Kierkegaard.* Milwau-kee: Marquette University Press, 1996.

Kirmmse, Bruce. *Encounters with Kierkegaard.* Princeton: Princeton University Press, 1996.

Kierkegaard in Golden Age Denmark. Bloomington and Indianapolis: Indiana University Press, 1990.

Law, David R. *Kierkegaard as Negative Theologian.* Oxford: Clarendon Press, 1993.

Lebowitz, Naomi. *Kierkegaard: A Life of Allegory.* Baton Rouge and London: Louisiana State University Press, 1985.

Lindström, Valter. *Stadiernas Teologie, en Kierkegaard Studie.* Lund: Haakon Ohlsons, 1943.

Lowrie, Walter. *Kierkegaard.* London and New York: Oxford University Press, 1938.

A Short Life of Kierkegaard. Princeton: Princeton University Press, 1942.

McCarthy, Vincent A. *The Phenomenology of Moods in Kierkegaard.* The Hague and Boston: Martinus Nijhoff, 1978.

MacIntyre, Alasdair. *After Virtue.* South Bend, Ind.: University of Notre Dame Press, 1981.

Mackey, Louis. *Kierkegaard: A Kind of Poet.* Philadelphia: University of Pennsylvania Press, 1971.

Points of View: Readings of Kierkegaard. Tallahassee: Florida State University Press, 1986.

Maheu, René for UNESCO, ed. *Kierkegaard Vivant.* Paris: Gallimard, Collection Idées, 1966.

Malantschuk, Gregor. *Kierkegaard's Thought.* Ed. and trans. Howard V. Hong and Edna H. Hong. Princeton: Princeton University Press, 1971.

Marino, Gordon D. *Kierkegaard in the Present Age.* Milwaukee: Marquette University Press, forthcoming.

Matuštík, Martin J., and Merold Westphal, eds. *Kierkegaard in Post/Modernity.* Bloomington and Indianapolis: Indiana University Press, 1995.

McKinnon, Alastair, ed. *Kierkegaard: Resources and Results.* Waterloo, Ont.: Wilfrid Laurier University Press, 1982.

Minear, Paul, and Paul S. Morimoto. *Kierkegaard and the Bible: An Index.* Princeton: Princeton Theological Seminary, 1953.

Mooney, Edward F. *Knights of Faith and Resignation: Reading Kierke-*

gaard's Fear and Trembling. Albany: State University of New York Press, 1991.

Selves in Discord and Resolve: Kierkegaard's Moral-Religious Psychology from Either/Or *to* Sickness unto Death. New York and London: Routledge, 1996.

Müller, Paul. *Kierkegaard's Works of Love: Christian Ethics and the Maieutic Ideal.* Trans. C. Stephen Evans and Jan Evans. Copenhagen: C. A. Reitzel Boghandel, 1993.

Nielsen, H. A. *Where the Passion Is: A Reading of Kierkegaard's* Philosophical Fragments. Tallahassee: Florida State University Press, 1983.

Nordentoft, Kresten. *Hvad Siger Brand Majoren? Kierkegaards Opgør med sin Samtid.* Copenhagen: G. E. C. Gad, 1973.

Kierkegaard's Psychology. Trans. Bruce Kirmmse. Pittsburgh: University of Pittsburgh Press, 1978.

Pattison, George. *Kierkegaard: The Aesthetic and the Religious: From the Magic Theatre to the Crucifixion of the Image.* New York: St. Martin's Press, 1992.

ed. *Kierkegaard on Art and Communication.* New York: St. Martin's Press, 1992.

Perkins, Robert L., ed. *International Kierkegaard Commentary:* The Concept of Anxiety. Macon, Ga.: Mercer University Press, 1985.

International Kierkegaard Commentary: Concluding Unscientific Postscript. Macon, Ga.: Mercer University Press, 1997.

International Kierkegaard Commentary: The Corsair Affair. Macon, Ga.: Mercer University Press, 1990.

International Kierkegaard Commentary: Either/Or, Part II. Macon, Ga.: Mercer University Press, 1995.

International Kierkegaard Commentary: Fear and Trembling *and* Repetition. Macon, Ga.: Mercer University Press, 1993.

International Kierkegaard Commentary: Philosophical Fragments *and* Johannes Climacus. Macon, Ga.: Mercer University Press, 1994.

International Kierkegaard Commentary: Two Ages. Macon, Ga.: Mercer University Press, 1984.

Kierkegaard's Fear and Trembling: *Critical Appraisals.* Tuscaloosa: University of Alabama Press, 1981.

Pojman, Louis. *The Logic of Subjectivity: Kierkegaard's Philosophy of Religion.* Tuscaloosa: University of Alabama Press, 1984.

Poole, Roger. *Kierkegaard: The Indirect Communication.* Charlottesville: University Press of Virginia, 1993.

Poole, Roger, and Henrik Stangerup, eds. *The Laughter Is On My Side: An Imaginative Introduction to Kierkegaard.* Princeton: Princeton University Press, 1989.

Roberts, Robert C. *Faith, Reason and History: Rethinking Kierkegaard's* Philosophical Fragments. Macon, Ga.: Mercer University Press, 1986.

Rosas, L. Joseph, III. *Scripture in the Thought of Søren Kierkegaard.* Nashville, Tenn.: Broadman and Holman, 1994.

Rudd, Anthony. *Kierkegaard and the Limits of the Ethical.* Oxford: Clarendon Press, 1993.

Shestov, Lev. *Kierkegaard and the Existentialist Philosophy.* Trans. E. Hewitt. Athens: Ohio University Press, 1969.

Sløk, Johannes. *Kierkegaard – humanismens tænker.* Copenhagen: C. A. Reitzel Boghandel, 1978.

  Da Kierkegaard tav: Fra forfatterskab til kirkegstorm. Copenhagen: C. A. Reitzel Boghandel, 1980.

Smith, Joseph H., ed. *Kierkegaard's Truth: The Disclosure of the Self.* Vol. 5 of *Psychiatry and the Humanities.* New Haven: Yale University Press, 1981.

Smyth, John Vignaux. *A Question of Eros: Irony in Sterne, Kierkegaard, and Barthes.* Tallahassee: Florida State University Press, 1989.

Spiegel, Shalom. *The Last Trial.* New York: Pantheon Books, 1967.

Stott, Michelle. *Behind the Mask: Kierkegaard's Pseudonymic Treatment of Lessing in the* Concluding Unscientific Postscript. Lewisburg, Pa.: Bucknell University Press, 1993.

Swenson, David F. *Something about Kierkegaard.* Minneapolis, Minn.: Augsburg Publishing House, 1941; 2nd ed., rev. and enl., 1945.

Tanner, John S. *Anxiety in Eden: A Kierkegaardian Reading of* Paradise Lost. New York and Oxford: Oxford University Press, 1992.

Taylor Mark C. *Kierkegaard's Pseudonymous Authorship: A Study of Time and the Self.* Princeton: Princeton University Press, 1975.

  Journeys to Selfhood: Hegel and Kierkegaard. Berkeley and Los Angeles: University of California Press, 1980.

Theunissen, Michael. *Der Begriff Verzweiflung. Korrekturen an Kierkegaard.* Frankfurt am Main: Suhrkamp, 1993.

Thomas J. Heywood. *Subjectivity and Paradox.* Oxford: Basil Blackwell, 1957.

Thompson, Josiah. *Kierkegaard.* New York: Alfred A. Knopf, 1973.

  The Lonely Labyrinth: Kierkegaard's Pseudonymous Works. Carbondale: Southern Illinois University Press, 1967.

Thomte, Reider. *Kierkegaard's Philosophy of Religion.* Princeton: Princeton University Press, 1949.

Thompson, Josiah, ed. *Kierkegaard: A Collection of Critical Essays.* New York: Doubleday, 1972.

Thulstrup, Niels. *Commentary on Kierkegaard's* Concluding Unscientific Postscript, *with a New Introduction.* Trans. Robert J. Widenmann. Princeton: Princeton University Press, 1984.

Kierkegaard's Relation to Hegel. Trans. George L. Stengren. Princeton: Princeton University Press, 1980.

Thulstrup, Niels, and Marie Mikulová Thulstrup, eds. *Bibliotheca Kierkegaardiana.* 16 vols. Copenhagen: C. A. Reitzel Boghandel, 1978.

Wahl, Jean. *Études Kierkegaardiennes.* Paris: Fernand Aubier, éditions Montaigne, 1938; 2nd ed., J. Vrin, 1949.

Walker, Jeremy D. B. *Kierkegaard: The Descent into God.* Kingston and Montreal: McGill-Queen's University Press, 1985.

To Will One Thing: Reflections on Kierkegaard's "Purity of Heart." Montreal and London: McGill-Queen's University Press, 1972.

Walsh, Sylvia. *Living Poetically: Kierkegaard's Existential Aesthetics.* University Park: The Pennsylvania State University Press, 1994.

Weston, Michael. *Kierkegaard and Modern Continental Philosophy: An Introduction.* London and New York: Routledge, 1994.

Westphal, Merold. *Becoming a Self: A Reading of Kierkegaard's* Concluding Unscientific Postscript. West Lafayette, Ind.: Purdue University Press, 1996.

Kierkegaard's Critique of Reason and Society. University Park: The Pennsylvania State University Press, 1991.

Wisdo, David. *The Life of Irony and the Ethics of Belief.* Albany: State University of New York Press, 1992.

Wyschogrod, Michael. *Kierkegaard and Heidegger: The Ontology of Existence.* New York: Humanities Press International, 1954.

INDEX